VOICES OF CRIME

EDITED BY
LUZ E. HUERTAS,
BONNIE A. LUCERO, AND
GREGORY J. SWEDBERG

FOREWORD BY
RICARDO D. SALVATORE

VOICES OF CRIME

Constructing and Contesting Social Control
in Modern Latin America

THE UNIVERSITY OF
ARIZONA PRESS
TUCSON

The University of Arizona Press
www.uapress.arizona.edu

Printed in the United States of America
21 20 19 18 17 16   6 5 4 3 2 1
ISBN-13: 978-0-8165-3304-6 (cloth)

Cover design by Carrie House, HOUSEdesign LLC
Cover photograph: *Emilio Salvanesqui in Galeria (1887)*, Galería de Ladrones Conocidos.

Publication of this book is made possible in part by the proceeds of a permanent endowment created
with the assistance of a Challenge Grant from the National Endowment for the Humanities, a
federal agency.

Library of Congress Cataloging-in-Publication Data
Names: Huertas Castillo, Luz, editor. | Lucero, Bonnie A., editor. | Swedberg, Gregroy J., editor. |
  Salvatore, Ricardo Donato, writer of foreword.
Title: Voices of crime : constructing and contesting social control in modern Latin America / edited
  by Luz E. Huertas, Bonnie A. Lucero, and Gregory J. Swedberg ; foreword by Ricardo D. Salvatore.
Description: Tucson : The University of Arizona Press, 2016. | Includes bibliographical references
  and index.
Identifiers: LCCN 2016008671 | ISBN 9780816533046 (cloth : alk. paper)
Subjects: LCSH: Crime—Latin America—History. | Justice, Administration of—Social aspects—
  Latin America—History.
Classification: LCC HV6810.5 .V65 2016 | DDC 364.98—dc23 LC record available at https://lccn
  .loc.gov/2016008671

♾ This paper meets the requirements of ANSI/NISO Z39.48-1992 (Permanence of Paper).

CONTENTS

FOREWORD

THE VOLUME THAT READERS HAVE BEFORE THEIR EYES is a selection of the wonderful new work on the history of crime and justice being undertaken by a younger generation of scholars. Here readers will find studies on a variety of topics: on Southern Cone police conferences; on the adaptation of European criminological theories to Peruvian reality; on the Chilean police's long-standing preoccupation with drug use and drug trafficking; on the emergence of sensationalist crime journalism in Lima; on the murder of a black patriot general in Cuba in the aftermath of the 1898 U.S. occupation; on the contrasting visions of insecurity and police work in the city of Buenos Aires in 1920; on the prosecution of rape cases in the state of Veracruz, Mexico, during the period 1920–1950; and on the interpretations given to lynching events in Mexico in the 1930s and 2000s.

While the first chapters are devoted chiefly to the social and cultural construction of criminality, the subsequent chapters move toward the contestation, alternative visions, and excluded voices in the construction of crime and policing. While all of the contributors use a diversity of written records to speak authoritatively about the crimes under examination, in the second part of the volume the reader will find that representations themselves (crime statistics, crime reports, newspapers, and other written sources) are the privileged object of historical reflection. But this is only the middle terrain, for the volume moves toward the deployment of new voices that contest expert-state views of crime and its causes. And when this happens, the narratives become inflected not only with regional, local, or transnational views about crime but also with the constitutive elements of race, gender, and ethnicity, displacing from the center of the scene narratives of crime formerly conceived of as "Peruvian" or "Cuban" or "Argentine."

The contestation between elite-constructed visions of crime and order and those presented by nonstate agents, the socialist and anarchist press, mothers of sexually abused girls, lower-class patrolmen, black Cubans, Mexican peasants, and other non-elite actors, is perhaps the most salient achievement of this book. Strictly speaking, this is not a subaltern history of crime and policing in Latin America. But it comes close to it, to the extent that the authors endeavor to put into dialogue elite and non-elite perceptions of and perspectives about criminality. And, in comparison with earlier edited books on the subject, this new scholarship pays more attention to the intersections of race, gender, and nation. In the conclusion to the volume, Bonnie Lucero calls this approach an "intersectional vision," as these studies attribute an important role to the intersection of different regimes of inequality.

As someone who has argued for a long time on the necessity to view subalternity in all its plurality and to examine what different subaltern identities bring to the discussion of the national community, I could not agree more with this emphasis on "intersections." Social and cultural reality results from the interaction and overlapping of different regimes of domination/subalternity; culturally and socially constructed visions of crime cannot be an exception to this rule.

The editors claim to have extended the frontiers of the subdiscipline (the history of crime and justice), by incorporating: (a) alternative (popular, subaltern, ethnic, and subnational) conceptions of order, crime, and justice; (b) new geographical areas or countries formerly understudied; and (c) new complex ways of analyzing the "criminal question" that draw insights from feminist and race-studies critiques. They also argue that this multilayered and more complex rendition of historical criminality could help us understand the problems posed by contemporary crime and "insecurity." I can only confirm that all these claims are true and offer some examples.

The complexity of crime as a social and cultural construct is masterfully deployed in Bonnie Lucero's rendering of the 1899 assassination of black General Dionisio Gil. The Afro-Cuban general, a patriot of the independence struggle, found himself trapped in the webs of various institutional and social forces he could not control; among them: the constitution of a new police force in Cienfuegos under the guidance of American occupation authorities, and the reconstruction of local elite power after the end of the Spanish-Cuban-American war. A white-dominated police force began to move toward the enforcement of the old racial order, bringing to an end José Martí's promise of a "racial brotherhood." Afro-Cuban policemen were displaced, most of them falling into poverty. In this context, black veterans, previously considered national heroes, were suspected of immoral and criminal behavior. While the police officer who killed General Gil was arrested and prosecuted, black workers were gradually pushed out of the public sphere, their protests now met with harsh police repression. As a result of this, Afro-Cubans from Cienfuegos had to find less combative methods of self-assertion. So, they started to promote the building of a public monument in honor of the murdered patriot general. In this way, the murder of a black patriot generated a series of tensions and debates involving Cuban nationalism, promises of racial equality, workers' rights, U.S. imperialism, and the question of historical memory.

In making a more complex assessment of something previously narrated in simplified terms ("Peruvian" criminology), the essay by Luz Huertas also hits a high point. The author tells the story of how different experts and opinion-makers borrowed from distinct branches of European criminological theory—in particular what she calls "psychological heredity"—in order to paint a picture of Peru's criminality that was attentive to region, ethnicity, and race. These writers found that the crime threat was different in the coastal areas than in the highlands, and consequently started to project a view of "Peruvian crime" segmented by region and race. In this way, the traditional association of the coast with progress and civilization and of the highlands with backwardness and uncivilized behavior translated into regionally distinct "crime problems." Mixing into their interpretations environmental/social explanations and insights drawn from psychology and biology, Peruvian experts located the dangers posed by Indians and cholo delinquents in a regional/civilizational divide. Contemporaneously, other writers on crime "discovered" a new threat to social order posed by Chinese immigrant workers. Also, the postindependence concern with black and mestizo banditry migrated into a deep preoccupation with the criminal propensities of urban "cholos." That is, a matrix of European ideas about crime was creatively adapted to Peruvian regions and racial-ethnic groups in order to generate a rather complex discursive field for understanding the constitutive fragments of the crime problem in Peru. These creative adaptations produced visions of criminality that went beyond the simple overcoming of Cesare Lombroso's theory or the adoption of those of Gabriel Tarde and Alexandre Lacassagne.

In Juandrea Bates's analysis of the public repercussions of the 1920 police conference in Buenos Aires, the reader will find elements to compare with contemporary problems of crime and security. We learn that police work means different things to different people. Police chiefs and experts seemed absorbed by the idea of fighting labor unrest, while ordinary patrolmen thought, like their working-class neighbors, that police forces should invest in providing security to ordinary folks (i.e., protecting them from common theft and assaults). There was growing discontent in the city because the rich center (downtown) got better police protection than the working-class barrios in the south. In short, the article projects at least three distinct perspectives of police work (an expert-bureaucratic view, a middle-class view, and a working-class view). These distinct visions of policing represent the tension between community safety and the control of workers' protest differently. And such different views of the proper role of the police force in a modern city such as Buenos Aires speak to contemporary problems, where popular "punitive passions" usually confront progressive, more lenient views about delinquents. Bates's essay shows these conflicts of interpretation existed in the past, but were presented in a different form. *Porteños* in the 1920s discussed the social function of policing in relation to the question: Is the police's function to protect capitalists from workers' protests, or is it to protect the public from common crime?

These are examples of the carefully contextualized and well-documented cases examined in the book. In addition, the reader will find an interesting alternative reading of lynching events in Mexico. Gema Santamaría revisits the question of the lynching of hundreds of "socialist teachers" in Mexico in 1935–36 to argue against the traditional interpretation that presents these acts of "popular justice" as carried out by "Indian fanatics" influenced by Catholic priests. Other essays quite in tune with contemporary preoccupations are those about drug trafficking in Chile and sexual abuse in Veracruz, Mexico. These essays on crimes that have been underresearched document the geographic and thematic expansion of the frontiers of inquiry, as claimed by the editors.

The same concern with complexity and multivocality inhabits the whole volume. The essays give true attention to the question of regions and localities, to the social and political conjunction, and of course to the influence of gender and race in the making of "crime problems." The volume is called "Voices of Crime" in part because it extends the construction of criminality to a diverse array of voices or, better, to perspectives different from those of criminologists, penologists, police chiefs, and other state agents. One expected result of the extension of the territory to new margins and of the incorporation of additional voices within the construction of criminality is that the existing mosaic of crime discourse gets radically diverse and, hence, difficult to characterize with simple generalizations.

Expert disciplinary knowledge, being the muse of modernity, often tends to produce a proliferation of categories of "social danger" that can appear confusing to the uninformed reader. In this selection of essays we learn about the construction of several of these categorical others: "the traveling criminal" (Galeano); the "coastal" versus "highland" bandit (Huertas); the Bolivian, Peruvian, and Chinese "drug users" in Chile (Fernández Labbé); the "sexual abuser" of Veracruz (Swedberg); or the unruly "black veteran" in Cuba (Lucero). What this selection of essays tells us is that elite constructions of crime were at the time contested by different enunciations and that the dynamic of social, political, and cultural change transformed the impact and meaning of these stereotyped categories. By reading the multiple voices of criminality, it is possible to have a more comprehensive understanding of the problem of crime and policing in the history of Latin America.

Ricardo D. Salvatore
Buenos Aires, November 2015

ACKNOWLEDGMENTS

THIS VOLUME WAS FIRST CONCEIVED in January 2012, when the members of a panel organized for the American Historical Association 126th Annual Meeting discussed possible ways to contribute to the historiography on crime, justice, and social control in Latin America. Our goal was successfully achieved in the form of a volume thanks to the support, advice, and enthusiasm of several colleagues and friends. James Garza provided invaluable guidance in the planning stage of this project. Pablo Gomez and Ricardo Salvatore, with patience and generosity, encouraged us to carry on and improve the volume. We also express our special thanks to Cassia Roth, Mercedes García Ferrari, and anonymous reviewers for the time invested in reading and commenting on the chapters.

VOICES OF CRIME

INTRODUCTION

ॐ

Studying the Construction, Negotiation, and Repression of Crime

LUZ E. HUERTAS, BONNIE A. LUCERO,
AND GREGORY J. SWEDBERG

IN THE UNITED STATES, popular conceptions of Latin America are often over-run with stereotypes linking the region and its residents to crime, insecurity, and violence. People associate the region with drugs and drug trafficking, organized crime, illegal immigration, indiscriminate killings, and political and legal corruption. These simplistic generalizations paint a harrowing picture of chronic instability, perpetual danger, and a culture of deviance.

This volume emerged from the authors' common goal to challenge these stereotypes and *simplismos* in order to foster greater mutual understanding and specifically a more nuanced vision of crime in Latin America among scholars and general readers alike. In order to accomplish this collective vision, the eight essays presented here reintroduce critical historical analysis in discussions of crime, reinvigorate some foundational debates in the historiography, and offer new trajectories for conversation on this important topic. In this introductory chapter, we offer a working definition of crime, a brief examination of the development of the field, and an overview of the major questions this book asks and the contributions it makes.

Let us begin with a simple question: How do we define crime? A good starting point is to understand that crime is conventionally defined as the violation of state codes. Defining an act as criminal sets in motion a host of processes involving law enforcement, courts, and possible punitive action against the offender. Yet, this simple definition, though seemingly intuitive, prompts more questions. Who defines what constitutes a crime in the first place? How are crimes and their perpetrators identified? How should a society punish or rehabilitate criminals? These questions, in one way or another, are at the heart of each of the following chapters.

The main premise of this book is that crime cannot be understood simply as a violation of law but rather as a reflection of a society's values. But it would be naïve to
assume that a uniform vision of crime exists in any particular time and place. Rather,
the diversity inherent in the racially and culturally heterogeneous Latin American societies gives rise to multiple, evolving, often competing ideas about crime.
Although the institutionalization of particular notions of crime, order, and punishment has historically served to legitimize the dominant sociopolitical and cultural
values, the act of criminalizing individuals and actions is not, ultimately, the exclusive
domain of one particular stratum of society or even of the state.[1] Definitions of crime,
we contend, are continually (re)produced through ongoing negotiations among
diverse actors, whether they operate as agents of the state, are subject to the powers of
the state, or exist on the state's margins. These ongoing points of contact, conflict, and
fissure grow out of and also influence prevailing visions of what is harmful and what
is not, of what should be punished and what should be forgiven or even ignored: they
help constitute definitions of crime and criminality. Thus, our goal in this book is to
interrogate the ways in which these diverse views and representations of crime encap-
sulate and reinforce certain historically and culturally specific notions of race, class,
nationality, and gender.

In short, this book examines these "official" and "unofficial" perceptions of deviance, justice, and social control and how they have informed notions of crime in Latin
America since the late nineteenth century. We highlight the persistence of colonial
institutions and the perpetuation of systemic inequalities even during the consolidation of the independent Latin American republics. In other words, these enduring
structures of inequality influenced the ways the state interacted with diverse segments
of society and shaped the criminalization of specific racial, classed, and gendered bodies. However, our research also paints a nuanced portrait of Latin America as a region
in which different sets of values and ideas about deviancy and order coexisted even
within seemingly coherent social groups. In this way, we challenge simplistic notions
of "elites" and "plebeians." Both the construction and contestation of crime stemmed
from these diverse views about order and justice, which transcended the legal realm
to enter the fears, anxieties, and everyday practices of men and women of popular and
elite backgrounds alike.

Our emphasis on crime as a lens of social analysis draws on the pathbreaking historiography on Latin American crime that has developed since the late twentieth
century. These studies emphasize not only the antagonistic relationship between
state and society, but also the classist and racist nature of national states. They focus
mostly on the social and political continuities and ruptures between the colonial and
national periods, centering on the institutionalization of mechanisms of social exclusion and marginalization.

Latin America's crime history has developed in continual dialogue with European approaches to these topics. Of particular importance has been the influence of nontraditionalist British Marxist historians who, starting in the late 1950s, promoted the study of individuals and sectors criminalized by capitalist societies in order to reconstruct the history of popular struggle. Latin American historians drew upon the work of British legal historians, who presented justice systems as class-biased products of capitalism.[2] Collectively, these approaches not only established a new methodological language for discussing criminals and crime, which incorporated concepts such as class, class struggle, and resistance, but they also set up banditry, smuggling, and rioting, among other ways of "fighting the system," as new topics of inquiry. Among these studies, the works of George Rudé (1910–93) and Eric Hobsbawm (1917–2012) proved to be the most influential in the region.[3] In particular, Hobsbawm's model of the bandit as a premodern rebel prompted enthusiastic discussion across Latin America beginning in the 1980s. Historians such as Richard Slatta, Paul Vanderwood, Carlos Aguirre, Charles Walker, and Louis A. Pérez Jr. applied, tested, and critiqued these early insights on banditry in their studies, reexamining Hobsbawm's theory about banditry and rural criminality and challenging the idea of bandit-peasant relationships being based on solidarity.[4] Latin American historians also engaged European political and cultural perspectives on the rise of the modern state. Also, the studies of European scholars such as Norbert Elias (1897–1990) and Jürgen Habermas (1929–) had a profound impact on Latin American scholarship. Their theses on the emergence of modernity and the consolidation of power attempted to explain both the oppressive rule of the state over the common people and the cultural roots of bourgeois identity and the marginalization of the poor.[5] These studies reinvigorated discussions about criminalization and the imposition of moral values and views of order from the top down, while reorienting scholarly attention toward the role of the elites and the state.[6] In the late 1970s and early 1980s, for example, Michael Scardaville and Gabriel Haslip introduced these topics into the debate on criminality in colonial Mexico City, emphasizing the prerepublican roots of the state's interest in policing social order and control as well as in strengthening punishing mechanisms in the urban milieu.[7]

Since the late 1970s, poststructuralist studies have offered important theoretical insights for scholarship on crime in Latin America and beyond. In particular, Michel Foucault's (1926–84) attention to the body, surveillance, the changing mechanisms of repression, and, most importantly, the cultural structures that made specific punishing systems logical and sustainable provoked new studies on prisons, elite ideas about crime and punishment, and the normalization of society.[8] Historians of crime such as Robert Buffington, Pablo Piccato, Ricardo Salvatore, Carlos Aguirre, and James Garza have established the foundations for exploring the production and legitimization of ideas about crime and social order in Mexico, Argentina, and Peru. Their studies present these discourses as expressions of the modernizing projects that involved the elite's criminalization of the lower classes.[9] Jorge Salessi, Eugenia Scarzanella, Ricardo Pérez, and Claudia Agostoni have also examined the application and impact of those discourses and their manifestations in state policies. Some of these studies have explored the development of public policies that criminalized homosexuality, immigrants, and the production and consumption of drugs, while others have emphasized the practice of illicit types of work, including prostitution, in Argentina and Mexico.[10]

While Latin American histories of crime have consistently engaged with foreign intellectuals, the ways they contributed to these theoretical debates, applied the theories of these intellectuals, and critiqued their assumptions have depended heavily on the specific lines of inquiry already developing in each country. One of the most pronounced patterns in scholarly work on the history of crime across the region has been an emphasis on the production of criminalizing discourses in the nineteenth and early twentieth centuries. Whereas the Bourbon Reforms of the late eighteenth century catalyzed the modernization of social control, discourses of social order gained momentum only with the consolidation of independent states in the Spanish American mainland. More recent studies, though still largely confined within the boundaries of the nation-state, have expanded the geopolitical parameters of study, reoriented attention to nonstate actors, and begun to challenge earlier assertions about the elite's monopoly over criminalization. Elisa Speckman, for example, examined both official and popular discourses on crime as well as the criminalization of the working classes, whom Mexican elites viewed as inherently deviant. Likewise, in his study of law enforcement in Rio de Janeiro, Marcos Bretas disputes the idea that the elites directly controlled the police force, depicting the modern state as less cohesive and coherent. Similarly, Pablo Piccato's study of the mechanisms of social control in Mexico City emphasizes that neither the elite nor the state monopolized the construction of criminality because the lower classes had their own "unofficial" means and methods to fight crime. By harnessing the methodologies of history "from below," these scholars offer a more critical view of the supposedly antagonistic relationship between state and society and question the actual cohesiveness and coherence of the national state.[11]

The contributors to this volume build on this transition in the historiography on crime by privileging the diverse "voices of crime" in the history of Latin America. *Voices of Crime* makes three important interventions in the existing scholarship on crime. First, our main emphasis is not only on the state but on individuals and groups allegedly involved in crime, its construction, and its repression. The chapters herein take a closer look at the conflicting discourses within the state and among elites but also take into account popular conceptions of crime and "plebeian" approaches to justice. Building on recent scholarship on women, law, and crime in Latin America, we likewise advance the view that the realm of justice was not exclusively masculine and suggest that criminalized men might also be fruitfully examined as gendered subjects.[12] Thus, we explore the ways people constructed, contested, navigated, and negotiated notions of crime, criminality, and justice. Hence, the volume's title *Voices of Crime* emphasizes the plurality of alternate articulations, interactions, and experiences with criminality that are equally important for understanding the relationship between crime and society.

Second, this volume combines new work on well-documented regional hubs like Argentina, Mexico, and Peru with pioneering investigations of crime in Chile and Cuba. It also introduces a novel transnational approach to the history of crime with a study of cooperative policing in Brazil, Argentina, Uruguay, and Chile. In addition, although the volume follows the lead of earlier scholarship in emphasizing the centrality of urban spaces in visions of crime, several chapters examine regional hubs, provincial cities, and rural areas. Such geographical breadth highlights important continuities across the region, such as the ongoing tensions between local and central/federal governments in the perceptions of crime and law enforcement. At the same time, juxtaposing these diverse cases also unveils salient differences, such as the varying ethno-racial and geo-racial constructions of supposed criminal types and the diverging roles and perceptions of the foreign presence in prevailing understandings of crime.

Third, by emphasizing the linkages between past and present, this volume offers careful explorations of changing ideas and values related to crime, violence, order, and punishment in their specific geographic and cultural contexts and historical moments. This volume thereby facilitates a more nuanced and long-ranging understanding of the roots of contemporary crime. We examine popular interactions with the state in its continuous process of development and the conflict inherent in the state's attempts to consolidate a monopoly on the use of violence. Unpacking power relationships unveils complex and multilayered discourses about crime and the use of particular actors and events by the agents of the state, media, and popular actors alike as both products for public consumption and political tools.

The book is organized into two sections, each examining a different set of voices on crime beyond the confines of the law. The first section, entitled "Constructing Criminality," explores the elaboration of notions of crime and the strategic criminalization of particular sectors that either confronted the national state or represented an alleged menace to morality according to certain standards. The four essays in this section challenge the notion that definitions of crime came uniformly and neatly from a unified "elite" and present a more complex view of the way these discourses developed. These essays also examine the various power-wielding groups—and their needs, fears, and interests—behind the production of these discourses.

Diego Galeano's "Traveling Criminals and Transnational Police Cooperation in South America, 1890–1920" introduces a new view of criminalization and police action. A comparative analysis of the efforts of several South American police forces, this chapter reveals the strategies and technologies used and shared against the seemingly increasing menace of international criminals. Galeano focuses on these collaborations as a response to the large influx of immigrants arriving in Buenos Aires and Rio de Janeiro at the turn of the twentieth century. His innovative analysis of the discourses about the "travelling thief" and the capacity of police forces to act brings to light aspects of social control and international action that have been hardly explored in Latin America, such as the international influence of locally developed technologies and the efforts to standardize narratives on dangerousness.

While Galeano's chapter highlights the centrality of a discourse on foreign criminals for the development of police action, Luz Huertas's "Imagining Criminality: Race, Identity, and Crime in Peru, 1890s–1930s" explores the coexistence of several discourses about criminal subjects in Peru. Her study reveals a surprising degree of selectivity in the theories developed by criminologists and criminology enthusiasts. It also highlights the importance of theories that scholars have hardly examined but were greatly influential in the region, such as psychological heredity, which helped to link distinct criminal traits to specific racial groups. According to Huertas, Peruvian criminologists combined foreign theories with their own views about race, class, gender, and, more importantly, regional identity and created sophisticated discourses that interpreted dangerousness differently according to which "criminal subject" they addressed. They also interpreted increasing urban violence and crime as the result of progress and modernization, which made necessary the intervention of professionals on crime prevention.

In "Police Imagination: The Construction of Drug Users and Drug Trafficking in Chile, 1900–1950," Marcos Fernández Labbé also examines the way "expert" discourses focused on the criminalization of specific individuals and practices. Here, Fernández Labbé studies the discursive strategies of Chilean policemen and penologists, who labeled specific people, particularly foreigners such as Bolivian and Peruvian workers, as criminals by tying them to the illegal drug trade. Fernández Labbé skillfully analyzes the discourses that constables and jurists used to construct the drug trade, drug traffickers, and drug addicts, finding that their discourse emphasized dangerousness and contagiousness to justify far-reaching repression. Ultimately, he finds that the discursive constructs created by the police proved unhelpful for law enforcement because they were far removed from the realities of the trade when it emerged and, especially, when domestic consumption of illegal substances peaked between the 1970s and 1990s.

Indeed, fear of crime was even used to create a market of "fear consumers," as Sönke Hansen demonstrates in "Between Fiction and Reality: *Policiales* and the Beginnings of the Yellow Press in Lima, 1940–1960," the fourth chapter in this section. Hansen analyzes the world of the *crónica roja* in Lima and argues that, while newspaper articles on murders or robberies were short and precise at the beginning of the twentieth century, by the 1940s, journalists' narratives became almost fictional. Filled with sensationalist details, their biased writings appeared in high-circulation newspapers and managed to become an important component of popular culture in Lima by the 1950s. By examining the world of good and evil captured in the *sección policial*, Hansen demonstrates that the conventional emphasis on a surge in criminality in 1960s Lima actually had its roots much earlier. This important shift in media reporting on crime responded to rising popular literacy in the city. Together, Galeano, Huertas, Fernández Labbé, and Hansen show the way official discourses on crime developed from competing factions of elite actors who attempted to impose dominant ideas about activities and individuals that were supposedly dangerous.

The second section, "Navigating Criminalization," explores popular engagement with diverse state and public institutions. The chapters in this section reveal the ways socially subordinate groups deployed their alternate perspectives on crime, punishment, and morality to traverse the justice system, which was often skewed against them. These chapters show that while some fortunate individuals did present compelling challenges to their criminalization and sometimes managed to thwart state-directed policies of social control, the dangers of confronting the state remained profound. Several chapters show that individuals struggling for the renegotiation of rights, spaces, and social mobility sometimes met with the powerful forces of state or extralegal violence.

The second section begins with "Order in an Occupied City: Police and Antiblack Violence in Cienfuegos, Cuba, circa 1899." Bonnie A. Lucero highlights the limits of negotiation and the consequences of systemic state violence in a period of political transition. Her in-depth analysis of the murder of black General Dionisio Gil by white policemen in Cienfuegos reveals that this event marked a transformation in the relationship between the police and the Cienfuegueros because, as the force shifted from a multiracial to an almost exclusively white body, policemen increasingly targeted poor and working-class urban residents. Thus, the assassination of General Gil established the criminalization of the racially heterogeneous urban poor as a state tactic for maintaining the social order as Cuban political elites increasingly collaborated in the occupying government's vision of social order.

In the following chapter, "Visions of Order: Criminality, Class, and Community Conceptions of the Police in 1920s Buenos Aires," Juandrea Bates explores the

paradoxes of the modernization of the police force in early twentieth-century Buenos Aires. By examining the visions of criminality among police administrators, the
middle and working class, and patrolmen, she forcefully argues that the diverging
perceptions of order, security, and citizenship translated into conflicting visions of
criminality. The contradictory perceptions of local criminality, particularly the rift
between police administrators and patrolmen, and the growing alienation of the middle and working classes from state agendas of reform caused a stagnation and even
reduction in police efficiency despite the increasing attention of the authorities to
police reform. The failure of the modernizing measures enacted by the central state
resulted from this dislocation and directly affected the relationship between police
officers and the local community.

In chapter 7, "Prosecuting Deviance: Sexual Violence in Postrevolutionary Veracruz, 1920–1950," Gregory Swedberg critically examines the differences between
state policies and the practices of legal officials in cases related to sexual violence. He
contends that the consolidation phase of the Mexican Revolution marked greater
continuity with, rather than a complete break from, colonial and early republican
perceptions of sexual violence. Critically, both penal and civil laws were more concerned with maintaining the state's role of safeguarding families. Therefore, young
working-class women with stained reputations and mothers who defended them
usually fell outside the auspices of state protection. Ultimately, the courts demonstrated more concern for preserving the integrity of familial honor than they showed
for prosecuting sexual violence. This study suggests there was greater social and legal
continuity amid the political transition of the Mexican Revolution than is usually
acknowledged.

In the last chapter, "Between Barbarity and Tradition: Past and Present Representations of Lynching in Mexico," Gema Santamaría examines two chronologically
distanced cases of lynching in postrevolutionary Mexico. Combining sociological
and historical perspectives, she emphasizes the disparity between state and popular
notions of criminality by comparing the reactions of officials and the media to episodes of "popular justice" in the 1930s and the 2000s. Santamaría shows that, in both
periods, a certain "discourse on traditions" served as the main means to represent and
pigeonhole popular sectors as backward and religiously fanatical. In Mexico's historical present, where race has become a somehow "unsayable" marker of social difference, references to the alleged "traditions" of certain communities associated with collective acts of violence may speak to the persistence of a certain discourse that sees and
produces racialized subjects through naturalized or reified cultural markers.

Lucero, Bates, Swedberg, and Santamaría expose the complex character of the
negotiations between diverse nonelite social sectors and the state, particularly during

periods of political transition, when definitions of citizenship and national belonging themselves became tense battlegrounds. All the contributions herein demonstrate that the construction of crime and the resulting assigned, assumed, and contested roles it imposes cannot be explained as a unidirectional process. In addition,
our search for the historical voices that have forged not only modern perceptions of
criminality but the way the national state functions has also revealed the great gaps
still existing in the historiography. The concluding chapter provides a historiographical assessment of the ways scholars have examined the role of social hierarchy in studies of crime in Latin America and outlines some trajectories for future scholarship
inspired by intersectional feminist scholarship.

The eight chapters in this volume contribute to the development of a greater dialogue among historians and between scholars and society in general. Taken together,
this research represents some of the newest approaches to the history of crime in
Latin America, with our innovative approaches infusing new energy into the historical debates over crime, social control, and punishment. By focusing on the experiences and interactions of popular sectors with various criminalizing discourses in
major urban centers and peripheral spaces alike, the contributors to this volume offer
a vivid account of the complexities, nuances, and ambiguities of historical processes
of crime, criminalization, and criminality. In this way, the volume provides the reader
with the tools to examine and challenge stereotypical depictions of crime and criminality in Latin America.

NOTES

1. Pablo Piccato, *City of Suspects: Crime in Mexico City, 1900–1931* (Durham, NC: Duke
    University Press, 2001), 34–49, 73–102.

2. Douglas Hay, Peter Linebaugh, John G. Rule, E. P. Thompson, and Cal Winslow, *Albi-
    on's Fatal Tree: Crime and Society in Eighteenth-Century England* (New York: Pantheon
    Books, 1975).

3. George Rudé, *The Crowd in History: A Study of Popular Disturbances in France and En-
    gland* (New York: Wiley, 1964); Eric J. Hobsbawm, *Primitive Rebels: Studies in Archaic
    Forms of Social Movement in the 19th and 20th Centuries* (Manchester: Manchester Uni-
    versity Press, 1959); Eric J. Hobsbawm, *Bandits* (New York: Delacorte Press, 1969).

4. Paul J. Vanderwood, *Disorder and Progress: Bandits, Police, and Mexican Development*
    (Lincoln: University of Nebraska Press, 1981); Richard W. Slatta, ed., *Bandidos: The Va-
    rieties of Latin American Banditry* (Westport, CT: Greenwood Press, 1987); Louis A.
    Pérez Jr., *Lords of the Mountain: Social Banditry and Peasant Protest in Cuba, 1878–1918*

(Pittsburgh: University of Pittsburgh Press, 1989); Carlos Aguirre and Charles Walker, eds. *Bandoleros, abigeos y montoneros: Criminalidad y violencia en el Perú, siglos XVIII–XX* (Lima: Instituto de Apoyo Agrario / Instituto Pasado y Presente, 1990).

5. Norbert Elias, *The Civilizing Process* (New York: Urizen Books, 1978); Jürgen Habermas, *The Structural Transformation of the Public Sphere: An Inquiry into a Category of Bourgeois Society* (Cambridge: Cambridge Polity Press, 1989).

6. On justice systems and social control, see Sarah C. Chambers, *From Subjects to Citizens: Honor, Gender, and Politics in Arequipa, Peru, 1780–1854* (University Park: Pennsylvania State University Press, 1999); Lila Caimari, ed., *La ley de los profanos: Delito, justicia y cultura en Buenos Aires (1870–1940)* (Buenos Aires: Universidad de San Andrés: Fondo de Cultura Económica, 2007).

7. Michael Scardaville, "Crime and the Urban Poor: Mexico City in the Late Colonial Period" (PhD diss., University of Florida, 1977); Gabriel Haslip-Viera, "Crime and the Administration of Justice in Colonial Mexico City, 1616–1810" (PhD diss., Columbia University, 1980).

8. Michel Foucault, *Discipline and Punish: The Birth of the Prison* (New York: Pantheon Books, 1977). Among the most important studies representing this trajectory are Ricardo D. Salvatore and Carlos Aguirre, eds., *The Birth of the Penitentiary in Latin America: Essays on Criminology, Prison Reform, and Social Control, 1830–1940* (Austin: University of Texas Press, 1996); Carlos Aguirre, *The Criminals of Lima and Their Worlds: The Prison Experience, 1850–1935* (Durham, NC: Duke University Press, 2005); and Robert Buffington, *Criminal and Citizen in Modern Mexico* (Lincoln: University of Nebraska Press, 2000).

9. Robert Buffington, "Revolutionary Reform: The Mexican Revolution and the Discourse on Prison Reform," *Mexican Studies/Estudios Mexicanos* 9, no. 1 (1993): 71–93; Buffington, *Criminal and Citizen*; Pablo Piccato, "La construcción de una perspectiva científica: Miradas porfirianas a la criminalidad," *Historia Mexicana* 47, no. 1 (1997): 133–81; Pablo Piccato, "'El Chalequero,' or the Mexican Jack the Ripper: The Meanings of Sexual Violence in Turn-of-the-Century Mexico City," *Hispanic American Historical Review* 81, no. 3–4 (2001): 623–51; Piccato, *City of Suspects*; Ricardo Salvatore, "Criminology, Prison Reform, and the Buenos Aires Working Class," *Journal of Interdisciplinary History* 23, no. 2 (1992): 279–99; Carlos Aguirre, "Crime, Race, and Morals: The Development of Criminology in Peru (1890–1930)," *Crime, History, and Societies* 2, no. 2 (1998): 73–90; and James Alex Garza, *The Imagined Underworld: Sex, Crime, and Vice in Porfirian Mexico City* (Lincoln: University of Nebraska Press, 2007).

10. Donna J. Guy, *Sex and Danger in Buenos Aires: Prostitution, Family, and Nation in Argentina* (Lincoln: University of Nebraska Press, 1991); Jorge Salessi, *Médicos, maleantes, y maricas: Higiene, criminología y homosexualidad en la construcción de la nación Argentina (Buenos Aires, 1871–1914)* (Rosario: Beatríz Viterbo, 1995); Eugenia Scarzanella, *Ni grin-*

gos ni indios: Inmigración, criminalidad y racismo en Argentina, 1890–1940 (Buenos Aires: Universidad Nacional de Quilmes Ediciones, 2002); and Claudia Agostoni, *Monuments of Progress: Modernization and Public Health in Mexico City, 1876–1910* (Boulder: University Press of Colorado, 2003).

11. Elisa Speckman Guerra, *Crimen y castigo: Legislación penal, interpretaciones de la criminalidad y administración de justicia (Ciudad de México, 1872–1910)* (Mexico City: El Colegio de México, 2002); Marcos Bretas, *Ordem na cidade: O exercício cotidiano da autoridade policial no Rio de Janeiro, 1907–1930* (Rio de Janeiro: Rocco, 1997); Piccato, *City of Suspects.*

12. Steve Stern, *The Secret History of Gender: Women, Men, and Power in Late Colonial Mexico* (Chapel Hill: University of North Carolina Press, 1995); Guy, *Sex and Danger in Buenos Aires*; Chambers, *From Subjects to Citizens.*

PART 1

CONSTRUCTING CRIMINALITY

૨૬

Otherness in the Discourses and Policies on Order and Progress

1

TRAVELING CRIMINALS AND TRANSNATIONAL POLICE COOPERATION IN SOUTH AMERICA, 1890–1920

꩜

DIEGO GALEANO

IN SOUTH AMERICA in the late nineteenth and early twentieth centuries, numerous archival documents, newspaper articles, and police bulletins refer to the question of "traveling criminals." According to these accounts, crimes against property transcended national boundaries in a time of massive immigration and the improvement of transportation. Whenever police mentioned this incipient transnational crime, they alluded to the inferior capabilities of the police to pursue the criminals. The police were always slower, less dynamic, anchored to rigid, antiquated procedures, and above all ill suited to the pace of the emerging world of crime. This chapter examines the main responses to this disparity between policing and international crime, focusing on the transformation of policing practices. I argue that in the first decades of the twentieth century, increasing international cooperation among police forces emerged, first between Brazil and Argentina, then expanded to include Uruguay, Paraguay, Bolivia, and Peru. This study demonstrates that the development of emergent networks of police cooperation offered a direct response to the transformation of criminal practices in an era of massive transoceanic and international movement.

The emergence of a network of cooperation among South American police forces manifested in three interconnected developments. First, the sharing of police handbooks, photographs, and the identification cards of subjects who crossed borders emerged as a key mechanism of exchange, fortified by the arrival of anthropometric methods in the region, and consolidated with the implementation of the dactyloscopic (fingerprinting) system developed by Juan Vucetich in Argentina.[1]

Second, the expansion of travel by police, who visited neighboring countries to study policing technologies and produced texts about their experiences, contributed to the formation of a field of common concerns and the invention of the very concept of a "South American police force."[2] Finally, a series of police encounters took place in the Brazilian and Argentine capitals, initiating an ongoing dialogue among the police chiefs of both capitals in the wake of the visit of the Argentine president to Rio de Janeiro in 1899 that reached its apogee in the International Police Conference in Buenos Aires in 1905.

This research enables us to build on the historiography on police repression in Latin America in at least two ways. First, various studies have argued that the consolidation of the national states in countries like Argentina and Brazil provided the legal foundation to expand the power of their police forces, which in turn targeted the most radical sectors of the labor movement. In this sense, deportation laws are emblematic because they were implemented in large measure as repressive tools against anarchists and communists.[3] Although this research does not deny the existence, much less the importance, of the suppression of labor activists as a factor affecting the policing profession, it shows that the deportation laws and the police networks that implemented them also targeted international thieves and swindlers. Like Marcos Fernández Labbé's research (this volume), mine underscores the increasing internationalization of ideas of crime and practice of policing in South America. Second, this research, albeit indirectly, suggests the need to rethink the historicity of cooperation among police forces. In contrast to the conventional wisdom that international policing collaboration emerged under the region's infamous dictatorships in the context of the Cold War, this research points to earlier antecedents.[4]

To analyze the emergence of police cooperation and transnational crime in South America, this study relies on diverse sources. First, it includes documents that police forces themselves produced, such as institutional memoirs, photo albums of "known criminals," collaborative agreements, and acts of international conferences. Second, this study utilizes documents that individual policemen and officials produced, including chronicles published in police journals and papers presented at conferences, as well as unofficial material like travel accounts and letters. Finally, it relies on an intensive use of newspapers to follow the trajectories of subjects whom the police labeled as "traveling criminals."

The chapter is divided into four parts. The first part uses police records, judicial documents, newspaper articles, and literature to reconstruct the life history of a suspected international criminal known as Minga-Minga. The second part focuses on the development and tightening of ties between the police forces of Brazil and Argentina during the visit of the Argentine president to Rio de Janeiro, Brazil, in 1899. By examining a series of exchanges of photographs of criminals, this section demonstrates that the case of Minga-Minga was neither isolated nor exaggerated. The third part analyzes an event of tremendous importance for the history of South American police cooperation: the International Police Conference convened in Buenos Aires in 1905, which helped expand the international policing network beyond Argentina and Brazil. Finally, the fourth part traces a series of concrete exchanges among South American police forces following an agreement drafted at the International Police Conference and signed that same year. As a result of the tensions that this agreement later produced, police forces expanded their collaborative work. The chapter closes with the conference of 1920, also in Buenos Aires, which opened a new era in the history of this network of cooperation, more focused on political policing. The history of South American police cooperation remains understudied. Analyzing its development, as we will see, casts a light on significant aspects of everyday policing in the region as well as on the emerging mechanisms for monitoring people's social and political practices in these countries.

MINGA-MINGA: TRAVELING THIEF

Ángel Artire was an Italian who, like many others, immigrated to South America in the final quarter of the nineteenth century. The date of his arrival and his port of arrival are uncertain, although police records show that he began to experience a long series of arrests, penal judgements, and jail terms around 1875, the beginning of a period of intense immigration. Indeed, over six million Europeans immigrated to Argentina and over four million to Brazil between 1870 and 1930, rates surpassed only by immigration to the United States and Canada. Indeed, although the United States received the largest total number of immigrants, the relative proportion of immigrants to native-born people was far higher in Argentina, where in 1914 immigrants constituted 30 percent of the total national population, and approached 50 percent in Buenos Aires.[5] Such high indices of European immigration made Buenos Aires, whose population surged from 200,000 to 1.5 million in a matter of decades, one of the most important metropolises of the Americas, second only to New York. The period between the 1880s and the early 1920s marked the heyday of Italian immigration to Argentina.[6] Police records also suggest that Artire had been born around 1860 and that he was better known by his nickname: Minga-Minga. Because he used various names over the course of his life to evade apprehension, this pseudonym is the thread that connects the multitude of clues about his travels through South America's Atlantic cities. From Buenos Aires and Montevideo to Rio de Janeiro and São Paulo, the life history of Minga-Minga illustrates the emergence of a transnational space in which thieves, swindlers, counterfeiters, and sex traders operated.

Stories like that of Minga-Minga elucidate one of the most important factors triggering the process of international police cooperation, which the Chilean delegate to the 1905 International Police Conference called "traveling criminals." Thanks to the "easy methods of transportation," these individuals "immigrated in ever-greater numbers from Europe to these prosperous cities of the Atlantic, from Rio de Janeiro and Montevideo to Buenos Aires, and from there to Santiago de Chile, returning to each of those previously visited [cities] when threatened with prison."[7] One of the major historiographical views of Latin American police treats policing discourse as an object of suspicion that often conceals the "true intentions" of police authorities. Nevertheless, the words of this Chilean delegate reflect the anxieties of local elites who worried about preserving order in a changing society, in which nonelite actors' practices of resistance threatened the status quo. At least some of these threats were real. Certainly the prospect of "traveling anarchists" wandering through South America's major Atlantic cities and weaving ties of solidarity tormented elites.[8] Yet, interpreting criminalization solely as an expression of elite fears fails to capture the whole picture. Evidence from the period suggests that we need to rethink this reductionist narrative focused on political policing and take more seriously the idea that an international network of criminals affected society at large.

It is necessary, then, to return to the story of Minga-Minga and examine the vestiges of his activities in order to unveil the spaces of international crime. The *Galería de ladrones de la capital* (1887), a collection of two hundred mugshots of suspects whom Buenos Aires police detained on various occasions, provides us with some important clues. Among the first mugshots in the *Galería* was that of Minga-Minga, under which appeared the criminal history of Ángel Artire.[9] At that time, he was twenty-eight years old and had arrived in Buenos Aires in the early 1870s. He had white skin, blue eyes, and a blonde mustache and beard, according to the description. Between 1875 and 1886, he had accumulated a record of thirty-nine arrests for various charges, including robbery and disorder. Sometimes he was set free, but occasionally he ended up serving his sentence locked away in the National Penitentiary of Argentina.[10]

At the end of the list of arrests, the chief of the Bureau of Investigations (Comisario de Pesquisas) gave a brief description of the subject: "He is an accomplished *punguista* [pickpocket], that is, an individual able to pick someone else's pockets without being detected. He has never attempted large or dangerous business. He has traveled throughout Brazil and the Estado Oriental [Uruguay] for several years and he is a man of more or less civilized manner. Now he tends to occupy himself as a swindler too, because the fact that he is too well known to the police inhibits him from going about on the streets."[11]

The above chief was José Sixto Álvarez, who would later become an emblematic writer of Argentine *costumbrismo* (a literary genre focused on the depiction of everyday

No. 1

Angel Artire

FIGURE 1.1A AND 1.1B. Ángel Artire, 1887. *Galería de ladrones de la capital*, Centro de Estudios Histórico Policiales "Francisco Romay," Policía Federal Argentina (Buenos Aires, 1887).

Núm. 1

ANGEL ARTIRE

(á) Minga-Minga

—

Italiano, 28 años. soltero, sin ocupacion, blanco, ojos azules, pelo rubio corto, bigote id, boca grande, lábios algo pronunciados, naríz regular, estatura 1 m. 74 1|2. Sabe leer; residencia 15 años.

———

Ha tenido 39 entradas, 18 por desórden

En Mayo 29 de 1875—Seccion 1 ≈, por vago y sospechoso; Correccional.

En Noviembre 20 de 1875—Seccion 1 ≈, por hurto; Correccional.

En Julio 24 de 1876—Seccion 4 ≈, por robo, Correccional, condenado á dos meses de trabajos; Juez Doctor Boneo.

En Octubre 12 de 1876—Seccion 2 ≈, por tentativa de hurto, Correccional, condenado á dos meses de trabajo; Juez Doctor Boneo.

En Abril 18 de 1877—Seccion 3 ≈, por conato de robo, Correccional, condenado á dos meses de Penitenciaria; Juez Doctor Boneo.

En Octubre 28 de 1877—Seccion 3 ≈, por conato de robo, Correccional, condenado á dos meses de Penitenciaria; Juez Doctor Boneo.

En Enero 1 de 1878—Seccion 6 ≈, por desórden, Correccional, condenado á dos meses de Penitenciaria; Juez Doctor Boneo.

En Abril 10 de 1878—Seccion 1 ≈, por desórden, Correccional, condenado á tres meses de Penitenciaria; Juez Doctor Boneo.

En Julio 26 de 1878—Seccion 11 ≈, acusado de robo, Correccional, condenado á cinco meses de Penitenciaria; Juez Doctor Boneo.

En Marzo 21 de 1879—Seccion 3 ≈, por sospechas de robo, Penitenciaria.

———

FIGURE 1.1A AND 1.1B. *(continued)*

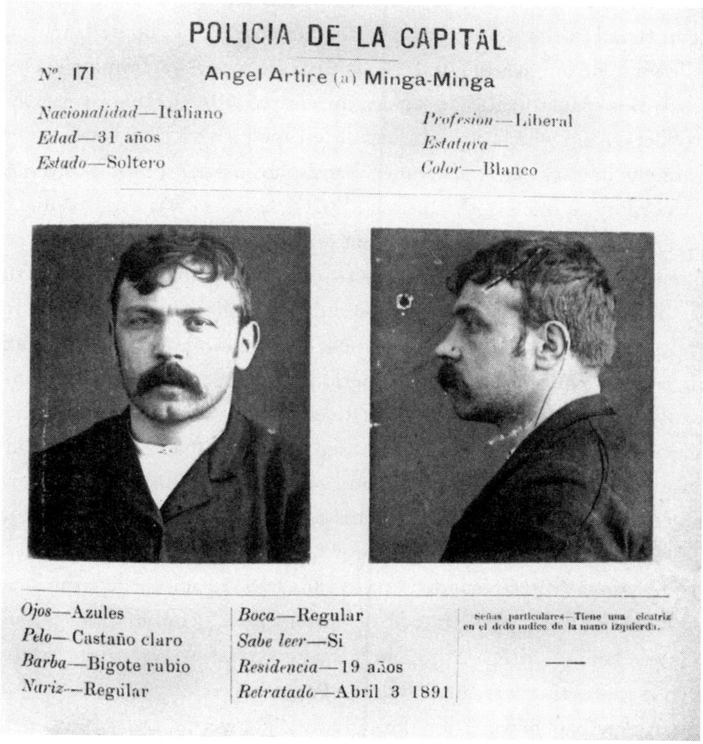

POLICIA DE LA CAPITAL

N°. 171   Angel Artire (a) Minga-Minga

Nacionalidad—Italiano   *Profesion*—Liberal
Edad—31 años   *Estatura*—
Estado—Soltero   *Color*—Blanco

Ojos—Azules   *Boca*—Regular   Señas particulares—Tiene una cicatriz
Pelo— Castaño claro   *Sabe leer*—Si   en el dedo indice de la mano izquierda.
Barba—Bigote rubio   *Residencia*—19 años
Nariz—Regular   *Retratado*—Abril 3 1891

FIGURE 1.2. Minga-Minga, 1904. *Galería de ladrones conocidos*, Centro de Estudios Histórico Policiales "Francisco Romay," Policía Federal Argentina (Buenos Aires, 1904).

life) through his stories in the magazine *Caras y Caretas*, which he signed with his pseudonym of Fray Mocho. One of his books, *Memorias de un vigilante* (1897), described the city of Buenos Aires from the perspective of a beat policeman. In a chapter on punguistas, Fray Mocho noted that one thief who had been taken to jail for stealing a watch was "none other than Ángel Artire, alias Minga-Minga."[12] In contrast to the *Galería*, whose portraits Álvarez was in charge of describing, *Memorias de un vigilante* mentions very few thieves by name, last name, and pseudonym. The words "none other than" were an indication of Minga-Minga's renown. He would reappear in a new *Galería* of "known criminals" published in Buenos Aires in 1904, but with a mugshot taken by police in 1891.

Diverse documents produced in Brazil confirm that Minga-Minga indeed traveled through this country as Chief Álvarez asserted, and that he employed a strategy of Atlantic travel to evade arrests and long prison sentences. Some clues as to his presence in Brazil in the 1890s appear in the newspapers of Rio de Janeiro and São Paulo following the publication of the *Galería* of Buenos Aires criminals. On July 12, 1892, a daily newspaper in Rio de Janeiro implicated Minga-Minga as the author of a bank robbery, from which he had allegedly escaped with a large sum of money. He was "a young man of elegant appearance, handsome, a perfect *dandy* of the *Encilhamento*," according to one police chronicle.[13] *Encilhamento* was the Brazilian expression describing the feverish speculation that surrounded the financial crisis (1889–92) during the early years of the republic (1889–1930). This term was also the title of the Visconde de Taunay's novel, which criticized the proliferation of diverse forms of white-collar crime exploiting the frantic movement of money in the then-capital city of Rio de Janeiro. The chronicles of the period often described traveling criminals as gentlemanly thieves who lived at the interstices of that world of speculation.

Evidence suggests that Minga-Minga used the name João Sanguinette in Brazil. Brazilian authorities suggested that the imprisonment of Minga-Minga following the 1892 robbery described above prevented his escape to Buenos Aires, a trip for which he had purchased tickets to depart the following day. Other criminal episodes in Brazil involving Minga-Minga included one in 1895 in São Paulo, where the local newspapers referred to a crime perpetrated by a "known thief [*gatuno*]."[14] In an incident in 1897 in Rio de Janeiro, Minga-Minga and other criminals were cornered at the Hotel do Comércio just as they were fleeing to São Paulo.[15]

Brazilian newspapers were not the only media covering the exploits of Minga-Minga. The same alias graced the lists of the most famous criminal pseudonyms of Brazil, published in a book of urban memoirs by Alexandre José de Melo Morais Filho.[16] In another book, *Os ladrões no Rio* (1903), written by the police commissioner of Rio de Janeiro, Vicente Reis, Minga-Minga appeared as one of the "gentleman bandits" (*bandidos de casaca*) who traveled to rob, donning fine clothing and good manners to feign "honesty in the social class in which they lived."[17] The same book contains a lithographic portrait of Minga-Minga (fig. 1.3).

Minga-Minga also appeared in the memoirs of a famous thief known as Dr. Antonio, who worked Brazilian hotels. He wrote while imprisoned in Rio de Janeiro's House of Detention, where he would have had the opportunity to meet and converse with Minga-Minga. Dr. Antonio included his prison mate in a list of "notable" thieves, some of whom had already established themselves "very well in Buenos Aires."[18] We know very little about the fate of Ángel Artire, João Sanguinette, or Minga-Minga beyond the first years of the twentieth century, but it is evident that the constant movement of criminals defined the route between Rio de Janeiro and Buenos Aires. It also emerged as the site of unprecedented connections among police forces of the region.

Minga-Minga

FIGURE 1.3. Minga-Minga, 1903. Vicente Reis, *Os ladrões no Rio, 1898–1903* (Rio de Janeiro: Laemmert, 1903), 96.

INTERNATIONAL POLICING NETWORKS

Though eventually gaining continental support, cooperation among South American police forces began with exchanges between the forces of two countries: Brazil and Argentina. The growing ties between the two emerged in the 1890s through two main mechanisms. First, the creation of the first offices of identification in South America fostered the adoption of the anthropometric technique created by the French police officer and researcher Alphonse Bertillon. Anthropometrics offered a solution to the problem of the false names that delinquents like Minga-Minga often used to escape legal action and evade longer sentences due to recidivism. In 1889, Buenos Aires became the first city outside of France to found an anthropometric office in a public police department. From that point forward, various police chiefs in Brazil suggested that Rio de Janeiro should follow Argentina's example in order to facilitate the exchange of information between both countries and combat international crime with greater efficiency. Finally in 1899, after several failed attempts amid the political instability of the first decade of the Brazilian republic, an anthropometric department was established within the Rio de Janeiro police force under the leadership of João Silvado.[19]

The second mechanism strengthening the ties between Argentine and Brazilian police forces was a shift in the way republican elites in Brazil viewed their Argentine counterparts. In contrast to their imperial predecessors, Brazilian elites in the early republic stopped viewing Argentina as an example of Spanish American disorder and began to see it as a symbol of regional modernity.[20] After the abolition of slavery in Brazil in 1888 and the proclamation of the Republic the following year, a significant portion of the Brazilian press began to construct a discourse of "brotherhood" with the other nations of the Río de la Plata region. The visit of Argentine president Julio A. Roca to Rio de Janeiro in 1899 and the reciprocal visit of Brazilian president Manuel Ferraz de Campos Sales to Buenos Aires in 1900 marked the beginning of a period of strengthening bilateral relations between the two countries.[21] These presidential visits served various diplomatic purposes. Among the most salient agendas was Roca's attempt to prevent an impending alliance between Brazil and Chile in the context of heightened political tension between Argentina and the trans-Atlantic country over an international border dispute. Nevertheless, within the substantial entourage that accompanied the Argentine president on his visit to the Brazilian capital, each of the numerous actors pursued his own agenda, which was not always subsumed within the political objectives of the highest echelons of government.

To be sure, the Buenos Aires police officials sought to establish connections with their Brazilian counterparts. In Rio de Janeiro, detailed coverage of Roca's visit graced the front pages of some of the most important newspapers for several days. This coverage evinced broad interest in this potential police collaboration. Even before the official commission embarked from the Argentine port toward Brazil, telegrams communicated the news in Argentina. On July 31, 1889, the *Jornal do Commercio* published a telegram sent by its correspondent in Buenos Aires, in which he explained that the police chief of that city, Francisco Beazley, would travel with the official commission to discuss with his Brazilian counterpart "important matters of international policing."[22] The Brazilian police chief who received Beazley was precisely João Silvado, the man responsible for installing the anthropometric department the same year. In a subsequent telegram, the correspondent added that on August 2, around midnight, Roca and his commission had embarked for Rio de Janeiro on the steamboat *Patria* and that Beazley brought with him albums containing the mugshots of five hundred delinquents.[23]

Several days after the arrival of the commission, the same newspaper published an extensive interview with the Buenos Aires police chief, conducted by the journalist Félix Pacheco. Years later, Pacheco became director of the Office of Identification in Rio de Janeiro's police force and assumed a leading role in organizing the first South American Police Conference in Buenos Aires in 1905. In the interview, Pacheco confirmed the correspondent's assertions, explaining that the inclusion of Beazley in the Argentine commission was not a coincidence nor "merely [a matter] of courtesy." According to the reporting in the *Jornal do Commercio*, before Beazley assumed the position as chief in 1896, the police forces of Rio de Janeiro and Buenos Aires rarely engaged in dialogue. In contrast, following his appointment, the communication between the two chiefs intensified.

For Beazley, it was crucial for these ties to be direct, without intervention of consular authorities, because the information needed to travel quickly, without bureaucratic impediment. In any other scenario, the police would be unable to match the speed with which international criminals traveled through the Atlantic cities of South America. Indeed, Beazley theorized that the spatial distribution of thieves was directly related to the intensity of police activity: "Rio de Janeiro and the capital of the Argentine Republic are the two great epicenters of South American delinquency. Pursued with rigor by agents of the law [in Buenos Aires], the criminal moved toward Rio de Janeiro. Contrarily, when the police here insistently surveilled and pursued delinquents [*amigos de lo ajeno*] with all the rigor of the law, they seek refuge in Buenos Aires."[24] This zero-sum hypothesis attempted to explain the rapid movement of delinquents in the Atlantic cities of South America. At the time of the interview, the journalist interrupted Beazley to tell him a fact that supported his theory. Roca's visit to Rio de Janeiro had just been announced when, according to investigations conducted by Rio de Janeiro's police, thieves began to arrive from Buenos Aires, with the intention of taking advantage of the celebration to commit crimes. To demonstrate the dense flow of traveling criminals between the two cities, Beazley ordered "three old, experienced agents" who knew "absolutely all the criminals who infected Buenos Aires" to depart toward Rio de Janeiro in a separate ship from the official commission. Chief Silvado, in turn, authorized these Argentine investigators to make their rounds in distinct prisons throughout Rio de Janeiro to identify criminals.

Two days after the interview, the *Jornal do Commercio* reported the arrival of four rather than three secret agents, whom the journalist described as "perfect gentlemen" who spoke different languages. The same day, the agents visited the Central Department of Police, the House of Detention, and the House of Correction, in which they identified approximately twelve thieves who had apparently also operated in Buenos Aires. Among these thieves were Felippe Monfo, alias "el Brasilerito" (the Little Brazilian); Francisco Taborda, alias "Ojo de Buey" (Ox Eye); Manoel de Oliveira, known in the Argentine capital as "Segundo Lobo" (Second Wolf); José Ferrari and his wife and accomplice in robbery, Theresa, "who felt very embarrassed and confused upon being recognized."[25]

Moreover, the journalist of the *Jornal do Commercio* gained access to the two volumes of photographs of known criminals Beazley had presented to Silvado and was able to make his own visual observations. Flipping through the pages of the photograph albums, the journalist was surprised to find in the plethora of Argentine criminals some of the "most illustrious" personalities of the "chronicles of our *gatunagem* [delinquency]."[26] Delinquent number forty, he explained to his readers, who appeared in the Buenos Aires album as Luciano Ludeña, Pantaleón Gómez, or Pedro Ruiz, was known by the Fluminense police as "Julio Madurano." Similarly, Alberto Gomensoro boasted criminal records in both cities.[27] Another of these traveling criminals was Emilio Salvanesqui, alias Narigueta, also known in Brazil as Emilio Silvano.[28] Like Minga-Minga, Narigueta's mugshot appeared in the *Galerías* of Argentine criminals as well as in the book of the Rio de Janeiro police commissioner Vicente Reis.

The case of Narigueta appeared to confirm Beazley's hypothesis. A police chronicle in the Brazilian *Diário de Notícias* noted that in April 1890, Narigueta arrived in Rio de Janeiro on a train from São Paulo, guarded by two policemen from that city. According to this narrative, Narigueta had fled to São Paulo to escape pursuit by João Batista Sampaio Ferraz, Rio de Janeiro's police chief known for his ferocious campaign against various individuals considered dangerous.[29] Narigueta's appearance in the *Galería* of criminals of Buenos Aires in 1904, with a mugshot taken in February 1891, just after his arrest in São Paulo, suggests that he traveled frequently between Argentina and Brazil. As his criminal record included in the *Galería* of 1887 demonstrated, he had been arrested several times in Buenos Aires between 1871 and 1886 for robbery and fraud. A short time after the police chronicles appeared in Rio de Janeiro's press, news of his deeds in Brazil came to light.[30]

No. 100
Emilio Salvanasqui

FIGURE 1.4A AND 1.4B. Emilio Salvanesqui, 1887. *Galería de ladrones de la capital*, Centro de Estudios Histórico Policiales "Francisco Romay," Policía Federal Argentina (Buenos Aires, 1887).

Núm. 100

EMILIO SILVANI Ó SALVANESQUI

(a) Narigueta

Italiano, 33 años, casado, sastre, blanco, ojos castaños, pelo castaño claro lácio, bigote ral idem, boca chica, nariz grande, estatura 1 metro 66 centímetros, sabe leer, 18 años d residencia. Tiene una pequeña cicatriz en el codo del brazo izquierdo figurando un punt negro.

Ha tenido 15 entradas; 2 por desórden

En Octubre 24 de 1871—Seccion 1ª, por robo; Correccional, condenado á 2 meses de arresto en Noviembre 29 de 1871.

En Setiembre 4 de 1874—Seccion 3ª, por conato de robo; Correccional.

En Octubre 23 de 1873—Seccion 13ª, por conato de estafa; Correccional.

En Abril 22 de 1878—Seccion 12ª, por agresion á mano armada; 8 dias de arresto.

En Octubre 19 de 1878—Seccion 13ª, por robo; Correccional, condenado á 2 meses de arresto.

En Febrero 14 de 1879—Seccion 2ª, por robo; Correccional, condenado á 5 meses de prision.

En Agosto 24 de 1879—Seccion 2ª, por raterías; Correccional, condenado á 5 meses de prision.

En Julio 30 de 1880—Seccion 3ª, por robo; Correccional.

En Enero 23 de 1881—Seccion 4ª, por hurto; Correccional, en libertad por no estar justificado su delito.

En Agosto 15 de 1881—Seccion 10ª, por sospechas de hurto; Correccional, condenado á 8 meses de prision.

En Agosto 15 de 1881—Seccion 10ª, por sospechas de robo; Penitenciaría, en libertad, sobreseida la causa; Juez Doctor Torres.

En Julio 2 de 1884—Seccion 4ª, por complicidad en hurto; Correccional, en libertad, sobreseida la causa.

FIGURE 1.4A AND 1.4B. *(continued)*

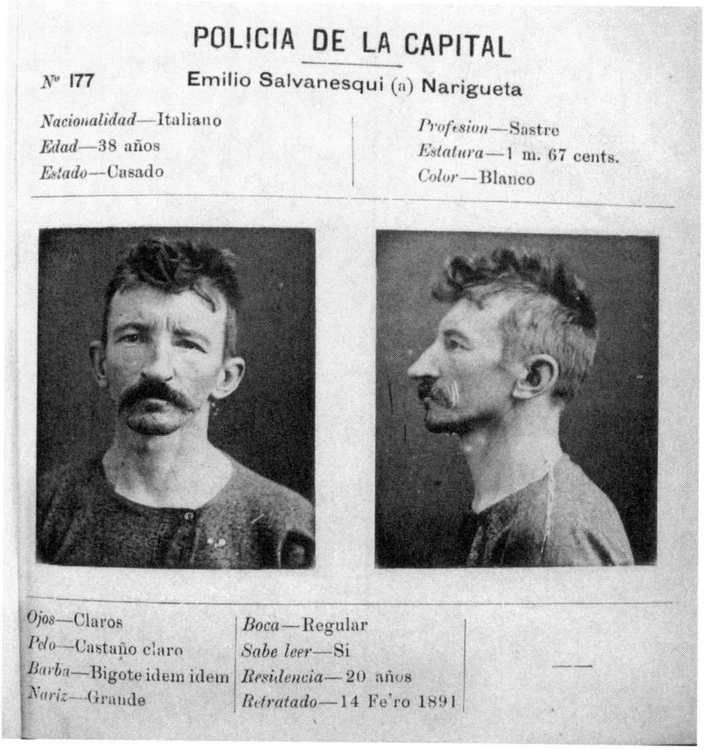

FIGURE 1.5. Emilio Salvanesqui, 1904. *Galería de ladrones conocidos*, Centro de Estudios Histórico Policiales "Francisco Romay," Policía Federal Argentina (Buenos Aires, 1904).

Beazley affirmed during his visit that his tenure as police chief was defined by the tenacious pursuit of the "known thieves" of Buenos Aires, to the extent that many of them fled to Montevideo. Agreements with the Uruguayan police regarding the exchange of mugshots and telegrams enabled authorities to arrest traveling criminals as they crossed the Río de la Plata. Beazley suspected that their new preferred destinations were Brazilian Atlantic cities. Consequently, the objective of the Buenos Aires police chief was to extend informal police agreements to the three countries involved in the South American Atlantic routes. "With such a service, internationally coordinated, but independent and harmonious, Brazil, Argentina, and Uruguay would end up returning to Europe the pernicious element it sends us."[31] Beazley's objective was to defend what we could call the "South American Atlantic space," an area defined by the international route that united the two principal ports of the Río de la Plata

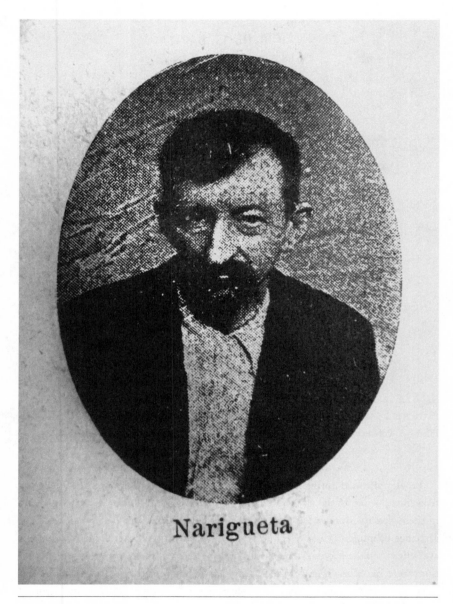

Narigueta

FIGURE 1.6. Salvanesqui, 1903. Vicente Reis, *Os ladrões no Rio, 1898–1903* (Rio de Janeiro: Laemmert, 1903), 141.

(Buenos Aires and Montevideo) with Brazilian port cities and with Lisbon, Oporto, Vigo, Barcelona, Geneva, Naples, and other European cities across the Atlantic Ocean.

This zone of trans-Atlantic movement was further stimulated by an intense wave of immigrants, who transformed the social and demographic makeup of the most important cities of Atlantic South America, facilitated in large part by improved means of transportation.[32] In 1895, the future chief of Rio de Janeiro's police wrote that, in Europe, he had seen the way the criminals exploited the "advantages trains provided, as well as their abundance and speed." Trains easily connected various countries on a continent where "locomotion was an easy thing" and a passenger could "drink a coffee in Berlin, eat lunch in Liége [Belgium], and have dinner in Paris, all on the same day."[33] Exactly one decade later, an Argentine policeman declared that "today the greatest criminals, whose life becomes impossible in one country, change [locations] with breathtaking ease thanks to the increasingly effortless and quick methods of transportation."[34] The problem of the traveling criminal, and the need to respond to it with increasing police cooperation, were topics of interest in various countries of the Atlantic world during this period.

For this reason, the most significant aspects of Beazley's 1899 visit were the meetings between police chiefs. According to the daily Brazilian newspaper *O País*, the main objective of these encounters was to sign a reciprocity agreement to facilitate "the necessary means for the repression of criminality."[35] This news, diffused in Rio de Janeiro's press, similarly graced the pages of a Buenos Aires police journal, which implied the success of Beazley's visit to Rio de Janeiro. "Agreements have not been signed, treaties have not been written," explained the author, but the police had arrived at a common understanding regarding the exchange of communications, facts, warnings, and diverse information about the "active and natural interchange of outlaws and all kinds of evil-doers, which is maintained constantly between the two cities."[36] Additionally, this journal printed a photograph of one of the meetings, in which the two chiefs can be seen surrounded by various officials of the Rio de Janeiro police force. "We believe we are not mistaken to declare that . . . the way in which, from this point forward, communication between the police forces of the two great capital cities of America will be carried out has been definitively decided between the two police chiefs, Doctors Beazley and Silvado," lauded the journalist in the *Jornal do Commercio*.[37]

Both chiefs represented reformist tendencies in their own forces. Silvado, after travelling to France to interview Bertillon, had established an Office of Identification in Rio, paving the way for the exchange of anthropometric files. Beazley, who had already managed an anthropometric office for over a decade, was more skeptical of the potential of this technology, but he insisted on the necessity of exchanging photographs and telegrams between the police forces of the region. Both men, nevertheless,

FIGURE 1.7. Beazley's visit to Rio de Janeiro, 1899. "La Policía de Río de Janeiro: El viaje del Doctor Beazley," *Revista de Policía* (Buenos Aires) 55, September 1, 1899.

agreed on one fundamental point: it was no longer possible to pursue traveling criminals without mechanisms of international policing.

INTERNATIONAL POLICE CONFERENCE

A series of police conferences convened in Montevideo, Rio de Janeiro, and Buenos Aires in the early twentieth century helped crystalize the proposal Beazley had raised at the Rio meeting. The renewed interest in policing technology was forged by supporters of dactyloscopy, who, with Juan Vucetich's leadership, sought South American support in their international challenge against Alphonse Bertillon's method. Creator of the "Argentine Dactyloscopic System," Vucetich was the director of the Office of Identification of the Buenos Aires Provincial Police, headquartered in the recently founded city of La Plata. This was a policing institution created in 1880 following the disintegration of the former Buenos Aires police, which subsequently became the Police of the Capital and operated within the city limits of Buenos Aires. Vucetich was a Croatian immigrant, a self-taught man without university education, who earned his place in the provincial police first in the 1890s as a specialist in anthro-pometric identification and then as an inventor of a new system, which at the beginning of the twentieth century began to challenge the regional hegemony of bertillonage.[38]

In the Juridical and Social Sciences section of the Second Latin American Scientific Congress in Montevideo in 1901, convened by the Brazilian law professor Manoel Alvaro de Souza Sa Vianna, Vucetich introduced the basic ideas of his new system of identification to a foreign audience for the first time, boasting of its numerous advantages over Bertillon's system. One of the most important advantages was the possibility of facilitating "the international exchange of detentions and request of criminal records, given that the dactyloscopic system can be considered a viable lingua franca for all the police forces in the world."[39] The ties Vucetich forged with the Office of Identification of Rio de Janeiro, directed by Pacheco since August 1901, were crucial in the advancement of his project to construct an international South American police force based on the exchange of dactyloscopic records. Indeed, the close cooperation between Vucetich and Pacheco facilitated in 1902 a formal agreement for the exchange of records between the identification services of Rio de Janeiro and La Plata, before dactyloscopy was accepted by the police of the Argentine capital in November 1903.

All these achievements laid a crucial foundation for a successful bid by proponents of dactyloscopy. It is no coincidence that this strategy, carefully prepared by Vucetich and Pacheco, took place at the Third Latin American Scientific Congress in August 1905 in Rio de Janeiro. There Vucetich and his assistant Alberto Cortina publicly presented the idea circulating between the police forces of Argentina and Brazil: the configuration of a "South American Police Conference."[40] According to the delegates from La Plata, this would be an effective strategy to advance the formation of an international police force, a universal need that, for geopolitical reasons, South America could accomplish with greater success than any other continent in the world. These reasons justified "limiting the formation of the Congress only to South American countries," including the ten republics of Venezuela, Colombia, Ecuador, Peru, Bolivia, Chile, Argentina, Uruguay, Brazil, and Paraguay. The initiative emerged with the increasing cooperation between the police forces of Argentina and Brazil, but eventually extended to the remaining South American countries. "The fact and right of international service" could be considered "established with legitimate predominance in the entire continent" only when six of the ten republics were represented.[41] This proposal was unanimously approved at the first police conference, where delegates also moved to adopt "a universal professional terminology" and standardize policing procedures. One of the Brazilian delegates, Antônio Bento de Faria, also proposed systematizing South American policing. Because the increasing ease of transportation enabled thieves to effect a "rapid change in their field of operations," he opined, one of the principal challenges facing the police forces was "to impede the passage of the escaping delinquent."[42] This jurist from Rio de Janeiro considered "the collective policing of American countries, linked to the establishment of identical and general precepts [which are] uniform and efficient," to be the only way to combat the problem of traveling criminals.

International crime was a central theme in the conference proposals and agreements between South American police forces. José Gregorio Rossi, commissioner of police of the Argentine capital, declared that the principal obstacle in the fight against criminality was the growing trend toward "internationalism." The professional delinquent had "launched himself into a tour of the world," a phenomenon that had already constituted a truly "global network of delinquency." Rossi argued that these networks demonstrated a profound spirit of solidarity, to the point that when a traveling criminal arrived at his destination, he was received by a guide "to show him the city." Rossi concluded that "the Argentine Republic, like all the South American nations subject to the enormous currents of immigration, is subject to receive—and surely receives—a great part of the scum of Old Europe, which bounces around the jails from Brazil to the [Río de la] Plata, to the Pacific and vice versa."[43]

Eurico Cruz, lawyer and commissioner of the Rio de Janeiro police, thought that the coming police conference constituted a "real and true league against the recurring threat to South American countries," which had been transformed into an "asylum for the surplus of criminal and degenerate populations from other nations." Across the borders that separated these countries, Cruz opined, "delinquents hold hands." For this reason, it was necessary for police to confront "the international associations of criminals, whose existence is evident . . . with the combined strength, courage, intelligence, and international solidarity of the various police forces."[44] These thunderous declarations called for the rest of the South American countries to subscribe to the agreement already celebrated between Argentineans and Brazilians. In fact, as declared in a bulletin of the provincial police of Buenos Aires, "mutual cooperation between the police forces" of Brazil and Argentina already existed.[45] Another article about the first South American Police Conference, convened in the city of Buenos Aires in October 1905, admitted that the "general outlines" of the agreement were already "recognized." It included establishing a reciprocal exchange of dactyloscopic records and agreeing on rapid transmission of information "with policing objectives."[46]

When the Rio de Janeiro conference ended in mid-August, the police chief of that city asked Vucetich to postpone his return to Argentina so he could travel with Pacheco. Once in Argentina, Pacheco visited the Office of Identification recently established in the city of La Plata. For Argentine police, Pacheco had become the principal South American advocate for international cooperation among police forces. He was an untiring "Brazilian propagandist," as the writers of the Buenos Aires police bulletin called him when, on the eve of the Buenos Aires conference, they celebrated the achievements of Pacheco and Vucetich, "both energetic champions of scientific policing and of the defense of social efficiency."[47]

Nevertheless, Pacheco's visit to Argentina was not limited to improving Rio de Janeiro–La Plata relations. In the brief interlude between the conference in Rio de Janeiro in August 1905 and the one in Buenos Aires in October of that year, Rossi revealed the existence of an "exchange pact" between the police forces of both capitals, negotiated in January of that year. The Buenos Aires police bulletin reprinted a series of correspondence between the police chiefs of Argentina and Brazil, in which they agreed to "trade criminal records by means of dactyloscopy." A few days after the end of the conference in the Brazilian capital, the Rio de Janeiro police chief wrote his colleague again, explaining that he was sending Pacheco to Argentina with orders to propose "a meeting of chiefs of dactyloscopic identification services from La Plata, Buenos Aires, Montevideo, and Rio de Janeiro."[48]

The same chief sent other letters to his peers in the Montevideo police and the provincial police of Buenos Aires, informing them of his proposal, which he did not consider his work alone but rather a natural result of the "increasing friendship between the Brazilian and Río de la Plata police administrations."[49] Vucetich suggested that these four policing institutions from the three countries of the South American Atlantic space also invite the police force of Santiago de Chile, which had recently joined the dactyloscopic system, to participate.[50] The representative designated by the Chilean government was Luis M. Rodríguez, a lawyer who, as secretary of the Santiago de Chile police prefecture, played an active role in advocating the use of dactyloscopy in his home country.[51]

Shortly after the late inauguration of the conference in October 1905, delegates began to outline a formal agreement for collaborative policing.[52] The objective of the agreement centered on installing a mechanism for "exchanging of the useful records for policing purposes, with respect to classified persons or ones considered dangerous to society."[53] The delegates intensely debated the meaning of the phrase "policing purposes" (fines policiales). The Chilean representative disagreed with the others, requesting that the information circulated among police forces have an "absolutely confidential character." Rodríguez feared that the publication of incriminating information about an individual without a judicial sentence could be interpreted as a humiliating practice. For Pacheco, in contrast, "the greater interest of the defense of the social collective" took precedence over individual rights and justified preventive vigilance.[54] Despite this disagreement, the final text of the agreement included the warning to maintain "in strict confidence" the records transferred and to limit their use to "policing purposes." This last phrase implied surveilling individuals with recognized criminal antecedents or perceived criminal tendencies in order to prevent new crimes and eventually provide the justice system with information in criminal trials.

The second series of debates centered on defining the category of "dangerous person," which enabled the circulation of information among police forces. By developing a broad definition that applied to a wide spectrum of suspects, police authorities sought to target urban thieves as well as international delinquents and labor activists. Any individual who had "served at any time as the author, accomplice, or accessory in crimes against property" was considered dangerous. Moreover, "anyone lacking licit means of subsistence," who maintained relations with thieves, associated with "habitual delinquents," or utilized "instruments or objects known to be intended for the commission of crimes against property" fell in the same category. The criteria of dangerousness also included individuals who participated in "crimes of counterfeiting or falsification of stock market securities [*valores mobiliarios*]." Likewise, foreigners who left the country only to return with criminal records, sex traffickers (*trata de blancas*), "habitual inciters of social subversion," and lastly "agitators of the labor unions," who through "acts of violence or by force" intervene in the freedom of work, were also included under the concept of dangerous individuals, given that such activities represented a "habitual occupation and a source of profit."[55]

The ninth article of the 1905 agreement established that police officials in these South American countries should communicate "as soon as possible the departure of any dangerous individuals who are going to a [neighboring South American] territory."[56] This article would become a crucial linchpin in the effective practices of police cooperation, especially between Argentina and Brazil, which sanctioned laws permitting the deportation of "undesirable" foreigners in the early twentieth century. The deportation of thieves, swindlers, sex traffickers, and political agitators would pose concrete challenges for the exchange of information and the surveillance of South American ports.

THE WEB OF COOPERATION

One of the principal sources of tension in the implementation of international policing cooperation emerged with the increasing reliance on deportation as a repressive tool against traveling criminals. Two years after the 1905 conference, Brazil sanctioned the so-called Gordo Law, joining Argentina, which had approved it in 1902. This law instituted a mechanism for summary deportations of "undesirable" foreigners. As has been noted by numerous historians, officials routinely made use of the law to repress known criminals, pimps, militant anarchists, and communists.[57] Yet, the

lack of communication between the police forces of the region about these deportations enabled many of these individuals to seek refuge in neighboring countries,
where they continued committing crimes.

Police chiefs of the Río de la Plata noted some undesirable consequences of the
Brazilian deportation law. Immediately after the first Brazilian deportations, Ramón
Falcón, then chief of police of Buenos Aires, sent a letter to the Rio de Janeiro police.
Therein, he expressed his anxiety that frictions would develop in the following years
despite the official declarations of fraternity, cooperation, and friendship among the
police forces. For example, shortly after Brazil implemented its deportation law, a
large number of individuals bound for Rio de Janeiro took up residence in Argentina. These recent transplants were surprised by the local police "in circumstances
of intending to commit robbery in the streets or in public places."[58] For this reason,
and invoking the ninth article in the 1905 agreement, Falcón requested that when the
Rio de Janeiro police had "knowledge of the departure of any dangerous individual
headed for the territory of any of the allied police forces," that telegraphic notice be
given, specifying the name of the traveler and the ship on which the suspect traveled.
At the same time, he asked allied police forces to send the criminal records and relevant facts to help identify the suspects at the ports of entry.

Evidence confirms that the concerns Falcón expressed resulted in two concrete
consequences for the exchanges between Brazilian and Argentine police forces. Both
postal and telegraphic correspondence between Brazil and Argentina intensified as
police shared dactyloscopic records by mail and cabled the names and particulars of
the deportees. Toward the end of 1907, Falcón wrote another letter to the chief of the
Rio de Janeiro police, accompanying the dactyloscopic records of various individuals deported from Argentina, who had embarked on the steamship *Citá de Milano*.
It seemed to respond to a telegram received from Rio de Janeiro. Falcón also took
advantage of the opportunity to insist on a previous request for the list of deportees
expelled by the Brazilian government, an appeal Brazilian authorities had neglected.[59]

According to the Argentine chief, the police forces of the Brazilian states with
ports of call from which the deportees frequently embarked should also be involved
in the network of information sharing. In a new letter, this time to the police of São
Paulo, Falcón made explicit that the principal objective of these announcements was
to "defend our respective jurisdictions from the incorporation of antisocial elements"
by preventing their disembarkation at the Atlantic ports of South America. "My proposal," he wrote, "consists simply in establishing in the first place, as a regular procedure, that the deportations we undertake not be directed toward any South American
country, if it is not the original domicile of the deportee, and in the second place, that
we all communicate the cases of deportation, providing the identifying elements (fingerprints, photographs, particulars, etc.), and the judicial, police, and moral records

of the subject."[60] Brazilian and Argentine police forces came to this agreement infor-
mally rather than following established diplomatic channels. Nevertheless, it aligned
with the anti-European sentiment of the deportation laws: to protect the South
American region was the primary objective. In practice, this protection combined a
dense exchange of telegrams between the police forces of capital cities and the daily
work of the maritime police, who sought to impede the landing of passengers who
perpetually traveled through neighboring ports. Nevertheless, a discrepancy existed
between the work of the maritime police and the stated objectives for the cooperation of South American police forces. Frequently, Brazil denied entry to passengers
coming from Europe, but allowed them to continue their passage to the Río de la
Plata.[61] In order to address this disparity, greater cooperation was required.

Among the documents on the Rio de Janeiro police preserved in the Brazilian National Archives, there is a large quantity of letters and telegrams exchanged
between the police forces of Argentina and Brazil. This dense web of correspondence
reveals that police cooperation increased following the 1905 police conference. A significant portion of the letters and particularly the telegrams relate to the implementation of deportation laws. Falcón's intention to "return the undesirables to Europe,"
thereby protecting the Atlantic South American space, required strict control over
the ports, particularly with deportations from the south to the north. This cau-
tion resulted from the fact that deportees beginning their journey in Buenos Aires
boarded the same passenger ships that stopped in Montevideo and various Brazilian
ports (Santos, Rio de Janeiro, Recife, and others). Consequently, police perceived it
to be a big risk that the deportees might disembark imperceptibly among the crowd
and remain in South America. Telegrams from Buenos Aires warned the Brazilian
police when thieves and sex traffickers embarked. The documentation also demonstrates that Brazil's maritime police prevented a significant number of disembarka-
tions in the first decades of the twentieth century.

The telegrams also reveal the types of social practices that inspired such exchanges.
Traveling thieves continued to preoccupy the police of the region and were subject to
numerous deportations. Nevertheless, at the same time, deportations of labor activists
also increased, especially following the anarchist plot that killed Falcón in November
1909. This murder awakened Brazilian vigilance because the Argentine capital was one
of the major centers of anarchist activity on the continent, and the criminals deported
from Buenos Aires invariably traveled through Brazilian ports. Between 1909 and the
inauguration of the second South American Police Conference in 1920 in Buenos
Aires, "the labor problem" occupied an increasingly central role in international police
correspondence.[62]

Between the first South American Police Conference in 1905 and the following
one held in Buenos Aires in 1920, the police pursuit of traveling criminals, sex traf-

fickers, and anarchists increased considerably. Yet, the tenor of policing debates was also changing. At the 1920 meeting, representatives from Peru, Bolivia, and Paraguay joined the former delegates, expanding police cooperation to new parts of the continent. Nevertheless, the context, following the Russian Revolution of 1917, was very different from that of the 1905 meeting. The events transpiring in Europe were not the only developments affecting the climate of the conference. In South America, the growing labor movement emerged with significant anarchist and communist participation.

The political tone of the meeting showed less commitment to safeguarding individual rights. It was no coincidence that the meeting was in Buenos Aires. There, authoritarian groups increasingly dismissed the participants in any labor struggle as enemies of society.[63] The anxiety over the escalation of labor conflicts provided the main reason for a new official announcement. "Recent developments of a socially subversive nature" shaking the Río de la Plata region, noted the Buenos Aires police chief, have evinced the international nature of labor activism: "Their leaders maintained relations with sects located in various countries."[64] Shortly after the conference of 1905, Falcón had assumed the position of police chief and, from the Special Section, waged a war against anarchism, which included infiltrations into the realms of organized labor and the fierce repression of street protests. A massacre during a general strike on May 1, 1909, and the subsequent anarchist plot that claimed Falcón's life, unleashed a wave of repression that led to the enactment of the 1910 Social Defense Law. From then on, even the events of the so-called Tragic Week of January 1919 could be used to justify a shift in the direction of police cooperation toward "a true crusade of social prophylaxis," as one Peruvian delegate called it. A letter of invitation telegraphed to the various police headquarters also noted the immediate link between the conference and these political developments.[65]

Vucetich, an indisputable protagonist in the 1905 meeting, had distanced himself from the police since 1912, when he engaged in an open confrontation with police authorities of the city and province over his intention to create a general registry of civil identification. Since 1909, he had declared the necessity of establishing national organizations for independent identification in the police departments in order to avoid possible political uses of dactyloscopic information. Without questioning the widespread international acceptance the fingerprinting system had gained by then, the organizers of the 1920 meeting sought to link the conference more closely to the sphere of political repression than to the discussions of scientific policing that had predominated in 1905. This conference culminated in the reform of the 1905 agreement. The new version centered on cooperation in a more specific policing matter: the exchange of data about "plots or the execution of anarchical deeds attempting to alter the social order," the "circulation of dailies, newspapers, pamphlets, images

FIGURE 1.8. South American Police Conference, 1920. Conferencia Sudamericana de Policía, 1920, Archivo General de la Nación Argentina, sección de fotografías, inv. 189.824.

or pictures [*grabados*]," "resolutions of legal or administrative character referring to social defense," and information about the preparation or perpetration of *common crime*."[66]

Since the 1905 conference, the main problem identified by the police forces had been the growing geographic mobility of crime, but they had not developed solutions other than circulating photographs and dactyloscopic records. This time, police authorities attempted to narrow the gap between the dynamic capabilities of the criminal work and the antiquated police resources. The explanation of this discrepancy was simple: criminals fled at high speeds aided by the ease of transportation, relocated to one or another country with absolute freedom, frequently changed their names, and claimed different nationalities. In contrast, the police forces were required to comply with all legal procedures in order to travel from one country to another: they always arrived too late; the criminals were always one step ahead of them.[67] Besides, the reality of labor unrest clearly demanded modernized international policing methods.

In the face of this dilemma, the proposed solutions focused "purely" on the terrain of policing. The Argentine delegation proposed a plan to facilitate the pursuit of delinquents, suggesting that police who wanted to cross into any of the countries belonging to the conference to arrest a suspect should be exempted from gathering all the necessary documentation usually required in those cases. A "simple telegraphic announcement" from police headquarters, it was suggested, should be sufficient to allow an agent to cross borders, with the promise of mailing the necessary documentation within an agreed time frame. Another police official, the Comisario de Órdenes of the Police of the Capital, Miguel Denovi, additionally formulated a proposal outside the formal agreement to authorize postal and telegraphic resources to the chiefs of large policing institutions in order to accelerate communication. Delegates approved the proposal as a "recommendation to the government."[68]

CONCLUSIONS

Between the first interactions of Argentine and Brazilian police in the late 1890s and the 1920 South American Police Conference, the meaning of the term "traveling criminal" underwent substantial change. International criminals, from pickpockets and swindlers to counterfeiters, remained a central concern for South American police. Nevertheless, over the first two decades of the twentieth century, police aiming to limit the circulation of "undesirables" increasingly focused their attention on trans-Atlantic networks connecting militant communists and anarchists.[69] At the time, South American police considered the anarchist plots plaguing Europe to be a disturbing but distant reality. During his interview with Beazley, Pacheco noted that "happily, anarchism does not exist yet" in Rio de Janeiro.[70] But several years later, as a Brazilian delegate at the International Police Conference of 1905, Pacheco showed greater concern as he narrated the events of the first general strike of 1903.[71] These anxieties continued to grow in response to the increasing anarchist presence in Buenos Aires, Montevideo, São Paulo, and Rio de Janeiro.

Months before the Argentine police chief visited Rio de Janeiro, the international community had participated in an important International Conference against Anarchy in Rome, an event many historians consider the dawn of transnational police cooperation. Nevertheless, focusing exclusively on police pursuit of labor activists neglects an entire dimension of police activity concerned with traveling criminals and international networks of sex trafficking. The 1905 and 1920 conferences in Buenos Aires formed part of a broader global trend toward police cooperation in Europe and the Americas, where police jointly discussed diverse ways to combat transnational crime. Despite the particularities of each meeting, these South American conferences formed part of the trajectory of international cooperation that began in Rome and continued with the 1914 Conference of Criminal Police in Monaco and the 1922 International Police Conference in New York. This process culminated in the formation of the International Criminal Police Commission, headquartered in Vienna during the interwar period. After Nazis co-opted the institution in 1938, the Allied powers rebuilt the institution, naming it Interpol following their victory in World War II.[72]

Undergirding this emergence of an extensive network of police was a phenomenon sociologist Paul Knepper called the "invention of international crime," which emerged in the wake of the massive trans-Atlantic migratory routes.[73] Recall that both Minga-Minga and Narigueta had been born in Italy. Consequently, we can consider the history of traveling criminals and South American police cooperation as an integral part of circum-Atlantic history: "the history of the people who crossed the Atlantic, who lived on its shores and who participated in the communities it made possible."[74] This chapter has demonstrated that the exchange of criminal records, mugshots, and telegrams among South American police forces generated crucial records that permit us to reconstruct the social history of criminal practices across national borders. The traveling criminals were much more than figments of police imagination and fears. They lived complex lives full of daring, ambition, and survival.

NOTES

Translated by Bonnie A. Lucero

1. About the first point, see Simon Cole, *Suspect Identities: A History of Fingerprinting and Criminal Identification* (Cambridge: Harvard University Press, 2001); Kristin Ruggiero, "Fingerprinting and the Argentine Plan for Universal Identification in the Late Nineteenth and Early Twentieth Centuries," in *Documenting Individual Identity: The Development of Practices in the Modern World*, ed. Jane Caplan and John Torpey, 184–96 (Princeton, NJ: Princeton University Press, 2001); Julia Rodríguez, "South Atlantic Crossings: Fingerprints, Science, and the State in Turn-of-the-Century Argentina," *American Historical Review* 109, no. 2 (2004): 387–416; Mercedes García Ferrari, "Dissemination of the Argentine Dactyloscopy System in the Early Twentieth Century: Local, Regional, and International Dimensions," in *Identification and Registration Practices in Transnational Perspective: People, Papers, and Practices*, ed. Ilsen About, James Brown, and Gayle Lonergan, 40–58 (London: Palgrave, 2013).

2. Diego Galeano, "Voyages de policiers: Une route entre Paris et les villes sud américaines, 1880–1905," in *Circulations policières en Europe, 1750–1914*, ed. Catherine Denys, 41–62 (Lille: Presses Universitaires du Septentrion, 2012); Diego Galeano, "As polícias estrangeiras," in *Criminosos viajantes, vigilantes modernos: Circulações policiais entre Rio*

de Janeiro e Buenos Aires, 1890–1930 (PhD diss., Universidade Federal do Rio de Janeiro, 2012), 100–137.

3. See, for example, Juan Suriano, *Trabajadores, anarquismo y Estado represor: De la Ley de residencia a la Ley de defensa social (1902–1910)* (Buenos Aires: Centro Editor de América Latina, 1988).

4. This case of cooperation between police forces and soldiers is known as Operation Condor. Alejandro Paredes, "La Operación Cóndor y la guerra fría," *Universum* 1, no. 19 (2004): 122–37; Samuel Blixen, "La Operación Cóndor y la internacionalización de la represión en el Cono Sur," in *Memorias de la violencia en Uruguay y Argentina: Golpes, dictaduras y exilios (1973–2006)*, ed. Eduardo Rey Tristán, 125–32 (Santiago de Compostela: Universidad de Santiago de Compostela, 2007); J. Patrice McSherry, *Predatory States: Operation Condor and Covert War in Latin America* (New York: Rowman and Littlefield, 2005).

5. Dudley Baines, *Emigration from Europe, 1815–1930* (Cambridge: Cambridge University Press, 1995), 1–2; Samuel L. Baily and Eduardo José Míguez, eds., *Mass Migration to Modern Latin America* (New York: Rowman and Littlefield, 2003); Jose Moya, *Cousins and Strangers: Spanish Immigrants in Buenos Aires, 1850–1930* (Berkeley: University of California Press, 1998), 45–59.

6. May E. Bletz, *Immigration and Acculturation in Brazil and Argentina, 1890–1920* (New York: Palgrave, 2010); Eugenia Scarzanella, *Ni gringos ni indios: Inmigración, criminalidad y racismo en la Argentina, 1890–1940* (Buenos Aires: Universidad Nacional de Quilmes Ediciones, 2002).

7. Conferencia Internacional de Policía, *Convenio celebrado entre las policías de La Plata y Buenos Aires (Argentina), de Rio de Janeiro (Brasil), de Santiago de Chile y de Montevideo (R. O. del Uruguay)* (Buenos Aires: Imprenta de la Policía de la Capital, 1905), 20.

8. In a decade marred by abundant anarchist plots, traveling anarchists provoked intense debates over the need to create networks of police cooperation to facilitate the exchange of information. Regarding the links between the anarchist plots and the rise of police cooperation after the International Conference in Rome in 1898, see Richard Bach Jensen, *The Battle Against Anarchist Terrorism: An International History, 1878–1934* (Cambridge: Cambridge University Press, 2014).

9. For photographic galleries of Argentine delinquents, see Mercedes García Ferrari, *Ladrones conocidos/sospechosos reservados: Identificación policial en Buenos Aires, 1880–1905* (Buenos Aires: Prometeo, 2010), 55–111.

10. One of the cases against Ángel Artire can be found in the Buenos Aires Municipal Criminal Court archive; he was charged with stealing money from a Frenchman in 1883. The trial record confirms Artire's age (when he was sentenced, he was twenty-five years old) and also mentions his alias, Minga-Minga. Archivo Nacional de la República Argentina, Tribunal Criminal (Juzgado del Crimen de la Capital), proceso A-11-3, 1884.

11. República de Argentina, *Galería de ladrones de la capital, 1880 a 1887*, vol. 1 (Buenos Aires: Imprenta del Departamento de Policía, 1887), 8.

12. José S. (Fray Mocho) Álvarez, *Memorias de un vigilante* (Buenos Aires: Vaccaro, 1920), 97.

13. "24:000$000," *Diário do Comércio*, Rio de Janeiro, July 12, 1892, p. 1.

14. "Gatuno conhecido," *Correio Paulistano*, São Paulo, June 11, 1895, p. 2.

15. "Que quadrilha!" *Gazeta de Notícias*, Rio de Janeiro, October 6, 1897, p. 2. The events also appear in two other untitled articles: *Cidade do Rio: Jornal da tarde*, Rio de Janeiro, October 6, 1897, p. 1, and *A Notícia*, Rio de Janeiro, October 6, 1897, p. 1.

16. Alexandre J. de Mello Morais Filho, *Factos e memórias* (Rio de Janeiro: Garnier, 1904), 343.

17. Vicente Reis, *Os ladrões no Rio, 1898–1903* (Rio de Janeiro: Laemmert, 1903), 96.

18. Dr. Antonio, *Memórias de um rato de hotel: A vida do Dr. Antonio narrada por elle mesmo* (Rio de Janeiro: Gazeta de Notícias, 1912), 100.

19. Diego Galeano and Mercedes García Ferrari, "Cartographie du bertillonnage: Le système anthropométrique en Amérique latine: Circuits de diffusion, usages et résistances," in *Aux origines de la police scientifique: Alphonse Bertillon, précurseur de la science du crime*, ed. Pierre Piazza, 308–31 (Paris: Karthala, 2011).

20. Ori Preuss, *Bridging the Island: Brazilians' Views of Spanish America and Themselves, 1865–1912* (Frankfurt/Madrid: Iberoamericana-Vervuert, 2011); Boris Fausto and Fernando Devoto, *Brasil e Argentina: Um ensaio de história comparada (1850–2002)* (São Paulo: Editora 34, 2004).

21. Preuss, *Bridging the Island*, 116.

22. *Jornal do Commercio*, Rio de Janeiro, July 31, 1899, p. 1.

23. *Jornal do Commercio*, Rio de Janeiro, August 3, 1899, p. 1.

24. "Entrevista com o Dr. Beazley," *Jornal do Commercio*, Rio de Janeiro, August 10, 1899, p. 3.

25. "Agentes da polícia secreta de Buenos Aires," *Jornal do Commercio*, Rio de Janeiro, August 12, 1899, p. 3. The lineup formed by the Buenos Aires secret police also made the news. "Na polícia," *Jornal do Brasil*, August 12–13, 1899.

26. "A polícia argentina," *Jornal do Commercio*, Rio de Janeiro, August 13, 1899.

27. "A polícia argentina," *Jornal do Commercio*, Rio de Janeiro, August 13, 1899, p. 2. Indeed, the pictures of these thieves could be found in an 1892 photographic gallery: República de Argentina, *Galería de ladrones, 1888–1891* (Buenos Aires: Imprenta de la Policía de la Capital, 1892), 1:159–61, 1:335–37.

28. Both Minga-Minga and Narigueta were Italian by birth, arriving in South America during the height of European immigration. In Argentina and Brazil, Italians were among the immigrants labeled as "undesirable ethnicities," and consequently they faced persecu-

tion through deportation laws amid an increasingly xenophobic nationalist fervor. See Julia Kirk Blackwelder and Lyman L. Johnson, "Changing Criminal Patterns in Buenos Aires, 1890 to 1914," *Journal of Latin American Studies* 14, no. 2 (1982): 359–79; Boris Fausto, *Crime e cotidiano: A criminalidade em São Paulo (1880–1924)* (São Paulo: Edusp, 2001), 71–81; Scarzanella, *Ni gringos, ni indios*.

29. "Narigueta," *Diário de Notícias*, Rio de Janeiro, April 6, 1890, p. 2. About Sampaio Ferraz's campaign, see Marcos Luiz Bretas, "A queda do Império da Navalha e da Rasteira: A República e os capoeiras," *Estudos Afro-Asiáticos* 20 (1991): 239–56.

30. One report implicated him in the theft of an actress's jewelry (*Diário do Comércio*, Rio de Janeiro, April 21, 1889, p. 2). Narigueta was also accused of committing robbery at the Niterói racetrack (*Diário do Notícias*, Rio de Janeiro, Feb. 18, 1889, p. 1). Robberies on electric trams also showed traces of Narigueta's work, with the complicity of other crooks (*Jornal do Brasil*, Rio de Janeiro, March 26, 1895, p. 1). Perhaps the best-known case was the 1893 robbery, after which he attempted to kill an officer while resisting arrest, a confusing episode in which one national guardsman lost his life ("Assassinato," *Gazeta de Notícias*, Rio de Janeiro, March 23, 1893, p. 1).

31. "Entrevista com o Dr. Beazley," 3.

32. Throughout the nineteenth century, transoceanic migration assumed unprecedented proportions, particularly the flow of migrants from Europe to America. Between 1815 and 1930, more than five hundred million people left Europe for the American continent. The United States received the largest number of immigrants during the period (32.6 million), followed by Canada (7.2), Argentina (6.4), and Brazil (4.3). Baines, *Emigration from Europe*, 1–2.

33. João Brasil Silvado, *O serviço policial em Paris e Londres* (Rio de Janeiro: Imprensa Nacional, 1895), 112.

34. Alberto Cortina, *La Policía en Sudamérica* (La Plata: Talleres Gráficos "La Popular," 1905), 21.

35. "O Dr. Beazley," *O Paiz*, Rio de Janeiro, August 10, 1899, p. 1.

36. "La Policía de Rio de Janeiro: El viaje del Doctor Beazley," *Revista de Policía* (Buenos Aires) 55, September 1, 1899, p. 100.

37. "Polícia Argentina," *Jornal do Comércio*, Rio de Janeiro, August 18, 1899, p. 1.

38. Regarding the conflict between dactyloscopy and anthropometry, see García Ferrari, "Dissemination of the Argentine Dactyloscopy System," 40–58.

39. Juan Vucetich, *Dactiloscopia: Cuál debe ser la idoneidad del identificador: Su prueba legal en la reincidencia: Congresos Científicos* (La Plata: Joaquín Sesé, 1909), 19–20.

40. Juan Vucetich, "Congreso Policial Sudamericano: Su necesidad y manera de promoverlo," in Terceiro Congresso Científico Latino-americano, *A Polícia Argentina e a Polícia Brasileira* (Rio de Janeiro: Imprensa Nacional, 1905), 53–79.

41. Ibid., 79.

42. Antônio Bento de Faria, "Da necessidade e uniformizar a ação da polícia dos países americanos," in Terceiro Congresso Científico Latino-americano, *A Polícia Argentina e a Polícia Brasileira*, 81–87.

43. José G. Rossi, "La policía internacional," *Boletín de Policía* (Buenos Aires) 1, no. 10, September 15, 1905, pp. 5–6.

44. Eurico Cruz, "Necessidade da fundação de um Congresso Policial Sul-Americano," in Terceiro Congresso Científico Latino-americano, *A Polícia Argentina e a Polícia Brasileira*, 91–94.

45. "Del Doctor Félix Pacheco," *Boletín de Policía de la Provincia de Buenos Aires* (La Plata) 1, no. 3, September 30, 1905, pp. 3–4.

46. "Convención Interpolicial," *Boletín de Policía de la Provincia de Buenos Aires*, 1, no. 4, La Plata, October 31, 1905, p. 4. "La próxima conferencia policial internacional," *Revista de Policía* (Buenos Aires) 9, no. 201, October 1, 1905, p. 70.

47. "Sr. Juan Vucetich y Dr. Félix Pacheco," *Boletín de Policía* (Buenos Aires) 1, no. 10, September 15, 1905, pp. 1–2.

48. José G. Rossi, "La policía internacional," 7–9.

49. "Convenio Interpolicial Sudamericano," *Boletín de Policía de la Provincia de Buenos Aires* (La Plata) 1, no. 3, September 30, 1905, p. 6.

50. Regarding Vucetich's reception in Chile, see the dossier published in the *Boletín de la Policía de Santiago* 9, no. 79 (Santiago de Chile: Imprenta de la Prefectura de Policía, enero de 1909).

51. Cristian Palacios, "Entre Bertillon y Vucetich: Las tecnologías de identificación policial: Santiago de Chile, 1893–1924," *Revista Historia y Justicia* 1 (2013): 1–28.

52. Conferencia Internacional de Policía, *Convenio celebrado entre las policías de La Plata y Buenos Aires (Argentina), de Rio de Janeiro (Brasil), de Santiago de Chile y de Montevideo (R. O. del Uruguay)* (Buenos Aires: Imprenta y Encuadernación de la Policía de la Capital Federal, 1905).

53. "Conferencia internacional de policías," *Revista de Policía* (Buenos Aires) 9, no. 202, October 16, 1905, p. 78.

54. "Actas de la Segunda Sesión," in Conferencia Internacional de Policía, *Convenio celebrado*, 33.

55. Cf. art. 2, inc. a-g. "Actas de la Segunda Sesión," 5–6.

56. Ibid., 11.

57. Cristiana Schettini, "South American Tours: Work Relations in the Entertainment Market in South America," *International Review of Social History* 57 (2012): 129–60; Lená Medeiros de Menezes, *Os indesejáveis: Desclassificados da modernidade: Protesto, crime e expulsão na Capital Federal (1890–1930)* (Rio de Janeiro: Eduerj, 1996); Cristiana Schet-

tini, *Que tenhas teu corpo: Uma historia social da prostituição no Rio de Janeiro das primeiras décadas republicanas* (Rio de Janeiro: Arquivo Nacional, 2006).

58. Ramón Falcón, "Carta al Señor Jefe de Policía de Rio de Janeiro, Buenos Aires, Abril de 1907," in *Memoria de la Policía de Buenos Aires: 1906–1909, Jefatura del Coronel Ramón L. Falcón* (Buenos Aires: Imprenta y Encuadernación de la Policía, 1909), 130.

59. Ramón Falcón, "Carta al Señor Jefe de Policía de Rio de Janeiro, Buenos Aires, Noviembre de 1907," in *Memoria de la Policía de Buenos Aires*, 154–55.

60. Ramón Falcón, "Carta al Señor Secretario de Negocios de Justicia y Seguridad Pública del Estado de San Pablo, Diciembre de 1907," in *Memoria de la Policía de Buenos Aires*, 159.

61. Diego Galeano, *Criminosos viajantes, vigilantes modernos*, 227–30.

62. Archivo Nacional de Brasil, Secretaría de Policía, GIFI 6C, carpetas 252 y 308.

63. This position was aligned with the escalation of police repression in Rio de Janeiro and the hardening political vigilance that had been discussed earlier at the conference convened by Aurelino Leal. Pedro Tórtima, *Polícia e justiça de mãos dadas: A Conferência Judiciária-Policial de 1917* (master's thesis, Universidade Federal Fluminense, Niterói, 1988).

64. "Congreso Sudamericano de Policía: Sus orígenes: Constitución y desarrollo," *Revista de Policía* (Buenos Aires) 23, no. 523, April 1, 1920, p. 177.

65. Conferencia Internacional Sudamericana de Policía, *Convenios y actas* (Buenos Aires: Imprenta J. Tragant, 1920), 52.

66. Ibid., 125.

67. About the relationship between communication and transportation technologies, international delinquency, and the transnationalization of the police, see David F. Bell, "Technologies of Speed, Technologies of Crime," *Yale French Studies* 108 (2005): 8–19; Mathieu Deflem, "Technology and the Internationalization of Policing: A Comparative-Historical Perspective," *Justice Quarterly* 19, no. 3 (2002): 453–75; Paul Knepper, *The Invention of International Crime: A Global Issue in the Making, 1881–1914* (London: Palgrave, 2010), 12–42.

68. Conferencia Internacional Sudamericana de Policía, *Convenios y actas*, 25.

69. Richard Bach Jensen, "The International Anti-Anarchist Conference of 1898 and the Origins of Interpol," *Journal of Contemporary History* 16, no. 2 (1981): 323–47.

70. "Entrevista com o Dr. Beazley," p. 3.

71. Conferencia Internacional de Policía, *Convenio celebrado entre las policías*, 47. During the strike of 1903 in Rio de Janeiro, newspapers and police officials denounced the "foreign anarchists' infiltration of the Brazilian working class." Francisca Nogueira de Azevedo, *Malandros desconsolados: O diário da primeira greve geral no Rio de Janeiro* (Rio de Janeiro: Relume Dumará, 2005), 179.

72. Mathieu Deflem, *Policing World Society: Historical Foundations of International Police Cooperation* (New York: Oxford University Press, 2004), 97–110. Peter Andreas and Ethan Nadelman, *Policing the Globe: Criminalization and Crime Control in International Relations* (Oxford: Oxford University Press, 2008), 59–104.

73. Knepper, *The Invention of International Crime.*

74. David Armitage, "Three Concepts of Atlantic History," in *The British Atlantic World, 1500–1800*, ed. David Armitage and Michael J. Braddick, 11–27 (Basingstoke: Palgrave Macmillan, 2002), 16.

2

IMAGINING CRIMINALITY

᠄᠄

Race, Identity, and Crime in Peru, 1890s–1930s

LUZ E. HUERTAS

IN 1934, Peruvian political scientist and lawyer Juan Luis Hague argued that, scientifically speaking, biology ruled people's behavior. While dismissing the idea that free will determined criminality, Hague denounced prevailing criminal law for its aprioristic methods, which he believed disregarded the powerful relationship between psychological and physiological phenomena, particularly in relation to criminality.[1] Hague's musings were part of a broader pattern of Peruvian intellectuals engaging in and appropriating positivist theories of crime in an attempt to interpret the causes and characteristics of local criminality beginning in the late nineteenth century.

Historians including Carlos Aguirre and Deborah Poole, who have examined the ideas of these criminologists and criminology enthusiasts in depth, have argued that Peruvian elites used positivist theories to criminalize indigenous peoples and the *plebe* more generally and to justify exclusionary policies of social control.[2] Existing studies mainly trace the sociological or biological orientation of the Peruvian criminological discourses and their institutional impact. This chapter connects this historiography on crime and social control with the scholarly conversations on the flexibility and malleability of the concept of race.[3] I argue that rather than shifting from biological to sociological explanations of the etiology of crime, Peruvian criminologists dissected European theories and adapted them to preexisting notions of identity that were usually geo-racially determined—that is, notions that emerged out of geographically specific racial categories based mostly, in the case of Peru, on the dichotomy of the predominantly mestizo and white coastal lowlands, on the one hand, and the indigenous highlands on the other.[4] The political dominance of Lima and other coastal cities from the second half of the nineteenth century onward enhanced this dichotomous view of the country and its inhabitants.

By (re)examining the interpretations of race and crime in theses, dissertations, judicial studies, essays, specialized books, and scientific theoretical treatises from the period, this study demonstrates that, rather than choosing a single theoretical orientation, these intellectuals appropriated and selectively applied these theories according to the racially specific "criminal subject" they constructed. At the same time, scientific studies on psychological heredity influenced Peruvian intellectuals, as they developed a complex view of race that combined regionally rooted views of identity with biology and culture. This practice shows that intellectuals ultimately transformed theories spread throughout Latin America into specific and local explanations of race and crime. Also, this practice made it easier to link specific psychological characteristics—interpreted also as biological—to broad racial groups. In fact, between the 1890s and the 1930s, psychology became the main vehicle through which certain facets of biological determinism continued to shape scholarly explanations of crime. In their attempts to define the biological, moral, or cultural causes of local criminality, specialists also sought to connect Peru to what they imagined to be the core of modernity by interpreting "increasing" criminality as a sign of progress.

This chapter is structured in three parts. First, I focus on the ways in which the conceptual flexibility of racial thinking influenced criminologists' construction of local criminal subjects, particularly with internal racial others. The second part contrasts these ideas with those produced by the criminalization of Asian foreigners. The last section examines the connection between modernity and criminality by analyzing the criminologists' interpretation of their own role in the fight against crime, which they perceived as part of the elites' civilizing mission.

ON THE FLEXIBILITY OF THE CONCEPT OF RACE IN PERUVIAN DISCOURSES ABOUT CRIME

European theories of crime prevention were particularly popular in Peru after the War of the Pacific (1879–83) as the country struggled to recover from postwar devastation and the humiliation of losing its southern territories. The increasingly export-oriented nature of its economy during the late 1890s and its successful reinsertion into the world market made the development of new modernizing projects feasible, which in turn renewed the elites' interest in social control. The Limeño intelligentsia became particularly fond of discussing positivist ideas of order and progress as the city underwent major population growth (from 107,114 inhabitants in 1892 to 223,807 in 1920), the gradual transformation of its infrastructure, and the expansion of the middle and working classes.[5]

Profound political and administrative centralism also made Lima the country's political core, especially following the electoral reform of 1896, which mandated literacy as a precondition for political participation. Because most of the literate population lived on the coast—according to the census of 1876, for instance, 64 percent of Lima's population was literate—the main cities of this area, especially the capital city, wielded disproportionate power in electing national authorities.[6] Political centralism and the alliance between foreign capital, the coastal oligarchy, and provincial *gamonales* (provincial landed potentates) facilitated the political dominance of the Partido Civil, the political party of the *costeño* upper classes.[7]

During this period, positivist theories became a new item of scholarly interest at San Marcos University in Lima, the elites' main center of higher education from which the Partido Civil drew its intellectual core.[8] From the 1890s to the 1930s, the Peruvian intelligentsia, already imbued with hygienist theories, discussed the ideas of the positivist school of criminology and its variations. The Italians Césare Lombroso, Raffaele Garofalo, and Enrico Ferri, and the Frenchmen Gabriel de Tarde and Alexander Lacassagne, among others, became mandatory authors to read or cite when debating local criminality or possible reforms of the justice system, police, prisons, and other normalizing institutions.

Carlos Aguirre has argued that Peruvian intellectuals initially took keen interest in the Italian School of Positivist Criminology, which initially promoted biologically deterministic identification of criminals through physical features.[9] Yet, soon enough, these intellectuals began to reject these Lombrosian theories in favor of seemingly competing French theories, which emphasized the social rather than biological causes of crime. The appropriation of these theories, according to Aguirre, led to the evolution of racial ideas among the elites, who ultimately eschewed biological forms of racism.[10]

Nevertheless, recent research on the European criminological schools that gained popularity in Latin America during the end of the nineteenth century demonstrates that the prevailing assumption of a clear and complete separation between the French-sociological and Italian-biological theoretical perspectives did not actually exist.[11] Although French scientists, such as Tarde and Lacassagne, rejected the Lombrosian biologically deterministic idea of a born criminal, their social interpretation of deviancy did not completely abandon the role of heredity in its etiology.[12] Tarde's theory of imitation certainly argued that individuals were never born into criminality but rather socialized into it; yet, he also stated that some people had innate tendencies toward deviant behavior that predisposed them to crime.[13] In the same vein, Lacassagne's theories on environmental influence suggested that the modification of the social environment could lessen criminality, but his concept of the social relied on the hygienic influences of climate and diet and their effects in turn on the brain and body more so than it emphasized poverty or injustice.[14]

Furthermore, by the end of the century, Italian criminologists had adjusted their theoretical repertoire on the causes of crime by establishing biology as one of several factors that determined criminality. Peruvian criminologists actively discussed the ideas of Lombroso's disciples, Ferri and Garofalo, who proposed social defense and crime prevention as criminology's main mission and fostered the incorporation of this doctrine into actual regulations of criminal procedure. Therefore, although criminological theories "available" for Peruvian intellectuals did have points of disagreement, they were not mutually exclusive, and the legacy of Italian positivism continued to play an important role in scholarly and political debates.

More importantly, prior to the discussion of these theories, the circulation of studies on criminal psychology and psychological heredity that had had a great impact among scholars interested in scientifically identifying the sources of the "Peruvian national character" also influenced the debate about local criminality. Most of these theories proposed a Lamarckian view of heredity, which emphasized the capacity for generational improvement. Peruvian scholars' perspective on the so-called biological and social factors of criminality was not necessarily consistent, and they often used psychology to explain aspects of local criminality that escaped more general social and biological explanations.

The lack of consistency among these scholars was also related to the fact that they accommodated their theories depending on the shifts in academic and political interests. At the beginning of his career, Javier Prado y Ugarteche, the author of *El método positivo en el derecho penal* (1890)—the first text that discussed positivist theories of crime in Peru—criticized the seeming obsession of Italian scholars with biology, arguing that "in fact, they have been dazzled almost totally by the biological causes of criminality, studying only superficially its social causes."[15] Yet, he agreed with the idea that heredity was as important as environmental and social factors in the production of criminal tendencies among individuals, embracing theories that interpreted psychological heredity as a biological by-product. Later in his career, he even recommended "modify[ing] [the Peruvian race], to renew our blood and our inheritance" through whitening to improve the country's social condition.[16]

In 1895 another student at San Marcos University, Plácido Jiménez, a future deputy and minister of justice, wrote one of the most important theses about national criminality, in which he stated that, "thankfully for the country," social factors determined criminality, which meant that it was possible to improve the conditions of society and, therefore, decrease criminality.[17] Yet, in that same monograph he also argued that some individuals had an innate perversity: "why, then, don't we also admit that there are some people who are prone to goodness while others are prone to evil?"[18] Thirty years after the publication of his thesis, Jiménez developed a penal code draft that categorized "savages" and "semi-civilized" indigenous delinquents in the same group as physically disabled and degenerate criminals, which demonstrates that he limited his understanding of the "social" to certain social groups or circumstances.[19]

Rather than representing a shift from biological to sociological explanations of crime, the main transformation produced by these and other scholars' engagement with positivist criminological theories was a change of emphasis from crime to criminals as dangerous subjects as well as a new interest in crime prevention.[20] As Diego Galeano and Marcos Fernández Labbé argue in this volume, identifying specific types of criminals became crucial to agents in charge of fighting crime in Latin America. In Peru, this new emphasis conformed to predetermined though flexible notions of race stemming from the country's long colonial legacy, diverse ethnic and racial composition, variegated geography, and regional identities.[21] While deploying a cultural understanding of race in most cases, Peruvian elites tended to attribute specific characteristics to each social sector belonging to the popular classes, which ultimately allowed for detailed criminal characterizations. As a consequence, the flexibility of the notion of race played an important role in the construction of "othernesses," which in turn conditioned the use of theories about crime.

One telling example of the ways these notions of race influenced intellectual production outside the criminological milieu in Peru is the description of nonwhite populations by José Carlos Mariátegui, one of the most important Latin American thinkers of the twentieth century. When Mariátegui addressed the problem of race as a class issue in his pathbreaking *Seven Interpretive Essays on Peruvian Reality* (1928), he was certainly referring to indigenous peoples, whom he presented as national subjects oppressed by exploitative systems that had ultimately depressed them morally and physically. However, Mariátegui viewed blacks, mulattoes, and Asians as nonnational subjects incapable of contributing to the national life in a positive way.[22] In contrast to his interpretation of race in social and cultural terms when addressing indigenous populations, Mariátegui combined cultural and psychological elements when referring to other nonwhite races. He argued, for instance, that when African descendants mixed with Indians they bastardized the Indian race, as the Africans transferred to them their "morbid psychology."[23] In turn, his racial categorization of Asians depicted them as individuals "who grafted their race but not their culture" onto the Peruvian nation, "inoculating fatalism, apathy, and defects of the decrepit East in their descendants."[24] Thus, Mariátegui did not view all racial others as equal victims of classist systems of exploitation. Rather, he established differences between them based on a concept of race that defined human value in terms of an individual's proximity to the nation as well as on notions of psychological heredity.

Similarly, criminologists and criminology enthusiasts highlighted differences between indigenous, mestizo, black, and Asian deviants. The construct of the indigenous criminal subject, for example, tended to emphasize exploitation or inheritance, or both, as the cause of savagery or degeneration, which made tutelage mandatory for rehabilitation. Indeed, by 1900, lawyer Mariano Ignacio Prado y Ugarteche had examined several criminological theories in his search for the typical Peruvian criminal subject. Although the lawyer disregarded Lombrosian ideas about the supposedly distinctive physical features of born criminals, he, like his brother Javier, borrowed Théodule-Armand Ribot's evolutionist ideas on psychological heredity to explain that the character of indigenous peoples was resistant to change. According to Prado y Ugarteche, "the Peruvian indigenous individual is an irrefutable proof of the strength and intensity of this *biological* principle: time has passed and, despite the contact and influence of diverse civilizations and the profound political and social changes, [the Indian] continues to be dominated by his disgraceful heritage."[25] In the lawyer's view, this fact demonstrated the indigenous incapacity to act under civilized standards. Ribot, Prado y Ugarteche's model scholar, was a neo-Lamarckian French psychologist who in the 1870s had contended that biological heredity and its psychological counterpart defined fixed national characters.[26] He argued that although some nations had achieved higher levels of civilization by intermingling with other, "better" ones, there were some "survivors of a past age," such as the Roma, who were innately incapable of adapting to civilized life and, therefore, were also prone to lawless behavior.[27]

Another Peruvian intellectual who found psychological heredity a valuable theoretical resource was political scientist and lawyer Pio Máximo Medina. Between 1906 and 1907, Medina studied criminals and the stagnation of the indigenous race, arguing that the forced passivity imposed by the Inca Empire over indigenous peoples had altered these peoples' cerebral constitution over the generations.[28] The exploitation suffered during Spanish rule had triggered feelings of vengeance that could make them bloodthirsty, but, in general, the discouraging reality in which they lived had caused "organic defects" expressed in the natives' visible apathy. In contrast to the Prado y Ugarteche brothers, Medina considered Lombroso's born-criminal idea useful and even compared European cases of men with alleged congenital tendencies toward crime with indigenous men with homicidal impulses.[29] Because psychological heredity offered the possibility of "improvement," this comparison did not prevent Medina from suggesting that indigenous peoples' regeneration through education was a feasible means to reduce criminal behavior.[30]

The depiction of indigenous peoples as victims of historical oppression is also evident in Plácido Jiménez's writings, which blamed alcohol for the "stultification of two million Indians from the highlands" and the consequent proliferation of crimes due to intoxication.[31] Although Jiménez had superficially disregarded Lombrosian criminal taxonomies in his thesis, he had embraced Ferri's idea of the influence of physical factors, which allowed him to emphasize an apparent division between the "coastal *man* and the highland *indio*."[32] By doing so, he revealed his imaginings of Andean indigenous peoples as antithetical to the more acculturated coastal dwellers. This interpretation implied a de facto obliteration from his Indian construct of the corpus of faculties that made those dwellers "proper" human beings.

Jiménez was one of many scholars whose views about criminality, social control, and progress were deeply linked to regional perceptions of the national territory and its inhabitants. These perceptions, which established deterministic views of race, culture, and geography, became an important factor in the scholarly use of scientific theories throughout Latin America at the turn of the century. Euclides da Cunha's world-famous *Os sertões* (1902), for instance, shows a dichotomous relationship between the "civilized" southern coast of Brazil and the semibarbarous Brazilian backlands.[33] Previously, the renowned Brazilian criminologist Raimundo Nina Rodrigues had also highlighted the link between the "savage" races of Brazil and western and northern Brazilian states.[34]

With the advent of Indigenismo in Peru in the early twentieth century, critical voices about the role of indigenous peoples in Peruvian history challenged the construct of the degenerate indigenous subject. Yet, although *indigenistas* deployed explanations of indigenous deviancy that highlighted social causes such as exploitation and corrupt authorities, they did not necessarily reject biological explanations of crime. In fact, *Causas de la criminalidad indígena en el Perú* (1919), the outstanding example of a pro-indigenous criminological study, focused on proving that this population was neither degenerate nor deserving of the Lombrosian category of born criminal, though it accepted this category and most of Lombroso's biological proposals as valid.

Moreover, the author of this study, José Antonio Encinas—the most important Peruvian educator of the first half of the twentieth century—used psychological heredity theories to analyze the "Indian," who, according to him, suffered from a nuanced case of nervous wear (degeneration).[35] It is important to note that Encinas could not escape the already established convention of seeing physical and psychological phenomena as conjoined, which led him to claim that although the indigenous physical constitution was strong, indigenous peoples' nervous systems showed serious perturbations.[36] His objective was to reveal the expansion of *latifundismo* and economic exploitation as the causes of that condition.

In his attempt to highlight the social causes of indigenous afflictions, Encinas separated indigenous peoples from the "civilized" mestizos and whites, thereby reinforcing the existing racial stereotypes. However, Encinas also geo-racialized criminal activities such as banditry to emphasize positive indigenous traits. According to him, brigandage was a uniquely coastal phenomenon whose main agents were blacks and mestizos.[37] Indigenous banditry, although rare, was caused by contact between indigenous peoples and "civilization," which produced professional criminals.[38] Thus, Encinas took an inverse view of the coast/highlands dichotomy influenced by his own personal experience as a member of the provincial elite of the southern highlands (Puno), which had afforded him access to higher education in Lima. Although he acknowledged Lima and the coastal regions in general to be the center of modernity and "civilization," Encinas reinterpreted "civilization" also as a means for the spread and sophistication of deviancy.

The influence of Indigenismo in the decades that followed the publication of Encinas's study did not erase geo-racialized interpretations of criminality or the popularity of psychological heredity to explain its causes. As late as the 1930s, scholarly explanations of crime based on the coast/highland dichotomy persisted. For instance, after famous sociologist José Varallanos asked Enrique López Albújar to write a book on his experiences as a judge in the early 1930s, López Albújar addressed a list of questions developed by Varallanos that at first glance interpreted *bandolerismo* as a consequence of social and economic factors. Nevertheless, when it came to identifying the bandit, the sociologist asked whether he was "of Indian or mestizo race," assuming a priori only two possible racial backgrounds for this type of criminal subject.[39] López Albújar did not find this question illogical or contradictory. In fact, the core of his analysis is a rich combination of political, sociological, psychological, and biological trends, which he carefully dissected to explain specific regional phenomena and fit the geo-racial stereotypes that he (re)constructed. In a time when biological determinism had supposedly fallen out of use, his book *Los caballeros del delito* (1936) demonstrates the resilience of these theories, which were actually still circulating among Peruvian scholarly circles.

Los caballeros del delito presents the view of a coastal intellectual writing about a phenomenon that encompassed several regions as well as social groups in the national territory. According to López Albújar, although the Peruvian bandit was definitely nonwhite (indigenous, black, cholo, or mestizo), the most extreme examples of bandit types embodied deeply contrasting characteristics.[40] For instance, the *bandolero* of the Andean hinterlands at Huánuco was an "Indian" whose "senses react to all violent inspirations. The nose of this Andean criminal acquires a strange excitability[,] which immerses him in a hallucinatory intoxication for long hours. He gets drunk smelling; and the smell, and blood, and turmoil are the necessary stimulants that make his virility, softened by coca and alcohol, react. . . . That is why, when he assaults, he is not satisfied with stealing passengers' bags or taking their animals. . . . He rapes and kills, leaving in his destructive work a testimony of his unrestrained sexuality and his primitive fury."[41] In contrast to the above construct, the bandit from the coastal region of Piura was a mestizo, who was "less reflective than the Indian but more impetuous and faster [to] attack; less greedy and thoroughgoing, less cruel and bloodthirsty. He does not enjoy, with rare exceptions, the spectacle of blood and pain. He does not feel that sadistic and a slightly ritualistic pleasure that the Andean bandit feels; that [type of] pleasure that leads [the Andean bandit] to drink the blood of his victims, to take the heart and eyes out and eat them with an ideological end. He does not unleash his libido in his raids; not because he lacks the will, but because of his modesty."[42]

These extremely specialized categorizations of Peruvian bandits show, above all, the weight that stereotypical views of the inhabitants of broad natural regions carried for the author's concept of race. His depiction of the indigenous bandit highlights physical and physiological elements that are not present in the description of the mestizo bandolero, which ultimately helped the author depict the highland indigenous criminal subject as primitive (atavistic) and animal-like. More importantly, the features of the coastal mestizo criminal were posed in direct opposition to those of the indigenous brigand, which resulted from the author's perception of the two types of *bandidos* as antithetical. In his view, they represented the contradictory coexistence of a progressive coast and an unchanging highland—a dichotomy also present in the texts of Medina, Jiménez, and the Prado y Ugarteche brothers.

Likewise, the main psychological feature of this highland bandit, according to López Albújar, was his "retarded" mental condition, which, together with the exploitative Creole or *mestizo* local authorities, the absence of the central state, and the region's rough and remote geography exacerbated the violent character of the banditry endemic to this region.[43] In contrast, his explanation of the brigandage of the coastal *departamento* of Piura and especially of its littoral provinces highlighted environmental and social influences, such as the desert landscape, the development of agrarian capitalism, social inequalities, and the infamous link between brigands and the local networks of power.[44] López Albújar argued that those links were particularly harmful and ultimately created an ambience of impunity.

López Albújar also selectively used theories of heredity, alternating in his emphasis on biology or culture depending on the subject he analyzed. In his examination of the criminality of the southern coastal city of Tacna, for example, he argued that a high proportion of Italians and their descendants in the population had transformed Tacneño peoples—Creoles and indigenous—into a "more evolved" racial type through miscegenation. That racial improvement encompassed biological and cultural factors, which together with economic, social, and environmental ones such as the absence of haciendas, law-abiding behavior, reduced rural poverty, the Chilean coercive presence, and a benign climate had all contributed to making Tacna a banditry-free city.[45] López Albújar generally saw the Peruvian coast as the recipient of modernity, which made this region's banditry nonprimitive, even though his analysis lacked a comparable examination of the role of the haciendas and mostly dismissed criminal actions of white nationals.[46]

Scholarly perceptions of nonwhite criminal "others" and their linkage to the geographically diverse regions of the country also included constructs about peoples living in even more remote areas than the sierra. For instance, in the introductory lines of Augusto Peñaloza's *Prevención eugénica de la criminalidad en el Perú* (1916), the author commented on the dangerous growth of national criminality by constructing specific criminal subjects who were racially and culturally incompatible with his audience. In one particularly vivid passage, he described two criminals: "an individual of color, who boldly and determinedly broke into a well-located facility in daytime to suffocate an unfortunate wealthy old man in the arc of his brawny arms . . . [and] a woman native of our forests [*selva*], who in an attack of atavistic desire, [and] favored by the darkness of the night and the solitude of the hamlet, cruelly kills her patroness and[,] with the bloodlust that—according to Laugverné [Lauvergne]—characterizes the 'cold murderer,' sacrifices barbarously and unnecessarily two little children."[47]

Although Peñaloza provided his readers with two examples of brutality by nonwhite peoples, only the case of the indigenous female murderer from the Amazon basin implies pure irrationality resulting from irrepressible atavism as the cause of the criminal action.[48] Peñaloza, who considered himself a follower of adaptive eugenics, combined Lombrosian atavism with some of the ideas that prison physician and phrenologist Hubert Lauvergne had developed more than thirty years before the appearance of Lombroso's famous book *L'uomo delinquente*.[49] Lauvergne, whose *Les forçats: Considérés sous le rapport physiologique, moral et intellectuel* (1841) is considered the first semiscientific study of the criminal, was a student of Franz Joseph Gall and a proponent of the identifiability of criminal penchants through the analysis of physical features (skulls).[50] He was also a pioneer in the construction of the first criminal taxonomies and the analysis of inheritable psychological criminal traits. Peñaloza did not make use of either Lombroso's or Lauvergne's propositions about cranial examination but focused on the elements of their theories that defined criminal actions as the result of primitive tendencies when describing indigenous criminal behavior.

Curiously, Peñaloza's example also introduces the female criminal construct to his readers, a rare choice given criminologists' general silence about Peruvian gendered deviance. In fact, there was a strong tendency to avoid women as a topic in Peruvian criminology, which seems to be related to an apparent gender bias in arrests at the turn of the twentieth century. For instance, between 1890 and the early 1920s, less than 18 percent of the individuals arrested in Lima were women.[51] Also, my examination of more than five hundred criminal trials from the same period show that, at least in the capital city, police repression was directed mostly toward men, as they were arrested for even minor offenses, such as brawling, drunkenness, and scandals.[52]

The few criminologists who mentioned women in their studies portrayed them as victims of poverty and abandonment or as examples of honest behavior rather than as deviants. In Jiménez's writings, for instance, women emerge as an example of education's lack of effectiveness against crime because, according to him, Peruvian women's lack of education did not produce a tendency toward criminal activities.[53] Jiménez also praised women's religiosity because he believed that it fostered moral principles. Juan Luis Hague also made some comments on female criminals but only to stress that pregnant women had less responsibility when committing a crime because of their condition.[54] This silence could be attributed to the reinterpretation of the role of women in late nineteenth-century discourses on modernity, which, as historian Maria Emma Mannarelli argues, emphasized women's role as the producers of Peru's future citizens. As a consequence, they were supposed to foster moral principles and ideals of order and progress.[55] Also, the fact that criminology was a field dominated almost exclusively by men during the early twentieth century might have influenced the gender bias in these intellectuals' scholarly works.[56]

DEFINING THE NATIONAL, CONSTRUCTING THE FOREIGN CRIMINAL

The contrasts in the specific cultural, biological, and psychological features in the constructs of criminal subjects belonging to broad natural regions also influenced these scholars' ideas about their own role in the control of criminality and criminals. This role, defined in paternalistic terms, fit the elites' view of their own tutelary mission perfectly because it made their intervention necessary to "rehabilitate" geo-racially defined criminals. Yet, the tutelary character of this mission tended to disappear when the criminal subject examined was perceived as foreign. Because a sector of the elite idealistically agreed that the Peruvian national character was less prone to criminal action, potential foreign deviancy within the country appeared as an increasingly menacing threat.[57]

Similar to the Italian "problem" in Argentina, the immigration of several thousand Chinese immigrants to Peru during the second half of the nineteenth century became a source of concern for a sector of the upper classes who did not profit directly from it. Some members of the elite believed that the social price of Asian immigration outweighed the economic benefits generated by this foreign workforce.[58] The increasing concentration of Chinese immigrants in the main cities of the coast and especially in Lima did not help to ease these concerns.[59] Indeed, between 1878 and 1936, 48–52 percent of the total Chinese population in the country resided in the capital city.[60]

Before the arrival of positivist criminological theories, hygienists had opposed the presence of these foreigners—mainly the poor ones—arguing that their living conditions contributed to the spread of disease and caused moral degeneration. The waves of yellow fever in the 1850s and 1860s only exacerbated these fears, which evolved into demands for proscription. In this context, physician César Borja wrote a thesis that summarized these ideas and presented Chinese immigrants as deviant subjects who, besides promoting the consumption of opium and gambling, had begun to harm Peru's biological "quality."[61] Especially in Lima, argued Borja, Chinese men were producing a new generation of children who inherited no elements of their Peruvian mothers but all traits from their Asian fathers. Consequently, those children were ugly, weak, rachitic, and imperfect.[62] Thus, Borja's ideas reduced the multiplicity of geo-racial and cultural stereotypes assigned to nationals to a single and rather ambiguous construct of a pure "Peruvian" biological race.

This arbitrary opposition of the Chinese and Peruvian "races" strengthened when Chinese immigrants were compared with other foreign communities residing predominantly in coastal cities. In 1896, for example, sociologist Joaquín Capelo contended that of all immigrants living in Lima, the Italian "element" was most aligned with the national character and almost always stayed in Peru to form *completely Peruvian* families.[63] He did not define what the "Peruvian character" was, and this statement actually contradicted his own arguments about the multiple racial groups coexisting under the civilizing power of the "*raza mezclada*" (mixed race).[64]

Some intellectuals and criminology enthusiasts used these ideas to emphasize not only the alleged danger of Chinese criminality but also the incompatibility of the whole "Chinese race" with the "Peruvian" one. For example, in 1891, a connoisseur of criminological ideas published an article in *El Diario Judicial* in which he denounced the unhealthy conditions in which poor Chinese immigrants lived, but also described these people as having "abnormal physiognomies, which could enrich Lombroso's files."[65] Likewise, Plácido Jiménez, who had shown himself rather paternalistic in regard to the "Indian problem," showed a completely different attitude about Asian foreigners living in Lima. He argued that they were responsible for most of the serious offences registered by the police.[66] According to Jiménez, the Chinese were by far the most harmful foreign minority, as they were "the most despicable of the Asians," who transmitted "by inheritance or imitation all their vices to the ones that surround them."[67]

Drawing on the theories of Lombroso and Tarde and combining them with Borja's hygienist ideas, Jiménez characterized the Chinese immigrant as a criminal. This construct emphasized the potential contagiousness of their customs and their "incorrigible" tendency to consume opium, which made them prone to anemia, phthisis, "paralysis, and furious madness."[68] Yet, the worst quality of Jiménez's Chinese subjects was related to their sexual practices. He believed that not even the police's statistical data provided accurate information on the magnitude of sexual offences, including pederasty, committed in Lima's Chinatown.[69] In this analysis of the Chinese "problem," Jiménez did not mention, however, the government's ambiguous policy on the distribution of opium or the substantial contribution of the already established Chinese population to the local economy. His biggest fear was the spread of Chinese customs among the working classes, whom he believed it was the elite's responsibility to moralize.

Like Borja, Capelo, Jiménez, and, as previously mentioned, Mariátegui, other Latin American scholars also used available theories to categorize Asian immigrants as potential criminals. In this volume, for instance, Marcos Fernández Labbé provides valuable information about the characteristics of the Chilean discourse about Chinese immigrants in relation to the consumption of drugs. Also, in Cuba, famous ethnographer and writer Fernando Ortiz believed that both blacks and Chinese were inherently primitive and barbarous. However, he established differences between the criminal attitudes of these racial groups, developing a specialized discourse on criminality and foreign minorities, which pointed to Asians as the most dangerous foreign community in Cuba.[70] Like Javier Prado y Ugarteche, who had emphasized the need of whitening to improve the Peruvian national character, Ortiz adamantly opposed policies that promoted the immigration of both Africans and Chinese peoples while promoting European immigration to the island.

THE PLACE OF MODERNITY: DISCUSSIONS OF CRIMINALITY AND IDENTITY

In Peru, the main function of the discourses on racialized criminal subjects was to reinforce a moral-racial hierarchy, whose strata were defined as geographically specific. Criminology enthusiasts residing in Lima and other coastal cities placed themselves in a privileged geo-racial position in terms of proximity to civilization. Certainly, by emphasizing stagnation as the characteristic of the predominantly indigenous Altiplano while highlighting the modernity of the acculturated coast, the dominant coastal elite defended their self-assigned prerogative to lead the journey to progress, as Capelo had clearly stated.

For Limeño jurists, sociologists, and physicians who embraced criminological theories, that proximity to modernity also involved the appearance or consolidation of modern types of criminality, which they could certainly identify and, above all, prevent. Furthermore, like in other Latin American and European countries, crimi-nology specialists used their own works to highlight their centrality to the process of preventing criminality and, consequently, achieving progress. In their attempts to establish their scientific competence, these intellectuals used moral panics and chal-lenged the work of other agents officially charged with fighting criminality.[71]

Although historian Carlos Aguirre has demonstrated that the city's per capita arrest ratio remained stable at around one percent between the 1890s and the 1920s, late nineteenth- and early twentieth-century intellectuals depicted Lima as con-stantly threatened by chaos and crime.[72] They pointed to nonwhite foreigners as well as poor working-class housing conditions and plebeian leisure activities as the main agents of degeneration.[73] In the 1920s and early 1930s, for instance, physician Oscar Miró Quesada and sociologists Augusto Peñaloza and Victor Villavicencio presented Lima's overcrowded *callejones* (tenements with numerous rooms connected by a com-mon patio, where each room had a small pen or corral) as "frighteningly transcen-dent" schools of vice, factories of recidivists, and spaces of biophysical degeneration.[74] They portrayed this type of housing as a space that lacked righteousness, morality, and religiosity—the three elements they believed important for the development of virtuous workers.[75] In the same vein, brothels, gambling houses, hostels, and prisons were depicted as places of crime and degeneration par excellence while vagrants, pros-titutes, and the *plebe* in general were seen as potential deviants.[76]

Most of these examples of increasing degeneration were accompanied by demands for crime prevention rather than the simple repression of delinquents. Crime preven-tion was seen as necessarily scientific and, therefore, only achievable if directed by the intellectual elite, which contrasted with what these intellectuals saw as the unscien-tific, brutish, and defective performance of the police. This contrast between inef-ficient police action and a presumably more competent scientific approach to crime had also been clearly stated by Enrico Ferri in his *Criminal Sociology* (1884).[77]

Curiously, at the turn of the twentieth century, the police also used moral panics to highlight their own "heroic" performance to prevent crime. In an early 1892 edi-tion of *La Gaceta Policial*, a newspaper published by Lima's police, the editor wrote that "Never, in any era, have there been a greater number of crimes in Lima. Nor has criminality been flaunted with greater terror. . . . The police force has performed actively and diligently [to ensure that criminals] are safely kept to suffer condign pun-ishment."[78] With the multiple conflicts—including the recent war—affecting Lima in the 1890s, *La Gaceta* editor's assertion should be taken with a grain of salt. Yet, it still shows both that the spread of moral panics was seen as institutionally useful and that there was more than one actor claiming the leading role in the "fight" against crime.

But beyond the criminalization of spaces and peoples and the spread of moral panics that transformed Lima into a seemingly chaotic city, criminologists emphasized Lima's moral sickness as also symptomatic of a more complex phenomenon.[79] When these intellectuals were not directly "exposing" specific social threats, they tended to denounce a broader, less clear, and generalized criminal crisis, which did not necessarily have its epicenter in Peru but menaced the country with its "unstoppable growth."

Javier Prado y Ugarteche, for instance, argued in his pioneering thesis that the moral crisis afflicting Europe would reach Peru if intellectuals did not fight social diseases.[80] Five years later, Jiménez contended that crime had developed at an alarming rate that expressed itself in the "crime waves" that "swamped many countries" and that seemed to be approaching Peru.[81] Likewise, in 1896, lawyer Alfredo Solf y Muro warned that recidivism was acquiring "colossal proportions" in the West and was actually already affecting the country, whose statistical studies were still too rudimentary to show its real magnitude.[82] Even eugenics specialist Peñaloza contended a decade later that crime "condensed like a cloud" in the Peruvian social atmosphere.

All these statements were certainly subjective; yet the fact that these intellectuals included the capital city among the metropolises affected or about to be affected by what they imagined were criminal phenomena common to modern countries shows their intention of both legitimizing Lima's place within modernity and establishing a horizontal dialogue with their peers in the "civilized" world. Pharmacist and lawyer Juan Luis Hague, for example, noted in his study of scientific techniques for policing that it was "indubitable" that Peru itself and its capital were "cores of high civilization"; therefore, Peru's criminality had "similarities with analogous communities of the universe."[83]

These ideas joined comparable statements made by influential Latin American and European intellectuals in their search for their "typical criminal." For instance, Spanish positivist jurisconsult Manuel Gil Maestre argued in *Los malhechores de Madrid* (1889) that all great cities had particular types of criminality, while introducing Madrid as one of those "great cities."[84] His countrymen Constancio Bernaldo de Quirós and José María de Llanas Aguilaniedo made a similar argument in their studies on the psychological elements of the *hampa madrileña* (1901).[85] Likewise, in his famous *Hampa afro-cubana* (1902), Fernando Ortiz analyzed the racial particularities of Havana's criminal class while emphasizing that "the great civilized cities are all alike in their criminal life as much as in the honest life of their inhabitants" and even compared the racial character of Cuba's criminality to that of Europe.[86] All these scholars greatly influenced one another's work, which ultimately linked their "*grandes ciudades*" located at the periphery of modernity to that modernity's core, quite often geopolitically depicted as the main western European cities.

In Peru, Limeño scholars' claim to that coveted place near modernity did not go uncontested, as intellectuals who wrote *from* the highlands also developed their own views about the local and national character of criminality. On the one hand, some of them used positivist theories to reaffirm exclusionary views of indigenous peoples, as Deborah Poole found in her study of cattle theft in Cuzco. On the other hand, several sources show that some intellectuals and authorities did not echo the costeño geo-racial assumptions and stereotypes that separated coast and highlands but criticized, discarded, or appropriated criminological theories to develop their own discourses on crime and identity.

On the construction of the indigenous criminal subject, a rather innovative and critical view of the whole hegemonic intellectual discourse was proposed in Puno by Anfiloquio Valdelomar, an Iqueño judge who had become head prosecutor of the local superior court in 1923.[87] In his study of the judiciary statistics of this region, Valdelomar rejected the idea that local criminals—mostly Aymara—possessed either innate perversity or natural tendencies toward crime.[88] He even argued that attempting to study local recidivism was useless, as society should be the one punished for forsaking nationals living in that part of the country. More importantly, Valdelomar noted that there was no use in studying "the Indian" because "not even all the [indigenous peoples] from the highlands have enough elements of resemblance to enclose them in a single concept in order to judge them from the criminological viewpoint."[89] His overview of the criminal problem in Puno was, above all, an analysis of the lack of effective state presence in the region and the manipulation of power by landlords and dwellers. His strikingly critical ideas proved to be in many ways more advanced than those of José Antonio Encinas, whose defense of indigenous peoples still relied on the arbitrary obliteration of the many indigenous identities to speak in defense of *the* "Indian."[90]

A few years later, in Arequipa, another city of the Peruvian Altiplano, lawyer César Aibar creatively deployed positivist theories to reinforce regional identity and reinterpret the role of race and modernity. In his analysis of this region's criminality published in 1935, he "discovered" that climatic phenomena instilled in Arequipeños the desire to excel.[91] According to Aibar, that influence was active only in natives, and it endangered only individuals with weak and poorly formed organisms, who became prone to harmless madness. Thus, Aibar embraced Lacassagne's and Ferri's ideas about environmental influences to create a positive interpretation of his own regional identity. In the same vein, he rejected all theoretical positions that depicted indigenous peoples as naturally degraded and mestizos as naturally immune to criminal tendencies and emphasized rather that Arequipeño Indians and mestizos were qualitatively different from those of the rest of the country. Likewise, he saw the seemingly high crime rates of Arequipa's capital city as a confirmation of its own development because "crime is a consequence of the greater progress and of the greater complexity and difficulties that the great cities offer in the struggle for life."[92]

CONCLUSIONS

Peruvian intellectuals who embraced positivist criminology at the turn of the twentieth century did not randomly mix theories to create eclectic interpretations of crime. They dissected existing theories and chose the elements that were useful to construct criminal subjects who, above all, they envisioned as embodying geo-racially defined stereotypes. The fact that some of them tended to reject the Lombrosian born-criminal type did not mean that they disregarded biological forms of racism. In fact, by using theories such as psychological heredity, they managed to link primitivism both biologically and culturally to entire indigenous populations of the sierra and the rainforest. These discourses sought to enhance regional power through the use of the coast/highlands dichotomy, whose values were sometimes inverted or modified depending on the relationship between scholars and specific regions and regional identities.

Also, that most intellectuals interpreted racial evolution in Lamarckian terms when focusing on indigenous criminal subjects speaks not of an advancement of the elites' ideas about these topics but of their need to enhance a historically hierarchical relationship between themselves and a population that—for the sake of the elites' interests—ought to be in a perennial process of redemption. This condition ultimately secured the elites' exclusive access to the "modern" and "civilized" realm and also reserved for them the mission of "civilizing" the plebe. This view of the elites' role explains the fact that, in most cases, criminologists proposed instruction that sought to instill love for manual work rather than for science, letters, and arts to "regenerate" the working classes.

Despite their deeply specialized and geo-racially specific categorizations of criminal subjects, Peruvian scholars shifted from these selective constructs to a broad category of the Peruvian "race" when examining foreigners perceived as potentially dangerous. At the turn of the twentieth century, Chinese immigrants to Peru became that ultimate "other" for most criminologists and criminology enthusiasts, who depicted them as one of the main agents of the demoralization of the capital city. Finally, subjective depictions of Lima's high rates of criminality aimed to incorporate the city into a circuit of modern metropolises and insert criminologists into a conversation with foreign specialists on crime. Thus, Peruvian intellectuals also appropriated scientific theories in order to reinterpret their own role and that of their city or region of origin as leading the civilizing process.

NOTES

1. Juan Luis Hague, *Hacia un nuevo concepto de la responsabilidad criminal y de la pena* (Lima: Imprenta y Litografía T. Scheuch, 1934), 40.

2. Carlos Aguirre, "Mapping Lima's Morals: The Cultural and Political Construction of the Criminal Classes in Late 19th-Century Peru" (paper presented at the Latin American Studies Association Meeting, Chicago, September 24–27, 1998); Aguirre, "Delito, raza y cultura: El desarrollo de la criminología en el Perú," *Diálogos en Historia* 2 (2000): 179–206; Aguirre, *The Criminals of Lima and Their Worlds: The Prison Experience, 1850–1935* (Durham, NC: Duke University Press, 2005), 17–39; Deborah Poole, "Paisajes de poder en la cultura abigea del sur andino," *Debate Agrario* 3 (1988): 29; Poole, "Ciencia, peligrosidad y represión en la criminología indigenista peruana," in *Bandoleros, abigeos y montoneros: Criminalidad y violencia en el Perú, siglos XVIII–XX*, ed. Carlos Aguirre and Charles Walker (Lima: Instituto de Apoyo Agrario, 1990), 335–67.

3. Nancy Appelbaum, Anne S. Macpherson, and Karin Alejandra Rosemblatt, eds., *Race and Nation in Modern Latin America* (Chapel Hill: University of North Carolina Press, 2003), and Peter Wade, *Raza y etnicidad en Latinoamérica* (Quito: Abya-Yala, 2000), among others.

4. For an analysis of other geo-racial categories in Latin America, see Laurence E. Prescott, *Without Hatreds or Fears: Jorge Artel and the Struggle for Black Literary Expression in Colombia* (Detroit: Wayne State University Press, 2000), 24.

5. Pedro E. Muñiz, *Memoria del prefecto del departamento de Lima* (Lima: Imprenta del Universo, 1893); Fanny Muñoz, *Diversiones públicas en Lima, 1890–1920: La experiencia de la modernidad* (Lima: Red para el Desarrollo de las Ciencias Sociales en el Perú, 2001), 47–50; Peter Klarén, "The Origins of Modern Peru, 1880–1930," in *The Cambridge History of Latin America*, vol. 5, ed. Leslie Bethell (Cambridge: Cambridge University Press, 1986), 614–15.

6. Carlos Contreras, *Centralismo y descentralismo en la historia del Perú independiente* (Lima: JCAS–IEP, 2000). On the data related to literacy in Peru, see Alex Loayza and Ximena Recio P., "Proyectos educativos y formación de la república," in *Chile-Perú, Perú-Chile en el siglo XIX: La formación del Estado, la economía y la sociedad*, comp. Eduardo Cavieres F. and Cristóbal Aljovín de Losada (Valparaíso: Ediciones Universitarias de Valparaíso, 2005), 232–40.

7. The term *gamonal* is a Peruvianism that refers to a provincial boss whose power rested primarily on the control of land, mercantile monopoly, as well as on access to servile labor and military bands. Brooke Larson, *Trials on Nation Making: Liberalism, Race, and Ethnicity in the Andes, 1810–1910* (New York: Cambridge University Press, 2004), 164, 173–74.

8. Marcos Cueto, "La reforma universitaria de 1919: Universidad y estudiantes a comienzos de siglo" (tesis de Licenciatura en Historia, Lima, PUCP, 1982), 48.

9. Carlos Aguirre, "Mapping Lima's Morals," and *The Criminals of Lima*, 43–47.

10. Ibid.

11. Matei Candea, *The Social After Gabriel Tarde: Debates and Assessments* (New York: Routledge, 2010), 19n5; Piers Beirne, *Inventing Criminology: Essays on the Rise of "Homo Criminalis"* (Albany: State University of New York Press. 1993); Martin S. Staum, *Labeling People: French Scholars on Society, Race, and Empire, 1815–1848* (Montreal: McGill-Queen's University Press, 2003).

12. Césare Lombroso, *Criminal Man*, trans. and ed. Mary Gibson and Nicole Hahn Rafter (Durham, NC: Duke University Press, 2006), 6.

13. Beirne, *Inventing Criminology*, 160; Gabriel Tarde, *Penal Philosophy* (New Brunswick, NJ: Transaction, 2001), 256.

14. Staum, *Labeling People*, 167.

15. Javier Prado y Ugarteche, *El método positivo en el derecho penal* (1890; Lima: Universidad Ricardo Palma), 133.

16. Ibid., 52–81; Javier Prado y Ugarteche, "Estado social del Perú," in *Pensamiento positivista latinoamericano*, ed. Leopoldo Zea (Caracas: Biblioteca Ayacucho, 1980), 1:326–35.

17. Plácido Jiménez, "La sociedad y el delito," *Anales de la Universidad Mayor de San Marcos de Lima* 23 (1898): 117, Falcón, "Carta al Señor Jefe de Policía de Rio de Janeiro, Buenos Aires, Abril de 1907," 185.

18. Ibid., 170.

19. Comisión Parlamentaria Compuesta por Placido Jiménez y Gustavo Cornejo, *Proyecto de código penal* (Lima: Imprenta Minerva, 1928), art. 581: "Savages, semi-civilized, and deaf and dumb."

20. Robert Buffington, *Criminales y ciudadanos en el México moderno* (México: Siglo XXI Editores S.A., 2001); Carlos Aguirre, *The Criminals of Lima*.

21. Appelbaum, Macpherson, and Rosemblatt, eds., *Race and Nation in Modern Latin America*, 1–13.

22. José Carlos Mariátegui, *Siete ensayos de interpretación de la realidad peruana*, 3rd ed. (Caracas: Biblioteca Ayacucho, 2007), 277–84.

23. Ibid.

24. Ibid., 288; see also Nelson Manrique, *La piel y la pluma: Escritos sobre literatura, etnicidad y racismo* (Lima: SUR Casa de Estudios del Socialismo, 1999).

25. Mariano Ignacio Prado y Ugarteche, *El tipo criminal* (Lima: Imprenta de E. Moreno, 1900), 52.

26. Thédodule Ribot, *Heredity: A Psychological Study of Its Phenomena, Laws, Causes, and Consequences* (New York: Appleton, 1875).

27. "This race offers a curious instance of a native incapacity, preserved and transmitted by heredity, for adaptation to civilized life. The Gypsies are in our moral and social world what the dodo and the ornithorhynchus are in our physical world, the survivors of a past age." Ibid., 116.

28. Pio Máximo Medina, *Causas del estacionarismo de la raza indígena y el remedio eficaz para su regeneración* (Lima: Imprenta La Industria, 1906), 1–7.

29. Medina, *El tipo criminal* (Lima: Imprenta San Pedro, 1907), 14–15.

30. Medina, *Causas del estacionarismo de la raza indígena*, 16.

31. Jiménez, "La sociedad y el delito," 282–83.

32. Ibid., 172. Emphasis added.

33. Euclides da Cunha, *Os sertões: Campanha de canudos* (Sao Paulo: Atelié Editorial, 2001).

34. Raimundo Nina Rodrigues, *As Raças humanas e a responsabilidade penal no Brasil* (Sao Paulo: Companhia Editora Nacional, 1938); Marcia das Neves, "A concepção de raça humana em Raimundo Nina Rodrigues," *Filosofia e história da biologia* 3 (2008): 251.

35. José Antonio Encinas, *Causas de la criminalidad indígena en el Perú: Ensayo de psicología experimental* (Lima: E. R. Villarán, 1919), 9, 13.

36. Ibid., 36.

37. Ibid., 25.

38. Ibid., 25–26.

39. Enrique López Albújar, *Los caballeros del delito* (Lima: Editorial Juan Mejía Baca, 1973), 20.

40. Ibid., 14. About these contrasts, see Deborah Poole, "Paisajes de poder en la cultura abigea del sur andino," 29.

41. Ibid., 121.

42. Ibid., 196.

43. Ibid., 125–28; John Dawe and Lewis Taylor, "Enrique López Albújar and the Study of Peruvian Brigandage," *Bulletin of Latin American Research* 13, no. 3 (1994): 247–80.

44. A *departamento* is a geopolitical jurisdiction. Peru is divided into twenty-four departamentos and one constitutional province (Callao).

45. Ibid., 42.

46. Dawe and Taylor, "Enrique López Albújar," 250–55.

47. Augusto Peñaloza, *Prevención eugénica de la criminalidad en el Perú* (Lima: La Voce D'Italia, 1916).

48. Ibid., 3–4. A third example presents a domestic servant betraying the trust and generosity of his employers.

49. Hubert Lauvergne, *Les forçats: Considérés sous le rapport physiologique, moral et intellectuel* (Paris: Baillière, 1841); Staum, *Labeling People*, 56, 77.

50. On Lauvergne's work, see Robert A. Nye, *Crime, Madness, and Politics in Modern France: The Medical Concept of National Decline* (Princeton, NJ: Princeton University

Press, 1984); and Peter Gay, *The Bourgeois Experience: Victoria to Freud*, vol. 3, *The Cultivation of Hatred* (New York: Norton, 1993), 203.

51. Luz E. Huertas, "Whistles and Clubs: The Institutional and Social History of the Police of Lima, 1890s–1910s" (PhD diss., Texas Christian University, 2015), 255.

52. Ibid., chap. 6. 508 files from legajos 515 to 530 (1890), 600 to 602 (1895), 7 to 11 (1900), 33 to 38 (1905), and 49 to 52 (1910), Causas Criminales, Poder Judicial, AGN, Lima.

53. Jiménez, "La sociedad y el delito," 246.

54. Hague, *Hacia un nuevo concepto*, 60–61.

55. Maria Emma Mannarelli, *Limpias y modernas: Género, higiene y cultura en la Lima del novecientos* (Lima: Flora Tristán, 1999), 47.

56. The first important study written by a woman was Susan Solano's *El estado peligroso: Algunas de sus formas clínicas no delictivas* (Lima: Universidad de San Marcos de Lima, 1937). According to Deborah Poole and Carlos Aguirre, this study was deeply influenced by Italian positivism. Poole, "Paisajes de poder," 362; Aguirre, *The Criminals of Lima*, 54.

57. See Joaquín Capelo, *La sociología de Lima* (Lima: J. Garland, 1895), 3:23, 178; Alfredo F. Solf y Muro, "Penalidad de la reincidencia," *Anales de la Universidad Mayor de San Marcos de Lima* 25 (1898): 55; Jiménez, "La sociedad y el delito," 237, 320.

58. Eugenia Scarzanella, *Ni gringos ni indios: Inmigración, criminalidad y racismo en la Argentina, 1890–1940* (Buenos Aires: Universidad Nacional de Quilmes Ediciones, 2004).

59. About the Chinese immigration to Peru, see Humberto Rodríguez Pastor, *Herederos del dragón: Historia de la comunidad China en el Perú* (Lima: Fondo Editorial del Congreso del Perú, 2000); Wilma Derpich, "Sistema de dominación: Cimarronaje y fugas," in *Primer Seminario sobre Poblaciones Inmigrantes* (Lima: CONCYTEC, 1988); Derpich, *El otro lado azul: Empresarios chinos en el Perú (1890–1930)* (Lima: Fondo Editorial del Congreso del Perú, 1999); Fernando de Trazegnies, *En el País de las Colinas de Arena: Reflexiones jurídicas sobre la inmigración china en el Perú del S. XIX desde la perspectiva del Derecho* (Lima: Pontificia Universidad Católica del Perú, 1994).

60. Rodríguez Pastor, *Herederos del dragón*, 134.

61. César Borja, "La inmigración china es un mal necesario de evitar," *Anales Universitarios del Perú* 10 (1877): 47–92.

62. Ibid., 88.

63. Capelo, *Sociología de Lima*, 1:116.

64. Ibid.

65. Dr. Vidrieras, "La podre de Lima: La ciudad de los chinos," *El Diario Judicial* 2/462, December 1, 1891. Quoted by Aguirre, *The Criminals of Lima*, 37–39.

66. Jiménez, "La sociedad y el delito," 139.

67. Ibid., 321.

68. Ibid.

69. Ibid., 322.

70. Fernando Ortiz, "Consideraciones criminológicas positivistas acerca de la inmigración en Cuba," *Memoria oficial: Quinta conferencia de beneficencia y corrección de la isla de Cuba* (Havana: Librería y Papelería La Moderna Poesía, 1906), 351.

71. Moral panics are disproportionate social responses to the perception that the moral condition of society is deteriorating at a calamitous pace. See Allan G. Johnson, *The Blackwell Dictionary of Sociology: A User's Guide to Sociological Language* (Oxford: Blackwell, 1995), 184; Stanley Cohen, *Folk Devils and Moral Panics: The Creation of the Mods and Rockers* (New York: Routledge, 2002); and Cornel Sandvoss, "Moral Panic," in *The Cambridge Dictionary of Sociology*, ed. Bryan S. Turner, 400–401 (Cambridge: Cambridge University Press, 2006).

72. Aguirre, *The Criminals of Lima*, 80.

73. For the Limeño elite's discourses on diversions and their modernization, see Fanny Muñoz, *Diversiones públicas en Lima, 1890–1920: La experiencia de la modernidad* (Lima: Red para el Desarrollo de las Ciencias Sociales en el Perú, 2001).

74. Peñaloza, *Prevención eugénica*, 117; Victor Villavicencio, *Algunos aspectos de nuestra sociología criminal* (Lima, 1930), 40; Miró Quesada, cited by Aguirre, *The Criminals of Lima*, 50.

75. Peñaloza, *Prevención eugénica*, 118.

76. For depictions of hostels, see Juan Luis Hague, *"Estudios Policiales": Técnicas científicas aplicadas a la policiología y consideraciones sobre el mejoramiento de la institución policial en el Perú* (Lima: Impr. de la Escuela de la Guardia Civil, 1934), 46.

77. Enrico Ferri, *Criminal Sociology* (London: T. Fisher Unwin, 1895), 139.

78. "Crímenes al por mayor," *La Gaceta de Policía*, II/31, January 30, 1892, 1.

79. Pablo Piccato, *City of Suspects: Crime in Mexico City, 1900–1931* (Durham, NC: Duke University Press, 2001); Robert Buffington, *Criminales y ciudadanos en el México moderno* (México: Siglo XXI Editores S.A., 2001); Scarzanella, *Ni gringos ni indios*; Donna J. Guy, *Sex and Danger in Buenos Aires: Prostitution, Family, and Nation in Argentina* (Lincoln: University of Nebraska Press, 1991).

80. Prado y Ugarteche, *El método positivo*, 7–8.

81. Jiménez, "La sociedad y el delito," 184.

82. Solf y Muro, "Penalidad de la reincidencia," 54–55.

83. Hague, *"Estudios Policiales,"* 43–45.

84. Manuel Gil Maestre, *Los malhechores de Madrid* (Gerona: Imprenta y Librería de Paciano Torres, 1889), vi.

85. Constancio Bernaldo de Quirós and José María de Llanas Aguilaniedo, *La mala vida en Madrid: Estudio psico-sociológico con dibujos y fotograbados del natural* (Madrid: B. Rodríguez Serra, 1901).

86. He highlighted the presence of "gypsies" and their relationship with European societies. Fernando Ortiz, *Hampa afro-cubana: Los negros brujos* (Madrid: Editorial América, 1917), 19.

87. Carlos Ramos, *Historia del derecho civil peruano* (Lima: Pontificia Universidad Católica del Perú, 2005), 2:231.

88. Anfiloquio Valdelomar, *La criminalidad indígena en el departamento de Puno: Estadística Judicial Criminal* (Puno: Tipografía Fournier, 1923), 3–4.

89. Valdelomar, *La criminalidad indígena*, 5–6.

90. For a discussion of race and identity in Cuzco, see Marisol de la Cadena, *Indigenous Mestizos: The Politics of Race and Culture in Cuzco, Peru, 1919–1991* (Durham, NC: Duke University Press, 2000).

91. César Aibar Valdez, *Diez años de criminalidad en Arequipa (interpretación)* (Arequipa: Tipografía Librería Quiroz Perea, 1935).

92. Ibid., 27, 43.

3

POLICE IMAGINATION

ൟ

The Construction of Drug Users and Drug
Trafficking in Chile, 1900–1950

MARCOS FERNÁNDEZ LABBÉ

URING THE FIRST HALF of the twentieth century, Chilean criminologists
articulated a new social and political figure, the drug user, who was depicted
as a dangerous foreigner whose habits potentially threatened the virtuous Chilean nation. As a result of the increased international visibility of drug trafficking
and the beginning of the "war on drugs" following the 1919 Treaty of Versailles,
officials alleged that drugs threatened even remote regions such as Chile.[1] Consequently, Chilean authorities began to create the institutions and systems necessary
to track drug trafficking. Alongside depictions of the drug user, Chilean authorities also constructed the image of the drug trafficker and subsequently the police
force dedicated to controlling this vice. In nearly three decades, this trio of figures
(consumers, traffickers, and police officers) formed the foundation for an influential
set of opinions, knowledge, and police practices, despite the very low levels of consumption, trafficking, and legal prosecution of drug use in Chile. Police officials,
penal scientists, and forensic medicine practitioners deployed a series of strategies
to construct representations of figures enmeshed in drug trafficking. They employed
references to international criminological debates, legal precedents, fictional stories,
and legal norms to foreground the threat of drugs and their collateral damage in the
public consciousness and into the realm of state action.

Although the state expressly prohibited extra-medical consumption of substances
like opium, morphine, coca leaf, and cocaine in the 1930s, I argue that police officers
in Chile began constructing a series of traits, institutions, procedures, and social representations surrounding drug use that endured into the 1950s. Virtually nonexistent
in practice, these fictionalized attributes proved remarkably powerful in influencing

key institutions by mobilizing public opinion and state resources.[2] I identify the construction of drug trafficking as an entity that operated in discursive and preinstitutional form for nearly fifty years before drug use became widespread.

Through in-depth analysis of the national press, periodicals published by unions, police officials, pharmaceutical and criminological organizations, and right-wing organizations, as well as academic studies including theses from law and pharmacy schools produced during the period under study, I expose the contradictions between the discursive constructions and actual practices of drug users and trafficking. Paradoxically, by the time Chile became enmeshed in the international cocaine trafficking circuit in the 1950s and by the time marijuana consumption became widespread there in the late 1960s, the existing array of social representations proved anachronistic—a far cry from the realities of the Chilean drug trade. This disparity was particularly evident in the type of individual who used drugs—by the 1970s typically nonconformist youth, as opposed to the dangerous foreigners and degenerates imagined by police and penal scientists.[3] Moreover, once the police institutions dedicated to the prosecution of drug trafficking emerged, they were riddled with corruption, in spite of their moralistic rhetoric of "national salvation."

RACE AND NATION: DRUGS AS A FOREIGN VICE

Beginning in the first decades of the twentieth century, Chilean public health authorities established policies to regulate the production, manufacture, trade, and consumption of morphine, opium, coca leaves, and cocaine. Regulations limited the legal sale of these drugs to pharmacies. For this reason, some of the first people concerned with the extra-medical consumption and traffic of drugs were pharmacists, who argued in 1927 for greater "control of the alkaloids in pharmacies."[4] They recommended the restriction and oversight of morphine, cocaine, and opiates.[5] Authorities in the General Health Committee (Dirección General de Salud, DGS) implemented these measures through the 1936 Drug Regulation (Reglamento de Estupefacientes).

The first measures regulating substances targeted the foreign population, namely Peruvian, Bolivian, and Chinese workers.[6] This fact evinced authorities' perceptions that the Chilean "race" was less inclined toward intoxication, though they feared it might be susceptible to the contagion of vice. Indeed, as early as the 1920s, authorities implemented a complex regulatory mechanism to control the provision of coca leaves consumed by Peruvian and Bolivian workers living in the mineral fields in northern Chile.[7] The DGS permitted the importation and distribution of significant quantities of coca leaves from Bolivia with the condition that they be sold only to those foreign workers.[8] From the beginning, though, distributors flouted these regulations, owing to the absence of formal pharmacies near the mining offices and nitrate fields. Instead, general stores sold the coca leaves without a prescription, as the nitrate companies rejected any attempt by the DGS to oversee sales.[9] The opposition by the owners of the nitrate companies, whom pharmacy owners described as "feudal men," to regulating the dispensation of controlled substances, particularly coca, likely reflected their intention to keep the workers in their condition as a "pusillanimous, vicious, and degenerate race," easy to dominate and force into submission.[10]

The owners of nitrate companies justified their policies allowing foreign workers to consume drugs by citing characteristics that allegedly differentiated them from and rendered them inferior to Chilean workers. Peruvian and Bolivian workers relied on a dose of coca leaves, "without which they do not want to work," claimed one apologist. This same observer noted that the high demand for labor obliged Chilean employers to hire what he considered inferior workers: "presently so many workers are needed to power all the [nitrate and mining] industries of these regions, which until recently remained overrun by the most profound lethargy, that we must resort to Bolivian workers."[11]

Despite these racial justifications for the distribution of controlled substances like coca among foreign workers, Chilean authorities came to view the inconsistent regulation of drugs as a threat to the nation because of the possibility that drug use could spread to Chilean workers. In 1927, Doctor Victor Grossi warned that "in the nitrate fields of the pampas, coca has begun to affect our citizens, introduced and propagated by the Bolivians, many of whom worked and fraternized with our own workers."[12] Authorities also identified the presence of a significant number of inhabitants of Chinese origin in the country as another potential source of contagion in discourses that resemble those of Peruvian intellectuals, as discussed by Luz Huertas in the previous chapter. Indeed, authorities often represented these individuals as withered degenerates "overcome with a great sadness, indifferent to the point of being decrepit, [and] ending their days in marasmus and stupidity."[13] In 1927, one doctor indicated that 80 percent of the nearly five thousand Chinese inhabitants "used, trafficked, or dedicated themselves to the distribution of opium." The same doctor alleged that Chinese people frequented "saloons, gambling houses, meat markets, and brothels." Likewise, the Chinese maintained "numerous opium smokehouses, public and private . . . the most important being the Chinese Club Iquique." This venue "had been raided by order of the general director of police, who found various Asian people smoking, and seized pipes, lamps, and all types of ingredients used to attend to a large and diverse clientele," in which "a considerable number of Chilean opium smokers has not been found."[14] Police pursued opium smokers based on the 1917 Law of Residency (Ley de Residencia), deporting from the country individuals labeled as undesirable citizens.[15] According to the sources, the Chinese were labeled as a *race* of opium users, who "straggle behind development and intellectual progress." The lust for opiates "dominates the [Chinese man's] will and dulls his conscience."[16]

Thus, in Chile, the social representation of drug use in the first half of the twentieth century depicted foreigners as the principal users and denounced the potentially harmful effects they could have on the Chilean race. One author in a pharmaceutical newspaper recommended energetic action from the press, schools, and universities to help reveal the moral and physical threats of drugs and to protect the Chilean people from their harmful effects. He concluded that safeguarding the national race could only be achieved "by combating the vices that threaten it." Although he discounted the likelihood of reducing alcohol consumption in a country that produced wine, he sought to "extirpate those exotic poisons" so "relentlessly and immorally heaped upon our shores"[17] However, drug users were not the only foreign threats to the Chilean nation. Within the world of representations appearing in these historical documents, traffickers and instigators of vice were also foreign to the Chilean nation.

Even though there was no talk of organized bands or networks by the late 1930s, authorities did identify the nebulous presence of traffickers in the nightlife of big cities. According to one police publication, a few phantom distributers, "generally Argentineans or Central Americans," lurked in Santiago's and Valparaíso's brothels and nightclubs, where cocaine and ether use allowed "the excitement and fictitious enthusiasm to remain latent."[18] Once again, authorities blamed foreigners before Chileans and alluded to mysterious figures who presumably distributed drugs in places of vice amid the smoke and music of nightlife.

The first specific mention I encountered of any sort of permanent organized network illegally distributing controlled substances to the national market appeared in a fictional story published in an investigative police magazine in February 1943. It alludes to events that had occurred in late 1938. The short story, titled "The Case of the Botanist," takes place in the borderlands between Chile and Argentina called Los Libertadores, high in the Andes Mountains. Throughout the story, a band composed of eight foreigners smuggles significant quantities of controlled substances (especially cocaine) to Santiago. The story suggests that traffickers smuggled drugs into Chile from Argentina with the help of a gringo (North American) botanist known as an eccentric expert on high-altitude vegetation. They turn over the shipment to the botanist, who hides it in his backpack, before arriving at the border checkpoint. Amid inoffensive herbs, the shipment continues its journey through paths parallel to police control, after which it is turned over to another member of the organization, who takes it to the "Chino" (Chinese man), head of the contraband trade headquartered in the neighborhood of Recoleta in the capital.[19]

Several months later, the author published another installment of the story. The twist in the narrative at first glance seems farfetched, but the level of detail included suggests that the story may have been based on real-life events. Under the headline "The Road of Drugs," the author tells of the discovery of the Chino's hideout, located near a cemetery. In an underground bunker, bundles containing "a substance similar to salt, fine and shiny" and "hundreds of small boxes containing glass capsules full of liquid resembling distilled water" are hidden. The police discover and shoot the Chino (who speaks with a thick foreign accent and lives with a Bolivian woman) after he has murdered one of his accomplices in a street in the capital.[20] This narrative underscores popular perceptions that the threat of contagion emanated from foreign consumers dispersed among the Chilean population. Beginning in the 1930s, the Bureau of Investigations (Dirección de Investigaciones) noted the "extreme seriousness" of the extra-medical consumption of regulated substances. The situation, though having no comparison to the problems existing in other nations of "higher civilization and culture," could no longer be denied as a medical-social problem.[21]

In sum, forensic and policing knowledge presumed a clear relationship between nationality and race. The idea that drug use threatened to debilitate the Chilean population presupposed a racialized vision of the Chilean nation, one that would lend itself to eugenics-inspired policies characteristic of this period.[22] In this way, the association between a foreign race and vice depended on the opposing extreme—a virtuous Chilean race characterized by fortitude, health, and progress. In the same vein, official discourse suggests that the Chilean people are minors or childlike, in need of protection against the harmful influences of populations deemed either "less civilized" or degenerate (indigenous and Asian) as well as from those subject to accelerated processes of modernization, as would be the case of Argentineans and North Americans. The solution to this problem for the state was applying the concept of the antisocial individual, which included delinquents, prostitutes, undesirable foreigners, alcoholics, and drug users all in the same category.

PARASITE-MEN: SOCIAL EXCLUSION AND THE "IMAGINED COMMUNITY" OF DRUG USERS

Between the late 1920s and the 1950s there emerged in Chile a set of medical, criminological, and legal judgments and opinions aimed at establishing the precriminal state of certain social groups, like drug users, vagabonds, prostitutes, and alcoholics. These discourses set the stage for the development of social rehabilitation measures.[23] The government implemented this discourse in law by establishing the Defense of Society, a superior body charged with the right and duty to protect the nation from the contagion "of the vices that can push an individual toward the abyss of crime." For proponents of the Defense of Society, the dangers of potential criminal subjects were vast and "encompassed not only outward signs but . . . could also emerge in an imminent state of the individual."[24] In this way, they established a direct link between vice, crime, and, by implication, social danger. One result of this idea of needing to defend society was the criminalization of drugs, which in turn identified the drug user as a threat to society, subject to punishment.

The most explicit forms of this discourse of criminalizing drug use can be found in police records. For example, in 1935, the Chilean police magazine *Detective* defined the *parasitic population* as a police problem. This problem emerged following major social transformations, including the consolidation of a mass society associated with expanding participation in international finance, modern industrial production, and state administration. This expansion of the criminal subjects' sphere of influence, the birth of social security, the expansion of media outlets, and the transformation of predominantly rural and conservative public opinion into a secular one helped produce the image of the "parasite-man." This parasite-man allegedly lived off of his illegal activities "without producing anything positive in the way of progress." This individual was characterized by "irresponsibility, sometimes material, always moral; they are the failures of the world of business, of the classrooms, or are merely illiterate and immoral characters."[25]

Just as medical scientists studied bacteria or viruses, police had to study antisocial individuals in "a true laboratory that we could call the Institute of Investigations, where social parasites could be examined from a scientific perspective, to study the social failures that produce them and to determine the true educational procedures necessary to avoid the development of their moral monstrosity."[26] A logical result of these efforts would be the application of social rehabilitation measures, by way of "the creation of true centers of reeducation, centers in which to submit society's parasites to an energetic and profound treatment aimed at regeneration, that is, to transform the spirit and orientation of these individuals toward useful activities for the benefit and the progress of society."[27]

Beginning in 1917, Chilean authorities targeted supposed parasite-men with the Law of Residency, which sought to impede the entry or residence of individuals considered undesirable in the country. It should be noted that these types of laws were common in the Southern Cone. In chapter 1 of this volume, for instance, Diego Galeano examines the development of police discourses about traveling criminals and the networks of collaboration that police forces of several countries—Chile included—organized against them. From the very beginning, Chilean authorities swiftly applied this law to individuals involved in trafficking or using substances deemed to "violate good customs and public order," underscoring an early connection between smugglers, traffickers, and political agitators, all of whom they envisioned as "foreigners."[28] In this way, Chilean authorities directly invoked the logics of social control, eugenics, and social reform as explicit justifications for implementing categories like "foreigner" and "internal enemy" in legislative and policing initiatives that targeted these groups for their *antisocial states*.

By early 1936, the official organ of the Investigative Police of Chile, a policing unit established just three years earlier, cited among its tasks for the year "the necessity of rationally reforming our penal laws such that preventive police work is no longer useless." It also proposed the creation of labor camps or fishing and agricultural communities as "the solution to the problem of this floating population."[29] Until that time, the police had the power *only* to detain people on suspicion. Yet, "there, the judge, following legal norms, releases them or applies very light sentences. They continue their dubious ways in the streets until they are apprehended again . . . and the cycle continues." In the face of such difficulty, one police newspaper declared the need for preventive policing, defined by constant monitoring of the parasitic population. Society had the right to maintain surveillance of its potential enemies in order to reduce the parasitic population through judicial proceedings, since "it would be much more beneficial for the police to control the activities of 'dangerous' individuals" in order to safeguard the population. In this way, "the police officers would know at all times the true activities of their subjects, and this would prevent them from visiting dubious places and people." The paper declared that the police "defend society" through this "highly social mission" not only "by repressing and preventing crime when possible" but also by fostering "the rehabilitation of the delinquent" in the future.[30]

At its core, the social representation of drug users, starting with their dangerousness, centered on the ways the supposed social parasites threatened the entire society through their degenerative actions. As a reaction to that threat, the state forged a series of race protection policies, under the assumption that the collective task of defending the race united Chileans across class lines. Beginning in the 1930s, Chilean authorities represented the national population as the guardians of a common patrimony, independent of their social class and position in the productive system. This racial element gave the population its identity and strength, and both factors had to be protected to ensure collective well-being. Months before the outbreak of World War II, the institution called Defense of the Race and Management of Free Time (Defensa de la Raza y Aprovechamiento de las Horas Libres) was created based on the German NS-Gemeinschaft "Kraft durch Freude" (National Socialist Organization Strength Through Joy) and Italian Opera Nazionale Dopolavoro (National Leisure Hours Club). In an address before the Chilean congress, President Pedro Aguirre Cerda articulated the objectives of the institution as "strengthening, then, the race, making it healthy and vigorous, providing it with the love of life, the pride of feeling Chilean." He identified two interrelated ways to achieve this goal. On the one hand, the institution was charged with "fortifying the physical vigor of our fellow citizens though adequate athletic practice and fresh air and invigorating the moral health, promoting home life and relationships." According to Aguirre Cerda, the state's current efforts to combat "the plagues that degrade our race" were "insufficient." He declared it necessary "to undertake another campaign, innovate the systems according to the new conceptions existing, and institute effective procedures that enable the prompt application of a radical solution to the problem of fortifying the Chilean race."[31]

Lawyer Armando Roger advocated for highlighting drug users in the mission of the new institution, given that they were carriers of "degenerations and physical and psychic defects of such magnitude that they become socially maladjusted if not mentally alienated." What was even more concerning to Roger was the prospect that drug users could pass their illnesses to their offspring: "they engender sick progeny, by which they contribute in no small degree to the degeneration of man."[32] Later, the same author considered drug users as "inept for marriage," because they posed a threat to their descendants and a general danger due to their "tendency to win over converts and propagate their own vice. The drug user, it can be said, is a vehicle of contamination that should be eliminated."[33]

In 1943, the Institute of Penal Sciences, the principal space of criminological debate in Chile up until 1960, transformed this proposition into legislative form: a bill on antisocial states. This legislation prescribed preventive medical and police action, while considering danger a natural part of every individual. These assumptions led the bill's proponents to conclude that it was unnecessary to wait until a crime was committed. They envisioned the purpose of law as preventing "not only dangerous individuals from becoming delinquents but also regular people from turning into dangerous ones."[34] With or without legislative innovation, the police expanded their powers over "dangerous individuals." In 1948, a publication of the Institute of Penal Sciences described the ways the police incorporated new technologies into their tried-and-true policing techniques: After midnight, "the beat policemen of the precincts in each neighborhood of the capital" detain and bring to jail "the idle men, beggars, suspicious persons, and drunkards," later identifying them "scientifically through the registry of the fingerprints by Dactyloscopy."[35]

In the early 1950s, Chilean criminological discourse emphasized the urgency of preemptively repressing subjects considered to be antisocial. Authorities developed a new bill that, despite distinguishing between "antisocial individuals" and "delinquents," still sought to submit the former to "security measures, aimed at reeducating and rehabilitating them to society." The category of antisocial elements included "habitual drug users" because "they are imminently dangerous subjects, and they can be reincorporated into the social nexus as useful members of the community through an adequate detoxification treatment." In contrast, the bill placed drug traffickers, "individuals who proselytize vice and those who exploit it," in a separate category because these were "the true active element in this social sore of drug use." The bill proposed forced labor in agriculture or workhouses as punishment for individuals active in the drug trade. "This work should be remunerated but the proceeds should be kept in a reserve fund to enable those who once again obtain their freedom to earn an honest living," the legislation read.[36] With these assumptions, the Law of Antisocial States came into existence in Chile in late 1954. Under this law, the police and the institutes of mental rehabilitation were the central institutions.[37] It configured the legal context in which police prosecution would focus on drug trafficking. The path had its origins in developments occurring several decades earlier.

A plausible explanation for these developments is that the architects of the Chilean nation used threats of drug trafficking and drug use in order to forge a national identity characterized by racial vigor and health. This explanation appears even more compelling when we consider that these ideas developed alongside the first social policies addressing the modern work experience, which regulated labor relations and constructed a social security system.[38] The lazy drug user and spreader of vice provided a potent countertype to the worker devoted to his labor and his family and always mindful of national growth and progress. This opposition between degenerate, antisocial drug addicts, on the one hand, and virtuous national workers, on the other, evinced the rejection of the foreigner as a drug user. In this sense, it is important to recall that during the period under study, the concepts of race and nation, from an elite perspective, began to supersede the notion of class as the most significant categories by which to understand the social order.[39]

POLICE IN ACTION: DRUG REGULATION AND POLICE SPECIALIZATION

According to one publication for pharmacists, by the late 1920s a cocaine distribution network operated amid the urban nightlife. The drug trade allegedly catered to the worst elements of the urban underworld: "prostitutes, those who swarm around the brothels, dancers, hotel workers, boxers, and the heterogeneous population that lives at the edges of prostitution." The publication reported finding "in hotels of dubious reputation [and] cabaret restaurants" "undesirable elements from the dregs" of society, exploiting the sale of drugs, especially cocaine, in the late hours of the night."[40] That is to say, in cities like Santiago, Valparaíso, and Iquique, the extra-medical consumption of drugs started to become a visible feature of the nightlife.

Observers traced this pattern of extra-medical drug consumption to criminal, bohemian, and transgressive circles. Evidence of this appears in the reports of substance confiscation and seizure at pharmacies. For example, there was a clandestine drugstore on San Diego Street in the capital, a home goods store run by Arab immigrants in which "cocaine was found among the boxes of necklaces, buttons, and cheap products," and another home goods store dispensing morphine and cocaine.[41] One commentator argued the "necessity of having intelligent and experienced personnel dedicated exclusively to combating these expert criminals engaged in smuggling"—that is, a police division on illegal drugs, which did not yet exist.[42] In its absence, druggists denounced the clandestine circulation of the regulated substances.[43]

By the late 1920s, even when Chile was not a direct producer of the raw materials needed to manufacture drugs, visible albeit insignificant, isolated, and hidden consumption existed. This tendency would only become stronger as the twentieth century advanced. What is more, Chile did fall within the larger distribution networks, even if only as a "transit country" or a place for refining coca imported from the Andes. The entry of these substances into Chile resulted from insufficient legislation, the large expanses of coastline, and the porous borders of the country.[44] DGS reports to the multilateral organizations charged with combating drug smuggling confirmed these details. These reports exposed the fact that Chile lacked a police service dedicated to preventive control of trans-Atlantic traffic, which could easily supply Chilean distributers with internationally regulated substances after entering ports in that country.[45]

Following the approval of the 1936 Drug Regulation, the investigative police paid special attention to this type of work.[46] In 1929, a leader of a pharmaceutical union observed that "flipping through the pages of the newspapers, it is very frequent and increasingly [common to find] headlines referring to the clandestine sale of drugs, more or less successful investigations and discoveries of meeting places for individuals who use morphine and cocaine, and the discovery of considerable quantities of opium, etc."[47] The principal source of supply for the consumers seemed to be the pharmacies, or at least this was the opinion of the general director of Customs Police. He expressed his concern about the availability of stolen and adulterated pharmaceutical products, "the circulation and smuggling of which are easy to imagine."[48]

Although we cannot dismiss the importance of pharmacies as centers of distribution of substances on the clandestine drug market, trafficking on the street and in venues like night clubs and restaurants increasingly caught the attention of the police in the 1930s. One police newspaper published a review of crimes and delinquent types under the headline "The Story of Cocaine." The account told of an incident in which a dealer sold cocaine for a price much lower than usual to a trafficker known for his extensive clientele: "The man, who worked illicitly, becomes excited over the easy profit he will obtain and hands over the requested amount."[49] Commenting on the inadequacy of Chilean legislation on gambling, a police commentator noted that it was common to find drug traffickers in illegal gambling dens.[50] The development of drug regulation implied a direct connection between drugs and police, or in broader form, the understanding that extra-medical consumption was a crime worthy of police prosecution.

Distinct police corps participated in the repression of smuggling and the detention of consumers since at least the beginning of the twentieth century, with a particular focus on opium smokers and vigilance over pharmacies. The 1936 Drug Regulation only strengthened these patterns. For example, one police magazine noted that it published the complete text of the Drug Regulation because "our service was mainly charged with repressing the illicit traffic in drugs."[51] Moreover, in March 1928, Supreme Decree 1090 had created the division of international, politico-social, and informational investigation police, whose responsibilities included "taking control of international delinquents and investigating crimes of smuggling." By the end of that same month, the duties of the Investigative Police were defined as "surveillance over pharmacies, drug stores, and similar establishments to prevent the trafficking of drugs."[52]

Given that general narcotics control enforcement still fell under a public health institution (the DGS), the Chilean police repeatedly demanded greater responsibility for the prosecution of drug-related offenses. The official publication of the Bureau of Investigations explicitly urged the creation of "a specialized service of investigation" that might be called "the Drug Brigade." This new institution would work "in conjunction with the Public Health Board" to "help develop a harmonious plan of cooperation" for the enforcement of the Public Health Code, a plan that aimed to curtail "the alarming increase in vice."[53] That is to say, the set of regulatory arrangements in effect at that time forced the police to recognize the need to expand the resources it dedicated to the prosecution of drug use and trafficking, which had remained secondary up until then. With an extremist slant, the *Revista de criminología y policía científica* (*Journal of Criminology and Scientific Policing*) painstakingly enumerated the areas of influence that the legislation assigned to the police, requiring their vigilance even in the "locked shelves and enclosures" of pharmacies where cocaine, morphine, and their derivatives were stored. At the same time, police had to be aware of the multiple points through which drugs entered internationally. The bylaws of the Investigative Service, approved by Supreme Decree 3738 in late September 1944, established that the International Police section, dependent on the Department of the Exterior, should "know all facts related to international smuggling, drug trafficking, white slave trading, espionage and sabotage activities, etc." The law tasked the members of this section with gathering and filing information about foreigners considered suspicious as well as following matters of interest in the press.[54]

Nevertheless, according to a spokesperson for the police, the failure to implement the proposed measures exacerbated the problem in Chile, and this was in large part due to the lack of adequate legislation. Police officials recommended the prompt creation of an "institution, sanitarium, [or] hospital and the dedication of a special department in the national psychiatric hospital for the reclusion of these ill persons or addicted delinquents."[55] Along with this last suggestion, they insisted on surveillance and investigative measures directed at the sites where substances evidently circulated, including constant monitoring of sites flagged for habitual trafficking such as opium houses.[56]

According to the same source, the very directors of the Public Health Board supported the transition of drug control enforcement from a public health to a police jurisdiction. Doctors Castro Oliveira, Suárez Herreros, and Nacianceno Romero, then directors of the Public Health Board, signed on to and applied international treaties to control drugs. These regulations contained more rigorous measures than those established in Chilean legislation. By the mid-1940s, these international measures allowed justice to fall "implacably over the unscrupulous pharmacists."[57]

Part of the series of police measures that were created or reinforced during this time identified drug users as subjects of special investigation, their supposedly dangerous character being noted in the police registry. For example, in the classification cards for individuals accused of crimes against people, the investigative and identification units requested not "a medical diagnostic, but rather the identification of individuals who stood out to the eye: hardened alcoholics, insane persons, epileptics, individuals with incipient palsies (recognizable by the continuous trembling of the hands), visible syphilitics, people with tuberculosis, and those who show signs of opiate [use] and nervous ticks, etc."[58]

In a relevant milestone, in 1948, authorities proposed the appointment of a chemist-pharmacist for "criminal prosecution," whose role was to include the "expert investigation of crimes of drug and narcotics contraband."[59] At the same time, the Investigative Police seemed to resent the appointment, which kept the drug problem in the public health realm. In an overt criticism of this proposal, an official of the Bureau of Investigations cited the decentralized mechanisms and institutions for the prosecution of drug-related crimes as part of the gap between international policies and the participation of his department in the struggle against drug trafficking. "Unfortunately," he wrote, "certain aspects depended on different organizations and on different administrative structures. For example, the control of drugs is the jurisdiction of the General Board of Public Health and almost all of the other matters depend on different sections or departments of the General Bureau of Investigations."[60] Evidence of this consolidation and formalization of autonomous police control of drug trafficking can be seen in the congratulatory remarks various detectives and commissioners received in the early 1950s for their "careful, quick, and efficient work" in cases of drug trafficking.[61] In 1954, Commissioner Gustavo Basaure created the Joint Brigade against Speculation and Fraud, whose responsibilities included the establishment of the Campaign against Narcotic Drugs.[62]

Giving the police jurisdiction for controlling drug trafficking carried risks. In January 1959, a drug trafficking organization headed by Carlos Jiménez García, the subprefect chief of the Mobile Brigade of Investigative Police, was discovered and quashed. Jiménez had served for twenty-six years. His downfall exposed the degree to which networks of international drug traffickers had compromised the Chilean police. The press dedicated pages and pages to analyzing, speculating, and exaggerating every investigation. In brief, the case can be synthesized as follows: In late 1958 and early 1959, from the inside of the Investigative Police, there were strong suspicions about Jiménez's behavior. While participating in the resolution of famous criminal cases of the day, he enjoyed a lifestyle far above that of his fellow detectives; he was reportedly a lover of fine tailoring, owner of luxury cars, resident of the wealthy Barrio Alto, and generous contributor to the presidential campaign of Jorge Alessandri—a representative of the right wing in Chilean politics. He claimed that he financed these expenditures through his wife's money, as she owned a clothing factory in the very center of the capital.

Nevertheless, following his detention, 138 checks were confiscated that represented the bribes and commissions he had received from some of the most important drug traffickers of the time.[63] The fact that the detective maintained direct contact with these drug traffickers was what eventually gave him away as their accomplice. According to the newspaper *Vistazo*, he attempted to alert one of the most important Chilean drug traffickers at the time, Rubén Sacre Huasaf, of an impending raid. His call to Sacre was intercepted by his superiors, leading to his arrest and conviction. Once Jiménez was in prison, his case enabled the press to uncover the magnitude of drug trafficking.

First, this case exposed the persistent circulation of marijuana between the producing zones –the valley of Aconcagua—and the capital by way of improvised forms of transportation. This discovery shed light on the extent of drug trafficking in this early period. This early trade would develop with much greater force and breadth by the 1960s. Second, it revealed the frequency of the illicit exchange of cocaine between Bolivia, Peru, and northern Chile, as well as its exit from the country toward Havana and Miami through official correspondence of the Investigative Police and the commercial flights of Panagra Airlines, as well as by way of "human packages" that crossed from Tacna or La Paz into the city of Arica. This border city was compared with Tangiers, Macao, or Hamburg in the international geography of the drug trade. For one of the interviewees—Luis Gayán, chief of Bolivian secret police under the MNR government—Chile was the "silver bridge" through which Peruvian and Bolivian cocaine circulated to the rest of the world.[64]

In the same vein, the press alluded to the contacts Jiménez maintained with one of the most important families of organized crime and drug trafficking in Chile: the Huasaf clan. Composed of Rubén Sacre Huasaf, René Harb Huasaf, and their mother, Amanda Huasaf, this family of Arabic descent was known for its ownership of the most famous brothel in Valparaíso. By 1952, they had been charged with the illegal establishment of cocaine purification laboratories in Las Zorras and Villa Alemana, towns located near the port of Valparaíso. The press indicated that the Huasaf family trafficked and refined Bolivian cocaine. Yet, the detective provided protection and acted as the largest distributor, while the pharmacist Sergio Iglesias operated as a smaller distributor in his pharmacy. One kilo of Bolivian cocaine was converted into three kilos of *pichicata*, which the distributors quickly disseminated in nightclubs, hotels, and brothels of the city.

Years later, the Institute for Penal Sciences published the details of the police investigation that had ended in the conviction of Sergio Iglesias. He was sentenced to two hundred days confinement and issued a small fine in compliance with article 314 of the Penal Code. His pharmacy "Iglesias"—in the middle of the capital—dispensed cocaine without medical prescription to regular clients. One employee who knew these frequent clients served them regularly. Some witnesses—who were also buyers—indicated that it was common practice for them to order *papelillos* of cocaine from waiters at nightclubs near the pharmacy "for a price that fluctuated between 5,000 and 7,000 pesos at the time, that is, around 25 dollars today."[65]

What became evident with the "Jiménez case" was that corruption was endemic among the police and that contraband, illegal gambling, and drug trafficking on a massive scale were recent phenomena but had firm historical roots in Chile. As such, the beaches of the great north, with the constant flow of ships full of nitrate cargos offered the perfect opportunity for smuggling American cigars, women's clothing, and small transistor radios, all thrown into the waterproof bags of the merchant marines and distributed by small merchants in coastal cities. Even more serious, the investigation conducted by military attorney Carlos Leyton and his assistant Hugo Lewis revealed the systemic protection given by investigators and customs police in Chile to the clandestine gambling and drug trafficking, to such a degree that a former general director of Customs Police had been detained and former president Carlos Ibáñez del Campo was summoned to testify. Under such officials, subsecretaries as well as a multitude of other high-ranking officials—many of whom were out of active service—of the Investigative Police participated in the two essential mechanisms for gathering and distributing the bribe money: the so-called *canasta* (basket) that represented the set of periodic payoffs that certain organized crime bosses submitted to the police chiefs in exchange for silence and protection; and the *galardones* (rewards), understood as individual bribes that each detective could receive in exchange for their services, or more accurately for neglecting their duties.[66]

CONCLUSIONS

The consumption of controlled substances in Chilean society expanded starting in the 1970s with cannabis, in the 1980s with cocaine, and in the 1990s with cocaine-based paste. By the time drug consumption in Chile became a major problem, none of the social representations constructed by criminologists and police were useful for combating or preventing it. On the contrary, the gap between the fictional assumptions made by police in the first half of the twentieth century and the actual circulation and consumption of drugs in the 1970s and beyond could not have been greater. Similarly, the Chilean society that engaged with drugs once they were consumed on a massive scale was much different from what police imagined. Young marijuana users saw relatively little danger in the consumption of cannabis, while officials strongly associated the drug with certain groups and the construction of a rebel identity, which transcended the hippie subculture.[67]

This reality, useful to understand the distortions created by social representations of both the consumption and traffic of drugs in Chile, should not prevent us from acknowledging the fact that those representations later influenced official policy. It is likely that the police construction of criminality in the realm of drug trafficking in Chile led to the subsequent mobilization of economic resources, international alliances, and the penetration on all levels of society of the "war on drugs." In addition, the border between Chile, Peru, and Bolivia has been consolidated as a key point in the South American cocaine trade, while Chilean ports and airports have also been identified as points of drug circulation. Finally, the police have become more dedicated to the struggle against drug trafficking in the last two decades.

This example suggests that the dynamic relationship between discourse, social meaning, and practice transcends the mimetic character of meaning as a reflection of "reality." Rather, what is said about a certain phenomenon, the traces of its meanings, and the references that make its social meaning possible shape practices. Over time, these practices influence the phenomenon, its execution, and its daily reproduction, even after the fact.[68] If we call this process fictional or imaginary, we do so not because of its supposed fantastic or impossible character. On the contrary, we do so in an attempt to pinpoint its effective and not subordinate impact over the practices that it enables.

NOTES

Translated by Bonnie A. Lucero. This article was made possible by support from the Programa Fondecyt Iniciación from the National Commission of Science and Technology of Chile.

1. For an overview of international drug regulation, see Richard Davenport-Hines, *La búsqueda del olvido: Historia global de las drogas, 1500–2000* (Mexico City: Fondo de Cultura Económica, 2003), 183–281.

2. For more on this discursive construction in anticipation of historical phenomena—particularly throughout the period of the construction of the "social" as a category of social

cohesion and political mobilization, which coincided with the middle of the twentieth century—see Miguel Ángel Cabrera, *Historia, lenguaje y teoría de la sociedad* (Valencia: Frónesis, 2001); Geoff Eley and Keith Nield, *El futuro de la clase en la historia: ¿Qué queda de lo social?* (Valencia: PUV, 2010); Patrick Joyce, "¿El final de la historia social?" *Historia Social* 50 (2004): 25–45; Ernesto Laclau and Chantal Mouffe, *Hegemonía y estrategia socialista: Hacia una radicalización de la democracia* (Buenos Aires: FCE, 2004).

3. For an analysis of these topics in the period following this one, see Marcos Fernández Labbé, *Drogas en Chile, 1900–1970: Mercado, consumo y representación* (Santiago: Ediciones Universidad Alberto Hurtado, 2011); Paul Gootenberg, *Andean Cocaine: The Making of a Global Drug* (Chapel Hill: University of North Carolina Press, 2008).

4. *Boletín Farmacéutico* (hereafter *BF*), año I, tomo I, August–October (1927), 28.

5. *BF*, año I, n° 9 (April 1928), 293.

6. Sergio González Miranda, *El Dios Cautivo: Las Ligas Patrióticas en la chilenización compulsiva de Tarapacá (1910–1922)* (Santiago: LOM Ediciones, 2004); Diego Lin Chou, *Chile y China: Inmigración y relaciones bilaterales, 1845–1970* (Santiago: DIBAM, 2003).

7. *BF*, año II, n° 4–5 (November–December 1928), 477–78.

8. *La Farmacia Chilena* (hereafter *FCh*), año II, n°s 6–8, 115, 133, 159. For more on the express relation between narcotics and labor exploitation, see William Jankowiak and Daniel Bradburn, eds., *Drugs, Labor, and Colonial Expansion* (Tucson: University of Arizona Press, 2003).

9. *FCh*, año II, n° 12 (December 1928), 238; *FCh*, año III, n° 1 (January 1929), 9–10.

10. *FCh*, año III, n° 3 (March 1929), 48.

11. Archivo de la Dirección General de Sanidad (hereafter ADGS), doc. 2074, November 1927.

12. *FCh*, año I, n° 5 (May 1927), 60.

13. Emilio Belmonte, *Capacidad y responsabilidad del morfinómano, cocainómano y opiómano* (Santiago de Chile: Imprenta Lagunas & Cía, 1920), 44. For more on Chinese immigration and opium consumption in other latitudes, see Evelyn Hu-DeHart, "Opio y control social: Culíes en las haciendas de Perú y Cuba," *Istor* 7, no. 27 (Winter 2006): 28–45.

14. *FCh*, año I, n° 4 (April 1927), 46.

15. *FCh*, año I, n° 5 (May 1927), 63–64.

16. *FCh*, año II, n° 2 (February 1928), 21. See also Lessie Jo Frazier, *Salt in the Sand: Memory, Violence, and the Nation-State in Chile, 1890 to the Present* (Durham, NC: Duke University Press, 2007).

17. *FCh*, año I, n° 7 (July 1927), 91–92.

18. *Revista de Criminología y Policía Científica* (hereafter *RCPC*), año I, n° 4 (March 1938), 4–7.

19. *RCPC*, año IV, n° 47 (February 1943), 77–86.

20. *RCPC*, año IV, n° 50 (May 1943), 110–23.

21. *RCPC*, año I, n° 2 (December–January 1937–38), 18–20.

22. See Nancy Leys Stephan, *"The Hour of Eugenics": Race, Gender, and Nation in Latin America* (Ithaca, NY: Cornell University Press, 1991).

23. On the construction of antisociality as a legal category of exclusion, see Marcos Fernández Labbé, "Asociales: Raza, exclusión y anormalidad en la construcción estatal chilena, 1920–1960," *Revista de Historia Social y de las Mentalidades* 16, no. 2 (2012): 167–94.

24. Juan Cambiazo Díaz, *El sentido subjetivo del Derecho Penal y el estado peligroso* (Chillán: Talleres Gráficos La Discusión, 1930), 27, 36.

25. *Detective*, año II, n° 19 (July 1935), 7–8.

26. *Detective*, año II, n° 19 (July 1935), 7–8.

27. Ibid.

28. *Boletín Oficial de Investigaciones, Identificación y Pasaportes* (hereafter *BOI*), año II, n° 54 (July 1934), 7.

29. *Detective*, año III, n° 25 (January 1936), 4.

30. *Detective*, año IV, n° 37–40 (January–April 1937), 6–7.

31. *RCPC*, año II, n° 20 (July 1939), 9–13.

32. Armando Roger Zelada, *El problema de los estupefacientes* (Santiago: Imprenta El Imparcial, 1939), 7.

33. Ibid., 18, 21.

34. *RCPC*, año IV, n° 46 (January 1943), 13–24.

35. *RCPC*, año VIII, n° 112 (September 1948), 32.

36. *RCPC*, año XI, n° 147 (August 1951), 41–63.

37. *RCPC*, año XIII, n° 187 (December 1954), 3.

38. For an overview of social legislation during this period, see Juan Carlos Yáñez, *La intervención social en Chile, 1907–1932* (Santiago: Ril Editores, 2008).

39. Fernández Labbé, "Asociales."

40. *FCh*, año I, n° 6 (June 1927), 80.

41. *FCh*, año I, n° 6 (June 1927), 63–64.

42. *FCh*, año I, n° 6 (June 1927), 75.

43. *FCh*, año I, n° 12 (December 1927), 177.

44. *FCh*, año III, n° 4 (April 1929), 61–62.

45. *BOI*, año IV, n° 138 (February 1936), 11–12.

46. *BOI*, año IV, n° 161 (August 1936), 14.

47. *FCh*, año III, n° 10 (October 1929), 182–86.

48. *FCh*, año III, n° 12 (December 1929), 225.

49. *Detective*, año I, n° 2 (February 1934), 11–12.

50. *RCPC*, año I, n° 1 (October–November 1937), 34.

51. *Detective*, año III, n° 32 (August–October 1936), 11. For more on Chilean drug legislation, see Cristián Merino Rojas, *Evolución histórica de la legislación nacional sobre tráfico ilícito de estupefacientes* (Talca, 2000).

52. Patricio Morales Salinas, *La Dirección General de Investigaciones* (Santiago: Editorial Universitaria, 1956), 16–17.

53. *RCPC*, año I, n° 4 (March 1938), 4–7.

54. Morales Salinas, *La Dirección General de Investigaciones*, 43.

55. *RCPC*, año I, n° 4 (March 1938), 4–7. The third preventive director of the General Bureau of Investigations did keep a first registry. Shortly thereafter, at a conference for doctors at the Neuropsychiatric Clinic of the Public Jail of Santiago, at the Second Latin American Criminology Conference, the proposition was heard for "the operation of a clinic for drug users or an Institution of Reeducation. Preferably, the models adopted in Switzerland and in the United States, N.A. [Narcotic Farm, Lexington], of course, should be followed, preserving the needed proportions and according to our socioeconomic reality." *RCPC*, año III, n° 34 (March 1941), 39.

56. *RCPC*, año I, n° 4 (March 1938), 4–7.

57. *RCPC*, año V, n° 69 (January 1945), 31–32.

58. *BOI*, año VI, n° 267 (April 1939), 10.

59. *RCPC*, año VIII, n° 108 (May 1948), 28.

60. *RCPC*, año IX, n° 120 (May 1949), 38.

61. *BOI*, año XVII, n° 511 (December 1951), 5–6; *BOI*, año XVIII, n° 520 (September 1952), 6.

62. *RCPC*, año XIII, n° 180 (May 1954), 46.

63. According to the source cited here, this proximity to the world of organized crime had reached the point that the detective was the godfather of one of the daughters of Mario Silva Leiva, better known as "Cabro Carrera," who would become one of the most famous drug traffickers in Chilean history.

64. For the interviewee, the vast majority of the cocaine that passed through Chile did so in a transitory way: "this is a market of little importance, they pay little and sometimes nothing at all. What is consumed in Santiago is a mixture of bicarbonate with boric acid and with minimal quantities of cocaine." For indicators of the participation of Chilean drug traffickers in the arrival of cocaine to the United States, see Gootenberg, *Andean Cocaine*; Eduardo Sáenz Rovner, *La conexión cubana: Narcotráfico, contrabando y juego en Cuba entre los años 20 y comienzos de la Revolución* (Bogotá: Centro de Estudios Sociales, Universidad Nacional de Colombia, 2005).

65. *RCPC*, vol. XXV, n° 2 (May–August 1966), 122–26.

66. *Vistazo*, January 20–27 (1959); February 17, 1959.

67. Patricia Richard, Ana María Viveros, and Liana Ortiz, *¿Fuma marihuana el estudiante chileno?* (Santiago: Ediciones Nueva Universidad, PUC, 1972); Patrick Barra-Melej,

"Hippismo a la chilena: Juventud y heterodoxia cultural en un contexto trasnacional (1970–1973)," in *Ampliando miradas: Chile y su historia en un tiempo global*, ed. Fernando Purcell and Alfredo Riquelme, 305–25 (Santiago: PUC-RIL, 2009).

68. Hans Ulrich Gumbrecht, *Producción de presencia* (Mexico City: Universidad Iberoamericana, 2005); Alun Munslow, *Desconstruindo a história* (Rio de Janeiro: Editora Vozes, 2006).

4

BETWEEN FICTION AND REALITY

ૐ

Policiales *and the Beginnings of the Yellow Press in Lima, 1940–1960*

SÖNKE HANSEN

IN THE MIDDLE DECADES of the twentieth century, the Peruvian city of Lima underwent a wave of profound transformations, as the urban population expanded and the social ills of city life multiplied. Historians, sociologists, and anthropologists of twentieth-century Lima have typically focused on the 1960s as the period of greatest social and cultural change, due in large part to the massive migration from the highlands to the city during this decade. Peruvian social anthropologist José Matos Mar, among the first and most recognized proponents of this thesis, contended that migration from the Andean highlands caused a *"desborde popular"* in Lima—a bursting at the seams—that shook the society to its very foundations, catalyzing political instability and creating a flurry of social problems in the city.[1] Within a few years, the "colonial and oligarchic" city of Lima "mutated into a chaotic, dirty, dangerous, and culturally heterogeneous peruvianized megacity."[2] Subsequent scholars across the disciplines have concurred that the massive migration from the middle of the twentieth century constituted the most important development driving social and cultural change in Lima.[3]

Although the great migration of the 1960s did transform Lima's culture in significant ways, the process actually began much earlier. Indeed, profound demographic changes and urban growth that were under way as early as the 1890s led to a massive population growth in Lima over the first half of the twentieth century. The city's 1890 population of just 104,000 inhabitants expanded to over 141,000 in 1908, and grew to 540,000 in 1940.[4] The population growth renewed the ranks of the urban poor and working classes. By the 1940s and 1950s, many working-class men and women began to take on a greater role in the emerging mass society of twentieth-century Lima. Through their participation in the social and cultural life of the capital, workers helped to produce popular culture through their everyday practices and patterns of consumption, fostering greater demand for sporting events, cinemas, music halls, bars, and other leisure and amusement activities. Lima's working classes contributed to the emergence of new leisure practices and even began to infiltrate formerly elite cultural spheres such as horse racing.

Nowhere was the cultural shift more apparent than in the city's expanding base of low-priced newspapers.[5] This emerging form of popular media owed much of its success to the democratization of public education and, in turn, the rising literacy rates among the urban working classes over the course of the first half of the twentieth century.[6] The rising importance of popular consumption of the yellow press, as it was called, fundamentally transformed the way journalists reported the news. Perhaps the most salient marker of this change was the explosion of crime stories, typically called *policiales*, between the 1940s and 1950s. Prior to the mid-twentieth century, press coverage of current murders and robberies in the Lima newspapers consisted of short and precise notes. In contrast to the dry, fact-driven accounts of daily occurrences, policiales typically featured lurid anecdotes of delinquents, victims, and criminal offenses. Speculation about the motives of criminal suspects captured the attention of a broad audience and gained popularity among the expanding readership. The structure of the policiales resembled the modern "lead" style common in the United States: journalists explained the significance of the events—apart from place and time—in the opening lines. The articles no longer followed a chronological order but rather prioritized sensationalized content. The abundant photos and illustrations accompanying the policiales further distinguished this new form of media from its predecessors.

Thus, the cultural transformations occurring during this period in Lima created a change in the way news media covered crime. The marked change in the type, content, and cost of newspapers printed during the 1940s and 1950s evinced an expansion of working-class participation and consumption of media. It also led high-circulation papers to compete with each other for the readership, fostering an increased reliance on sensationalized stories that tended to use crime as a hook to lure in readers.

Massive popular consumption of this form of media led to a second important shift: the discourses and coverage around crime shifted away from stories that claimed objectivity and focused on facts and toward narratives that sensationalized the crimes, victims, and suspects. This shift occurred in two phases. First, between 1940 and 1950, newspapers presented fact-driven accounts of crime with only varying hints of sensationalism to arouse curiosity among their readers. This demonstrated a preliminary transition between detailed investigation and the beginnings of sensationalist journalism. The second period, from 1950 to 1960, was characterized by widespread sensationalism and showed increasing forms of exaggeration and a distinctive literary style in crime coverage. A key catalyst in this transformation was the establishment of the newspaper *Última Hora* in 1950. The paper challenged the hegemony of *La Crónica* among the popular classes and led to a vigorous competition for readers, which translated into increasingly embellished reportage. With its popular and colloquial style, *Última Hora* was totally geared toward the urban lower classes and soon became the newspaper with the highest circulation in Peru.[7]

In order to elucidate this shift in media depiction of crime from the more "objective" journalism of the 1940s to the sensationalized stories of the 1950s, I critically analyze three emblematic cases. Mamoru Shimizu, Jorge Villanueva, and the well-known criminal Tatán all committed egregious homicides in Lima and subsequently attracted great attention from the inhabitants of the city. These cases were some of the most representative of this period, and reporters wrote about them in newspapers for weeks instead of one or two days as with the usual smaller cases. Also, these cases provide a broader selection of material over a longer period of time, which helps reveal patterns in the ways in which journalists wrote policiales. By examining a sample of the best-known cases, I argue that these sensationalized crime stories, which became key features of urban popular culture, contributed to a growing popular perception of Lima as an increasingly dangerous metropolis.[8]

As a supplement to fragmentary source material, policiales can provide vital information for understanding Peru's legal culture. Thus, this article looks at the writing style, content, and methods employed by the newspapers. Policiales created a world of good and evil, of heroes and villains. The stories either favored or attacked the possible culprits, which caused fear and curiosity among their readers while evoking opinions, moods, resentments, and racist stereotypes among members of the same popular classes profiled in many of the stories. Although policiales fostered a sense of danger surrounding the poor and working-class residents of the city, the daily reading of this section also seemed to foster greater awareness among the lower and middle classes of their own rights as urban citizens.

POLICIALES IN THE 1940S: BETWEEN DETAILED INVESTIGATION AND THE BEGINNINGS OF SENSATIONALIST JOURNALISM

In the 1940s, most of the reports about local crimes in Lima newspapers delivered a detailed chronological abstract of the event and the work of police and courts. Untenable hypotheses and sensationalized content appeared only sporadically and indirectly, mostly through inclusion of transcribed interrogations in the detailed reports.

This style of writing reflected former editorial practices, such as providing state institutions, like the police, with a space for succinct reports on daily occurrences when
situations warranted it. Furthermore, there were still marked differences in coverage
between newspapers of the elite and upper-middle classes such as the socially conservative and economically liberal paper *El Comercio* and the liberal *La Prensa* and those
of the popular classes (such as *La Crónica* and *Universal*).

The preliminary incorporation of sensationalism within largely fact-based reports
of crime, particularly in relation to anti-Japanese sentiment, most clearly emerges in
the case of Japanese immigrant Mamoru Shimizu, the seven-time killer in the barrio of Chacra Colorada in November 1944. Articles about this crime drew on and
reinforced the abundant racial stereotypes about Japanese people during and after
World War II. At this time Peru had interrupted diplomatic relations with Japan, and
anti-Japanese sentiment, which existed before the war, became increasingly visible in
Lima.[9] For instance, in May 1940, lootings of Japanese businesses caused the deaths of
ten Japanese residents.[10] After the United States entered the war in 1941, about eighteen hundred Japanese were deported from Peru to U.S. internment camps.[11]

On the night of November 2, 1944, four adults and three children of Japanese
origin were killed in their home in Chacra Colorada. Just days after the murder, the
police presented Mamoru Shimizu, who lived in the house where the murders occurred and was the brother of one of the victims, as the murderer. The crime ignited
tremendous press coverage in the capital city.[12] Over several weeks the daily press provided extensive and somewhat sensationalistic reports of the police investigation. The
murder captivated popular attention for weeks and remained in the memory of many,
evident in the publication of several popular studies about the case to this day.[13]

The press unanimously pointed out the exceptional cruelty of the crime. *La
Prensa* and *La Crónica* wrote nearly identical accounts claiming that such a horren-
dous crime had not been committed in Lima for many years.[14] Although the motives
of the crime remained unclear, *La Prensa* speculated that since no objects of value
were stolen, it must have been an act of jealousy or revenge.[15] *El Comercio* concurred
in the motive of the crime and buttressed police suspicions about the survivors in
the house as the prime suspects.[16] Over the next several days, coverage focused on the
police investigation, the Japanese families involved, and the property where the crime
took place.

Apart from the relatively dry descriptions of the events in publicized police reports, prejudiced assumptions with a nationalist, xenophobic, or even an anti-Japanese
tone appeared. Some of these assumptions were deeply related to the negative view
that some Peruvians had about Asians, some of which Luz Huertas discusses in chapter 2 of this volume. In terms of media coverage of the crime, *La Crónica*, for instance,
wrote: "it seems very true that homicides . . . are [committed by those of] foreign

nationality, given the methods employed and the [fact that] they are done in cold blood."[17] However, these assumptions are not mentioned sensationalistically in the title but rather only in a section of the article. Two days later, seemingly key political details about the family were revealed, including the discovery of a copy of Adolf Hitler's *Mein Kampf* in a so-called secret room of the house of the Japanese residents.[18] In addition, the media made public a sensationalistic detail: the authorities had supposedly found a copy of a letter from the German ambassador in which he thanked Japan for the donation of two hundred sailors for a battleship—a piece of evidence that further suggested a link between Japan and Nazi Germany.[19]

Speculation that the ultra-nationalistic Japanese secret society Dragón Negro had committed the crime emerged as the most disturbing scenario. The newspaper *Universal* described Dragón Negro as an organization that was far more bloodthirsty than the Sicilian Mafia, the Camorra, or the Gestapo. According to that newspaper, their militants fought under the command of Japanese military officials and the Japanese aristocracy. Some articles claimed that the organization had more than one million members and was also popular among Japanese immigrants in Peru. Newspaper reports that the Shimizu family was reportedly on the brink of deportation to the United States sought to increase the readers' perception of the Japanese victims as either dangerous or linked to dangerous influences.[20]

To make the news appear sounder, newspapers typically hid their assumptions behind seemingly investigative questions, while subtly directing readers' attention toward the surviving Japanese men (Shimizu, the younger brother of a victim, and Naíto, a deaf man who worked and lived with the Shimizu family) and Japanese secret societies as the most probable culprits. Newspapers during this era also focused on meticulously incorporating documentation directly related to the police investigation, which made the articles appear reliable and gave the impression that reporters understood every single detail of the process as it developed.

A few days after the crime, newspaper reports of the evidence found by the police against Shimizu became more sensationalized. *El Comercio* and *La Prensa* wrote that Shimizu's wife did not have any doubt that her husband committed the crime.[21] In examining the possible motive of the crime, *La Crónica* quoted Shimuzu's wife, who said that the murdered brother had insulted Shimizu.[22] In the same article, the newspaper also mentioned other supposedly incriminating evidence: the discovery of a Japanese flag with the Dragón Negro sign in the so-called secret room as well as photos of Shimizu in Japanese military uniform.[23] The newspapers also discussed changes in Shimizu's behavior during the investigation. In contrast to the attitude he assumed in the first days after the crime, Shimizu had become increasingly dull and depressive.[24] *El Comercio* also compared the two suspects: while Naíto answered questions quickly in the interrogations, Shimizu kept his head down, remaining silent.[25] *Universal* even described Shimizu as desperate, crying before his arraignment.[26] *El Comercio* wrote that Shimizu was on the brink of giving a guilty plea and quoted him personally with the words: "I wants [*sic*] to tell the truth but I cannot."[27]

Whereas articles prior to Shimizu's detention typically presented details related to the case as elements that underscored possible hypotheses, after his detention, journalists became bolder in their assertions. Local writers emphasized negative characteristics of the two suspects, Shimizu and Naíto, and began to exploit prevailing prejudices or assumptions to attract more readers. Indeed, at least one newspaper suggested that Shimizu was suicidal. At the same time, the press did not seem to accept the possibility that Shimizu and Naíto might have acted independently and without the pressure of criminal organizations, even as evidence increasingly supported this idea.

Many newspapers exploited pervasive anti-Japanese sentiment. According to the press, the Japanese "character" itself was the cause of the murders. Anti-Japanese statements peppered reports of the crime, emphasizing, among other themes, the supposedly barbaric Japanese culture as a cause of the brutal episode. *Universal* suggested that Japanese conceptions of life undergirded the brutality of the crime.[28] Moreover, *El Comercio* still strongly suggested personal revenge as a possible motive and insisted that Japanese culture was to blame. Some articles even implied that the murder had been a Japanese "national decision."[29] Many newspaper articles included stereotyping and racist remarks against Japanese immigrants. For instance, *La Crónica* dismissed Shimizu's wife's denunciation of her husband as a hoax, apparently because Japanese culture was presumed to frown on betrayal.[30] Other articles transcribed the wife's statements phonetically to emphasize her broken Spanish.[31]

Despite Shimizu's confession to having committed the seven murders, which appeared in all newspapers on November 13, many of the editors and journalists speculated that Shimizu had not acted alone.[32] Immediately following the confession, the murders occupied an even greater proportion of news coverage. Detailed reports of the confession, the sequence of events, and the official reconstructions of the crime graced the pages of multiple newspapers, though noticeable differences in the way papers covered the confession emerged. While *La Crónica* and *Universal* provided their readers with about ten days of new revelations, coverage by *El Comercio* and *La Prensa* declined after a few days.

This case, quite typical in the way newspapers covered similar crimes in the 1940s, featured detailed descriptions that gave credibility to the articles. Clearly untenable hypotheses, bluntly racist comments, and lurid descriptions appeared only sporadically and indirectly during the 1940s. Although newspapers were not free of sensationalism and subjective journalism, these were not to be found as continually or as prominently as they were later, during the 1950s. In addition, the differences between the high-circulation newspapers and more elitist ones were neither as clear nor as pronounced as they became in the following decade.

POLICIALES IN THE 1950s:
WIDESPREAD SENSATIONALISM

In contrast to the press coverage of the 1940s, the policiales in the high-circulation newspapers of the 1950s no longer contained the detailed abstracts of the incidents that customarily accompanied judicial and police reports. Popular newspapers like *Última Hora* and *La Crónica* published anecdotes and stories about the cases. As competition for new readers increased, it became more important for the newspapers to report on spectacular news while keeping some level of credibility. For this reason, some newspapers fabricated interviews to back up their assumptions and employed language that implied veracity.

Coverage of important cases evinced a tendency toward storytelling and literary embellishment, rather than merely interpreting evidence. But this came at the cost of offering a coherent, fact-based account of the crime and the ensuing police investigation. Likely in an effort to increase sales, stories often emphasized sensationalistic details, some of which invariably contradicted information provided in previous articles. The 1950s saw a critical change in the way high-circulation newspapers crafted policiales, as fierce competition between *La Crónica* and *Última Hora* grew. In contrast, elitist newspapers like *El Comercio* usually published policiales in their tabloid-like afternoon editions. In fact, policiales rarely graced the pages of more serious morning editions, and in the exceptional case that they did, the coverage was rather reserved, short, and fact driven. The shift in press coverage, most apparent in the high-circulation newspapers attracting broad working-class readerships, emerged most clearly in the way *La Crónica* and *Última Hora* covered two important criminal cases involving Jorge Villanueva and well-known criminal Tatán.

JORGE VILLANUEVA:
EL MONSTRUO DE ARMENDARIZ

In September 1954, the murder of three-year-old Julio Hidalgo shocked the population of Lima. The small child was kidnapped during the day just outside of his parents' house. His body was found the next day in the ravine Quebrada de Armendariz, in Miraflores. After some days of uncertainty, the police presented Jorge Villanueva, a man of Afro-indigenous origin, as the perpetrator of the murder. Two years later he was sentenced to death, and in 1957 he was executed. This was the first time in sixty-seven years that someone was officially executed for a crime in Peru.[33]

The newspapers followed the case with high interest and reported nonstop on the murder. They competed with each other in the hunt for information and attempted to captivate an expanded readership by emphasizing the exceptional cruelty of the crime and the increasing dangers of the city. *La Crónica* called the delinquent the "Monstruo de Armendariz" and concluded that he was either a pervert or a demented person. The paper incoherently also reported that the mysterious and alarming disappearance of minors was ascribed to a criminal gang that kidnapped children, which demonstrates that the reporters aimed to incite moral panic in order to attract more readers rather than provide coherent information about the crime and the victim.[34] *Última Hora* called the delinquent the "Herodes de Barranco" and initially claimed that Lima's entire population craved a hunt for the "beast" who perpetrated the crime.[35] During the days after the murder, the press reported that a person of Afro-indigenous origin was suspected of having committed the crime.[36]

After the arrest of Villanueva, high-circulation papers immediately discussed the death sentence for the alleged murderer. With their style of coverage, the newspapers contributed to an increasingly hostile climate against him. *La Crónica* wrote that the death sentence would be well justified in this case, as it involved the murder of a defenseless child. In their view, people like Villanueva were inhuman and depraved and therefore deserved a penalty no lighter than death. Already declaring Villanueva guilty, these newspapers pointed at him as one of many "abnormal" people who were highly dangerous and for whom a jail sentence simply would not effectively to ensure rehabilitation.[37] *Última Hora* even quoted a priest—who wished to remain anonymous: "The beast should die as an example to others." It did not matter if Villanueva had mental problems; he was no more than "*escoria humana*" [scum] according to the newspaper, and therefore he had to be eliminated.[38] The anonymity of the speaker suggests a possible sensationalist fabrication by the journalists and editors. However, for noncritical readers of lower education levels, this type of statement offered a very strong argument in favor of the death penalty, because it was presented as the word of an ecclesiastical authority.

To increase support for the victim and animosity against the alleged culprit, the paper claimed that the neighbors of the Hidalgo family wanted Villanueva to be lynched or burned at the Plaza de Armas in downtown Lima.[39] *La Crónica* promoted the death penalty in its headlines, and that newspaper's writers even claimed that Hidalgo's mother had demanded the death penalty for Villanueva.[40] They also included the results of their own survey, claiming that a majority of the population asked for the death penalty.[41] All of the articles presumed that Villanueva was guilty.

This position momentarily changed after Villanueva's confession, when these newspapers offered mixed opinions about the crime to produce suspense and uncertainty. *Última Hora*, for instance, reported that only one of twenty witnesses had been able to identify Villanueva as the criminal. However, the suspected murderer had been charged previously with stealing and sexual crimes, including the assault of a teenager, just days before the murder.[42] Also, the ten-year-old brother of Hidalgo had almost accompanied Villanueva once before, not knowing that he soon would be known in Chorrillos as the "terror[izer] of the children."[43] The incoherence in the news coverage of *Última Hora* intensified the following day, when the newspaper reported that Villanueva never had been convicted for sexual offenses but only for robbery.[44]

Interestingly, the focus on Villanueva's abnormal behavior emerged in the press only after his own confession to the crime. Several newspapers reported on Villanueva's peculiarities, depicting him as an abnormal and crazy individual beyond the reaches of civilized society. *Última Hora*, for instance, wrote that Villanueva preferred to sleep on the floor rather than in a bed at the police station.[45] *La Crónica* even included a picture of Villanueva with the subtitle: "The mind resists believing that beings such as this one exist, but the reality is raw, scary, to say the least."[46] In contrast to popular papers like *Última Hora* and *La Crónica*, *El Comercio*, which catered to middle- and upper-class Lima residents, contended that Villanueva did not necessarily merit execution even if he seemed abnormal.[47]

At the end of September 1954 the case disappeared from the headlines.[48] Newspapers sporadically covered the trial in 1956. While *La Crónica* reported daily from the hearing, *Última Hora* published about it only occasionally, often without adding editorial commentary. However, the headlines of *Última Hora* were usually marked by their originality. On the day of the judgment, for instance, the paper printed that the "Monster has a date with destiny today."[49] After the issuance of the death sentence, the paper published a grim cartoon of the future execution of Villanueva.[50] *La Prensa* and *El Comercio* reported only irregularly about the process. They described the course of the trial without commenting on the possible verdict. Only after the pronouncement of judgment did *El Comercio* write that the death penalty was a fair sentence for the disgraceful criminal.[51]

During the hearing, *La Crónica* dryly reported the viewpoints of the prosecution and the defense. Nevertheless in certain sections, the paper foregrounded what the public surely understood to be its strong opinions on the case. A few days before the sentence was issued, the writers claimed that people wanted Villanueva to be strongly and exemplarily punished to avoid the murder of children in the future and to protect society.[52] After sentencing, the paper continued to report on Villanueva in a lurid way. A journalist with *La Crónica* even interviewed the convict, who swore his innocence from his jail cell. But the paper called Villanueva's claims pure bluff, taunting him and reiterating the need to punish him severely.[53]

A few days before his execution in December 1957, Villanueva became the focus of press coverage again. For many people, the daily newspaper and radio coverage of the case was not enough. In fact, their curiosity prompted them to visit the jail to learn more about Villanueva and the case, or even, with a little luck, to see the "villain" himself.[54] According to *La Crónica*, thousands of people waited outside of the jail to hear the shots of his execution.[55]

Even as the day of the execution approached, *La Crónica* did not back off its adamant position against Villanueva. Apart from talking about every detail of Villanueva's execution and his last days alive, the paper also mentioned that public opinion overwhelmingly supported—even demanded—the death penalty.[56] Statements such as "the Monster Villanueva is undoubtedly a human beast, a being without a soul who deserves no pardon from man or God," were not uncommon.[57] *Última Hora*, too, wrote in detail about Villanueva before the execution. It was equally as lurid, but the tone was more balanced than that of *La Crónica*. About the death penalty for Villanueva, it stated that the public opinion was divided into supporters and opponents.[58]

After the execution, *La Crónica* remarked that Villanueva had been a liar until the day he died because he had sworn his innocence.[59] Afterward the newspaper mentioned Villanueva's declaration of innocence in several articles and even let Villanueva's lawyer talk about his client's defense arguments. This was the first time that *La Crónica* completely refrained from doubting those arguments for Villanueva's innocence.[60] This change in the newspaper's attitude was likely a commercial strategy to keep the readers' interest by presenting information and opinions that could arouse doubt and concern. *Última Hora*, on the other hand, refrained from a final evaluation of the death penalty, preferring to continue its tabloid-like coverage on Villanueva's supposed son.[61]

Only the magazine *Presente* defended Villanueva, calling into question the evidence against him. What is more, the magazine reminded readers of the fact that Villanueva was not convicted for rape and murder but only for murder.[62] After the execution, the magazine printed a letter that criticized the congress for avoiding Villanueva's petitions for amnesty.[63] The author implies that racial and social discrimination could have been the reason: "Has he paid the offense of his color? If he had been white, wealthy, influential, would they have killed him? . . . Was he caught redhanded? . . . His poverty and sickly existence contributed to his downfall."[64]

Newspapers, especially *La Crónica*, with its one-sided coverage of the case, created a hostile atmosphere that incited collective fear of kidnappings and rapes of children. Prejudice and racism, likely also a strategy to increase circulation, intensified opinions against Villanueva because of his visible indigenousness and African ancestry. News about sexual crimes allegedly committed by Villanueva further fanned the flames of popular prejudice and rage against him, although there was no evidence that Hidalgo had been the victim of sexual violence. For these reasons, the execution cannot be understood without considering the ways press coverage shaped public opinion from the very beginning to demand the imposition of the death penalty. Almost a decade after Villanueva's death, doubts about his guilt arose and were dramatized by Francisco Lombardi in his movie *Muerte al amancer* (*Death at Dawn*, 1977). The persisting popular legacy of the case underscores the subtle changes in how press coverage defined popular notions of criminality and influenced the criminal justice system.

TATÁN: CRIMINAL AND MEDIA HERO

In contrast to the decidedly negative press coverage of Villanueva, another prominent criminal, Tatán (Luis D'Unián Dulanto), emerged as something of a media darling between the mid-1940s and the early 1960s.[65] Tatán was a mestizo who usually appeared to be well dressed and enjoyed the privileges of being photogenic and young. Although he was a criminal, he boasted the reputation of a gentleman or even a Peruvian "Robin Hood." Tatán's fame in the press lasted fifteen years, during which countless articles about his offenses and his private life appeared in newspapers and magazines. In contrast to the coverage of Shimizu and Villanueva, the case of Tatán is not about a single offense but about the whole life story of a young criminal, from his first offenses to his prison terms, escapes, discharges, and trials, finally ending with his murder in 1962. He was the star of high-circulation newspapers, but the increasing sensationalism of the news and stories about him worked against him, ultimately making it impossible for him to escape the unsavory reputation his crimes had earned him.

La Crónica published one of the first articles about him in 1946. It described Tatán's arrival as a prisoner alongside an accomplice at the port of Callao. La Crónica distinguished the young criminal from regular delinquents, who "showed evidence of depression."[66] Tatán was "the exception," as he seemed to enjoy giving interviews and greeting the crowd that had waited for him at the pier. After that first moment of fame, Tatán gradually earned an impressive reputation and gained a place in Lima's newspapers thanks to his skills as an ingenious escape artist.[67]

While the articles about Tatán often had an admiring tone, especially in the first years, journalists also included critical or almost educational lines in their stories. La Crónica, for instance, wrote that the young criminal had an "unfortunate reputation in the underworld."[68] Especially in El Comercio, disdainful judgments of the "sadly famous delinquent" appeared.[69] While in the 1940s even high-circulation papers criticized Tatán and were less sensationalistic, by the 1950s this fact-driven style predominated only in newspapers considered more serious, like El Comercio.

The newspapers wrote about Tatán not only when he was suspected of a crime or when he was captured but also during his trials and upon his releases from prison. In September 1954, for example, Tatán's trial for theft and the murder of a cellmate became a media event. Despite the presence of other important suspects, Tatán became the main attraction. La Crónica wrote daily about the proceeding. In addition, the paper published further details, including the claim that Tatán was tortured before he confessed to the murder and that he had been on a hunger strike. Other articles emphasized his repentance, claiming that he had sworn to be a better man after the death of his father.[70] The emphasis on the human side of this proven criminal contrasts deeply with the treatment received by Shimizu and Villanueva and, above all, makes clear that the press showed a preference for individuals with certain racial and class backgrounds.

Tatán was absolved of the murder and had to serve only a minor sentence for various robberies. After learning of the sentence, the newspapers emphasized that Tatán would devote himself to living an honest life, working as a carpenter, reading the Bible, playing chess, and writing his autobiography, which purportedly aimed to deter young adults from starting a criminal career.[71] Yet, stories about his simple home life as a carpenter lasted only a short while. The press searched for new stories about him. *La Crónica* quoted a psychiatric expert who described Tatán as a lunatic who committed crimes to acquire fame.[72] Some newspapers also reported on Tatán's prospective job as an actor in *radionovelas*, a probable future as a professional soccer player, or even a possible reclusive life in a monastery.[73] However, all these "news" stories were merely fabrications.

Journalistic interest also piqued during Tatán's 1959 trial. Again the papers focused on him although he had codefendants. Apart from the details of the trial, gossip about Tatán filled the pages of the newspapers. *Última Hora*, for instance, published one article titled "The Wife and a Harem Fight to See Tatán," which was ultimately a story about two women who fought vehemently for the right to visit Tatán in jail.[74] *La Crónica* entertained its readers by publishing a story about the fact that he had apparently worn a new gray suit that made him look "like a dandy."[75] The obsession with reporting on the minutiae of the popular delinquent's life continued for days, with the paper reporting that Tatán donned a brand-new suit with silver lining.[76] Indeed, he appeared in countless photographs, elegantly dressed and smiling. In comparison, his codefendants looked miserable and generally dressed poorly.[77]

During the trial, the media hype caused such tremendous public interest that the courtroom was always crowded and a television channel even asked for authorization to broadcast the trial. The request was denied, though, as captured in this statement from the judge published by *La Crónica*: "We are not dealing with a public spectacle, but rather a trial whose excessive diffusion could cause disruptions in the minds of adolescents by making Tatán important when, on the contrary, he is a pernicious subject who has made his bad reputation his trademark."[78] Besides this kind of coverage in high-circulation newspapers, which at least indirectly enhanced the fame and popularity of Tatán, press reports only seldom and sporadically included critical remarks about him. *La Crónica*, for instance, wrote: "D'Unián Dulanto, a character of the underworld, has again fallen into delinquency. His obsession with notoriety, his desire for stardom, has been the cause of his downfall."[79]

In mid-November, Tatán again made front-page news in high-circulation newspapers following his acquittal owing to lack of evidence.[80] *Última Hora* wrote that upon leaving jail, Tatán gave his first interview to a radio station right by the jail exit, as if he were a popular hero.[81] The area did not lack "people who took out their notebooks, asking for his autograph. Some women compared him to a movie actor," the article read.[82] Just like in 1954, the newspapers clamored in his defense, arguing that Tatán would study, work, and be honest from then on. Apparently, his autobiography would also appear soon.[83] *Última Hora* announced that Tatán had already found work as a guard in a shop.[84] *La Crónica* quoted Tatán's defender, listing the famous criminal's four goals after his release: he wanted his nickname to be forgotten, and he set out to finish his studies, work calmly, and marry the mother of his child.[85] The newspapers visited him at home to interview him and showed him as a loving family man.[86] But just like before, the idyllic picture of the new Tatán suggested by the papers did not last. He left his new workplace after only a few days and, a few months later, he was in jail again for robbery.[87]

The media's love affair with Tatán could not save the famed criminal from the horrible fate awaiting him in jail. In June 1962, he was murdered by a cellmate while serving his sentence. Following his slaying, the media plunged into a debate over whether the murder could have been avoided.[88] Tatán's last words, which were about his wife and daughter, were quoted in different versions, which again highlights the commercial strategies used by high-circulation newspapers.[89] *La Crónica* eulogized his death, writing, for instance, that Tatán had been a master in his business as a criminal, enjoying an impressive twenty-year career.[90]

The funeral was also transformed into a media event. *La Crónica* wrote that the funeral was paid for by a mysterious rich lady, possibly an Argentinean actress.[91] According to *Última Hora*, hundreds of people followed the coffin from Tatán's house to the cemetery.[92] *La Crónica* and *Correo* reported that more than a thousand people went to the funeral and added, ironically, that there were so many fellow criminals among the mourners that the amount of jail time they had collectively served totaled more than three thousand years. The burial ceremony included the singing of the national anthem and several speeches in which Tatán was called "an exemplary father and citizen" among other laudatory titles.[93]

In contrast to this reverential commemoration in high-circulation newspapers, there were critical voices, especially in more conservative periodicals. *El Comercio* wrote that "instead of having considered Tatán the king of the underworld, he should have been treated as a publicity addict, given that his desire for notoriety seemed to be what pushed him to commit the deeds."[94] *Última Hora* claimed that Tatán reflected the problems of society and warned its readers about the weakness of young people who were prone to be seduced by the criminal lifestyle. According to that newspaper, on the one hand, print media, movies, and television indirectly celebrated this way of life and, on the other hand, parents tended to fail in teaching their children wholesome values, thus placing them at risk of following in the footsteps of unsavory characters like Tatán.[95] In another article, *El Comercio* criticized the popular perception of Tatán as an honorable and exemplary young man and also blamed the police for his tragic end.[96]

Although the newspapers often speculated about the reasons for Tatán's popular fame, they themselves had played an important role in developing the starlike image that had ultimately defined Tatán's life and shaped the terms of his death.[97] Indeed, he had become a media hero not only because of his notorious desire to appear on the front pages of high-circulation newspapers but also because these newspapers had converted him into product of consumption. While traditional papers like *El Comercio* simply ignored him or treated him like any other criminal, high-circulation newspapers embellished and even invented the gossip surrounding his offenses. They fabricated details and exaggerated stories, leading to the trivialization of his crimes. In so doing, they painted a romantic image of an elegant, honorable, and smart criminal. The occasional condemnation of his offenses in these papers simply failed to attract the audience that all the lurid stories commanded. Thus, in a way, high-circulation newspapers countered the efforts of police and judges to make an example of Tatán and other criminals by transforming a criminal into a popular hero. These newspapers may have inspired others to imitate Tatán's exploits in the hopes of achieving similar notoriety.

Creating heroes and villains was a successful sales strategy for high-circulation newspapers. Readers certainly seemed to enjoy the clear identification of good and evil. Also, the stories about that smart and good-looking young plebeian criminal might have amused a part of the working classes who interpreted his deeds as challenges to repressive agents and state institutions. In that way, the articles about Tatán can be viewed in terms of their role in the depressurization of the political sphere. In the end, the fate of media darling Tatán did not differ much from Villanueva's destiny. Like the "Monstruo de Armendariz," Tatán became a victim of high-circulation newspaper policiales. His public fame made it difficult for him to turn back to a civic life.

CONCLUSIONS

This chapter has examined the emergence of the yellow press in Lima in the 1940s and 1950s. While the policiales in the 1940s were still mostly fact-driven and consisted of detailed chronological abstracts of the incidents, with only rare and indirect sensationalistic content, the high-circulation newspapers in the 1950s used the policiales above all to tell an exciting and interesting story. The newspaper publishing companies discovered that they could appeal to the sensibilities and experiences of the urban working class by presenting news in simple, often moralistic, and, above all, sensationalistic ways. While some newspapers experimented with these strategies in the 1940s, by the 1950s sensationalism defined high-circulation newspapers, expanding the readership to include, indeed specifically target, the increasingly literate urban working classes.

By the 1950s, reports on crime in high-circulation newspapers catering mainly to Lima's popular sectors had changed markedly. They were no longer written in chronological order and did not necessarily provide a complete overview of the incidents. With the policiales, the high-circulation newspapers elicited opinions, moods, resentments, and racist stereotypes among their readers and influenced the public mood surrounding police investigations and court cases. The yellow press covered criminal cases whose alleged perpetrators belonged to the same sector of society as the readers, one that was above all urban, working class, multiracial, and multiethnic. With their articles, they campaigned for or against a potential offender and created heroes or villains in true literary form. The differences in coverage between these newspapers and the ones with more elite and upper-middle-class readership also became more pronounced in the 1950s. These latter newspapers maintained a decidedly more fact-based tone and balanced coverage in contrast to the tabloid-like coverage aimed at working-class readers.

The embellishment and sensationalism of the mid-twentieth-century policiales made the people of Lima look at their city and their own social class with different eyes. With the growing number of spectacular reports on robberies, murder, and accidents, Lima appeared to be a more dangerous place every day.[98] In each of the three cases analyzed here, the criminals belonged to the same popular sectors that consumed the policiales of the high-circulation papers. The romanticization of the mestizo figure Tatán and the vilification of the Japanese Shimizu and the Afro-indigenous-descended Villanueva highlight the ways media reporting on crime drew upon, legitimized, and disseminated dominant ideas about the "natural" social hierarchy. They also foreground the ways members of the popular sectors consumed and even internalized these racialized ideas about working-class criminality, even as these same notions worked against them.

NOTES

Portions of primary source material included here have been translated from Spanish by Bonnie A. Lucero. This chapter is based on a translation of a revised version of a chapter of the PhD thesis and book *Die Arbeiterschichten von Lima (1940–1960): Eine Kultur- und Freizeitgeschichte* by the author.

1. José Matos Mar, *Desborde popular y crisis del Estado: El nuevo rostro del Perú en la década de 1980* (Lima: Instituto de Estudios Peruanos, 1984), 13.

2. Julio Cotler, *Clases, estado y nación en el Perú*, 5th ed. (Lima: Instituto de Estudios Peruanos, 1988), 289; Denise Leigh Raffo, "El miedo a la multitud: Dos provincianos en el Estadio Nacional, 1950–1970," in *El miedo en el Perú: Siglos XVI al XX*, ed. Claudia Rosas Lauro (Lima: Fondo Editorial PUCP, 2005), 267; and José Varallanos, *El cholo en el Perú: Introducción al estudio sociológico de un hombre y un pueblo mestizos y su destino cultural* (Buenos Aires: Imprenta López, 1962), 105–7.

3. Julio Calderón Cockburn, *La ciudad ilegal: Lima en el siglo XX* (Lima: Facultad de Ciencias Sociales–UNMSM, 2005); and Aníbal Quijano, *La emergencia del grupo cholo y sus implicancias en la sociedad peruana* (Lima: Universidad San Marcos, 1967).

4. Peter Klarén, "The Origins of Modern Peru, 1880–1930," in *The Cambridge History of Latin America*, vol. 5, ed. Leslie Bethell, 587–621 (Cambridge: Cambridge University Press, 1986); Fanny Muñoz, *Diversiones públicas en Lima, 1890–1920: La experiencia de la modernidad* (Lima: Red para el Desarrollo de las Ciencias Sociales en el Perú, 2001), 47–50; *Boletin Estadístico Municipal*, Octubre–Diciembre 1956 (Lima, 1957), 4; and Calderón Cockburn, *La ciudad ilegal*, 110.

5. For works on the history of the Peruvian media, see Rita Atwood and Sergio Mattos, "Mass Media Reform and Social Change: The Peruvian Experience," *Journal of Communication* 32, no. 2 (1982): 33–45; Willie Hiatt, "Indians in the Lobby: Newspapers and the Limits of Andean Cosmopolitanism, 1896–1930," *The Americas* 68, no. 3 (2012): 377–403.

6. Dirección Nacional de Estadística, *Censo Nacional de Población y Ocupación levantado el 9 de junio de 1940* (Lima, 1944–1949), 189.

7. Juan Gargurevich Regal, *Última Hora: La fundación de un diario popular* (Lima: La Voz, 2005), 65.

8. Jorge Salazar, *De matar y morir*, vol. 3 of *Historia de la noticia: Un siglo de homicidios en el Perú* (Lima: Universidad de San Martín de Porres, 2004), 79.

9. The Japanese began immigrating to Peru in the 1890s. At first, they worked in coastal plantations. However, in the next decades many Japanese immigrants were able to move to the cities and start their own small businesses.

10. Ulrich Mücke, *Asiaten in den Amerikas, 1850–1950* (Hagen, 2006), 54, 59, 63; Amelia Morimoto, *Los japoneses y sus descendientes en el Perú* (Lima: Congreso de la República del Perú, 1999), 94, 104–6; Oscar Chambi, Amelia Morimoto, and José Watanabe, *La memoria del ojo: Cien años de presencia japonesa en el Perú* (Lima: Congreso de la República del Perú, 1999), 101; and Guillermo Thorndike, *Los imperios del Sol: Una historia de los japoneses en el Perú* (Lima: Brasa, 1996), 87–88.

11. Morimoto, *Los japoneses y sus descendientes*, 102, 107; and Isabelle Lausent-Herrera, *Pasado y presente de la comunidad japonesa en el Perú* (Lima: Instituto Frances de Estudios Andinos 1991), 48–49.

12. Salazar, *Historia de la noticia*, 48.

13. Jorge Salazar, *La medianoche del japonés* (Lima: Universidad de San Martín de Porres, 1991); and Max Jiménez León, *La organización secreta el Dragón Negra en el Japón y los crímenes en Tingo María* (Lima, 1944).

14. *La Crónica*, November 4, 1944, 18–19; *La Prensa*, November 4, 1944, 9.

15. *La Prensa*, November 4, 1944, 9.

16. *El Comercio*, November 4, 1944, 12.

17. *La Crónica*, November 6, 1944, 19.

18. *La Crónica*, November 8, 1944, 19.

19. *El Comercio*, November 7, 1944, 7.

20. *Universal*, November 8, 1944, 11.

21. *El Comercio*, November 8, 1944, 5; and *La Prensa*, November 9, 1944, 12.

22. *La Crónica*, November 9, 1944, 18.

23. Ibid.

24. *La Crónica*, November 10, 1944, 18–19.

25. *El Comercio*, November 12, 1944, 12.

26. *Universal*, November 11, 1944, 13.

27. *El Comercio*, November 10, 1944, 12.

28. *Universal*, November 9, 1944, 11.

29. *El Comercio*, November 10, 1944, 12.

30. *La Crónica*, November 12, 1944, 18.

31. *La Crónica*, November 7, 1944, 19.

32. *La Crónica*, November 13, 1944, 21, and November 18, 1944, 18; *La Prensa*, November 13, 1944, 7; and *Universal*, November 16, 1944, 12.

33. *La Crónica*, December 13, 1957, 17.

34. *La Crónica*, September 11, 1954, 1.

35. *Última Hora*, September 10, 1954, 1.

36. *La Crónica*, September 11, 1954, 21; *Última Hora*, September 11, 1954, 3.

37. *La Crónica*, September 16, 1954, 2.

38. *Última Hora*, September 15, 1954, 4.

39. *Última Hora*, September 15, 1954, 2.

40. *La Crónica*, September 15, 1954, 1.

41. *La Crónica* (Tercera), September 15, 1954, 1.

42. *Última Hora*, September 15, 1954, 3.

43. Ibid., 2.

44. *Última Hora*, September 16, 1954, 3.

45. Ibid., 3.

46. *La Crónica*, September 15, 1954, 16.

47. *El Comercio*, September 16, 1954, 15.

48. *La Crónica*, October 15, 1955, 19.

49. *Última Hora*, October 8, 1956, 3.

50. *Última Hora*, October 10, 1956, 3.

51. *El Comercio*, October 9, 1956, 3.

52. *La Crónica* (Tercera), October 4, 1956, 14.

53. Ibid., 16; and *La Crónica*, October 10, 1956, 19.

54. *La Crónica* (Tercera), December 11, 1957, 1, 20; and *Última Hora*, December 11, 1957, 1.

55. *La Crónica*, December 13, 1957, 20.

56. *La Crónica*, December 10, 1957, 15; December 11, 1957, 21; and December 12, 1957, 21.

57. *La Crónica*, December 10, 1957, 15.

58. *Última Hora*, December 11, 1957, 2–3.

59. *La Crónica*, December 13, 1957, 16.

60. *La Crónica* (Tercera), December 12, 1957, 18; *La Crónica*, December 13, 1957, 16; and December 13, 1957, 17.

61. *Última Hora*, December 13, 1957, 3.

62. *Presente*, June 8, 1957, v. 1, no. 27, 21.

63. *Presente*, January 1, 1958, v. 2, no. 50, 3.

64. Ibid., 4. Literature about discrimination or racism against Afro-Peruvians in Peru is scant. For general studies about racism in Peru, see, for instance, Jorge Bruce, *Nos había-mos choleado tanto: Psicoanálisis y racismo* (Lima: Universidad de San Martin de Porres, 2007); and Marisol de la Cadena, "Silent Racism and Intellectual Superiority in Peru," *Bulletin of Latin American Research* 17, no. 2 (1998): 143–64.

65. Domingo Tamariz Lúcar, *Memorias de una pasión: La prensa peruana y sus protagonistas*, vol. 1 (1948–1963) (Lima: Campodónico, 1997), 117–18; and Salazar, *Historia de la noticia*, 198–99.

66. *La Crónica*, February 28, 1946, 8.

67. *La Crónica* (Tarde), January 3, 1947, 6; and *La Crónica*, January 4, 1947, 8.

68. *La Crónica* (Tarde), November 16, 1948, 7.

69. *El Comercio*, December 24, 1954, 24, and June 16, 1962, 1.

70. *La Crónica*, September 3, 1954, 21; September 16, 1954, 20; September 17, 1954, 20; and September 23, 1954, 20; *La Crónica* (Tercera), September 10, 1954, 11; *Última Hora*, September 17, 1954, 4.

71. *Extra* 1, no. 1 (1954), 27.

72. *La Crónica*, October 24, 1954, 18.

73. *La Crónica*, January 12, 1955, 1, and October 5, 1955, 18; *Última Hora*, February 10, 1956, 10, and February 16, 1962, 3; *Extra* 2, no. 53 (1955), 19.

74. *Última Hora*, November 17, 1959, 6.

75. *La Crónica* (Tercera), October 31, 1959, 18, and November 3, 1959, 24.

76. *La Crónica*, November 21, 1959, 22, and November 22, 1959, 20.

77. *La Crónica*, September 2, 1954, 21; September 3, 1954, 21; September 28, 1954, 1; November 18, 1959, 23; and November 21, 1959, 22; *La Crónica* (Tarde), November 2, 1959, 22; November 16, 1959, 22; and November 20, 1959, 1; *Última Hora*, November 6, 1959, 5.

78. *La Crónica*, November 9, 1959, 17.

79. *La Crónica*, November 19, 1959, 24.

80. *La Crónica*, November 21, 1959, 1; and *Última Hora*, November 21, 1959, 1.

81. *Última Hora*, November 21, 1959, 3.

82. Ibid.

83. *La Crónica*, November 21, 1959, 22.

84. *Última Hora*, November 21, 1959, 3.

85. *La Crónica* (Tercera), November 21, 1959, 1.

86. *La Crónica*, November 23, 1959, 6.

87. *El Comercio*, June 16, 1962, 3, 18.

88. *Última Hora*, June 20, 1959, 3.

89. *Última Hora*, June 16, 1962; and *La Crónica* (Tercera), June 16, 1962, 1–2.

90. *La Crónica*, June 16, 1962, 26–27; and *Última Hora*, June 16, 1962, 3.

91. *La Crónica* (Tercera), June 16, 1962, 1.

92. *Última Hora*, June 18, 1962, 5.

93. *Correo*, June 18, 1962, 3; and *La Crónica*, June 18, 1962, 20.

94. *El Comercio*, June 17, 1962, 5.

95. *Última Hora*, June 18, 1962, 9.

96. *El Comercio*, June 18, 1962, 6.

97. *La Crónica* (Tercera), June 18, 1962, 23.

98. Salazar, *Historia de la noticia*, 79.

PART 2

NAVIGATING CRIMINALIZATION

༜

Agency and Its Limits amid State Violence

5

ORDER IN AN OCCUPIED CITY

৵

Police and Antiblack Violence in Cienfuegos, Cuba, circa 1899

BONNIE A. LUCERO

SUSPECTED OF ASSAULTING a white civil employee, the celebrated black general Dionisio Gil was transformed from a war hero to a fugitive from the law in December 1899 in the central Cuban city of Cienfuegos. He fled the waterfront entertainment district, where the confrontation had occurred, reaching the northeastern margins of the city where two of his former compatriots in arms, dressed in their freshly minted police uniforms, intercepted him. He surrendered himself peacefully and handed over his pistol. As he walked back toward the city center in police escort, another compatriot, police sergeant Agustín Rabasa, approached and fired at Gil, killing him instantly.

In a time of mass revenge killings of former combatants following a three-year bloody conflict ending in Cuban independence from Spain in 1898, this murder was undoubtedly unique. One of the most remarkable, if baffling, aspects about this slaying was its decidedly racial character among a group of men, Cuban patriots, who supposedly exemplified the ideal of racial brotherhood. Of practical necessity for recruiting men to the Liberating Army during the protracted thirty-year struggle for independence from Spain (1868–98), this radical social ideology offered the possibility of a new, more egalitarian Cuban republic, one that promised to erase the inequities of slavery and colonial rule. The murder of Gil, however, told a different story.

Indeed, racial brotherhood posed as many problems as possibilities for Cuban patriots during the tumultuous transition from colony to independent republic, especially as the United States consolidated a largely unwanted military occupation over the island (1899–1902), following their brief intervention at the end of the Cuban War of Independence against Spain (1895–98). As thousands of Cuban veterans sought to crown their military successes with a position in the local government, the discourse of "for all and for the good of all" rapidly deteriorated into a very familiar social hierarchy: whites securing the most prestigious and well-paying positions such as that of mayor, city councilman, and public inspector, while black veterans often came up empty-handed.[1] One exception was the municipal police force, which employed a considerable number of black veterans. However, the presence of black men within the police force became problematic because it meant that a racial group that social scientists in Cuba (and elsewhere) increasingly associated with criminality was in charge of law enforcement and maintaining social order.[2] Even more troublesome, the preservation of order in American-occupied Cuba, which relied on an amorphous, socially constructed, and unevenly deployed notion of crime, quickly became a barometer for Cuban fitness for self-government. The most explicit manifestation of this link between order and the island's political future was the Platt Amendment, which was imposed on the Cuban constitution in 1901 and facilitated future American military interventions in the event that U.S. interests were threatened. However, this tension in many ways defined the entire period of U.S. military rule.[3] Indeed, it offered one of the most compelling justifications for the decision, announced in late 1899, to prolong the U.S. presence in Cuba with the inauguration of a civil government the following year.

Precisely during this tense transitional period of U.S. military rule, black patriots became the main targets of a state campaign against urban disorder in a society that once celebrated racial harmony as a key tenet of nationalism. The murder of Gil marked a critical shift in the relationship between the local state and the population in Cienfuegos as control over the island shifted from Spanish to American sovereignty and eventually toward Cuban rule. Contending political elites increasingly criminalized black veterans as a way to fulfill their own political aspirations. Employing discourses of criminality to uphold the racial order helped them consolidate their legitimacy in the eyes of the military government as the support of their former compatriots in arms waned. Nowhere was this shift in state policy more significant than in the police force. Civil authorities initially employed both black and white veterans in the force, reflecting their defiance of American authority as well as what appeared to be a tradition throughout colonial Latin America of employing men of lower social standing in a poorly remunerated police force.[4] American military officials charged that the racial heterogeneity of the police rendered it an incompetent institution and ordered civil authorities to employ better-quality personnel. The resulting marginalization of black veterans by the state unveiled in this research corroborates the general historiographical consensus that black Cubans faced increasing exclusion from citizenship at the turn of the twentieth century.[5]

This study moves beyond the observation that racial inequality defined the emerging Cuban republic by revealing the practical implications of this shift for poor and working-class urbanites. Through a case study of American-occupied Cienfuegos, this article traces the transformation of the police force from a multiracial institution that defended poor and working-class residents against American aggression to a white body dedicated to the defense of the occupied state. I argue that one of the most important practical results of the transformation of the police force was the parallel rise of state-sponsored violence against poor and working-class urbanites, especially black men. The police assassination of General Gil forms part of a pattern indicative of the consolidation of the state in the hands of an ever more conservative group of white Cuban veterans.

The wave of state violence against blacks encapsulates the renegotiation of the boundaries of citizenship in the emerging Cuban republic as emerging local elites sacrificed the ideals of the revolution for the promise of political power in the emerging republic. The presence of Americans—with all their culturally specific racial baggage from the Civil War and the subsequent rise of Jim Crow—certainly contributed to the consolidation of a racially exclusive Cuban state.[6] Nevertheless, it was white Cuban veterans-turned-political elites, who enforced a de facto criminalization of certain segments of the population. They transformed the police force into a tool of the local state, thereby enforcing a narrowly defined citizenship.

TOWARD A RACIAL DEMOCRACY IN POSTWAR CUBA?

The wartime discourse of racial brotherhood catalyzed a renegotiation of social and racial boundaries in the second half of the nineteenth century. Men (and even some women) of African descent not only joined the Cuban army en masse but ascended to positions of leadership, often wielding authority over lower-ranking whites. Although this renegotiation of social boundaries inevitably created frictions within the army, the color-blind Cuban nationalism, often associated with the slain Cuban martyr José Martí, became a central pillar of patriotic identity in Cuba.[7]

The discourse of racial brotherhood, though seeming to promise an inclusive, meritocratic postwar society, offered tangible gains only for certain sectors of the veteran population. During the first months of the military occupation, Cuban veterans struggled to secure formal employment with the state, particularly at the local and provincial levels. After facing acute criticism for favoring the continued employment of Spaniards, American military officials begrudgingly appointed white Cuban veterans to the highest local offices, including that of mayor and city councilman, as the population awaited the first round of local restricted-suffrage elections in June 1900.[8]

The vast majority of veterans, particularly those of African descent, remained marginalized from the new political order. For the thousands of veterans who returned home to the cities, or traveled to these urban centers to await their military payouts scheduled for June 1899, postwar life was exceedingly precarious. Gainful employment was scarce, and the prohibitive prices of basic subsistence items far outstripped the meager wages offered for available day labor or seasonal agricultural work.[9] The conditions were so extreme that the more than two hundred thousand rations supplied by the American government in Cienfuegos between January and June 1899 were insufficient to quench the hunger of local veterans.[10] These desperate conditions, which disproportionately afflicted veterans of African descent and the working classes, contributed to elite anxieties about the propensity of these groups for crime, banditry, and violence.[11] Drawing on long-standing assumptions about the links between blackness and criminality in Cuba, and likely aware of emerging European and American social scientific theses on race and crime, members of the former slave-owning planter class, American military officials, and even some prominent white Cuban veterans discursively transformed esteemed black military heroes into potentially dangerous vagrants.[12] A new class of potential criminal was created.

At the same time as postwar poverty fostered racialized suspicion toward black veterans, the disappointingly low salaries offered for certain municipal jobs, like law enforcement, created potential employment opportunities for black and working-class veterans. The municipal police force of Cienfuegos was one of the only local state institutions to employ significant numbers of black veterans, though the officers were all white.[13] More than any other local or provincial government employer, the police force reflected the demographics of the soldiers of the Brigade of Cienfuegos, from whence the majority of the recruits came.[14] Although the exact number of black veterans employed cannot be determined from the available sources, the comment by the American police inspector that the force contained "quite a number of negroes" gives an idea of the racial heterogeneity existing therein.[15] Police of varying degrees of African ancestry included Roberto Galarraga, Rogelio Celada Zayas, and Epifanio Ordoñez, who was wounded by American gunfire in June 1899.[16]

Americans judged the police force, as it stood in mid-1899, unable to render proper service. They described the men as "mostly negroes" and "unfit to discharge the responsible duties of their office."[17] Race was the most pressing, but not the only issue, however: "It is to be observed that the Cubans, as a rule, have not sufficient size, strength, and self-reliance to make first class policemen," remarked James H. Wilson, commander of the Santa Clara and Matanzas Provinces in his *Annual Report*. Wilson referred to prevailing ideas that "the white race cannot become acclimatized or maintain its social efficiency in the tropics."[18] The presence of men of African descent and the alleged inferiority of the Latin races doomed the force to incompetence, according to military officials.

The employment of black veterans in the police force posed two additional problems for American military authorities. First, since turn-of-the-century criminology linked blackness to innate criminality, the presence of black men within an institution of law enforcement seemed ironic, if not downright paradoxical. Presuming that racial affinities trumped class differences and notions of justice, American military officials feared that black police officers would act too leniently with criminals, whom they presumed would be disproportionately black as well. These suspicions reveal anxieties about what some American military officials saw as the diverging conceptions of justice and law enforcement between popular and elite sectors—a conflict Juandrea Bates (chap. 6, this volume) also finds in Buenos Aires during the same period. Indeed, a common theme in American discussions of the Cienfuegos police was that they were incompetent because of their perceived inclination to defend black residents at the expense of public order.[19] For this reason, military officials stationed at Cienfuegos considered the police force one of the main obstacles in their self-proclaimed civilizing mission.

Second, the alleged alliances between black and white veterans embodied most clearly in the white veterans' appointment of black veterans to the police force fueled American officials' fears that the "revolutionary," "tropical and barbaric" Cuban was unfit for self-governance.[20] The insistence of civil authorities on employing their compatriots, regardless of race, over white noncombatants or allies of Spain demonstrated an unremitting commitment to nationalism and an unwillingness to lay down claims to independence. This fierce nationalism potentially interfered with their allegiance to the occupying government, leading to conflicting visions of legitimate authority.

The discordance between patriotic cross-racial sensibilities of many (though not all) Cuban veterans and the preference among U.S. officers for white, propertied men in power was at the heart of a series of violent confrontations between Cubans and Americans on the streets of Cienfuegos in the first half of 1899. In May, a dispute over payment to dock laborers employed by the Americans devolved into a brutal beating of workers and police by American quartermaster employees. One worker, a black veteran, sustained serious injuries from gunshots.[21] In June, a San Juan Day celebration erupted into a riot after three American soldiers harassed a local sex worker and resisted arrest by a racially diverse group of Cuban police. The conflict escalated into a shooting match between American soldiers and local residents and police. Several men, including a police officer, were wounded, and one man was killed.[22] It is no coincidence that both conflicts occurred in predominantly black residential areas. Americans and many Cuban elites considered poor and working-class neighborhoods as hotbeds of "disorder and violence" and perceived "the poor and the idle" as the "class which trouble the police and fill the prisons."[23] Notably, black neighborhoods were also the poorest ones, often overlapping with vice districts, where prostitution, gambling, and drinking abounded.[24]

At their core, these disputes were about deciding who would be eligible to wield power in the emerging republic, and by extension the degree to which the patriotic allusions to an inclusive, socially just republic would actually materialize. Among Americans, these riots fostered a general distrust of the socially radical implications of Cuban nationalism. The prevalence of cross-racial patronage relationships in the local political landscape directly threatened the American neocolonial project. The police force was the key institution exemplifying these treacherous ties. American military officials targeted the multiracial police force composed of mostly veterans because its members allegedly sympathized with the "worst elements" of society at the same time that they were supposed to represent the state. The vilification of the police force by U.S. officials forced local civil authorities to recognize the constant threat of American intervention in civil affairs. Resistance to American rule, they increasingly concluded, was not only unproductive but also threatened their political status. This cynical calculation contributed to a shift in the way they approached the art of governance and especially their relationships with their supposed social subordinates.

BUILDING RESPECTABLE POLICE: RACE AND THE SOCIAL CONSTRUCTION OF CRIMINALITY

As urban protesters demanded vindication against American aggression, civil authorities attempted to prove their allegiance to the occupying government and demonstrate their ability to self-govern. In order to demonstrate their respectability to the occupying government, civil authorities severed their ties to the masses. Between July and November 1899, they avoided any major confrontations with occupying authorities, while facing increasing criticism in the local radical press for their alleged collaboration with the enemy.[25] In so doing, they came to rely increasingly on the occupying government for their political power instead of gaining legitimacy through the broader electorate, thereby alienating their compatriots.

An integral part of the construction of the local Cuban state was the transformation of the law enforcement bodies into supposedly respectable institutions of order. Wealthy planters, particularly native and naturalized American citizens, concurred with American military officials that the best way to ensure that the police fulfilled their mission of "maintaining order" was by staffing law enforcement units with men who represented the "respectable classes" of society.[26] This policy implied the exclusion of radical patriots—especially men of African descent. American military officials wrote of reforms to the police department in 1899, broadly characterizing them as an effort to improve the caliber of men employed in the force.[27] Military authorities also conceded property owners the right to employ private armed guards.[28] The greatest transformations occurred within the paramilitary institution of the rural guard, charged with patrolling the countryside to prevent banditry, in large part because military officials wielded direct influence over this body. They kept only the "best men," dismissing the "least efficient men."[29] By 1900, Wilson referred to the rural guard as "an intelligent, well-mounted body."[30] The American inspector assessing the rural guard explicitly equated "intelligence" with whiteness, claiming that former black rural guardsmen were mentally inferior but physically superior to their white peers.[31] This so-called improvement essentially amounted to whitening.

Americans had less direct control over the municipal police force because it fell under the jurisdiction of the municipal government. Nevertheless, civil authorities responded promptly to American pressure by reforming the social composition of the force. Although the mayor refused to compromise on the almost exclusive employment of Cuban veterans, he did reduce the visibility of men considered racially objectionable. The exact number of black veterans dismissed from the police is lost with the records of that institution, but the growing number of complaints against the police by local black residents indicates that a certain shift in policy, and likely in the personnel, was occurring.[32] By early 1900, two black veterans had publicly criticized local political elites for removing black veterans from public positions "for the sole reason of being black."[33]

American military officials applauded what they saw as important changes in the police force. Though some officials expressed skepticism that even the newly whitened police force could maintain order, Wilson was confident that the "improvements in personnel" would ensure that the police force "will prove equal to all demands placed upon it."[34] Even though the salaries were still too low to "attract the best material," by 1900, military officials described the deficiencies of the force largely in terms of age as opposed to *racial* unfitness as they had in 1899.[35]

In addition to whitening the force and concentrating policing more directly on people of African descent and workers, the transformation of the municipal police force centered on eliminating (white) men who did not readily bow down to American authority. This proved more difficult, however, because of the political connections and social status of these individuals in the postwar period. One of the main targets was police chief Joaquín Oropesa. Despite his prestigious record of military service and his agreeable socioracial background, military officials alleged that Oropesa was unfit for his post. Wilson continually urged civil authorities to dismiss him, citing his unbecoming conduct during the riots. Oropesa "failed to satisfy me of his capacity to command such a force," wrote Wilson in the aftermath of the San Juan Day riot. Moreover, he was "lacking in energy and in the power to enforce discipline."[36] He renewed his recommendation in October 1899, compelling provincial governor José Miguel Gómez to launch a benign "investigation" to quiet his concerns.[37] The timing and tone of his recommendations to civil authorities suggest that Wilson likely targeted Oropesa because of his aggressive and antagonistic confrontation with American authorities during the May and June riots.

His wartime alliances with high-ranking local and provincial government officials shielded Oropesa from immediate dismissal, however. In December 1899, he still served as chief, but he faced increasing pressure to prove himself fit for the job. The willingness of civil authorities to protect white veterans like Oropesa while unflinchingly dismissing their black compatriots accentuates the consequence of the whitening of the local state under American rule, namely the increasing marginalization of black veterans from power.

The continuity of patriotic loyalty and the abandonment of racial brotherhood highlighted a widening rift between the ideals of racial brotherhood and the increasingly conservative local politics that emerged with the renegotiation of relations between local ruling elites and American military officials. Local politicians collaborated with the occupying government by whitening the police force, marking the early demise of racial brotherhood as an inseparable feature of Cuban nationality. The growing racist current in local employment contributed to the "repressive and markedly racist character" of the police force in American-occupied Cienfuegos.[38]

MURDEROUS MUNICIPAL POLICE: CRIMINALIZATION AND THE JUSTIFICATION OF THE ASSASSINATION OF DIONISIO GIL

On the afternoon of December 29, 1899, General Dionisio Gil, a Dominican-born veteran of the Cuban army, clashed with city health inspector Enrique Quintana in the Fonda Mariposa, a local café. Although the dispute initially involved only Quintana and Antonio Achón, the Chinese Cuban owner of the Fonda, Gil promptly intervened on behalf of the latter. Gil admonished Quintana for his abusive behavior toward Achón, declaring that with him, the health inspector "could not behave as he had with the Chinese man."[39] According to some witnesses, Gil assumed "an aggressive insolent attitude in words and manner towards Quintana."[40] The partiality of the officially collected testimony in favor of Quintana suggests that the police had already determined Gil's guilt before investigating.

Reading this testimony against the grain suggests that Gil considered himself the defender of a raceless Cuban patriotism, correcting Quintana for trespassing against it. In an exchange that subsequently appeared in multiple reports from several different sources, Quintana assured Gil that he respected him as a patriot but that he did not recognize him as his boss—a statement that likely reflected an unwillingness to recognize black military authority in postwar civilian life. Gil reportedly proclaimed that "there was no other boss but him."[41] The careful linguistic distinction between "patriot" and "boss" suggests that these men held fundamentally different visions of social hierarchy. Whereas Gil sought to transpose his military authority onto civilian life, Quintana quickly defended his racial privilege by distinguishing past military authority from present civilian authority. According to Quintana, the civilian social order would have to transform from the chaotic racial disorder of the Liberating Army. At its core, this initial confrontation was not only a disagreement over local claims to authority. The dispute revealed divergent visions of authority in a period of national transition; Gil was drawing on the ideal of racial brotherhood to challenge colonial racial hierarchies, and Quintana was seeking to preserve his privileged position in the old order.

The men eventually parted ways, only to settle their dispute later that evening, this time with violence. Around nine o'clock, Gil and Quintana encountered each other again at the café. Quintana testified that he suddenly felt a hand around his neck, as Gil pulled him into the Fonda. Gil allegedly beat him over the head with the butt of his revolver, "making him fall to the ground."[42] At the sight of an armed black man, several bystanders intervened on behalf of Quintana, who escaped to the street where he blew his whistle for help. Eduardo Hernández García, a sworn guard from the nearby Dos Hermanos plantation, attempted to stop Gil from fleeing, but the general broke free, reportedly shooting the guard in the gut.[43] According to one report, the policeman Antonio Hernández also attempted to detain Gil, but received a shot in the right leg.[44] Although Gil successfully evaded apprehension, the multiple attempts by bystanders and residents to detain him suggest that these armed white men judged Gil a danger without necessarily knowing the details of the dispute.

The police were no exception in their ready conviction of Gil. Eager to quell any disorder before the Americans intervened, Oropesa ordered his men to capture the black general.[45] Officers Celada and José Vázquez found Gil on the outskirts of the city and subsequently disarmed and detained him. Another officer, Agustín Rabasa, approached the surrendered general and delivered a fatal shot in the face at close range. In the first official reports, Rabasa and Oropesa claimed that Gil had fired three shots without wounding them as he fled from police custody, and that Rabasa had fired in self-defense while pursuing the general on his horse.[46] The police allegedly sought to prevent further "crimes against the peace of the community" by employing lethal force.[47]

This narrative meshed well with the prevailing criminological association between blackness and deviance. Certainly, the story made sense to American military officials.

According to Captain F. J. Kernan, "the killing is justifiable and all should be at [la]rge."[48] American military officials depicted the black war hero as no more than a common criminal, seeming to condone the shooting. Alpheus Henry Bowman of the 2nd U.S. Infantry described Gil as "a disreputable character." He added, "I knew the man by sight as a fellow without occupation, of questionable reputation, and one liable to be engaged in disorder." Moreover, Bowman blamed the slaying on Gil's own "disorderly conduct."[49] Bowman depicted Gil as a natural criminal, a vagrant, thereby deploying the socially constructed notion of crime as a feature of alleged black deviance to condemn Gil. The depiction of Gil as a common criminal conveniently helped exonerate the supposedly improved police force from the murder.

Americans also sought to recast Gil's military achievements in a way that would confirm their image of him as a criminal. By describing his military activity in terms of crime, opponents of Gil attempted to strip him of the honor of his rank and patriotic service. Bowman described Gil as cowardly rather than valiant, claiming that he had "acquired a reputation as an expert forager rather than a fighter." Furthermore, he described Gil as a thief, who would appropriate "property without reference to whom it belonged."[50] By downplaying his history of military honor and constructing a fictitious criminal past, Bowman forced the incident into the preestablished conceptions of criminality and so justified the elimination of black authority as necessary for the consolidation of a modern (white) state in Cuba.

These unfavorable descriptions failed to resonate with those who knew Gil personally. His son, Perfecto, celebrated his father's military achievements and claimed that the only criminals were the police, whom he called a "bunch of bandits."[51] Generalíssimo of the Liberating Army Máximo Gómez described Gil as a hero, who "honorably defended the liberty of this land." In contrast to the decidedly negative image Americans painted, Gil was known in his home country and in Cuba as a military hero. Born in 1852 in the city of Concepción de la Vega, Dominican Republic, he served under the rule of Dominican president Ulises Heureaux (1882–84, 1887, 1889–99) following the nation's second independence from Spain, before joining the Cuban war of independence on August 6, 1895. Gómez noted that Gil "was a man of color who was able to make many friends." He described him as a well-adjusted and beloved member of a community, not a natural criminal.[52]

THE CRIMINALIZATION OF RACIAL PROTEST

Having likely been subjected to the same police brutality that claimed Gil's life, poor and working-class urbanites gathered outside the Center for Veterans, located in the predominantly black portside neighborhood of Marsillán in protest of the murder. They demanded that the body of the deceased Dominican general be turned over to them "for embalming, guarding, and burying it with honors."[53] Both civil and military authorities worried that the predominantly black protesters represented ipso facto a breach of order. Mayor José Antonio Frías reported considerable agitation among the "negroes" of the city, labeling the crowd of protestors as the "worst classes [of] colored people." When the courts refused to turn over the body, "the same colored classes made cries in the streets," Frías noted patronizingly.[54] Americans likened the protesters to animals rather than rational beings with legitimate demands. F. J. Kernan, who was sent to investigate the matter, worried that the racial tensions resulting from the murder would lead to an eruption of disorder.[55]

Part of the concern over the racial composition of the protesters originated from the clear centrality of race in the murder. Perfecto decried as racism the poor treatment Cubans had given his father "only because he was black."[56] Moreover, the lackluster burial of his father represented an insult to his military honor. "Not only did they kill him," he wrote to Gómez, "but they also . . . treated him like a dog in that [he did] not even [receive] a burial as a Liberating General that he was."[57] Even these rather high-profile observers were clear about the causes of the murder: racism had ended Gil's life and continued to disgrace him in death.

Even American officials recognized the racial motives of the killing but dismissed them as politically insignificant. Kernan reported that "considerable race prejudice is involved in this affair."[58] Despite the general recognition that the murder was racially motivated, military officials disparaged the efforts of blacks to protest this racial killing. Bowman claimed that the assassination lacked "any significance, political or otherwise," thus denying the importance of black opinion in local politics.[59] He dismissingly wrote that "there has been a good deal of inflammatory talk among the negroes growing out of Gil's killing," portraying the protesters as agitators rather than justice seekers.[60] This tactic illustrated a broader pattern of condemning racial protest as illegitimate, even criminal.

The imminent threat of American intervention to suppress the alleged racial protest prompted the mayor to take action to maintain an image of "order." First, Frías assured military officials that police were competent to ward off disaster without military intervention. The "police with modification will preserve order, avoiding disruption of [the] public order," Frías communicated in a frantic telegram to military authorities, seeking to head off their early intervention in the matter.[61] Second, he "recommended people disperse immediately," likely in an effort to prevent what many American officials feared might become criminal action. It was telling that Frías informed military authorities explicitly about his action to disperse the crowd.[62] Several prominent white officers of the Liberating Army from the eastern provinces had arrived in solidarity with the protesters, but upon the request of the mayor, they turned against their black compatriots.[63] One of these white leaders, former president of the Republic in Arms, Bartolomé Masó, who in a subsequent interview with American military authorities revealed his belief that the proper place of blacks was in the cane fields, gave a speech promising to take the greatest care in the situation.[64] Other insurgent officials, including Jesús Rabí and José Miró Argenter, cursorily demanded justice, then told the protesters to disperse. Even General José Braulio Alemán, the president of the Cienfuegos Center for Veterans, seconded the previous speeches and ordered the people to return to their homes.[65]

By urging the protesters to disband, Alemán and his white compatriots publicly abandoned support for the black protesters, instead presenting themselves as agents of order to local political elites and American authorities. Given his political stance in favor of absolute and immediate independence, Alemán likely urged the protestors to disband for two related though contradictory reasons: to prevent the intervention of American military authorities in civil affairs, and to disassociate himself from the agenda of racial protest, which many American military officials assumed to be inseparable from his radical political position. His self-interest in gaining access to the political realm under American rule meant distancing himself from his alleged black allies, by which he showed his commitment to absolute and immediate independence as solely political and not socially radical. Even among the most radical white veterans, commitment to racial brotherhood proved to be politically dangerous.

Alemán's actions in the wake of the frustrated demonstration highlight his continuing commitment to independence and gradual abandonment of racial brotherhood. His position as president of the Center for Veterans obliged him to address public outrage about the assassination of Gil—as a veteran, though not necessarily as a black man. He took advantage of his position as the editor of the radical newspaper *La Tribuna* to reveal a number of inaccuracies in the official version of events in a public letter to the judge of instruction. Therein, Alemán asserted that Gil had actually turned himself in to the police and handed over his weapon peacefully, before Rabasa had shot him. He named a half dozen witnesses, including José Morales, José Fernández, and Policarpo Lafont, who saw Gil peacefully in police custody before the shooting.[66] The police had not acted in self-defense; rather Rabasa had murdered Gil in cold blood.[67] Although Alemán publicly criticized authorities, civil and military, for the inaccuracies of the initial reports, the silences in his statement were equally revealing: nowhere in his letter did he mention race, which the protesters so vehemently claimed was at the core of the assassination.

Even though most white revolutionaries could agree that affiliation with radical black protest was politically dangerous for them, a visible political rift was forming even among *these* former compatriots in arms. Power holders like Oropesa and Frías sought to consolidate their own political power not only by abandoning the ideal of racial brotherhood but also by compromising their radical nationalist posture to collaborate with the occupying government. This increasingly intimate relationship with the Americans appears to have bolstered their political power, at least temporarily. Radical nationalists and political hopefuls like Alemán, on the other hand, attempted to balance their own political aspirations—which still relied on maintaining order—with a semblance of commitment to the radical vision of Cuban nationalism, which hinged on the support of other veterans, many of whom were black. The black protesters, however, viewed these conservative and moderate stances as self-interested and unacceptable corruptions of racial brotherhood, an ideal they perceived to be a core value of Cuban patriotism.

Perhaps because it neglected to mention racial discontent, the public letter Alemán published in *La Tribuna* compelled authorities to renew investigation of the murder. Eventually investigators confirmed popular suspicions that the police had, in fact, murdered Gil.[68] Although Gil reportedly did attempt to flee the city at first, he later surrendered to police. Celada and Vázquez spotted him and gave him the "alto."

"It is I, General Gil."

"Will you surrender?"

"If you are Cubans, you can advance."[69]

Gil agreed to submit to police and turn over his weapon "because they were Cubans," which likely gave him a sense of security that he would be treated justly. He proceeded back to town in police custody.[70]

As the detained general and his police escorts crossed the city, they encountered police sergeant Agustín Rabasa on horseback. He "rode forward to the prisoner, inquired who it was, and on receiving from Gil a reply that it was he, Gil, [Rabasa] thrust a revolver in the latter's face, and firing, killed the prisoner instantly."[71] Witnesses noted that Gil had placed his hand "in a capitulating manner resting on his chest" right before Rabasa shot him. The bullet pierced his face just below his left eye, fracturing his cranium, and killing him "like a lightning bolt."[72] The horizontal angle of the entry wound confirmed that Rabasa shot Gil point-blank, and not from his horse as he had claimed originally.[73]

Rabasa had subsequently fabricated a story to exculpate himself from a charge of murder. He ordered Celada to fire several shots from Gil's already confiscated revolver. "Celada refused and threw the pistol from him, whereupon someone picked it up, fired several shots, and subsequently placed it in or near the dead man's hand."[74] Rabasa later confessed: "I was the one who killed him," assured that the rounds he ordered to be fired from the general's gun would exonerate him.[75]

Subsequent police testimony highlighted key inconsistencies in the narratives of events leading up to the shooting. High-ranking police officers including Oropesa and jail warden Pablo Hernández confirmed the original story despite their late arrival at the scene. Oropesa reported that when he inquired what had happened, Celada declared that Gil "was firing at us and we had to kill him."[76] Celada later recanted this statement, claiming that he had been forced to sign it without knowing what was contained therein. José Morales also reported that he had been pressured to make a statement to exonerate the police. These small missteps began to unravel the police conspiracy to cover up the murder, gradually giving greater credibility to popular suspicions of police culpability and racism.

The confirmation that the police had slain Gil in cold blood forced civil authorities to apprehend the most immediate perpetrator, Rabasa, who was tried and found guilty of murder.[77] The court sentenced him to fourteen years, eight months, and one day in confinement, ordered him to compensate the family of the late general in the amount of five thousand pesos, and assigned him one-third of the costs of legal proceedings.[78] Moreover, Rabasa was excluded from the official list of Cuban veterans, published in 1901.[79] His absence from the rolls possibly reflects an attempt to defend the image of the Liberating Army as a bastion of racial brotherhood.

The other police officers implicated in the killing did not face punishment, indicating a level of complacency among civil authorities regarding the rising tide of racial violence. This incensed local protesters, not to mention the family members of the late general. Perfecto denounced the impunity with which the perpetrators were treated: "the murderers are walking the streets of Cienfuegos so satisfied, not knowing [the consequences of] the crime they have committed."[80] Years later, the impunity afforded to these two men would loom in the public memory, causing one black activist to contemplate the possibility of retroactively jailing them, though civil authorities predictably never acted on these demands.[81]

Like Celada and Vázquez, Oropesa avoided charges, although his alleged involvement in the murder did nothing to help his reputation among American military officials. Military officials cited this incident as grounds for his dismissal from the force, suggesting that even violent defense of the racial order was insufficient to redeem Oropesa for previous instances of militant patriotism in the eyes of American military officials. Local authorities agreed to remove him as chief, indicating both their increasing collaboration with the occupying government and a tacit admission of Oropesa's culpability in the matter. Frías refused to abandon his white compatriot, however, and offered him a place on the city council, a position even more prestigious than his last. The retention of Oropesa in a high-ranking government position revealed an unwavering commitment to wartime patronage alliances among the small circle of local ruling elites—a well-documented pattern of local politics in Cienfuegos.[82] It also highlighted a troubling degree of indifference about the perpetration of racial violence in an allegedly raceless society.

The hostility of U.S military officials toward Oropesa should not be read as punishment for the role he played in the murder. On the contrary, Oropesa's intellectual authorship of the murder was more likely an attempt to demonstrate his ability to preserve "order"—a performance aimed at redeeming himself in the eyes of American military officials. His dismissal, and the subsequent removal of Frías from the office of mayor, followed critical incidents in which each man failed to adequately suppress public demonstrations by black men. For Oropesa, this failure manifested in the protests over the murder. In the case of Frías, local military officials pressured him to resign as mayor after he failed to suppress a labor strike.[83] Next, they engineered a conservative shift in local politics. Socially conservative, pro-American city councilman Leopoldo Figueroa emerged to take his place, first as interim mayor, and then consolidated his political power through American-sponsored electoral fraud in June 1900.[84] Figueroa cultivated the police as his own political tool, and when they failed to support his candidacy in the subsequent 1901 elections, he dismissed dozens of men from the force.[85]

The relationship between the police and the mayor became the barometer of local politics. The short-lived mayoral stint of liberal-leaning Gonzalo García Vieta, a colonel of the Cuban army, was plagued by conflict with military authorities and the police force. Pro-Figueroa police chief Juan José Campillo y D'Wolf, Oropesa's successor, maintained a growing allegiance to the occupying government rather than to the interests of the civil government, resulting in acute antagonism with Vieta, who favored greater local autonomy from Americans.[86] Political protest covertly organized by Figueroa and supported by the occupying government forced Vieta to resign within months of his popular election. Higinio Esquerra, former chief of the repressive rural guard and a longtime favorite of General Wilson, succeeded him, consolidating even further the conservative shift in politics and law enforcement.

CONCLUSIONS

One of the most significant implications of this research is that it shows how a socially constructed vision of crime became the primary tool in consolidating elite political power. This power not only hinged on the exclusion of black men from citizenship; it also increasingly relied on the United States for a precarious political legitimacy amid widespread alienation among the electorate. The omnipresence of the United States in Cuban politics and the parallel preservation of a white republic would continue to define the republic for much of the twentieth century.[87]

The specter of crime and its racialized connotations served as both a pretense and a justification for the increasing marginalization of black Cubans from the emerging Cuban republic. Although it evinced dissident visions of criminality operating among poor and working-class people, the murder of Gil was an ominous preview of what was to come in an allegedly free Cuba. Collaboration with Americans in search of independence meant not only the sacrifice of racial equality. It also signified the violent reinforcement of racial order by whites. As military authorities and their allies in the municipal government supported an increasingly narrow vision of citizenship, black patriots sought to harness the memory of Gil to fuel a movement for racial justice.

The increasing intolerance for, even criminalization of, overt forms of racial protest, allowed racial discrimination to survive even though it was considered unpatriotic under the discourse of racial brotherhood. Consequently, black Cienfuegos residents developed new strategies to express their grievances. By employing more moderate forms of protest like patriotic discourse and public commemoration, black activists sought to avoid the violent retaliation levied against overt public racial protest under the guise of preserving order and stopping crime.

Black veterans recognized the criminalization and persecution of racial protest as part of a broader process of postwar racial exclusion. Black marginalization from the political sphere constituted a significant obstacle that prevented blacks from influencing state policies. In a leaflet titled "To the Colored Race, Glory to General Gil" shortly after the assassination, black veterans Captain Pedro P. Mutos and Commandant Juan Sardiñas y Villa claimed that the departure of local ruling elites from the true ideals of patriotism jeopardized the emerging republic. Cuba was becoming the domain of "a certain class, for an oligarchy without conscience, that gives people more rights for being white than to us for being black." Mutos and Sardiñas chastised Cienfuegos political elites for their complicity in the murder and for their collaboration with American military authorities against black and working-class veterans. "The great Dominican soldier," they wrote, "was our pride as he was a humiliation for some Cubans who were before with the Spaniards more Spanish than Santiago, and who are today with the Americans more American than Washington himself."[88] By juxtaposing pro-Spanish sentiment and collaboration with the Americans with racism, Mutos and Sardiñas argued that current leaders were unpatriotic because of their race prejudice.

They further chastised white veterans for betraying the Cuban cause and turning their backs on their black compatriots. After all, blacks had been the very core of the Liberating Army, Mutos and Sardiñas claimed. They had stood "alone in defending independence while the revolutionary rank was dwindling by the surrender of the timid ones [whites]."[89] This argument became emblematic of the black struggle for inclusion in the new republic throughout the twentieth century: the centrality of their role in the struggle for independence entitled blacks to an equal share of rights and benefits in the emerging republic.[90]

Although most of the manifesto articulated black grievances through a language of patriotism, the militant tone likely rendered their noble intentions unrecognizable in the eyes of white veterans, who increasingly privileged their own political self-interest over the wartime ideals. In one part of the leaflet, the veterans referenced one of the greatest fears among property owners: that black veterans would rise up to take control of the island. "As General Gil rests in eternal glory," it read, "we in this valley of bastardized and adulterated ambitions will always be disposed to die before consenting to be pariahs in our own land."[91] Despite the justifiable frustration with postwar exclusion and violence against black men, planters and U.S. military authorities used this allusion to violence as an excuse to vilify the entire cause of addressing racial inequality, fanning the flames of white fears of alleged black radicalism. The leaflet became the subject of a secret police investigation into and criminalization of its authors rather than greater public support for racial brotherhood.

Subsequent protest sought to secure broader support for raceless patriotism while correcting the injustices of the murder through public commemoration of the late general within an emerging pantheon of national heroes. Well after the immediate public outrage of the murder of Gil had subsided, prominent black residents attempted to immortalize the link between Cuban patriotism and antiracism in a statue of the late general, while correcting his undignified burial by building a mausoleum for him in the cemetery. Similar to the manifesto by Mutos and Sardiñas, this form of protest articulated a dissident vision of Cuba libre with a more passive tone, apparently less threatening to order. Among the leaders of this movement was Nicolás Valverde, a tailor and a prominent figure of the local black elite. He touted a long record of combating racism in Cienfuegos, including the publication of a weekly newspaper in defense of working-class interests.[92]

Continuing his activism, Valverde gave voice to a broader movement among black Cienfuegos residents to commemorate Gil despite the opposition of local ruling elites. In October 1901, Valverde wrote to prominent black patriot Juan Gualberto Gómez, outlining his negotiations with local authorities to obtain permission to organize a fund-raiser to collect monies for the monument. Permissions appear to have been withheld, because Valverde renewed his attempts the following year.[93] In 1902, a group of residents petitioned the city council to change the name of their street on which Gil was murdered from Hernán Cortés to General Gil Street. Valverde also asked the city council to donate some extra tiles for the construction of the monument. The council denied both requests.[94]

Lack of support from the city council delayed the construction of the monument and likely constituted part of a broader tendency to "whiten" the national pantheon of heroes.[95] The statue was inaugurated eleven years later, in May 1911, and to this day remains the forgotten centerpiece of the park called Panteón de Gil. Although he was less "aggressive" than the protesters and manifesto writers, Valverde did emulate their articulation of racial injustice in terms of patriotism. Nevertheless, the limited success of these claims revealed a fundamental shift in the meaning of patriotism. Once a core tenet of nationalism, racial brotherhood became a subversive counterdiscourse of patriotism that white elites feared would undermine their political power. The monument to Gil represented one example of a broader array of creative responses to the paradox confronting men and women of African descent in turn-of-the-century Cuba. These strategies, which tended to downplay direct references to race, served both to challenge and uphold the centrality of the discourse of racial brotherhood to the national image of Cuba. The public display of black war heroes tended to validate the claim that Cuba remained a color-blind society, even though the life of the man the monument commemorated confirmed the centrality of racism to the Cuban state. The deployment of patriotic discourse and symbolism in lieu of explicitly racial language helped to consolidate the culture of racial silence that continued to stifle black activism.

NOTES

The author wishes to dedicate this article to the Black Lives Matter movement, in solidarity with the fight against racist police violence.

1. Cienfuegos City Council Minutes, April 28, 1899, vol. 43, fol. 68, Actas Capitulares, Provincial Historical Archive of Cienfuegos (hereafter AHPC/AC). The case of black veteran and veterinarian Martín Reinoso, denied employment as a meat inspector, exemplifies a broader pattern of racial discrimination in political appointments. Another notable case is that of Quintín Bandera. See Abelardo Padrón Valdés, *General de tres guerras* (Havana: Editorial de Ciencias Sociales, 1991).

2. Gwendolyn Midlo Hall, *Social Control in Slave Plantation Societies: A Comparison of St. Domingue and Cuba* (Baltimore: Johns Hopkins University Press, 1971), 129–32; Ricardo D. Salvatore, "The Crimes of Poor *Paysanos* in Midnineteenth-Century Buenos Aires," in *Reconstructing Criminality in Latin America*, ed. Carlos Aguirre and Robert Buffington, 59–84 (Wilmington, DE: Scholarly Resources, 2000), 67; Richard Warren, "Mass Mobilization versus Social Control: Vagrancy and Political Order in Early Republican Mexico," in Aguirre and Buffington, *Reconstructing Criminality in Latin America*, 44, 53; Thomas H. Holloway, "Punishment in Nineteenth-Century Rio de Janeiro: Judicial Action as Police Practice," in Aguirre and Buffington, *Reconstructing Criminality in Latin America*, 86.

3. Louis A. Pérez Jr. *Cuba Between Empires, 1978–1902* (Pittsburgh: University of Pittsburgh Press, 1985), 316–27.

4. Sarah C. Chambers, "Crime and Criminality: Judicial Practice in Arequipa, Peru, During the Transition from Colony to Republic," in Aguirre and Buffington, *Reconstructing Criminality in Latin America,* 28; Holloway, "Punishment in Nineteenth-Century Rio de Janeiro," 89.

5. Melina Pappademos, *Black Political Activism and the Cuban Republic* (Chapel Hill: University of North Carolina Press, 2010), 67; Alejandro de la Fuente, *A Nation for All: Race, Inequality, and Politics in Twentieth-Century Cuba* (Chapel Hill: University of North Carolina Press, 2001); Thomas T. Orum, "The Politics of Color: The Racial Dimension of Cuban Politics During the Early Republican Years, 1900–1912" (PhD diss., New York University, 1975), 96.

6. Rubin Francis Westin, *Racism in U.S. Imperialism: The Influence of Racial Assumptions on American Foreign Policy, 1893–1945* (Columbia: University of South Carolina Press, 1972), 145–50; Gerald Horne, *Race to Revolution: The United States and Cuba Under Slavery and Jim Crow* (New York: Monthly Review Press, 2014).

7. Ada Ferrer, *Insurgent Cuba: Race, Nation, and Revolution, 1868–1898* (Chapel Hill: University of North Carolina Press, 1999); Lillian Guerra, *The Myth of José Martí: Conflicting Nationalisms in Early Twentieth-Century Cuba* (Chapel Hill: University of North Carolina Press, 2005); Rebecca J. Scott, *Degrees of Freedom: Louisiana and Cuba After Slavery* (Cambridge: Harvard University Press 2005); Michael Zeuske, "'Los negros hicimos la independencia': Aspectos de la movilización afrocubana en un hinterland Cubano: Cienfuegos entre colonia y República," in *Espacios, silencios y los sentidos de la libertad: Cuba entre 1878 y 1912,* ed. Fernando Martínez Heredia, Rebecca J. Scott, and Orlando F. García Martínez, 193–234 (Havana: Ediciones Unión, 2001).

8. Cienfuegos City Council Minutes, February 28, 1899, vol. 43, fols. 18–25, AHPC/AC; Alejandro de la Fuente and Matthew Casey, "Race and the Suffrage Controversy in Cuba, 1898–1901," in *Colonial Crucible: Empire in the Making of the Modern American State,* ed. Alfred W. McCoy and Francisco A. Scarano, 220–29 (Madison: University of Wisconsin Press, 2009).

9. James H. Wilson to Adjutant General, February 8, 1900, box 31, file 665, U.S. National Archives, Military Government of Cuba, Record Group 140, Entry 3 (hereafter USNA/MGC/RG 140/E 3); "Sundry Cuban Soldiers to General Brooke," June 10, 1899, box 14, file 3190, USNA/MGC/RG 140/E 3.

10. James H. Wilson, *Annual Report of Brigadier General James H. Wilson, U.S.V., Commanding the Dept. of Matanzas and Santa Clara* (Matanzas, 1899), 167, 156.

11. Guadalupe García, "Urban *Guajiros*: Colonial *Reconcentración,* Rural Displacement, and Criminalisation in Western Cuba, 1895–1902," *Journal of Latin American Studies* 43, no. 2 (2011), 211.

12. "Terrorized by Cuban Bandits," newspaper clipping, June 7, 1899, vol. II.60, fol. 49, Massachusetts Historical Society/Edwin Atkins Papers (hereafter MHS/EFA); "Testimony of Antonio Betancourt Díaz," March 25, 1904, case 293, box 142, pt. 4, folder 3, fol. 31, U.S National Archives, Spanish Treaty Claims Commission, RG 76/E 352 (hereafter USNA/STCC); Wilson, *Annual Report*, 1899, 74; George Clarke Musgrave, *Under Three Flags in Cuba: A Personal Account of the Cuban Insurrection and Spanish-American War* (Boston: Little, Brown, 1899), 163. For a discussion of ideas about race and crime in Cuba, see Alejandra Bronfman, *Measures of Equality: Social Science, Citizenship, and Race in Cuba, 1902–1940* (Chapel Hill: University of North Carolina Press, 2004).

13. Cienfuegos City Council Minutes, February 7, 1899; April 28, 1899, vol. 43, fol. 10, 68, AHPC/AC.

14. Juan B. Cabrera, "Reports Officers and Men of Cuban Army Employed by the US," March 26, 1899, box 2, file 2337, USNA/Records of the United States Army Overseas (hereafter RUSA), RG 395/ E 1466. To determine the racial backgrounds of the police, I cross-referenced the March 1899 list of veterans from the Brigade of Cienfuegos with military pension records, notarial records, military diaries and journals, and a database of Cienfuegos veterans created by Orlando García Martínez.

15. C. J. Stevens to Adjutant General, May 6, 1899, box 7, no file, USNA/RUSA/RG 395/E 1331.

16. Judge Advocate's Office to Adjutant General, Dept. of Matanzas and Santa Clara, July 3, 1899, oversize box 1, file 2, USNA/RUSA/RG 395/E 1331.

17. Judge Advocate's Office to Adjutant General, Dept. of Matanzas and Santa Clara, July 3, 1899, oversize box 1, file 2, USNA/RUSA/RG 395/E 1331; Major 2nd Infantry to Mayor, June 24, 1899, oversize box 1, file 2, USNA/RUSA/RG 395/E 1331.

18. Wilson, *Annual Report*, 1899, 230, 25.

19. Bonnie A. Lucero, "Engendering Inequality: Masculinity and Racial Exclusion in Cuba, 1895–1902" (PhD diss., University of North Carolina–Chapel Hill, 2013), 285–89.

20. James H. Wilson to J. B. Foraker, May 12, 1899, box 44, Library of Congress, Manuscript Division, James H. Wilson Papers (hereafter LOC/MD/JHW).

21. Walter B. Barker to J. H. Dorst, Adjutant General, "Depositions," June 19, 1899, box 12, file 5573, USNA/RUSA/RG 395/E 1331; Francisco de Ostolazo, "Transmits Depositions in the Shooting Affair at the Office of Capt. W. B. Barker," May 17, 1899, box 7, file 3915, USNA/RUSA/RG 395/E 1331.

22. Judge Advocate's Office to Adjutant General, Dept. of Matanzas and Santa Clara, July 3, 1899, oversize box 1, file 2, USNA/RUSA/RG 395/E 1331.

23. Wilson, *Annual Report*, 1899, 21; Tiffany A. Sippial, *Prostitution, Modernity, and the Making of the Cuban Republic, 1840–1920* (Chapel Hill: University of North Carolina Press, 2013), 114–31.

24. Lucero, "Engendering Inequality," 250–58, 273–80.

25. "Brooke, Wilson, y el Director de 'La Tribuna,'" *La Tribuna*, July 12, 1899, box 1, no file, USNA/RUSA/RG 395/E 1352; "Contra todos los tiranos," *La Tribuna*, June 13, 1899, box 21, file 4199, USNA/MGC/RG 140/E 3.

26. Wilson, *Annual Report*, 1899, 108.

27. Ibid., 230.

28. Capt. C. J. Stevens, "Report Relative to the Rural Police of the Province of Santa Clara," June 9, 1899, box 11, file 5062, USNA/RUSA/RG 395/E 1331.

29. Louis A. Perez Jr., *Army and Politics in Cuba, 1898–1958* (Pittsburgh: University of Pittsburgh Press, 1976), 3–20.

30. E. I. Helmick to Adjutant General, "Submits Reports of the Operations of His Officer [*sic*] for the Year Ending June 30, 1900," July 11, 1900, box 41, file 6367, USNA/RUSA/RG 395/E 1331; Mayor José Antonio Frías to Dorst, June 13, 1899, box 11, file 5354, USNA/RUSA/RG 395/E 1331; Antonio R. Mora to General James H. Wilson, June 14, 1899, box 11, file 5584, USNA/RUSA/RG 395/E 1331; José del Castillo (Abreus) to General James H. Wilson, June 17, 1899, box 11, file 5418, USNA/RUSA/RG 395/E 1331; Antonio Gallart (Rodas) to General James H. Wilson, June 17, 1899, box 11, file 5478, USNA/RUSA/RG 395/E 1331; R. Pérez (Cruces) to General James H. Wilson, June 15, 1899, box 11, file 5420, USNA/RUSA/RG 395/E 1331; "Statement of the Estates That Have Been Granted Authority to Maintain Private Guards, Under Decree 83," June 2, 1900, box 36, file 3238, USNA/RUSA/RG 395/E 1331; Lucero, "Engendering Inequality," 178–80.

31. Capt. C. J. Stevens, "Submits Report Relative to the Rural Police of the Province of Santa Clara," June 9, 1899, box 11, file 5062, USNA/RUSA/RG 395/E 1331.

32. Unknown author to Máximo Gómez, [n.d.], box 38, file 4719 (new 5392), Archivo Nacional de Cuba, Fondo Máximo Gómez (hereafter ANC/FMG); Orlando García Martínez, "Caciques, elites, clientelas, y los problemas raciales: Veteranos negros en Cienfuegos entre 1902 y 1912," *Revista del Centro de Investigaciones Históricas* 15 (2004), 107.

33. Captain Pedro P. Mutos and Commandant Juan Sardiñas y Villa, "To the Colored Race, Glory to General Gil," January 27, 1900, box 42, file 86, USNA/MGC/RG 140/E 3; see also Miguel Barnet, *Biografía de un cimarrón* (Havana: Ediciones Ariel, 1966), 188.

34. J. Kernan, Captain and Adjutant 2nd Infantry, to the Adjutant, Rowell Barracks, January 27, 1900, box 42, file 86, USNA/MGC/RG 140/E 3; Wilson, *Annual Report*, 1899, 230.

35. James H. Wilson, *Annual Report of Brigadier General James H. Wilson, U.S.V., Commanding the Dept. of Matanzas and Santa Clara* (Matanzas, 1900), 214.

36. José Antonio Frías, "The Mayor J. A. Frías States That the Lower Class of Colored People Asked to Have the Body of General Gil Turn [*sic*] over to Them for Embalming, Guarding and Burial with Honors . . . , 1st Endorsement," December 30, 1899, box 29, file 20, USNA/RUSA/RG 395/E 1331.

37. José Miguel Gómez to General James H. Wilson, October 14, 1899, box 20, file 9132, USNA/RUSA/RG 395/E 1331.

38. García Martínez, "Caciques, elites, clientelas," 107.
39. Tribunal Supremo, *Jurisprudencia del Tribunal Supremo en material criminal* (Havana: Rambla y Bouza, 1908), 3:70.
40. Brigadier General James H. Wilson to Adjutant General Hugh L. Scott, January 1, 1900, box 42, file 86, USNA/MGC/RG 140/E 3.
41. Tribunal Supremo, *Jurisprudencia del Tribunal Supremo*, 3:70.
42. Kernan to Adjutant, Rowell Barracks, January 27, 1900; Tribunal Supremo, *Jurisprudencia del Tribunal Supremo*, 3:70.
43. Possibly refers to Officer Ambrosio Hernández, as no officer by the name of Antonio Hernández appears on the roster. José Miguel Gómez, "States That the Mayor of Cienfuegos Has Notified Him of the Killing by a Policeman of the Ex-General Gil of the Cuban Army," December 30, 1899, box 31, file 24, USNA/RUSA/RG 395/E 1331. A sworn guard was a specific class of private guard hired by plantation owners with special permission of the military government.
44. "Hechos Lamentables," in *El Telégrafo: Periódico Político*, January ?, 1900, Archivo Municipal Histórico de Trinidad (hereafter AMHT), courtesy of Orlando García Martínez.
45. Tribunal Supremo, *Jurisprudencia del Tribunal Supremo*, 3:71.
46. Wilson to Scott, January 1, 1900.
47. Frías, "The Mayor J. A. Frías States . . . ," December 30, 1899, 6th Endorsement.
48. Kernan to Adjutant, Rowell Barracks, January 27, 1900.
49. A. H. Bowman, "Reports Circumstances Attending the Death of General Gil (Negro) Late of the Cuban Army," January 4, 1900, box 42, file 136, USNA/MGC/RG 140/E 3.
50. Ibid.
51. Perfecto Gil to Máximo Gómez, [n.d.], box 9, file 1265-B ANC, ANC/FMG.
52. General Máximo Gómez to General Leonard Wood, March 1, 1900, courtesy of Orlando F. García Martínez.
53. "Hechos Lamentables."
54. Frías, "The Mayor J. A. Frías States . . . ," December 30, 1899.
55. Kernan to Adjutant, Rowell Barracks, January 27, 1900.
56. Gil to Gómez, [n.d.].
57. Ibid.
58. Kernan to Adjutant, Rowell Barracks, January 27, 1900.
59. Ibid.
60. Ibid.
61. Frías, "The Mayor J. A. Frías States . . . ," December 30, 1899.
62. Ibid.
63. García Martínez, "Caciques, elites, clientelas," 106.
64. Musgrave, *Under Three Flags in Cuba*, 163.
65. "Hechos Lamentables."

66. Kernan to Adjutant, Rowell Barracks, January 27, 1900; "La muerte de Gil," in *El Telé-grafo: Periódico Político*, January 21, 1900, AMHT, courtesy of Orlando García Martínez.

67. José B. Alemán, "La muerte de Gil," in *La Tribuna*, newspaper clipping, [n.d.], file 382, box 42, MGC/RG 140/E 3.

68. Frías, "The Mayor J. A. Frías States . . . ," December 30, 1899, 6th Endorsement, February 3, 1900.

69. "La muerte de Gil," in *El Telégrafo*.

70. Ibid.

71. Kernan to Adjutant, Rowell Barracks, January 27, 1900.

72. "La muerte de Gil," in *El Telégrafo*.

73. Tribunal Supremo, *Jurisprudencia del Tribunal Supremo*, 3:72.

74. Kernan to Adjutant, Rowell Barracks, January 27, 1900.

75. "La muerte de Gil," in *El Telégrafo*.

76. Kernan to Adjutant, Rowell Barracks, January 27, 1900.

77. Ibid.

78. "Expediente relativo a la comisión del cónsul de Santo Domingo solicitando detalles sobre la muerte del General del Ejército Libertador dominicano Dionisio Gil," April 26–June 9, 1900, May 10, 1900, Archivo Nacional de Cuba, Fondo Secretario de Estado y Gobernación (hereafter ANC/FSEG). Thank you to Orlando García Martínez for pointing out this document.

79. Carlos Roloff y Mialofsky, *Indice alfabético y defunciones del Ejército Libertador de Cuba, guerra de independencia, iniciada el 24 de febrero de 1895 y terminada oficialmente el 24 de agosto de 1898* (Havana: Imprenta de Rambla y Bouza, 1901).

80. Gil to Gómez, [n.d.].

81. Nicolás Valverde to Juan Gualberto Gómez, May 18, 1902, box 48, file 32, no. 3831, ANC/Fondo Adquisiciones.

82. García Martínez, "Caciques, elites, clientelas."

83. Edwin F. Atkins, *Sixty Years in Cuba* (Cambridge, MA: Riverside Press, 1926), 316; José Miguel Gómez, "Telegram Advising That Doctor Frías Delivered Office to Leopoldo Figueroa," March 2, 1900, box 55, file 347, USNA/MGC/RG 140/ E 3.

84. Atkins, *Sixty Years in Cuba*, 322.

85. Inocencio Sarría, Lorenzo Cabrera, José Ayala, Gavino Crespo, Herminio Quirós, Manuel Sánchez, R. Rodríguez, Pastor Ruíz, Florentino Leon, Aniceto Soto, José López, Narciso P. Blanco, José González, Gustavo Lescano, José Pagola, Andrés Díaz, Marcelino Cabrera, Adalio Torre, Alejandro Torres, Abelardo González, Manuel Alduncin, Francisco Fernández, and others, "Application Stating They Have Been Discharged," June 17, 1901, box 195, file 1846, USNA/MGC/RG 140/E 3; Cienfuegos City Council Minutes, July 20, 1901, vol. 49, AHPC/AC; Walter B. Barker to Adjutant General, July 9, 1901, box 183, file 2698, USNA/MGC/RG 140/E 3.

86. Luis J. Bustamante, *Diccionario biográfico cienfueguero* (Cienfuegos, 1931).

87. Guerra, *The Myth of José Martí*, 257.

88. Mutos and Sardiñas y Villa, "To the Colored Race, Glory to General Gil."

89. Ibid.

90. Ibid.

91. Ibid.

92. For example, in January 1894, Valverde was one of the first to attempt attending a performance at the Tomás Terry Theatre, under the protection of a recent Spanish decree mandating racial integration in public establishments. Although the white public rejected his presence, shouting that he be expelled and ordering the police to disperse his followers on the outside, he asserted his rights under Spanish law. "Lo de Anoche," newspaper clipping, courtesy of Orlando García Martínez. Later, American military officials would accuse Valverde of conspiring to unify blacks into a solid political bloc in Cienfuegos in 1907. W. D. Beach, Major 15th Cavalry, to Chief of Staff, Army of Cuban Pacification, September 28, 1907, box 2, file 17.33, USNA, Records of the Army of Cuban Pacification, RG 199/E 5.

93. Nicolás Valverde to Juan Gualberto Gómez," May 18, 1902, box 48, file 32, no. 3831, ANC/FA.

94. Cienfuegos City Council Minutes, January 10, 1902, vol. 50, AHPC/AC.

95. Marial Iglesias, *Las metáforas del cambio en la vida cotidiana: Cuba 1898–1902* (Havana: UNEAC, 2003), 48.

6

VISIONS OF ORDER

ॐ

*Criminality, Class, and Community Conceptions
of the Police in 1920s Buenos Aires*

JUANDREA BATES

O N THE MORNING of February 20, 1920, Buenos Aires residents joined with reporters from across South America to watch as eighteen delegates from seven Latin American countries began the South American International Police Conference (SAIPC). Public interest surrounding the congress had been building for weeks, as newspaper columnists ranging from the conservative writers for *La Nación* to the anarchists at *La Vanguardia* speculated about what issues the summit would address. In his opening speech, the city's chief of police, Elpidio González, thanked delegates from Bolivia, Brazil, Chile, Paraguay, Peru, and Uruguay for their attendance and announced the most pressing items on his agenda. He declared: "The role of the police, as the distinguished arm of the State, has become even more fundamental to the maintenance of social order. We must improve their abilities to prevent crime, but also develop their methods of containment and capacity to provide assistance under the auspices of peace, wellness, and justice."[1]

González's speech met with vigorous applause from spectators in the gallery and his fellow delegates. Although the diverse crowd contained members of the city's elite, the middle class, unionized workers, and anarchists, most agreed that the police force was in dire need of improvements. For years, *porteños*, residents of Buenos Aires from across the socioeconomic spectrum, had complained about the growing sense of chaos and danger in the burgeoning metropolis, and anxiety over rapid demographic, social, and political changes made police reform seem even more critical.

Improvements to the city's police department were well under way by the time of González's speech. A municipal order in 1872 had created the first professional force. At the turn of the century, the national government increased salaries and began offering generous benefit packages to attract better employees. Police Chief Ramón Falcón amplified these efforts, opening a new cadet training school in 1906 and making literacy a requirement for all patrolmen ten years later. Furthermore, the police department received an exponential increase in its budget and personnel. Crime investigation technology in Argentina, already among the most advanced in the world, continued to improve. By 1919, the department headquarters had begun keeping a catalogue of fingerprints collected from past suspects, establishing a broader regional trend of integrating the new technologies into police work. Finally, department administrators organized and attended international police conferences to brainstorm methods to help decrease crime rates in the capital city. In the first decades of the twentieth century, criminologists, police administrators, and politicians alike identified the modernization of the police force as essential to national progress. Many of the capital's brightest minds dedicated themselves to solving Argentina's social problems, and significant portions of the city's budget were earmarked for recruiting new officers, improving personnel training, and obtaining surveillance technology.

Despite all these reforms, however, the police department's performance remained stagnant. Quarterly reports issued by the police department actually showed higher rates of crime.[2] As historians Pablo Piccato and Thomas Holloway have argued, many Latin American metropolises noted higher arrest rates for crimes against public order as a result of the state's growing concern over the control of public space, more efficient policing, and stronger policies criminalizing the urban poor.[3] Yet, although there was a larger police presence in Buenos Aires than ever before, residents of Buenos Aires reported increased rates of violent crime. In 1914, the department received 3.45 complaints of murder, assault, or rape per 1,000 people compared to only 1.46 in 1887. Furthermore, the police force's own statistics suggest that in the midst of reform officers became less efficient in capturing suspects. The success rate for police apprehension of suspects decreased from 71.3 percent in 1895 to 45.9 percent in 1914. It leveled off at 42.1 percent in 1924. The growing rates of violent crime and the inability of law enforcement to apprehend suspects present an interesting paradox: Why did crime rates and police inefficiency continue to grow despite these reforms?

In recent years, historians have revealed a wealth of new information about the plans politicians, administrators, and criminologists designed to reform and improve policing in Buenos Aires at the turn of the century. Ricardo Salvatore, Eugenia Scarzanella, and Julia Rodriguez have demonstrated that discourses of crime and delinquency enabled medical doctors, criminologists, politicians, and police administrators to disenfranchise workers, immigrants, and women.[4] Diego Galeano's pioneering investigation of Policía de la Capital's own imagery illuminates nativist and antiunion sentiments in the development of police technologies and international police cooperatives.[5] Casting their eyes toward the later twentieth century, Osvaldo Barreneche and Laura Kalmanowiecki argue that the structure and ideologies developed by police administrators in Buenos Aires in the early twentieth century set the stage for their increasingly militant operations in the century to come.[6]

While those studies have revealed much about the plans and ideologies shaping the development of state programs of surveillance and repression, they often overlook the ways the success of official programs also depended on employee and community support. This essay reveals that crime rates and police inefficiency continued to increase after the enactment of significant police reforms in large part because administrators held different conceptualizations of citizenship and criminality than did the middle class, workers, and even their own employees. While workers and the middle class hoped that political enfranchisement would ensure a more responsive police force, department administrators maintained a single-minded focus on suppressing labor militancy and creating order in public spaces reserved for the elite. According to this view, workers—largely foreign born and composing some of the most active unions on the continent—were not citizens like themselves who deserved police protection. Rather, they represented dangerous threats to private property and social order. Frustration mounted among the working class as administrators refused to create a police department that reflected the new, supposedly democratic, nature of society, focusing on violent crimes and theft. Though initially excited about the prospect of expanding citizenship and police reform, working-class and middle-class residents showed an increasing resentment toward officers and the government. For them, the meanings of citizenship expanded under the 1912 voting reform, which established compulsory, universal male suffrage, were continually eroded until the democratic regime fell in 1930.

This chapter is divided into four parts. First, an analysis of the debates taking place at the South American International Police Conference reveals that protecting preexisting economic and social hierarchies in the face of serious political change constituted a central aim of police reforms. The second part examines the attempts to operationalize the reforms, tracing the distribution of resources and police personnel across elite and working-class neighborhoods. Third, it explores the ways middle- and working-class populations challenged the elite's use of the police department as a tool of disenfranchisement.

The final section examines a frequently overlooked aspect of constructions of criminality and prosecution of crime: the police officers themselves. A comparison of the biographies of administrators with profiles of patrolmen reveals that officers often had more in common with the supposedly deviant working classes than with the heads of their departments. These differences led patrolmen to reject some of the administrators' initiatives while accepting others, further complicating negotiations between state officials and the local populations over the boundaries of legal and illegal acts and the nature of citizenship. Together these sections reveal the importance of community members and patrolmen in the administration of justice and meanings of criminality.[7]

ENVISIONING POLICE REFORM: ARGENTINE DELEGATES AT THE SOUTH AMERICAN INTERNATIONAL POLICE CONFERENCE

Between 1880 and 1930, Argentina's growing economy attracted over six million European immigrants through the port of Buenos Aires. A town of 171,000 in 1869, the capital transformed into one of world's largest metropolitan centers, with a population of 1.6 million by 1914.[8] That year, 75 percent of the working class had been born in Europe.[9] The demographic expansion caused serious strains on available housing, sanitation services, and public safety forces in Buenos Aires, and members of the middle and upper classes worried that the "vice" of the poor would infect their neighborhoods.[10] The large number of Spanish and Italian immigrants with anarchist and socialist backgrounds further fueled elite fears of disorder emanating from the working classes. By 1904, the anarchist Federación Obrera Regional Argentina had helped consolidate formerly disparate labor movements, leading to intensifying confrontations in the capital. Between 1910 and 1920, over 750 strikes threatened to paralyze the nation.[11]

Confrontations between workers and bosses gave rise to an alliance between the traditional landed oligarchy and reform-minded middle-class groups, represented by the Unión Cívica Radical (UCR, Radical Civil Union). Attempting to maintain their influence by co-opting the native-born middle class, the conservative oligarchy enacted sweeping voting reforms in 1912. The resulting Sáenz Peña Law endowed all male citizens with obligatory suffrage, while largely excluding the foreign-born anarchist and socialist working class. Growing democratic participation brought a reformist UCR candidate, Hipólito Yrigoyen, to the presidency in 1916.[12]

The expansion of voting rights did little to quell the demands of largely foreign-born workers' movements, who saw the democratic opening as a chance to translate political power into serious economic and social reform. Labor militancy culminated in the January 1919 Semana Trágica (Tragic Week), in which a series of violent clashes between strikers, strikebreakers, armed segments of the middle class, and the police and military left more than seven hundred dead and four thousand injured.[13] Amid a rapidly growing population, rising labor unrest, and the country's first experiment with democracy, the police department's ability to secure public safety seemed critical to shoring up political legitimacy and social stability.[14]

The South American International Police Conference held in Buenos Aires from January 20 to January 26, 1920, was the second of its kind. Fifteen years earlier delegates from Buenos Aires, La Plata, Rio de Janeiro, Santiago, and Montevideo had met in the Argentine capital intent on building international cooperation to monitor and apprehend *"personas peligrosas,"* or dangerous persons, who might try to flee across international borders. Both conferences kept detailed transcripts of speeches and the ensuing debates, and many delegates offered musings on the presumed intersections of labor activism and crime. At the conclusion of the conference, formal booklets were issued with suggestions on how to reform international and national policing systems. These records reveal administrators' top agendas for the police. As historian Diego Galeano notes, in the fifteen years between the two conferences subtle shifts occurred in delegates' priorities.[15] The 1905 conference had included discussions of both labor activities and "known criminals," those who were habitually apprehended for robbery, assault, or larceny. By 1920, however, Argentine delegates spoke very little about preventing or punishing violent crime or theft. Instead, the bureaucrats supervising the Policía de la Capital focused on foreign-led labor activism. Their agendas pushed the police department to focus its energy on suppressing labor unrest, screening immigrants, and repressing social disturbances that threatened areas intended for government business, international investors, and elite leisure.

In his opening speech at the SAIPC, González declared that "popular movements, hiding within issues raised by the labor unions against their bosses, have jumped into the arena of the revolutionary fight to violate social stability."[16] As the conference progressed, the Argentine delegates continued to emphasize their concerns about worker activism, which they equated with unrest and delinquency. Such threats, González argued, could not be mediated through compromise:

> As time has passed and the demands of the working class have advanced through strikes and threats, the government has granted concessions and passed protective laws for workers. . . . In this state of affairs, class struggles and hatred have fermented and turned the city into a battlefield.[17]

These speeches, filled with terms such as "revolutionary," "chaos," and "battlefield," indicate that police administrators would not view strikes as a natural part of negotiations between workers and their bosses. Instead, they painted labor activism as inherently criminal acts, attempts at revolution and the socialization of private property through armed conflict.[18] Applauding a speech made by a Chilean delegate, the Buenos Aires police department's Enrique Duffey affirmed that "whether we call them vulgar criminals or simple advocates—as they pretend to be—it is true they promote new social and economic doctrines that challenge the natural orders of society."[19] Dedicated to maintaining the "natural order" of oligarchic Argentina through the transition to democracy, police administrators showed an increased aggressiveness in limiting those movements that called for economic reform and social inclusion. Political policing and monitoring of labor movements, not preventing violent crime or theft, became the primary aim in reforming the police department.[20]

González concluded his oration by identifying the police as the arm of the state most suited to deal with strikes and labor protests. He declared: "It is undeniable that society has the right to defend itself from these agitators with any weapons required." He went on to pinpoint "mounting a defense" as a primary task for both the police conference and the police force as a whole, which society "created and armed for this very purpose."[21] Delegate Enrique Duffey went on to insist that "the police have the obligation to use any forces at their disposal to prevent social disturbance."[22]

In identifying the police as the front line of defense against the supposed revolutionary threat of workers, administrators criminalized the very act of protest. The authorizing of patrolmen to use "any weapons required" indicates the extent to which the oligarchy viewed workers' citizenship as different from their own. While workers saw their protests as a legitimate attempt to transform their new political rights into economic reform, these efforts received harsh condemnation from the delegates at the SAIPC police conference, who cast their actions as dangerous disruptions to public order, private property, and social order. The national congress had passed no formal legislation curtailing the right to organize, yet in practice the rhetoric of police administrators served to criminalize labor protest. In doing so, they both undermined workers' asserted rights to organize peacefully or push for economic reform and diverted much-needed resources away from those segments of the force dedicated to patrolling the streets to prevent violent crimes and theft.

Argentine police administrators associated labor uprisings and anarchist movements with recent arrivals from Europe. Although unions and anarchist groups contained both foreign and native-born members, the Argentine delegates' rhetoric cast outside agitators as the central problem in labor disputes. One representative, Alfonso Hotron Fernández, remarked that "when these expelled troublemakers enter our nations, they do so with the intention of organizing uprisings and creating chaos."[23] Such fears of international anarchist and communist movements, already prominent in the nineteenth century, only grew after the 1917 Russian Revolution.[24] Conference attendees evinced a particular fear of a Russian influence in the Southern Cone. Police Chief González declared: "It lit a spark that threatens to set the revolutionary proletarian masses of all countries on fire."[25] With an air of sarcasm, he warned that the Russian revolutionaries would encourage the urban masses to "rise up, socialize private properties, and punish those who have committed the serious crime of owning lands."[26] This hyperbolic rhetoric centered on a perception that immigrants desired to overturn social order. While native-born workers could be "contaminated by infiltrators" or "swept up by foreign doctrines," immigrant workers catalyzed social disorder.[27]

Argentine delegates at the SAIPC hoped to bolster recent laws restricting the freedom of foreign-born workers to organize and sought to give the police department a larger role in immigration screening. In 1902, the Law of Residency prevented anarchists from entering the nation. In 1910, months after a Russian-born anarchist shot and killed the city's police chief, Congress passed the Laws of Social Defense, allowing the deportation, without trial, of foreign-born residents suspected of anarchist activities.[28] Delegates at the SAIPC sought to push this legislation further, suggesting that all immigrants be logged into an international "criminal" database. The proposed catalogue would contain a set of fingerprints, a physical description, and the last known location of all people entering the country, regardless of whether they had ever committed a crime.[29] Delegates further proposed that the information be circulated among police forces around the country and the hemisphere. The database would, therefore, formally mark all immigrants as potential criminals. Convinced that these recent arrivals posed a threat to the standing social order, González insisted that expanding the database was critical to securing public safety.

In debating the merits of this criminal database, González's motivations became clearer. When the Uruguayan representative sought to clarify whether the catalogue would be used to monitor international workers' movements, González responded that "workers' or popular movements can produce social unrest," and that "it was widely known not only by the police, but also by the unions themselves, that the police habitually monitor their activities."[30] For Argentine delegates, monitoring labor and preventing the entry of activists represented an important objective of police reform.

Argentine delegates remained notably silent in discussions about the prevention of nonpolitical crimes or apprehension of violent offenders and thieves. Delegates from Peru and Brazil made lengthy speeches on the need to augment police salaries, increase budgets, employ more men on their task forces, and increase the punishments for people convicted of homicides and theft. Argentine delegates, so vocal through the rest of the conference, remained mute on these issues. When thinking about threats to the nation, they overlooked the threat of petty criminals and thieves and designed their improvement projects accordingly.[31]

FROM VISIONS TO ACTIONS: A MODERNIZED POLICE FORCE ON THE STREET

Speeches made at the South American International Police Conference indicate that top administrators identified labor activists and immigrants as key concerns for the newly reformed police department. Yet, understanding how these bureaucrats' visions of crime affected the efficacy of police reforms must go beyond an exploration of rhetoric. The allocation of patrolmen also provide important insights into the mean-ings of police reform and help explain its limited success. Departmental administra-tors divided the capital into forty-six administrative police divisions, each with its own precinct. At the end of each quarter, these subsections submitted statistics of the number of officers they employed, crimes reported, and resulting arrests, and these statistics were compiled and published in quarterly bulletins by the Ministry of the Interior. By layering the information found in these bulletins with census data and statistics on living standards, I discovered that a disproportionate number of police-men patrolled elite neighborhoods in the center and north of the city.[32]

This uneven allocation of police officers fundamentally shaped how reform played out in everyday life. The abundance of public safety forces in wealthy areas resulted in growing arrest rates for crimes against public order in those areas, nonviolent offenses that mostly revolved around prohibiting working-class men from intruding into the leisure spaces reserved for the wealthy. It did not, however, prevent violent crimes or crimes against property. Arrests for crimes against public order were very low in poor areas of the city, as the overall allocation of officers in wealthy neighborhoods created a dearth of officers in many other areas. A high number of complaints for violent crimes and theft remained unsolved. This sense of lawlessness carried over into wealthy neigh-borhoods, as the public came to view poor areas as places where criminals could act with impunity and patrolmen had no means to apprehend suspects once they sought refuge there.[33]

Much of the public insecurity and fear over crime was linked to the profound sociogeographic transformation taking place in Buenos Aires in the decades lead-ing up to the SAIPC. As the population grew and profits from agro-exports brought GNP on par with much of Western Europe, urban planners sought to remake the capital into a showcase of Argentina's development and prosperity. By 1910, Buenos Aires's city center reflected the country's commitment to refinement. In 1889, urban designers redesigned the Plaza de Mayo, the city's central plaza, extending a wide bou-levard through its center westward from the presidential palace, La Casa Rosada, to the newly constructed National Congress building. This Avenida de Mayo quickly became the political, economic, and cultural heart of the oligarchic city. The city's finest restaurants, the National Cathedral, City Hall, and the lavish offices of two of the country's leading newspapers, *La Nación* and *La Prensa*, all lined its boulevard. Heavily influenced by Georges-Eugène Haussmann's renovation of Paris, the sur-rounding blocks were outfitted with large plazas, wide boulevards, and neoclassical architecture that brought fresh air and sunlight and gave rise to the city's reputation as the Paris of South America. The surrounding blocks with their neatly laid streets, marble buildings, and spacious plazas created a sense of order and vigor for those who inhabited them and impressed visitors with a sense of beauty and grandeur.[34]

By 1910, Buenos Aires's city center boasted a commitment to modernization and showcased an increasing prosperity. However, the downtown façade hid rising social inequality.[35] In order to build the wide avenues, stunning plazas, and elegant halls of government that demarcated the core, planners demolished low-cost housing. While fifty-two tenement-style *conventillos* dotted the downtown in 1887, by 1910 there were only two. Increasing rental prices drove most working-class residents out of the center of the city, pushing them toward already crowded tenements in the south and west of the city.[36] In contrast to the open, ordered, and imposing spaces surrounding the Plaza de Mayo, poorer areas like La Boca, Flores, and Barracas were dominated by dilapidated apartment buildings where entire families or multiple households crowded into tiny, one-room dwellings. During steamy summers, people slept on fire escapes, sat in doorways, and talked on street corners, packing every inch of outdoor space.[37] Daily life blended seamlessly into the surrounding industries: slaughterhouses, meat packing plants, chemical production facilities, and textile factories. Residents awoke each morning to the harsh noises of industrial life and fell asleep amid the distinctly sour smells of the chemically polluted river and discarded hides left to decay outside slaughterhouses.[38]

These poorer areas received little of the attention officials lavished on the city center. In southern districts such as Barracas and La Boca, major thoroughfares remained unpaved. Stormy weather brought debris and human waste into the streets and under doorways. Long after mortality rates improved in the rest of the city, the south remained plagued by epidemics of cholera, yellow fever, and tuberculosis.[39] Elites and middle-class residents largely left the area. Seeking work in the industries and along the dock, semiskilled and unskilled laborers, particularly immigrants and migrants from the interior, poured into the waterfront, driving the population of these barrios from 32,413 in 1887 to 213,801 by 1914.[40]

The areas surrounding the Plaza de Mayo and La Boca represented two different sides of Buenos Aires's drive towards modernity; they also developed distinct relationships with the police department. A comparison of police activities in downtown districts one through four and La Boca districts fourteen and fifteen illustrates the ways in which the assignment of policemen shaped perceptions of crime and the efficiency of the police in different areas of the city. In the four districts surrounding the Plaza de Mayo, municipal authorities employed over 628 police officers. Population records for the first four voting districts for 1920 reveal that on average there was one police officer for every 124 residents.[41] In contrast, the fourteenth and fifteenth divisions of the city had significantly lower standards of living and a smaller police presence. These areas contained a much larger number of residents, but police administrators assigned them almost the same number of police officers as the first through fourth divisions. On average, there was approximately one policeman for every 463 people in the fourteenth and fifteenth divisions. This difference in the number of policemen patrolling upper-class versus working-class neighborhoods reveals police administrators' attempts to provide middle-class and elite *porteños* with increased protection while denying working-class neighborhoods the same services.[42]

Police administrators' understanding of workers as potential suspects, not equal citizens, is also evident from the arrests rates in affluent neighborhoods.[43] Besides detailing where administrators stationed police officers, police bulletins also listed arrest rates and the demographics of the perpetrators. Over 78 percent of people arrested in affluent neighborhoods held working-class occupations.[44] While day laborers, tailors, machine operators, and seamstresses rarely saw security forces in their own neighborhoods, when they entered wealthy zones they became objects of police suspicion and subject to arrest.

A consideration of the types of crimes for which officers apprehended people and what time of day the arrests occurred makes the criminalization of workers in affluent barrios even more evident. When classifying types of crimes in their quarterly police bulletins, administrators divided them into five categories: crimes against people, against property, against the state, against morality, and against public order. While victims sometimes reported crimes against people or property, those against public order—which include public drunkenness, promoting drunkenness, scandal, disorder, carrying arms, firing arms without injury, and vagrancy—are ideal for understanding police initiatives. Individual police officers, influenced by their own understandings of crime, criminality, and belonging, distinguished between legal and illegal actions, thereby redefining these very categories.[45] For example, the officers' perceptions of suspects and communal norms determined the difference between a law-abiding citizen enjoying an after-work pint and someone criminally intoxicated. Consequently, rank-and-file officers played a substantial role in shaping the rates of arrest for these crimes. Furthermore, activities defined as crimes against public order became crimes only when performed in the public sphere. While the criminalization of activities defined as crimes against property and people represent the state's attempts to control and eradicate certain *behaviors*, the prosecution of these activities more accurately represents an attempt to control what activities took place in public spaces—and as such to eliminate certain purportedly undesirable *people* from privileged spaces.[46]

In the first through fourth districts, where working-class men made up less than 20 percent of the population, they were arrested for over 79 percent of crimes against public order. These districts contained less than one-quarter of the city's population, yet accounted for almost 58 percent of the arrests for crimes against public order in the city. These statistics cannot provide conclusive evidence of the correlation between occupational background and police officers' perceptions of behavior. Yet, they suggest that the police demarcated these neighborhoods as middle- and upper-class residential domains, and the mere presence of workers aroused suspicion.[47]

Statistics on what punishments resulted from the apprehension of people accused of crimes against public order in different parts of the city further demonstrate the criminal justice system's attempts to prohibit workers from spending their leisure time in elite neighborhoods. In the first district, approximately two-thirds of people accused of crimes against public order served some time in jail. Approximately 18 percent paid a fine and were released. The police released the remainder of subjects without any punishment. In the fourteenth and fifteenth districts, the areas of the city previously described as working-class neighborhoods, judges proved more lenient. Only 38 percent of people arrested served jail time; another 30 percent paid fines; and judges released the remainder. These numbers indicate that when in elite spaces, police officers defined a wider variety of activities as criminal behavior and subject to more strident punishment. For police officers, location as much as behavior contributed to understandings of criminality and of who constituted a suspect.[48]

COMMUNITY RESPONSES TO POLICE DEPARTMENT REFORMS

If administrators hoped their programs would generate public support, a quick read through any of the city's periodicals would have left them disappointed. In the weeks leading up to the SAIPC, newspapers from around Buenos Aires optimistically speculated about what reforms would result. As the conference continued, however, such enthusiasm faded. An analysis of periodicals with largely middle-class and wealthy readerships, such as *La Nación*, *El Diario*, and *La Prensa*, demonstrates that while members of the middle class agreed with police administrators that workers' unions could be dangerous, they demanded more attention for other types of criminal activities.[49]

Articles in *La Razón* and *La Nación* indicate that members of the middle class viewed labor movements, particularly those associated with the anarchist-led Federación Obrera Regional Argentina (FORA), as criminal threats to public safety and their own security. Commending Argentine delegate Elpidio González's speech about the need to control workers, a columnist from *La Epoca* wrote: "These delegates have begun to address factors that threaten us all."[50] Likewise, an article in *La Prensa* claimed a link between social disorder and immigrants that closely resembled the view of the police department's administration: "Our great city has attracted the expelled riffraff of Europe. This created an enormous disorder among the working class and challenged the social peace so that there has been a terrible explosion of uprisings and a perversion of social order."[51] Many articles in these middle-class newspapers blamed labor militancy on the presence of outside agitators and suggested that the police should screen and suppress militancy. A writer from *La Prensa* commented: "The need to prevent criminals from coming over the border should serve as a top priority for the police."[52] These periodicals, in turn, likely supported the SAIPC's suspicion of foreigners and the proposal to develop databases to catalogue immigrants and apprehend criminals.

While these periodicals expressed support for the SAIPC's goals of monitoring labor activities, they also pushed reformers to focus more on increasing *porteños'* safety, particularly in regard to theft. Two days before the SAIPC began, an article in *El Diario* included optimistic speculation that "through this congress the Policía de la Capital might find new modes to protect the people from the bands of stock thieves within the city."[53] A further article in *La Nación* asked reformers to think about the possibility of establishing regular patrols in areas notorious for robbery as a means to prevent it or, at least, capture its perpetrators.

As the SAIPC progressed, conservative periodicals began criticizing delegates for their lack of focus on city safety. A columnist in *La Argentina* revealed this discontent, writing: "These men seem out of contact with the citizens of the nation, who suffer from the threat of organized bands of thieves."[54] Two days later the editors of *La Nación* commented: "Thus far the conference has made no provisions to apprehend those thieves, murderers, or pickpockets who at present make the city unsafe."[55] These complaints reveal growing annoyance with the bureaucrats' unwillingness to address those threats, whether real or imagined, that the middle class found most pressing.

TO PROTECT AND SERVE? WORKERS' REACTIONS TO POLICE REFORM

If the middle-class periodicals showed irritation by the end of the conference, working-class publications leaned more toward outrage. Historians have frequently attributed the dramatic clashes between members of the urban proletariat and police officers to popular resentment of police surveillance and state intrusion into their neighborhoods. However, socialist and anarchist newspapers indicate that the proletariat welcomed and even celebrated the idea of more policemen stationed in poor neighborhoods.[56] On February 18, 1920, a columnist from the socialist newspaper *La Vanguardia* wrote: "If [the delegates] are concerned, as they say they are, with preventing crimes and restraining criminals in general, we welcome the congress and support its resolutions." Clarifying the role of the police, he said, "If the Congress will appoint the men to come to patrol our neighborhoods and protect its people, we support it in its entirety."[57] As this statement indicates, local populations hoped that the reforms to the police department would result in the creation of citywide security forces, ensuring safety for all residents of the capital.

Working-class communities complained about the prevalence of violence and theft in their neighborhoods and believed that the police department could be a critical ally in preventing these crimes. The columnist from *La Vanguardia* went on to clarify that the social disturbances of most concern in working-class neighborhoods were theft of property and physical assault. "Too long we have been victims of thieves . . . neighborhoods fill with violence," he stated.[58] While police administrators may have seen themselves at odds with the working class, local communities saw the relationship in a different light. In asking for increased patrols in their neighborhoods, members of the working class insisted on distinguishing themselves from criminals and that as citizens they should have equal access to state security forces.

When they believed that elite concerns about crime could mirror their own, the working class welcomed the police into their communities.[59] However, even amid this initial excitement, they remained suspicious of officers' intentions. The final sentences of an otherwise optimistic column in *La Vanguardia* warned: "If [the delegates] are working only to organize a system of espionage and the international persecution of men who are involved in the workers movement and politics, then we rescind approval."[60] Working-class periodicals, such as *La Tribuna Proletaria*, *La Vanguardia*, and *La Montaña*, expressed hopes that the summit would generate more patrols in their neighborhoods and reduce police corruption, but they were quickly disillusioned.[61] Attitudes toward the summit shifted even more when the public learned that administrators' goals for reform contrasted sharply with their own. In an article appearing in *La Montaña*, the editors had applauded the congress's "efforts to ensure the safety of Argentine citizens" when the conference began, but two days later complained: "This congress has no other point around which they unify except to persecute the workers for their character, intellectual currencies, and activities in economic struggle."[62] They further objected to the delegates' willingness to equate labor movements with violence or theft. "Here people who commit robbery and murder are the same as those people who want to make themselves a better life," they wrote critically.[63] Workers refuted elites' conflation of labor movements and crime and insisted that as citizens they too had the right to police resources.

Disappointment with the SAIPC undermined the legitimacy of a number of government institutions. An article in *La Tribuna Proletaria* questioned the bureaucrats' dedication to democratic institutions, raging, "Our government enacts increasingly violent actions and arbitrary laws that all serve as examples that the laws of our country are not meant to protect its citizens but to repress its workers."[64] In particular, the belief that police administrators were corrupt and had little interest in protecting their safety or property engendered resentment toward the police department as a whole. In a January 26 article, *La Vanguardia*, which days earlier had celebrated the possibility of expanding the police force, denounced the possibility that the police would increase security in working-class communities: "What will cure the 'disease' of radicalism will be equality, not government brutes roaming our streets."[65] Tensions between proletarian barrios and police officers were not inherent. Rather, as periodicals aptly pointed out, police administrators' decisions to allocate resources to political activities rather than street patrols served to further degrade officers' ability to prevent crime and further degraded relationships between the working class and the modernizing police department.

The decision of police administrators to provide ample services to wealthier areas reflects their attempts to contain some types of crime rather than eradicate them. While assigning police resources in this way limited crime in affluent neighborhoods, theft and violence flourished in poorer areas of the city. Furthermore, while members of the middle and upper class saw police officers as a daily representation of the state's desire to protect them and their property, members of the working class rarely saw police officers, who usually only appeared when breaking up strikes, putting down uprisings, or searching out suspects. Therefore, for the working class the uneven police presence served as a constant reminder of the state's repression and the unequal citizenship they held, not its ability to offer services. These tactics undermined the legitimacy of the police force among the working classes.[66]

Working-class periodicals had expressed excitement about the prospect of increased police presence in their neighborhoods. Although historians typically envision the police force as solely dedicated to control and punishment, some segments of the working class saw it as a social service. Allocating such a public resource fairly may have allowed the state to promote a sense of loyalty among workers under the pretense that it cared for the safety and protection of all citizens. Instead, by allowing crime to proliferate in working-class neighborhoods, police administrators undermined their own projects and increased animosity between the state and the working class. This allocation of police resources may have also reduced support for police projects among more affluent social groups. In their media outlets, voices from the middle class expressed a desire for the police to eradicate professional thieves in the city. However, by avoiding working-class neighborhoods, the police left the majority of the city unmonitored, creating easy escape routes and asylums for many suspects. Although reports of theft remained high in 1926, less than a quarter of them ended in the apprehension of a suspect. Finally, while statistics do not reveal the inner thinking of these administrators, the constant threat of urban vice provided them with a convenient specter that ensured their jobs and the power and prestige that accompanied them.[67]

Members of the middle class supported elite attempts to curtail labor movements and increase public order, but disagreed with the elite initiative to criminalize all immigrants and urban poor, insisting that reformers should focus on prosecuting thieves and violent criminals. The working class, on the other hand, sought police reforms that would help transform their newly obtained suffrage into economic and social inclusion. Insisting that police protection was their entitlement as citizens, workers pushed administrators to extend patrols into their neighborhood and allow for peaceful labor organizing.

POLICE OFFICERS' PERCEPTIONS OF CRIMINALITY AND CITIZENSHIP

An analysis of the views held by patrolmen in various neighborhoods provides further insights into the police department's underlying objectives and the sources of their shortcomings. The rank-and-file members of the police department, whose voices remain absent from the police conference or newspapers, played a critical role in determining how law enforcement projects played out. When criticizing the SAIPC, the socialist newspaper *La Crítica* suggested that the delegates "do not begin to know what it is like to work as a police officer on the street."[68] The article pointed out what many have ignored: the people who ran the police department had never worked as patrolmen.[69] In fact, the men who ran the department had little in common with the men who worked in it. Just as the general public understood crime differently from police administrators, so too did police officers. While this subject requires further investigation, a brief comparison of members of the police administration and regular officers underscores the stark differences between the two. Furthermore, considering the links police administrators perceived between criminality and immigrant communities, a statistical sketch of rates of arrest based on nationality suggests that members of the rank and file failed to internalize the agendas of administrators.

Police administrators came from wealthy, well-educated backgrounds. Every one of the men present—Police Chief González, Police Commissioner César Echeverry, Chief of Identification Eduardo Santiago, Director of the Ramon Colón School for Police Cadets Alfonso Hotron Fernández, and Chief of Social Order Duffey—were born in Argentina to families who had the financial resources to send them to college. None of them had ever worked as a patrolman. Instead, each had received his position by appointment. After graduating from the university with a degree in law, González and Duffey received appointments from the Minister of the Interior. Before taking his position as chief of police, González practiced and taught law in Buenos Aires and studied in some of the best schools in Europe. Santiago and Fernández had worked as bureaucrats in the Ministry of Agriculture and the Ministry of the Interior and were appointed by the chief of police. All of these men had university degrees.[70]

The education and background of the police department's administration stand in sharp contrast to the humble origins of many patrolmen.[71] While personal histories of the rank-and-file members of the police force have proven more difficult to locate, statistical data reveal that police officers were overwhelmingly native born. Though immigrants made up 63 percent of the population, only 71 of 3,604, or 1.9 percent, of the police force were born outside the country.[72] During the 1910s, police administrators advertised patrolmen positions in rural Buenos Aires, seeking to attract migrants looking for better wages. Although police work would have paid considerably more than wages as a farmhand, the higher cost of living in the city quickly erased surplus earnings. Rank-and-file members of the police force received low wages for long and strenuous work.[73] Entrance into the police training school required that candidates be between eighteen and thirty years of age and literate. However, of the thirty-six police commissioners who entered the force as regular cadets, only one had ever entered a university. This, coupled with the high turnover in the police force, indicates that the vast majority of men were young, usually in their twenties and early thirties.[74]

Although these members of the police force had different places of birth than the majority of people in the city, they had more in common with their fellow members of the working class than they did with the department's administration.[75] This fact was not lost on police administrators. In fact, as historian Sandra Gayol points out, higher-ups in the department often complained that the humble origins of patrolmen constituted the biggest obstacle in providing the capital with a well-functioning modern police force.[76]

The stark disparity between those people who created police projects and those who implemented them meant that in order to ensure the integrity of these reforms, men on the ground had to internalize, or at least be willing to enforce, elite ideas about what constituted crime and who fit the profile of a criminal. While a full analysis of the extent to which patrolmen internalized the administrators' rhetoric regarding the threatening nature of labor activism and the criminalization of immigrants is beyond the scope of this chapter, an examination of rates of arrest for foreign-born *porteños* indicates that police officers did not criminalize foreign-born residents of the city in the same way as did police administrators.

In their patrols, 1,922 officers made 2,506 arrests for public drunkenness in 1924. Native-born Argentines made up 831 of those arrests. Another 475, or 18.6 percent of arrests, were of people born in Spain. Italians made up another 410, or 16.3 percent of perpetrators. Other immigrant groups made up the remainder. Considering that in 1920 native-born Argentines constituted approximately 63 percent of the city's population, it would first appear that either Argentine natives drank less than immigrants or that officers were more likely to arrest immigrants. It also appears that police prejudices against Spanish and Italian immigrants, who composed 18 and 12 percent of the population, respectively, may have led officers to prosecute them more rigorously.[77]

However, these assumptions do not take into consideration the age and gender ratios in the city and their relationship to arrest rates. Of the 2,506 cases of public drunkenness in the city, men committed 88 percent. The majority also identified themselves as single. Furthermore, 73 percent of perpetrators declared occupations that would make them members of the working class. From these statistics, it appears that young, single, male members of the working class were the most common group to be arrested for public drunkenness. When considering that the waves of immigration coming to Argentina contained significantly more young male members who had working-class occupations, Spanish and Italian immigrant men were arrested at a rate proportional to their population in the city. Statistics for arrest for disorder, which could range from loud arguing to lewd language to public brawling, demonstrate a similar trend.[78]

The disproportionate rates of arrests of young men holding working-class occupations most likely resulted from both a higher number of young working-class men drinking and interacting within the public spaces of the city and preconceived ideas among police officers that working-class men were likely perpetrators of crime. These statistics, however, do not indicate that officers, despite their backgrounds and teachings, internalized their superiors' links between the immigrant community and criminality. While this statistical data cannot explain why police officers did not criminalize and prosecute foreign-born residents of the city in the way upper-class rhetoric directed, it does indicate a need to explore further how lower-ranking members of the state apparatus influenced larger projects intended to regulate working-class populations and control urban space.

CONCLUSIONS

The prevalence of crime and seeming inability of Buenos Aires's Policía de la Capital to foster a sense of legitimacy among the urban population has long been of interest to scholars.[79] In the last fifteen years, histories of the police, crime, and the criminal justice system in Latin America have emphasized the ways elites utilized discourses of science, medicine, and civilization to justify their expanding projects to survey, catalogue, and reform the behaviors and norms of the proletariat.[80] Many of these works, however, consider only elite discourse. Influenced by Foucauldian ideas of surveillance and control, these studies portray the liberal state as forever focused on their influence over workers' spaces and activities, with clashes arising when the poor resisted such intrusions.

However, this study contributes to a growing literature revealing a contrary pattern.[81] Utilizing political scientist Guillermo O'Donnell's notion of urban spaces as divided between blue zones, "where the state has a high degree of presences [and thereby] effectively sustains the rule of law and regulates behaviors," and "brown zones," where the state is virtually absent and the use of local sources of power pervades, this chapter has historicized a phenomenon that is well recognized in contemporary cities: an unswerving devotion of security forces to a perceived social threat—be it communism, drugs, or terror—and unequal allocation of public safety resources, serving as a powerful means of creating stigma and exclusion.[82] In doing so, this study has emphasized that the distrust between the urban populace and the government was frequently the result of unequal access to the benefits of modernizing projects and citizenship rights.[83]

This chapter has revealed that different conceptualizations of citizenship and criminality undermined the legitimacy of the police force as well as its ability to apprehend violent offenders and thieves. While administrators saw the police department as a critical tool to maintain social and economic hierarchies during a time of rapid demographic and political change, workers hoped that public security forces and an improved police department would help to expand their rights as citizens. Despite improvements in the technology of policing, increased funding of the police department, and police administrators' declared dedication to finding ways to preserve order within the city, during the 1920s residents of Buenos Aires reported growing feelings of danger, and officers proved less likely to apprehend suspects. Members of the middle class continued to express fear about the vices of the lower classes, and strikes continued to interrupt commerce in the city. Structural factors such as crowded living conditions, urban poverty, and a well-organized working class certainly contributed to Police Chief Elpidio González's failure to develop efficient means of "prevention and essential containment, but also . . . provide assistance under the auspices of peace, wellness, and justice."[84] However, as this chapter has shown, not only the uneven geographical distribution of police personnel but most significantly the divergence between police administrators' understandings of criminality and those of the middle or working classes undermined the success of their projects. In failing to make the prosecution of professional thieves and the eradication of urban crime a central platform of their reforms, police administrators lost middle-class support for their plans. By criminalizing labor movements, prosecuting immigrants, and failing to implement a stronger police presence within working-class neighborhoods, departmental bureaucrats also missed an opportunity to limit crime in urban spaces and alleviate tensions between the working class and the state. Finally, administrators failed to consider how their own employees' perceptions of crime might shape their ability to carry out their projects. As a result, members of the middle class lost enthusiasm for police projects, working-class *porteños* became increasingly hostile toward law enforcement agents on the ground, and police officers failed to carry out police initiatives.

NOTES

1. *La Nación* (Buenos Aires), February 20, 1920; *La Ultima Hora* (Buenos Aires), February 20, 1920; *La Argentina* (Buenos Aires), February 20, 1920; *La Razón* (Buenos Aires), February 20, 1920; *La Vanguardia* (Buenos Aires), February 20, 1920; quotation from Conferencia International Sudamericana de Policía (CISP, SAIPC in English), *Conferencia International Sudamericana de Policía: Argentina-Bolivia-Brasil-Chile-Paraguay-Perú-Uruguay Convenio y Actas* (Buenos Aires: 1920), 32.

2. Julia K. Blackwelder and Lyman Johnson, "Changing Criminal Patterns in Buenos Aires, 1890 to 1914," *Journal of Latin American Studies* 14, no. 2 (1982): 359–70.

3. Pablo Piccato, "Urbanistas, Ambulantes, and Mendigos: The Dispute for Urban Space in Mexico City, 1890–1930," in *Reconstructing Criminality in Latin America*, ed. Carlos Aguirre and Robert Buffington, 113–49 (Wilmington, DE: Scholarly Resources, 2000); Thomas Holloway, "Punishment in Nineteenth-Century Rio de Janeiro: Judicial Action as Police Practice," in Aguirre and Buffington, *Reconstructing Criminality in Latin America*, 85–112.

4. Eugenia Scarzanella, *Ni gringos ni indios: Inmigración, criminalidad y racismo en Argentina, 1890–1940* (Buenos Aires: Universidad Nacional de Quilmes Ediciones, 2002); Ricardo Salvatore, "Sobre el surgimiento del estado médico legal en la argentina [1890–1940]," *Estudios sociales* 20, no. 1 (2005): 81–114; Sandra Gayol, "Entre lo deseable y lo posible: Perfil de la policía de Buenos Aires en la segunda mitad del siglo XIX," *Estudios sociales* 10, no. 1 (2005): 123–38.

5. Diego Galeano, *Escritores, detectives y archivistas: La cultura policial en Buenos Aires, 1821–1910* (Buenos Aires: Teseo, 2009).

6. Osvaldo Barreneche, "De brava a dura: La policía de la provincia de Buenos Aires durante la primera mitad del siglo XX," *Cuadernos de antropología social* 32 (2010): 31–56; Laura Kalmanowiecki, "Origins and Applications of Political Policing in Argentina," *Latin American Perspectives* 27, no. 2 (2000): 36–56.

7. Like Pablo Piccato's work regarding Porfirian Mexico City and public policy studies regarding officers in major U.S. cities, this article points out the importance of patrolmen in shaping the administration of criminal justice as well as public perceptions of the state. Pablo Piccato, *City of Suspects: Crime in Mexico City, 1900–1931* (Durham, NC: Duke

University Press, 2001); Elizabeth Reuss-Ianni, *Two Cultures of Policing: Street Cops and Management Cops* (Livingston: Transaction, 1993): Steven Maynard-Moody and Michael Musheno, "Social Equities and Inequities in Practice: Street-Level Workers as Agents and Pragmatists," *Public Administration Review* 72 (2012): 16–23.

8. Nicolás Moreno, *Buenos Aires: Estudio critico de su población, 1536–1936* (Buenos Aires, 1939), 430–31.

9. David Rock, *Argentina 1516–1987: From Spanish Colonization to Alfonsin* (Berkeley: University of California Press, 1987), 167–72; Jose C. Moya, *Cousins and Strangers: Spanish Immigrants in Buenos Aires, 1850–1930* (Berkeley: University of California Press, 1998), 24.

10. James Scobie, *Buenos Aires: Plaza to Suburb, 1870–1910* (New York: Oxford University Press, 1974), 13–66.

11. For the number of strikes in the capital, see Ronald Munck, "Cycles of Class Struggle and the Making of the Working Class in Argentina, 1890–1920," *Journal of Latin American Studies* 19, no. 1 (1987), 34. For a discussion of labor activism in the early twentieth century, see Rock, *Argentina*, 172–77; David Rock, "Machine Politics in Buenos Aires and the Argentine Radical Party, 1912–1930," *Journal of Latin American Studies* 4, no. 2 (1972): 233–56; Sandra McGee, "The Visible and Invisible Liga Patriótica Argentina, 1919–1928: Gender Roles and the Right Wing," *Hispanic American Historical Review* 64, no. 2 (1984): 233–58.

12. For shifts in the political system, see Richard Walter, "Municipal Politics and Government in Buenos Aires, 1918–1930," *Journal of Interamerican Studies and World Affairs* 16, no. 2 (1974): 173–97; David Rock, *State Building and Political Movements in Argentina, 1860–1916* (Stanford, CA: Stanford University Press, 2002), 193–216. These members of the urban middle class represented a specific group both in terms of their geographic location within the city of Buenos Aires and their desire to carve out a sphere of influence within the state.

13. On the lessening of strikes during World War I, see Richard Walter, "Municipal Politics," 181. For La Semana Trágica, see David Rock, "Lucha civil en la Argentina: La Semana Trágica de enero de 1919," *Desarrollo Económico* 11, no. 42–44 (1971–72): 165–215.

14. *La Nación* (Buenos Aires), February 19, 1920; *La Vanguardia* (Buenos Aires), February 22, 1920; Laura Kalmanowiecki, "Police, Politics and Repression in Modern Argentina," in Aguirre and Buffington, *Reconstructing Criminality in Latin America*, 199–202.

15. Galeano, "Las conferencias sudamericanas de policías y la problemática de los 'delincuentes viajeros,' 1905–1920," in *La policía en perspectiva histórica: Argentina y Brasil (del siglo XIX a la actualidad)* (Centro de Estudios Latinoamericanos, Universidad Nacional de San Martín, 2009), 14–18.

16. CISP, *Conferencia International*, 38.

17. Ibid., 42.

18. The criminalization of labor activity has been widely noted by scholars. See Julia Rodrí-
    guez, *Civilizing Argentina: Science, Medicine, and the Modern State* (Chapel Hill: Uni-
    versity of North Carolina Press, 2006), 144; Juan Suriano, *Anarquistas: Cultura política
    y libertaria en Buenos Aires, 1890–1910* (Buenos Aires: Manantial, 2001); Sandra McGee,
    "The Visible and Invisible Liga Patriótica Argentina"; Kalmanowiecki, "Origins and Ap-
    plications"; Diego Galeano, "En nombre de la seguridad: Lecturas sobre policía y for-
    mación estatal," *Cuestiones de Sociología: Revista de Estudios Sociales*, no. 4 (Winter 2007):
    102–25.

19. CISP, *Conferencia International*, 88.

20. Diego Galeano also notes Argentina's growing concentration on political policing in the
    decades between the Conferencia Internacional de Policía in 1905 and the Conferencia
    Internacional Sudamericana de Policía in 1920. Galeano, "Las conferencias sudamerica-
    nas de policías," 18–19.

21. Ibid., 47.

22. Ibid., 122.

23. Ibid., 66.

24. Kalmanowiecki, "Origins and Applications."

25. Ibid., 72.

26. Ibid., 73.

27. Ibid., 70.

28. Rock, *Argentina*, 172–81.

29. Recent studies of fingerprinting and the development of police technology include Julia
    Rodriguez, "South Atlantic Crossings: Fingerprints, Science, and the State in Turn-of-
    the-Century Argentina," *American Historical Review* 109, no. 2 (2004): 387–416; Kris-
    tin Ruggiero, "Fingerprinting and the Argentine Plan for Universal Identification in the
    Late Nineteenth and Early Twentieth Centuries," in *Documenting Individual Identity:
    The Development of State Practices in the Modern World*, ed. Jane Caplan and John Tor-
    pey, 184–96 (Princeton, NJ: Princeton University Press, 2001); Mercedes García Ferrari,
    "El rol de Juan Vucetich en el surgimiento transnacional de tecnologías de identificación
    biométricas a principios del siglo XX," *Nuevo Mundo Mundos Nuevos*, no. 14 (2014).

    Most recently Diego Galeano and Mercedes García Ferrari have situated these devel-
    opments in the context of international policing in South America. Galeano and Ferrari,
    "El bertillonage en el espacio Atlántico sudamericano," *Criminocorpus* (online).

30. CISP, *Conferencia Internacional*, 144.

31. Ibid., 73–74, 81–83.

32. Pablo Piccato used a similar methodological approach in his study of patrolmen. Piccato,
    City of Suspects, 43–45.

33. All information throughout this section about the assignment of police officers comes
    from Rafael Bielsa, *Cuestiones de administración municipal* (Buenos Aires: J. Lajouane,

1930). Statistics on arrest rates come from Departamento de Policía de Buenos Aires, *Boletín mensual de estadística* 7, no. 55–68 (1922): 114–17.

34. Scobie, *Buenos Aires*, 24–62, 114–59; Rock, *Argentina*, 122–26; Richard Walter, *Politics and Urban Growth in Buenos Aires, 1910–1940* (New York: Cambridge University Press, 1993), 12, 23; Charles Sargent, *The Spatial Evolution of Greater Buenos Aires, Argentina, 1870–1930* (Tempe: Center for Latin American Studies, Arizona State University, 1974); Kindon T. Meik, "Disease and Hygiene in the Construction of a Nation: The Public Sphere, Public Space, and the Private Domain in Buenos Aires, 1871–1910" (PhD diss., Florida International University, 2011).

35. Moya, *Cousins and Strangers*, 128–44; Leandro Gutierrez and Juan Suriano, "Workers' Housing and Living Conditions in Buenos Aires, 1880–1930," in *Essays in Argentine Labor History*, ed. Jeremy Adelman, 35–51 (Oxford: Macmillan Press, 1992), 39–42.

36. Scobie, *Buenos Aires*, 70–113. *Buenos Aires, Censo General de Población*, 1909, 92.

37. Scobie, *Buenos Aires*, 142–59; Adolfo Carranza, *Argentinas* (Buenos Aires: G. Mendesky é Hijos, 1913), 114.

38. Scobie, *Buenos Aires*, 142–59; Sargent, *Spatial Evolution*, 62–65; Lilian E. Elliot, *The Argentina of Today* (London, 1926), 31; Walter, *Politics and Urban Growth*, 9, 24.

39. Contrasts between the wealthy sectors of the city and the poor come from Scobie, *Buenos Aires*, 112–59. Jose Moya also notes the lack of city services outside the urban center. Moya, *Cousins and Strangers*, 128–43.

40. Population density: Buenos Aires, *Censo General de Población*, 1887, 37; Buenos Aires, *Censo General de Población*, 1909, 77.

41. Dirección General de Estadística Municipal, *Anuario estadístico de la Ciudad de Buenos Aires* (Buenos Aires: Imprenta y Litografía, 1920), 13–19.

42. Ibid., 20; Bielsa, *Cuestiones de administración municipal*, 193. Statistics on arrest rates come from Departamento de Policía de Buenos Aires, *Boletín mensual de estadística* 7, no. 55–68 (1924), 114–17.

43. Ibid.

44. Ibid.

45. My understanding of the ways that police officers interpret crime has been heavily influenced by Pablo Piccato's studies of Mexico City in the first years of the twentieth century, particularly Piccato, "Urbanistas, Ambulantes, and Mendigos," 113–48, and *City of Suspects*, 40–45.

46. Departamento de Policía de Buenos Aires, *Boletín mensual de estadística*, 114–17.

47. Ibid., 119–20.

48. Ibid., 132–40.

49. William Garrett Jr., "From Reading to Reality: Print Culture, Collective identity, and Nationalism in Uruguay and Argentina" (PhD diss., University of North Carolina–Chapel Hill, 2007).

50. *La Epoca* (Buenos Aires), February 20, 1920; *La Nación* (Buenos Aires), February 20, 1920.

51. *La Prensa* (Buenos Aires), February 23, 1920.

52. Ibid.

53. *El Diario* (Buenos Aires), February 22, 1920.

54. *La Argentina* (Buenos Aires), February 26, 1920.

55. *La Nación* (Buenos Aires), February 26, 1920.

56. Pablo Piccato's work on Mexico City stands as a model for interrogating tensions between modernizing police departments and rapidly growing urban populations. Piccato demonstrates that neighborhoods often saw city patrolmen as allies against theft or violence and that local officers often depended on neighborhood allies to report crime and help them apprehend suspects. Piccato, *City of Suspects*, 33–44.

57. *La Nación* (Buenos Aires), February 26, 1920.

58. *La Vanguardia* (Buenos Aires), February 20, 1920.

59. Ibid.

60. Ibid.

61. Garrett, "From Reading to Reality."

62. *La Montaña* (Buenos Aires), February 21, 23, 1920.

63. Ibid., February 23, 1920.

64. *La Tribuna Proletaria* (Buenos Aires), February 22, 1920.

65. *La Vanguardia* (Buenos Aires), February 21, 1920.

66. A similar argument appears in Joseph J. Vargas, *Hell's Kitchen and the Battle for Urban Space: Class Struggle and Urban Reform in New York City, 1894–1914* (New York: Monthly Review Press, 2013), 106–8.

67. Departamento de Policía de Buenos Aires, *Boletín mensual de estadística*, 114–17.

68. *Crítica* (Buenos Aires), February 26, 1920.

69. Recent scholarship has given more weight to the differences between police patrolmen and officials in Buenos Aires. Diego Galeano, "'Caídos en cumplimiento del deber': Notas sobre la construcción del heroísmo policial," in *Mirada (de) uniforme: Historia y crítica de la razón policial*, ed. Diego Galeano and Gregorio Kaminsky (Buenos Aires: Teseo e Universidade Nacional Rio Negro, 2011), 191–92. Marcos Bretas makes this point a central feature of his history of Rio de Janeiro in the Imperial period. Bretas, "La policía de la capital del imperio Brasil," in Galeano and Kaminsky, *Mirada (de) uniforme*, 87–110. Pablo Piccato also makes this point explicit in his earlier study of Mexico City. Piccato, *City of Suspects*, 42–45.

70. Profiles of delegates appear in *La Prensa* (Buenos Aires), February 19, 1920; *La Nación*, (Buenos Aires), February 20, 1920; *La Prensa* (Buenos Aires), February 21, 1920.

71. In chapter 5 of this volume, Bonnie A. Lucero identifies a similar trend in turn-of-the-twentieth-century Cuba.

72. Moya, *Cousins and Strangers*, 489. Kalmanowiecki, "Police, Politics, and Repression in Modern Argentina," 195–202.

73. Diego Galeano also notes the low pay, long hours, and minimal prestige that patrolmen received. Galeano, "Caídos en cumplimiento del deber," 191–92.

74. Ibid., 191–93.

75. Bielsa, *Cuestiones de administración municipal*, 193.

76. Sandra Gayol, "Entre lo deseable y lo posible: Perfil de la policía de Buenos Aires en la segunda mitad del siglo XIX," *Estudios sociales* 10, no. 1 (2005): 123–38.

77. Departamento de Policía de Buenos Aires, *Boletín mensual de estadística*, 114–22.

78. Departamento de Policía de Buenos Aires, *Boletín mensual de estadística*, 122.

79. Leopoldo López, *Reseña histórica de la policía en Buenos Aires* (Buenos Aires: Imprenta y Encuadernación de la Policía, 1911); Enrique Fentanes, *Cuatrocientos años de Policía de Buenos Aires* (Buenos Aires: Biblioteca Policial, 1981); Julia Kirk Blackwelder, "Urbanization, Crime, and Policing: Buenos Aires 1880–1914," in *The Problem of Order in Changing Societies: Essays on Crime and Policing in Argentina and Uruguay*, ed. Lyman L. Johnson, 65–88 (Albuquerque: University of New Mexico Press, 1990); Kristin Ruggiero, "Passion, Perversity, and the Pace of Justice in Argentina in the Turn of the Last Century," in *Crime and Punishment in Latin America: Law and Society Since Late Colonial Times*, ed. Ricardo D. Salvatore, Carlos Aguirre, and Gilbert Joseph, 211–33 (Durham, NC: Duke University Press, 2001); Lila Caimari, "Remembering Freedom: Life as Seen from the Prison Cell (Buenos Aires Province 1930–1950)," in Salvatore, Aguirre, and Joseph, *Crime and Punishment in Latin America*, 391–414. On the failure of Buenos Aires's police department to fight corruption or build legitimacy, see Kalmanowiecki, "Police, Politics, and Repression in Modern Argentina," and Daniel M. Brinks, "Informal Institutions and the Rule of Law: The Judicial Response to State Killing in Buenos Aires and Sao Paulo in the 1990s," *Comparative Politics* 36, no. 1 (2003): 1–19.

80. Rodríguez, *Civilizing Argentina*; Ricardo D. Salvatore, "Criminology, Prison Reform, and the Buenos Aires Working Class," *Journal of Interdisciplinary History* 23, no. 2 (1992): 279–99; Donna J. Guy, *Sex and Danger in Buenos Aires: Prostitution, Family, and Nation in Argentina* (Lincoln: University of Nebraska Press, 1991). For similar arguments in Brazil and Peru, see Thomas Holloway, *Policing Rio de Janeiro: Repression and Resistance in a Nineteenth-Century City* (Stanford, CA: Stanford University Press, 1993); Carlos Aguirre, *The Criminals of Lima and Their Worlds: The Prison Experience, 1850–1935* (Durham, NC: Duke University Press, 2005).

81. Recent studies have begun to challenge views of the liberal state as entirely interventionist. See, for example, Nara Milanich, *Children of Fate: Childhood, Class, and the State in Chile, 1850–1930* (Durham, NC: Duke University Press, 2009), introduction.

82. Guillermo O'Donnell, "On the State, Democratization, and Some Conceptual Problems: A Latin American View with Glances at Some Post-Communist Countries," *World Development* 21, no. 8 (1993): 1357.

83. Pablo Piccato, *City of Suspects*, 34–45; Alexandra Mina Stern, "Nationalism on the Line: Masculinity, Race, and the Creation of the U.S. Border Patrol, 1910–1940," in *Continental Crossroads: Remapping U.S. Borderlands History*, ed. Samuel Truett and Elliot Young, 299–324 (Durham, NC: Duke University Press, 2004); Miguel Castells, *The City and the Grassroots: A Cross-Cultural Theory of Urban Social Movements* (Berkeley: University of California Press, 1983); Teresa Meade, *"Civilizing" Rio: Reform and Resistance in a Brazilian City, 1889–1930* (University Park: Pennsylvania State University Press, 1999).

84. CISP, *Conferencia International*, 38.

7

PROSECUTING DEVIANCE

֎

Sexual Violence in Postrevolutionary Veracruz, 1920–1950

GREGORY J. SWEDBERG

O N NOVEMBER 30, 1939, in Cordoba, Veracruz, Carmen Huerta,[1] married and eighteen years of age, recounted to legal officials the beating and rape she had suffered three days earlier. According to her testimony, she was on her way home after bringing lunch to her husband, who worked as a campesino near Huatusquito. On an isolated rural path she encountered a man she claimed she did not know, Francisco Lopez, who grabbed her arm and threw the basket that had held her husband's lunch to the ground. In the struggle, Huerta stated, no one could hear her screams for help, and Lopez finally overpowered her, put his hand over her mouth, tore her clothes, and raped her.[2]

Huerta reported the assault to Fernando Dominguez, presidente de la junta vigilancia, who immediately ordered a search for Lopez and apprehended him quickly. Lopez was confined to prison while evidence was gathered. According to Dominguez, Lopez was known to be a "bad element" in the community, as he had committed robberies and assaults in the past, mostly against women. Lopez, who was twenty-four years old and illiterate, testified that he did in fact encounter Huerta on his way back from "the city" to his home near Huatusquito. He explained that he caught up to "a woman" who was walking ahead of him who carried a basket. He approached Huerta and took her hand, and when she pulled away she tripped and fell, breaking the basket and tearing her clothes. He maintained that he did not beat or rape her.

The evidence from the doctor, in part, supported Lopez's account. The cut that she sustained on her cheek was not severe (would heal within fifteen days), and there was no evidence of semen or forced penetration. The doctor also noted that she was not a virgin, an obvious conclusion since she was in fact married.[3] After weighing the accounts, Judge Efraín Angeles Sentíes ruled that there was not ample evidence to charge Lopez with rape.[4] Instead, based on Lopez's testimony that he had accosted Huerta and probably on his previous criminal record as well, the judge claimed that a charge of *atentado al pudor* (a lewd act committed without the person's consent that does not result in rape) was appropriate.

Many scholars have explored sexual violence in both the colonial and republican periods, but few studies have explored regions outside of Mexico City during the immediate postrevolutionary era. This chapter juxtaposes emerging revolutionary penal laws and how officials in Veracruz, Mexico, interpreted and applied these laws in specific cases of sexual abuse following the Mexican Revolution (1910–20). I argue that despite nascent feminist movements and progressive legal changes, which appeared to elevate women's status in society, the postrevolutionary period shows greater continuity with, rather than a complete break from, colonial and early republican views of sexual violence, a finding that matches with the narrative of Cuba between empires in Bonnie A. Lucero's chapter in this volume. Moreover, some cases reveal the difficulties that single mothers faced when litigating on behalf of their children, suggesting a clear intersection of gender and class in cases of sexual abuse. The outcomes indicate that victims, or the families of the victims, could attain a favorable verdict, but required proof of virginity, honorability, and chastity—qualities presumed to be the domain of the wealthy.

Poor women's legal protection depended, in part, on how officials viewed cases of sexual assault among the poor and working classes. Concurrently, new laws and civil codes empowered women through husbands and fathers, but this came at a price. The state, in its drive to modernize Mexico, embarked on extensive scrutiny of women's bodies, for which Veracruz governor Adalberto Tejeda (1920–24 and 1928–32) was a champion.[5] Legal officials associated sexual violence with the working classes, whose "morality and customs" had become relaxed as a result of poverty, urbanization, and industrialization. Consequently, Tejeda supported eugenics, sterilization (Veracruz had the only sterilization law in Mexico), sex education, prohibition of alcohol, and the eradication of the influence of the Catholic Church, which he believed created many of Veracruz's social ills.[6] Tejeda's 1932 Civil Code codified equal rights between husbands and wives but also stipulated that racial improvement and eugenics would be implemented "for the good of the veracruzano proletariat."[7] Tejeda's perceptions of the proletariat were at times reflected in legal proceedings. As an Orizaba attorney noted when presenting a case of spousal violence in 1939, "certain social classes" are accustomed to this type of abuse.[8] Women's demands for equality during and following the revolution and subsequent legal changes clashed with the continued perception of poor or working-class women as morally suspect and prone to sexual attack. Despite the progressive rhetoric, women's rights in Veracruz, much like in Yucatán, were still predicated on the perception of the victim's honorability and their ability to prove virginity and chastity.[9]

The state of Veracruz was home to a large rural and indigenous population, yet no references to ethnicity appear in any of the cases I explored for this chapter, which is not surprising. The postrevolutionary discourse of inclusivity and unity (a mestizo nation) trumped ethnic categorizations despite their cultural persistence. Notwithstanding the silences, the intersection of class and ethnicity did not fade following the violent phase of the revolution, despite efforts to cast Mexico's indigenous past in a more favorable light. Marjorie Becker and Claudio Lomnitz have argued that postrevolutionary Indigenismo upheld *mestizaje* as ideal, pointing the way toward a new Mexico removed from its barbaric and ignorant past.[10] Instituting clear judicial processes and laws was part of this modernizing project.

In my research, litigation of rape was not common, which squares with much of the scholarship on sexual violence in postindependence Latin America. Police officials and defense attorneys sought to undermine the veracity of the victims' claims and forced them to recount their loss of honor.[11] Therefore the legal process placed women (especially poorer women who may have lacked education and resources) at a disadvantage. In addition, the reputation of the victim, her family, her social class, and the witnesses who testified often determined the outcome of sexual abuse cases.[12] The increased reliance on medical inspection of a woman's body was also probably a deterrent to reporting incidents of rape. Medical inspection became increasingly common in the 1920s, although the inspection of women's bodies (most notably prostitutes) was a hallmark of the Porfirian positivist era.[13] With the advent of new scientific methods, doctors were called to testify about the condition of a girl's or woman's hymen to determine both the virginity of the plaintiff and the veracity of their claims.[14] This was often problematic because doctors and judges often did not take into consideration that a woman's hymen could have been torn in other ways and that simply examining the condition of the hymen could not reveal how and when she had been "deflowered."[15]

The cases also reveal the voices of the plaintiff, defendant, and witnesses as filtered through court officials and attorneys, whose recounting of the facts were informed by their own cultural biases pertaining to class, ethnicity, and gender during the consolidation phase of the Mexican Revolution.[16] Court officials conducted cases orally while a legal secretary processed the testimony in writing. Transcripts were chronological following the order of events and stages of the legal proceedings.[17] In the hundreds of criminal cases that I examined in the Archivo General del Estado de Veracruz (AGEV), only thirty-two pertained to rape or *estupro* (twenty-one estupro and eleven rape). Two cases specifically addressed rape of a female adult. Judges ruled on behalf of the plaintiffs in twenty-three cases, against them in five, and four were indeterminate.

Some municipalities, due to storage and other constraints, transferred their penal records (juzgado de primera instancia) to the AGEV. In the cases I examined, there was either tremendous detail or simply the part of the trial record with the ruling. In some instances the record indicated who brought charges, while in others it is not clear. In at least six of the cases, the mother of the daughter brought charges, which would indicate that the father was not present. Fathers, with masculine authority, usually filed the charges. Estupro rarely was litigated because an agreement was usually reached between the parties involved, which commonly entailed marriage or payment to the victim's family.[18] My research indicates that when it was litigated, the court often sided with the victim's family. The percentage of victories in this sample may seem unusual as much of the research on sexual violence indicates that women and girls were at a disadvantage in a legal system that favored men.[19] But the details of the cases reveal complexities that extend well beyond court rulings. Many of the charges were reduced, and in some instances the men or boys admitted that they had had sexual relations, making it easier for the judge to reach a determination. Moreover, the burden of proof in these cases always disproportionately fell on the woman's or girl's family.

The litigants in the cases I examined were largely (when mentioned) poor or working class. These cases, while not entirely conclusive, provide insight into the intersection between a culture that continued to associate women's value with their honor and public reputation and the challenges that families confronted (especially single mothers) if they decided to seek legal recourse on behalf of their daughters. This chapter builds on research conducted in other regions of Latin America and provides insight into the difficulties single mothers faced in sexual abuse cases, which have received little scholarly attention.

Many scholars have noted the partial openings that the revolution created for women. New laws advanced women's protection in the workplace and the family, while feminist movements pushed for women's suffrage and legal equality. However, Mexican penal law and the actions of police continued to predicate women's legal protection on public reputation and often viewed cases of sexual assault as the inevitable degradation of working-class life, mirroring cultural perceptions in other regions of Latin America.[20] Reputation, familial stability, honor, and the patrimony of the family took precedence over addressing the physical and emotional pain associated with sexual violence.[21] The following section delves into how women's sexuality, class, and gender roles impacted laws pertaining to sexual violence.

WOMEN'S BODIES AND THE LAW

Following the Mexican Revolution, legal processes and cultural norms continued to base a woman's honor (or *honra*, public perception of honor) on virginity and chastity. Therefore, penal codes continued to stipulate that honesty and chastity were vital in determining culpability in cases involving rape and especially estupro. Under Spanish colonial law, estupro (from the Latin *stuprum*, which means to disgrace or defile) was defined as an act of sexual intercourse with a virgin that involved seduction or deceit.[22] Because girls were part of the family patrimony (in the republican period as well), the accused could marry the victim or provide compensation.[23] Colonial law and codes of honor survived into the republican period and shaped Mexico's first penal code. In 1831, a committee charged with drafting a criminal code divided criminality into two categories. The first pertained to crimes against security, order, and "tranquility," while the second addressed personal safety, good name, property, or honor. In 1835, Veracruz became the first state to enact a criminal code that addressed crimes against "honor."[24] The outcome of litigation involving sexual abuse or seduction (crimes involving honor) was often determined by virginity and public reputation.[25]

During the second half of the nineteenth century, reform-minded liberals introduced new penal codes that were supposed to erode the last vestiges of "barbarism and fanaticism" associated with colonial Mexico. Veracruz's Penal Code of 1896, based largely on the 1871 Federal Penal Code, stated that sexual assault was a crime against "the order of families, public morality, and good customs," and as a result, men who committed such acts should be confined to prison.[26] However, the introduction of protective legislation spoke more to the concerns about family stability and honor than violence against women. State-led efforts to protect women and children emerged largely from scientific research that increasingly noted the importance of motherhood to the stability and health of children. Officials underscored the dangers working women and children faced due to disease and the toxic effects of hard labor. These conditions undermined their reproductive role, which was vital to the stability and prosperity of the nation.[27] Working women (most who labored as seamstresses, domestics, and laundresses) were heads of the household and also confronted the problems associated with child care. The challenges working women faced in protecting their daughters coupled with men's "urges" could make it difficult to attain legal recourse if, in fact, a charge of sexual abuse went to court, not to mention the stress and economic consequences for women.

Kathryn Sloan notes in her research on nineteenth-century Oaxaca that a girl's sexual purity in cases of deflowering was vital to determining honorability.[28] This persisted well into the twentieth century, as revised labor laws and those concerning the family reflected the state's increased concern for the welfare of Mexican women and children and their potential contribution to the state's postrevolutionary modernization project. These initiatives were, in part, grounded in a nineteenth-century positivist ideology of order and progress, vestiges of colonialism that underscored women's probity and modesty, and postrevolutionary philosophy that emphasized the importance of women's education, motherhood, and community activism.[29] Porfirian education minister Justo Sierra noted that education would prepare women for the home. "She will be the companion and collaborator of man in the formation of the family," which Sierra argued perpetuates the "creation of the nation."[30] Sierra's prescription reflected late nineteenth-century sentiments that centered on reforming the poorer classes in Mexican society, many of whom were also indigenous. Porfirian criminologist Carlos Roumagnac posited theories of criminal behavior that reinforced elite ideas about the degeneracy of the lower classes and their propensity to commit criminal acts.[31]

DEBATING LAW AND MORALITY

Following the Mexican Revolution, laws pertaining to criminality again emerged as a source of debate. In 1925, President Plutarco Elías Calles created revision committees to reform Mexico's Federal Penal Code. Positivist scholars such as José Angel Ceniceros and Miguel Macedo believed that criminal acts such as sexual abuse were pervasive in all societies and that social and cultural factors informed criminal behavior.[32] As a result, the punishment should fit the individual and not the crime. However, this theory had far-reaching implications. Positivists insisted on attaining a better understanding of who would commit certain crimes. Positivist and legal reformer José Almaraz led the charge for a social Darwinist perspective that called for the protection of society from those who might threaten the social order whether they had committed crimes or not.[33] This meant targeting citizens who might become criminals, such as vagrants and alcoholics. The 1929 Federal Penal Code reflected these changes and produced a firestorm of debate. Two years later, state officials reformed the penal code so as to protect society from dangerous criminals, yet also provide citizens protection from arbitrary arrest. The 1931 Penal Code also gave judges greater discretionary power and allowed them to consider social and personal circumstances in the sentencing phase of the trial.[34]

The flexibility in the new penal code also expanded the paternal role of judges. Judges were able to use their discretionary power to take into consideration the background of the criminal, his or her social circumstances, and the likelihood that this person would commit another crime. Judges increasingly became paternal figures who presided over Mexico's expanded surveillance of social and family life. The new penal code balanced the state's desire to crack down on crime with the social realities of Mexican society, to placate both modernists and traditionalists.[35] Judges no longer adhered to mandatory sentencing of sexual offenders if they believed that there were mitigating circumstances. When the code was adopted in Veracruz in 1932, Tejeda explained the partial rejection of positivist criminology that derided pure retribution as a method of reform:

The social attitude with respect to delinquency and crime, modified in this body of law, considers that delinquency is like a social pathological problem, which should not be a reason simply for vindication and punishment. In this way the penal code postulates principles and norms of defense that separate it from the old punitive conception of simple punishment and repression.[36]

This perhaps explains the relaxation of criminal codes pertaining to sexual abuse, as sentences for all forms of sexual assault were reduced in the new penal code.[37]

The theories of international "experts" on women's sexuality also contributed to how lawmakers and citizens understood sexual violence. The work of Césare Lombroso, Richard von Krafft-Ebing, José Ingenieros, and Havelock Ellis, although differing in some respects, maintained that women, and certainly girls, were susceptible to immoral influences.[38] Ingenieros, for example, was a noted champion of women's rights, but he also argued that inequalities between men and women were natural, undeniable, and as a result moral.[39] While reformers underscored women's potential as national educators and moralizers, scientists continued to make a case for biological differences that confirmed women's weakness and corruptibility.[40] Researchers claimed that women's cranial shape or menstrual cycles predisposed them to degeneracy. Using emotion rather than reason made them unfit for dangerous and masculine responsibilities and made them susceptible to moral corruption.[41] These ideas meshed with the vestiges of Spanish and Porfirian law as well as with regional realities in Mexico that shaped how legal officials and citizens understood rape and estupro. Educational and social reform during the 1920s and 1930s also addressed officials' growing concerns that the postrevolutionary state's anticlericalism undermined morality. Reformers such as education secretary José Vasconcelos (1920–24) believed that women could extend their maternal influence from the family into the classroom.[42] Therefore thousands of women became teachers following Mexico's revolution in order to instill postrevolutionary values in young minds. With proper guidance, women could carry the values of sobriety, hard work, and devotion into the family and the classroom.

However, sex education became part of a much larger debate over girls' morality. Patience Schell explains that feminine modesty was a concern for the Ministry of Public Education, which thwarted efforts to educate young girls about sex. This stood in sharp contrast with the position of the Department of Public Health, which maintained that young women "did not realize their virginity was threatened and, according to social workers, became prostitutes as a result."[43] This was an affront to middle-class sensibilities, which continued to maintain the salience of girls' morality and women's familial example. Similar to the late colonial period, girls' perceived reputation could either undergird or undermine their legal defense in cases of estupro. This represents a clash between a culture that was reticent to expand women's sexual education and state officials who believed that some form of instruction was necessary to prevent young girls from falling prey to sexual desire or corrupting forces.

Clearly the revolution did not erode cultural perceptions that women could also corrupt men. In 1925, Secretary of Defense General Joaquin Amaro noted that the *soldaderas* were "the main cause of vice, diseases, and disorder," and he barred them from the barracks.[44] The transgressive behavior of the soldaderas (women who travelled with revolutionary combatants and at times took up arms, thus locating themselves in masculine spaces) underscored men's seeming inability to control themselves. So while postrevolutionary reformers sought to modernize patriarchy in ways that did not condone sexual violence, they also continued to affirm women's ability to tempt and corrupt men. In so doing, they set up a duality that was difficult for women to navigate.[45] As former Zapatista Antonio Díaz Soto y Gama noted in 1919:

> Is it not painful for all Mexicans to see the low depths to which our women have fallen? I admire the woman in two forms———rather, I admire her in one form but understand that the woman has two roles: to provide pleasure, a very humble role but one that appeals to men because we are all sinners, and a high role, that of bearing the future generations and in that capacity the woman is the most superior being, the most sanctified of all, the mother.[46]

This double standard trapped women in a culture that often portrayed women as sexual objects for men's pleasure while demanding that they remain honorable and chaste. While state officials such as Tejeda or Aguilar in postrevolutionary Veracruz did not condone sexual violence and sought to reform perceptions of women as merely "beasts of pleasure," they also were slow to encroach on men's authority to control women sexually.[47] The next sections will examine the implementation of laws in cases of sexual abuse.

LITIGATING SEXUAL ABUSE

Most cases of sexual abuse did not see the inside of a police station, not to mention a courtroom. In Pablo Piccato's research on Mexico City, he notes that sexual crimes often were not litigated because officials did not recognize sexual violence as violent in nature. In addition, family members often did not view forced sexual intercourse as a form of violence.[48] In regions such as Veracruz, officials associated sexual violence with poor and uneducated social classes as evidenced by Tejeda's observations at the beginning of this chapter. When cases did reach a courtroom, social class was indeed a factor. It was far easier to dismiss charges based on the presumption that the lower classes had a propensity for violence, due to their poverty and lack of education. In the case of marital violence in Orizaba in 1939 mentioned earlier, the attorney defending the husband's actions argued that there were women who "are emotionally malad-justed and do not resent the blows of a brutal husband. These women can be perfectly calm and then suddenly explosive, leading to fleeting violent encounters which are common among certain social classes."[49] The following case demonstrates how many single or widowed mothers in Veracruz not only struggled against public perceptions of the poorer classes' assumed propensity for violence and immorality, but also the economic demands of meeting their families' needs.

On October 24, 1930, a criminal case was filed in Orizaba (juzgado de primera instancia) against Marcelino Gomez for estupro and atentado al pudor of his niece Galinda Villa.[50] The mother of the young girl, Antonia Villa, claimed that when her older daughter, Claudia, returned home late in the afternoon, she found her uncle (Gomez) in bed with her ten-year-old sister. In the trial record, Villa stated that she had left Galinda in Gomez's care while she and her oldest daughter went to work. Gomez's profession is not mentioned, although the trial record notes that he had friends in the municipal government. Villa, whose husband had died several years ear-lier, worked as domestic servant in Orizaba, and her daughter made tortillas to help support the family. Villa also had a third daughter who was at church during the time of the incident. Late that afternoon, Claudia and the victim, Galinda, rushed to the home where their mother was working and described what had happened. In riveting detail, Villa recounted the traumatic crime. "He threw her [Galinda] onto the bed, undid his trousers, placed his right hand over her mouth so she could not scream, and placed his penis between her legs while she struggled in pain to free herself."[51] That same evening Villa took her daughter to the hospital and informed the police.[52] Police then arrested Gomez pending criminal charges. Under these circumstances, if the state found Gomez guilty, he could face up to six years in prison.[53]

In the case against Gomez, the court heard evidence from witnesses and a doc-tor against the defendant. Gomez denied the charges and claimed that it was in fact Galinda, whom he said was thirteen or fourteen years old, who tried to seduce him.[54] Such a defense was logical because, according to Veracruz's penal codes, the sentence was not as severe if the girl was at least fourteen years old and if it could be proven that she was not "honest." Gomez explained that Galinda initiated sexual contact and deliberately tried to arouse him. Gomez's attorney, in graphic detail, explained that the defendant had been alone with Galinda when she "began to play with the defen-dant, passing her hand over his genitals three times thereby exciting him."[55] Gomez then testified that when he gave in to her overtures, Galinda's sister interrupted them before they could have intercourse. He claimed the girl was not as young as Villa stated, that she initiated sexual contact, and that he had done nothing wrong because they did not have sex. Galinda's sister Claudia, however, testified that when she came home the door to the bedroom was open. When she entered the room she found her uncle in bed with her sister who was crying. "He [Gomez] immediately stood up and put on his trousers. When I asked him what he was doing he did not answer me."[56]

The age of the victim also complicated the case. A doctor testified that he believed the girl was older than ten but not older than twelve. The court was not able to locate the registry to determine Galinda's exact age. Gomez's attorney also questioned Claudia's testimony, arguing that the door to the bedroom was closed and therefore she could not have seen what happened. If there was no eyewitness, then it was in fact Galinda's word against her uncle's. This, however, did not preclude Gomez from confessing that he had had sexual contact with Galinda, but they did not have sex. Despite character witnesses who testified that Gomez was a decent and respectable man in the community, and medical evidence that suggested that Galinda had not been raped, the judge found Gomez guilty of atentado al pudor (attack against modesty) and sentenced him to six months in prison.[57]

Decoding a judge's decision in a case such as this one is difficult. Judges were essentially bound by the parameters established in legal codes even if they did enjoy a degree of flexibility in weighing evidence and sentencing. Ana Maria Alonso found in her research on Namiquipa, Mexico, that judges could use their power "to support women who represented themselves as sexually passive."[58] Judges, clearly attuned to the maneuverings of litigants and attorneys, operated within legal and cultural parameters that favored chaste and honorable women over those who were of poor public reputation. Yet judges, however paternalistic and patriarchal, also had to weigh the veracity of the evidence in accordance with legal codes or risk a ruling being overturned in a higher court. In cases of estupro and rape, there is a fundamental tension between the need to protect women and children, beliefs that women and girls could instigate their own sexual abuse, and men's traditional rights to control women and girls sexually. Moreover, penal law and judges' adjudication in cases of estupro demonstrate the legal system's continued preoccupation with preserving sexual difference since the benefits of state protections were contingent on women's proper moral conduct and public reputation. Indeed the penal code indicates that the crime must be committed with a "chaste and honest" woman or girl.[59] Officials were obviously wary of the supposed sexual power of women and girls and may have accepted men's claims that they had been seduced. This was clearly the strategy that Gomez's attorney employed. The fact that an attorney would accuse a woman (a young girl in this case) of inciting an attack indicates an inability (or unwillingness) on the part of state officials to break with customs that assumed women were temptresses and therefore might deserve an attack. Undoubtedly, ideas about girls' or women's honorability influenced the framing of subsequent penal codes that retained "*honestidad*" (honesty) as a key factor in determining culpability. Gomez's attorney, therefore, had no problem insinuating Galinda's sexual prowess despite her young age.

This case also demonstrates the complexities of daily life for poorer families. Villa was a widow who, along with her daughters, struggled to maintain their home in an Orizaba neighborhood.[60] Her life was centered on family, labor, community, and church.[61] Women who worked outside of the home often relied on extended family for the care of their children. Gomez had a responsibility to provide protection for his extended family in the absence of Villa's husband and to help alleviate the hardships of daily life. However, he shirked his honorable responsibility to protect Galinda. This also may have factored into the court's decision.

While sexual abuse was difficult to prove and a woman's poor reputation could easily provide exculpatory evidence, the judge in this case convicted Gomez.[62] However, it was probably Gomez's confession that he had had sexual play with the young girl that resulted in the ruling. Gomez did not deny his sexual contact with Galinda, only clarified that they had not had intercourse. The attorney's defense of Gomez, however, adds another dimension to the legal and social implications of Mexico's revolution and how it informed perceptions of "deviant" social behavior, class, and gender:

> The social climate in which we find ourselves is due to the modernism that the revolution has brought, which has relaxed the morality that existed many years ago. . . . The government, far from being a [moralizing force], is a source of corruption. Now because a man is subjected to the nature of his own weakness based on his psychological functions which are irresistible, the government proposes careful education to provide a means to attain morality among inmates . . . something which the government cannot provide because of its sad financial situation. Do you think you can moralize this town by filling the prisons? Impossible, because this is a crime of nature . . . the defendant never considered that what he did was a crime because he is unconscious of any concept that would indicate that this was a crime.[63]

Gomez's attorney not only revealingly cites the deleterious effects of the Mexican Revolution on community morality, but also situates his argument within much of the psychosexual research that not only explored men's sexual proclivities and women's role in encouraging abuse but also affirmed sexual difference.[64] The only solution therefore was for the state to provide proper education to enable men to resist their urges, while instructing women about the dangers of temptation. The attorney is also perhaps referring to the state's conflict with the Catholic Church that angered many Catholic conservatives. Tejeda was a vehement anticleric and blamed the church for what he believed to be Veracruz's fanaticism and ignorance.[65] Opponents believed that Tejeda's attacks undermined morality.

This case also demonstrates how science, tradition, and the postrevolutionary mission to create stable, productive, and hardworking families clashed with the state's increased interference in relationships between men and women. Early studies exploring the changes in family life following the revolution note the damaging effects it had on morality, some of which were blamed on the decline of church power. For example, an article appearing in the journal *Social Forces* in 1936 reaffirms the belief that the Mexican Revolution led to the deterioration of morality. Therefore, officials needed to fill the vacuum left in the wake of the Catholic Church's decline. The author notes that the "high percentage of illegitimate births, the striking prevalence of syphilitic infection, and the acknowledged amorality and immorality of the great masses are clear evidence of the need of sex instruction of a systematic nature."[66]

This observation, while faulting state officials for not doing enough to create sex education programs, also notes the supposed degradation of the poor and working classes. Officials believed that poor or working-class men and women behaved differently from their upper-class counterparts and that therefore licentiousness was part of working-class life. Women or girls who claimed they were raped or assaulted had to establish their honorability, while the legal process, in many ways, stripped them of dignity, respect, and honor. As Carlos Monsiváis explains, legal officials continued to argue that if women understood the importance of "guarding their modesty" and dressing responsibly, they would not have to endure violence and humiliation.[67]

Gomez's attorney's argument also reflected mounting changes in criminology. Much of the research that was emerging during the 1920s and 1930s affirmed that men were libidinous. If the state could not provide education and proper moral guidance, then there was no reason to assume that poorer men's behavior would change. Gomez's attorney explained that the state's efforts had failed to remedy Mexico's social problems, which explained his client's inability to grasp his crime.[68] Gomez's attorney did not condone or defend his client's conduct, but rather associated his behavior with men's inability to control their sexual desires, behavior that authorities associated with the depravity of the poorer classes. This argument points to the dichotomous nature of tradition and law as well as to the incongruities of state rhetoric that portrayed women and children as "vulnerable" while still implicating them in their own sexual abuse. Another case, also from 1930, mirrors many of the circumstances in the case against Gomez.

On March 18, 1930, María Antonio Santiago filed an appeal with the state supreme court in Xalapa (tribunal superior de justicia) to overturn the lower court's ruling in Orizaba that exonerated Federico Breton for the *violación* (rape) and *rapto* (kidnapping) of her daughter Josefina Santiago.[69] The mother claimed that the municipal court (juzgado de primero instancia) did not adequately consider her case due to her inability to prove that Josefina was in fact her daughter. Officials in Tlaxcala, Veracruz, where the girl was born, apparently never notarized her daughter's birth. In addition, Josefina's legal name and the name that the mother used in the affidavit complicated matters. The mother explained that the priest gave Josefina part of her name, María Apolonia, while her mother gave her the name Josefa. At home everyone called her Josefina. Confusion over the girl's name baffled court officials in Orizaba and led them to question the mother's legitimacy.[70] Much of the documentation is dedicated to sorting out the daughter's real name and who her biological mother and father were. Josefina was a *"hija natural,"* meaning she was born out of wedlock. The document also indicates that the father was not involved in her life. María's appeal, while addressing the problems of legitimate birth and her daughter's name, also carefully constructed her daughter's honor while detailing the confusing circumstances of this case. The mother explained that her daughter spent her childhood in Huamantla, Veracruz, which was a "very Catholic town and contains one chapel for every person who lives there."[71] She also explained that her daughter, "a young and innocent creature," was baptized with all the sacraments. María noted that she lamented the lower court's refusal to find Breton guilty and that this had caused "great pain, dishonor, and suffering."[72] The municipal court did not find Breton culpable based on several technicalities, which the mother sought to remedy.

In the trial record, María recounted the events that led to her daughter's ordeal. She argued that Breton tricked her "naïve" daughter, who was probably seventeen at the time, into chasing him to a room where he brutally beat and raped her. According to her complaint, she sent her daughter out one evening to run some errands, which involved determining the value of two rings that she had in her possession. While Josefina was out, she met Federico, who commented on the two rings she had and wanted to know where she had purchased them. When Breton asked if he could look at them more closely, the mother explained, "my daughter being naïve, handed them over. Federico then ran off with the rings and my daughter ran after because she feared that I would punish her if she lost them."[73] When she caught up to him, she discovered that he had lured her to a "dingy room where he abused and violently raped her." María's complaint, several pages long, indicates not only what she believed happened, but moreover what she thinks will be important to legal officials. Her meticulous recounting of events came as a result of the state's "abundance of obfuscations," which has "obstructed justice" for her young daughter. Her testimony reconstructed her young daughter's honor and chastity as well as the religiosity of her hometown and her devotion to the Church, qualities she believed would be important to court officials despite the secular bent of many postrevolutionary officials. (Not all embraced the state's anticlericalism and most surely were not atheists.) María saw to it that her daughter received the sacraments and that she was baptized so as to guarantee her piety and sanctity. Thus, the description of her rape heightens the brutal act forced on an honorable, young, and chaste body. María explains, "The act of rape removed the honor of my daughter, who was a virgin."[74] The defendant denied the charge and maintained that the girl was of legal age and consented to his overtures. The final ruling in the appeal is missing.

Despite the gaps in the court record, this appeal shows the complexities involved in rape and kidnapping cases involving poorer citizens as well as the importance of constructing a woman's honor and chastity within an emerging bureaucratic legal system that underscored the importance of chastity and honesty, especially among the poor and working classes. If Josefina had not been a virgin, then it would have been very difficult for her to attain a favorable verdict. Josefina's honor was in part tied to her affiliation with a "very Catholic town with many chapels," which heightens the violence of Sanchez's sexual attack. In addition, the mother's defense of her daughter contains no reference to social class (it was obvious they were poor) but rather emphasized piety, baptism, and sacraments.

This case exposes the clash between modernity and tradition in regions such as Veracruz. Many who lived in rural areas were quite poor and often did not legitimate their marriages or births with state officials, which placed them at a serious disadvantage in criminal cases. However, María's position as a mother defending the honor and innocence of her daughter is particularly important for how both society and the state understood behavior associated with class and gender. In this case, much like that of Galinda Villa, there was no father to defend the honor of his daughter or family. While this could have garnered the court's sympathy, her social class could have led officials to question whether she had properly "guarded her modesty."

The cases of single mothers confronting the sexual abuse of their daughters demonstrate the complexity of a changing legal system as well as perceptions that continued to associate the poorer classes with immorality and depravity. Throughout the first two decades following Mexico's revolution, women's chastity and modesty were integral factors in cases of sexual abuse or estupro. Because the family was the basic unit of social organization, officials were more concerned with preserving familial integrity and reducing the numbers of illegitimate children than they were with prosecuting men for committing acts of sexual violence. The case of Federico Breton is very instructive in this regard. Breton did not deny the encounter, but rather claimed that the girl was of legal age and that their sex was consensual. It was his word against hers. When medical evidence was inconclusive, it was difficult to prosecute the defendant.

Family honor was another factor that played into how citizens understood sexual violence. Penal codes stipulated that charges of estupro could be reversed if the perpetrator married his victim and if the girl was at least fourteen years old. This could restore her and her family's honor. If the offender refused to do so, the state had the right to incarcerate the offender for up to four years.[75] A front-page story of forbidden love in an issue of *Los Sucesos*, one of Orizaba's most widely circulated newspapers, told of such a case. In August of 1934, Vicente Sanchez ran away with his young lover Isabel Chavez. Vicente, seventeen years of age, came to collect Isabel from her home and take her to the train station. The article did not disclose Isabel's age. According to Isabel's testimony, she was the one who pressured Sanchez to run away. As they approached the train station, Isabel's father and the police caught up with them and arrested the boy. Sanchez explained that he wanted to marry Isabel, but his parents had convinced him that he did not have the means to support a wife.[76] Because Sanchez was shirking his duty to preserve the honor of Isabel's family, he would face a lengthy jail sentence. Sanchez had "deflowered" the young girl. If the court believed that Isabel was "chaste and honest," then the only option was for Sanchez to preserve Isabel's honor and the honor of her family by marrying her. While many of the details do not appear in the article, and the case does not appear in the judicial record, the ruling was clear. The court sentenced Sanchez to two years and four months in jail. His family appealed the court's decision to the state supreme court in Xalapa, but the judge in that case refused to overturn the lower court's ruling. The judge's ruling fit within the statutes laid out in Veracruz's penal code, which provided sanctions for men who would not restore the honor of the girl and family in question.

Clearly, cases of estupro could be more complicated when they involved consensual sex. Nonetheless, if the girl was a virgin, not legally an adult, and did not have blemishes on her reputation, the court usually assumed that she was naïve and that the offender took advantage of her to pursue "carnal pleasures." These assumptions persisted into the 1940s. For example, in the case of Porfirio De Valle and Carmen Alegre, the court sentenced the boy to three and half years in prison in 1941 for the rapto and estupro of Carmen Alegre, who was fifteen years of age.[77] Despite Alegre's testimony that she did not resist De Valle and that she was attempting to escape a difficult home situation, the court did not sympathize with her. The mother of the girl pressed charges, authorities arrested the boy, and the judge sentenced him to three and half years. De Valle's attorney filed an appeal with the state supreme court arguing that the sentence of three and half years was not constitutional according to penal law because the sex was consensual and violence was not involved. In addition, he argued that the girl was fifteen and that she had consented; therefore there was no kidnapping. More importantly, however, the attorney claimed that during the time the defendant was out on bail following the initial charges, he married the girl and therefore had complied with the penal statutes that stated that marriage would absolve him of all charges. The attorney also maintained that the marriage had the mother's blessing. The appeal, which the court litigated one year later, did not overturn the previous ruling.[78] The state supreme court ruled that the boy was not in fact free to marry the girl when he was out on bail. However, the judges did find that the sentence of three and half years was excessive, given the details of the case, and therefore reduced it. The circumstances of the trial indicate that when a boy or a man took possession of an honorable girl's virginity, he was required to marry her or suffer incarceration, at least in theory. This suggests that women continued to secure familial honor and patrimony. As long as a young man could legally offer marriage, a familial stain could be removed. In both of the previous cases, the court, following statutes stipulated in the state penal codes, ruled that premarital sex among minors could be transformed from licentious acts to honorable relations only through marriage. In the second case, it is clear that the attorney and defendants believed they had upheld their obligations, both culturally and legally. Regardless, the state supreme court would not recognize that the boy had the legal right to marry because he could not engage in a legal contract while out on bail.

The state's passage of the Law of Social Defense in 1944 and a new penal code in 1948 continued to stipulate a girl's honesty if the family was to have any hope of attaining legal recourse in cases of sexual violence.[79] In cases that I examined that involved appeals to the state supreme court in Xalapa and in some cases the federal supreme court, officials had to be sure that there was no evidence that the victim was sexually questionable. For example, in 1947 Angel Ortiz was charged with the kidnapping and rape of his fourteen-year-old sister-in-law. While the court sentenced him to two and half years in prison, and this ruling was upheld in the appeals process, the language in the case is fascinating. Similar to the previous cases, the family was working class and the mother was not married. According to testimony, the defendant claimed that his sister-in-law asked him to "ravish her several times." As a result, he had not done anything wrong because she "asked for it."[80] Following the court's conviction, he appealed to the state supreme court and finally the federal supreme court. The judge argued that despite the defendant's claim that the girl had instigated sexual contact, there was no evidence of any "lustful provocation" on the girl's part. In other words, had she been suspected of initiating contact, her morality would have been called into question and could have provided exculpatory evidence according to penal codes.

The language in the supreme court's decision mirrors another ruling from Tuxpan, Veracruz. In 1949 the court in Tuxpan (juzgado de primero instancia) found Roberto Dimas guilty of estupro of Maria Velazquez and sentenced him to two years in jail and a fine of five hundred pesos to be paid to the girl's family. The details, however, reveal a more convoluted story that parallels cases of seduction from generations earlier. The judge ruled that because two male neighbors had testified to Maria's honorability, that Roberto was in fact her boyfriend, that the circumstances of the sexual encounter indicated that Maria prudently "guarded her virginity until Roberto had promised marriage," and that Maria had never worked as a house servant (work that was often associated with poorer and disreputable women), they found him guilty.[81] However, in the ruling, the prison sentence and the order of apprehension were "provisionally suspended." No reason was given. Roberto's family still appealed the decision to the state supreme court in Xalapa, where the lower court's ruling was upheld. Roberto was ordered to pay a fine to both the court and the family. No mention of arrest or imprisonment appears in the appealed ruling. Roberto "deflowered" Maria and was forced to pay a fine, but no further punitive action was noted.[82]

What connects all of the cases presented in this chapter is that while legal codes changed over the years, the criteria for guilt or innocence and the process by which that was determined seem to have changed very little. Yes, scientific methods were employed more frequently, and the language used in documents became increasingly bureaucratized and sterile. But the expectation that women needed to be honorable persisted. In the case of rape that opened this chapter, a medical exam indicating that the married woman in question was not a virgin and that her injuries did not appear severe led the judge to hand down a lenient sentence despite the defendant having a record of violent behavior. In the case of estupro committed against Galinda Villa, it appears that only the uncle's admission that he had sexual contact with his niece moved the judge to find him guilty, though he handed down a lenient sentence. In the final case, the judge suspended the sentence even though Maria Velazquez was known to be an upstanding girl who had guarded her virginity.

Legal debates about sexual violence led some to argue, quite presciently, that implementing more severe punishments for sexual crimes would not have an effect on the numbers of crimes committed. Beda Ponce de Mendez noted in 1947 that

> educating women in the school and in the home through various scholastic institutions . . . would destroy societal prejudice that held that women were weak. [This] is the best method to avoid sexual crimes . . . without having to resort to new penal codes. We ask for the [state] to quickly include women in social life in the same way that has been done for men as laws continue to stipulate that women are weaker than men and need protection.[83]

The emphasis on sexual difference and women's weakness facilitated a culture of violence against women and girls. De Mendez noted that labor inequalities between men and women also exacerbated the problem.

CONCLUSIONS

The legal processes captured in this chapter shed light on how both litigants and state officials viewed sexual relations and crimes in postrevolutionary Veracruz. Under the governorship of Tejeda, Veracruz was not only a social laboratory for agrarian and clerical reform, but a region where the legal system grappled with the forces of poverty and presumed immorality and social decay. While judges did in fact punish sexual crimes, litigation focused on class, family, and public reputation, or in cases of consensual sex, restoring familial honor. In the case that opened this chapter, chastity was not a factor because Huerta was married. However, her honesty was called into question as the judge did not accept her account that she was raped despite evidence that she was struck and her clothes torn. The charge was reduced based on a doctor's conclusion that there was no evidence of forced sexual relations or semen residue. In other words, Huerta's testimony was moot because her body had been properly inspected by medical officials. This was also the case in the suit brought by Antonia Villa. The ways the women litigated these cases provide a window into how state officials viewed the morality of marginalized groups and the veracity of their claims. The way in which litigants structured their arguments in a court of law, not to mention the fact that girls remained a central part of the family patrimony, also demonstrates the persistence of tradition as represented in legal codes in regions such as Veracruz, despite the "modernizing" rhetoric of state officials. While the revolution created new spaces for women to address labor and family inequalities, not to mention issues of citizenship and suffrage, sexual crimes and perceptions of sexual abuse marked greater continuity with, rather than a break from, colonial and early republican perceptions of sexual violence.

NOTES

1. Some of the names of the plaintiffs and defendants have been changed to protect the identities of those families who may still live in the regions examined in this chapter.
2. Archivo General del Estado de Veracruz (AGEV), Tribunal Superior de Justicia, Juzgado Primero, Penales, año 1939, Cordoba, December 2, 1939.
3. Ibid.
4. Ibid., March 16, 1940.
5. Alexandra Minna Stern, " 'The Hour of Eugenics' in Veracruz, Mexico: Radical Politics, Public Health, and Latin America's Only Sterilization Law," *Hispanic American Historical Review* 91, no. 3 (2011): 431. Adalberto Tejeda's 1932 Civil Code was progressive at the time, codifying married women's equality with their husbands. See Tejeda, *El Nuevo Código Civil del Estado de Veracruz-Llave* (Xalapa: Talleres Gráficos del Gobierno del Estado, 1932).
6. Nancy Leys Stepan, *"The Hour of Eugenics": Race, Gender, and Nation in Latin America* (Ithaca, NY: Cornell University Press, 1991), 132. Also see Alexandra Minna Stern, *Eugenic Nation: Faults and Frontiers of Better Breeding in Modern Latin America* (Berkeley: University of California Press, 2005).

7. Tejeda, *El Nuevo Código Civil*, 21, cited in Stern, "'The Hour of Eugenics,'" 440.

8. AGEV, Fondo, Tribunal Superior de Justicia Sección: Ciudad, Orizaba: Serie, Juzgado Segundo, exp. 194, March 27, 1939. For a thoughtful examination of sexual violence and the law, see Ana M. Alonso, "Love, Sex, and Gossip in Legal Cases from Namiquipa, Chihuahua," in *Decoding Gender, Law, and Practice in Contemporary Mexico*, ed. Helga Baitenmann, Victoria Chenaut, and Ann Varley, 43–58 (New Brunswick, NJ: Rutgers University Press, 2007). For the colonial period, see Patricia Seed, *To Love, Honor, and Obey in Colonial Mexico* (Stanford, CA: Stanford University Press, 1988).

9. Yucatán's governors Carillo Puerto and Salvador Alvarado instituted progressive legal reforms in the area of women's rights. However, this did not seem to impact litigation of cases of sexual abuse, where women remained at a disadvantage. See Stephanie Smith, *Gender and the Mexican Revolution: Yucatán Women and the Realities of Patriarchy* (Chapel Hill: University of North Carolina Press, 2009).

10. Marjorie Becker, *Setting the Virgin on Fire: Lázaro Cárdenas, Michoacán Peasants, and the Redemption of the Mexican Revolution* (Berkeley: University of California Press, 1995), 75; Claudio Lomintz-Adler, *Exits from the Labyrinth: Culture and Ideology in the Mexican National Space* (Berkeley: University of California Press, 1992).

11. Pablo Piccato, *City of Suspects: Crime in Mexico City, 1900–1931* (Durham, NC: Duke University Press, 2001), 125.

12. See Smith, *Gender and the Mexican Revolution*. Smith notes that Yucatán revolutionary tribunals provided opportunities for women to seek justice until 1917, when they were replaced by the bureaucratic court system laid out in the constitution of 1917. While some women were discouraged from seeking recourse, some filed charges despite the odds against them. See also Alonso, "Love, Sex, and Gossip," 43–58. For regions outside of Mexico, see David Carey, "Forced and Forbidden Sex: Rape and Sexual Freedom in Dictatorial Guatemala," *The Americas* 69, no. 3 (2013): 357; Carey, *I Ask for Justice: Maya Women, Dictators, and Crime in Guatemala, 1898–1944* (Austin: University of Texas Press, 2013); Tanja Christiansen, *Disobedience, Slander, Seduction, and Assault: Women and Men in Cajamarca, Peru, 1862–1900* (Austin: University of Texas Press, 2004), 129. For the early nineteenth century, see Eugenía Rodríguez, "'Tiyita Bea lo que me han echo': Estupro e incesto en Costa Rica (1800–1850)," *Anuario de Estudios Centroamericano* 19, no. 2 (1993): 71–88.

13. Smith, *Gender and the Mexican Revolution*, 77; Mark Overmyer-Velázquez, "Portraits of a Lady: Visions of Modernity in Porfirian Oaxaca City," *Mexican Studies* 23, no. 1 (Winter 2007): 75. For an examination of sexual violence against children of both sexes, see Jorge Alberto Trujillo Bretón, "Los excesos del deseo: Incontinencia y violencia sexual contra niños y jóvenes en Jalisco, 1885–1911," *Relaciones: Estudios de Historia y Sociedad* 32, no. 127 (Summer 2011): 153–94.

14. Carey, "Forced and Forbidden Sex," 357.

15. Smith, *Gender and the Mexican Revolution*, 76–77.

16. For an in-depth analysis of Mexican law, see Stephen Zamora et al., *Mexican Law* (Oxford: Oxford University Press, 2004). Issues of public reputation were of course not limited to Mexico. Up until the 1970s, a plaintiff's sexual history was presented as evidence to undermine the credibility of victims in the United States. See Jennifer Temkin, *Rape and the Legal Process*, 2nd ed. (New York: Oxford University Press, 2003).

17. Alonso, "Love, Sex, Gossip," 51.

18. Ibid., 54–55.

19. See Piccato, *City of Suspects*, 120.

20. It should be noted that libertinism was associated with poorer men and women. Even in Porfirian-era novels, victims of seduction were usually poor women. See Pablo Piccato, *The Tyranny of Opinion: Honor in the Construction of the Mexican Public Sphere* (Durham, NC: Duke University Press, 2010).

21. Honor and *honra* (the public perception of one's honor or virtue) were colonial constructs, which implied a hierarchy based on status, blood line, class, chastity, gender, and piety. Honor was defined differently for men and women. Men's honor, in part, was associated with their ability to control the sexual behavior of women. For women, chastity defined honorability or decency/modesty (*honestidad*). Women who were faithful in marriage or chaste before nuptials safeguarded their honor. Piccato, *The Tyranny of Opinion*. See also Susie S. Porter, *Working Women in Mexico City: Public Discourses and Material Conditions, 1879–1931* (Tucson: University of Arizona Press, 2003). For the colonial period, see Anne Twinam, *Public Lives, Private Secrets: Gender, Honor, Sexuality, and Illegitimacy in Colonial Spanish America* (Stanford, CA: Stanford University Press, 1999).

22. Catherine Komisaruk, "Rape Narratives, Rape Silences: Sexual Violence and Judicial Testimonies in Colonial Guatemala," *Biography* 31, no. 3 (2008): 373.

23. Alonso, "Love, Sex, and Gossip," 54. See also Arlene J. Díaz, *Female Citizens, Patriarchs, and the Law in Venezuela, 1786–1904* (Lincoln: University of Nebraska Press, 2004).

24. Victor M. Uribe-Uran, "The Great Transformation of Law and Legal Culture: 'The Public' and 'the Private' in Transition from Empire to Nation in Mexico, Colombia, and Brazil, 1750–1850," in *Empire to Nation: Historical Perspectives on the Making of the Modern World*, ed. Joseph W. Esherwick, Hasan Kayali, and Eric Van Young, 68–105 (Lanham, MD: Rowman and Littlefield, 2006), 91.

25. Komisaruk, "Rape Narratives, Rape Silences," 378–79. See also Rebecca Earle, "Rape and the Anxious Republic: Revolutionary Colombia, 1810–1830," in *Hidden Histories of Gender and the State in Latin America*, ed. Elizabeth Dore and Maxine Molyneux, 127–46 (Durham, NC: Duke University Press, 1999). For a comparative analysis of criminal seduction cases, see Brian Donovan, "Gender Inequality and Criminal Seduction: Prosecuting Sexual Coercion in the Early-20th Century," *Law and Social Inquiry* 30, no. 1

(Winter 2005): 61–88. Donovan argues that women could at times successfully bring charges again men who reneged on their promises to marry. However, success was often limited because seduction cases were legally a gray area.

26. *Código penal del Estado de Veracruz Llave: Proyecto formado por las Comisiones Unidas de la honorable Legislatura y del honorable Tribunal Superior de Justicia, aprobado y mandado observar por la Ley núm. 32 de 15 de agosto de 1896* (Xalapa, Veracruz: Enriquez, 1896). For thoughtful analysis of domestic violence in nineteenth-century Mexico, see Ana María Alonso, "'What the Strong Owe to the Weak': Rationality, Domestic Violence, and Governmentality in Nineteenth-Century Mexico," in *Gender's Place: Feminist Anthropologies of Latin America*, ed. Rosario Montoya, Lessie Jo Frazier, and Janise Hurtig, 115–34 (New York: Palgrave, 2002).

27. "State Labor Office Charged with Investigating the Unhealthful Conditions at the Cigarette Factory El Progresso," Archivo Municipal de Orizaba (AMO), Salubridad, caja 561, exp. 20, June 13, 1919.

Department of Labor records indicate that inspectors believed that women were more susceptible to tuberculosis and other illnesses. State officials often used such claims to argue that women who worked in jobs that were normally male dominated threatened the health and stability of the family.

28. Kathryn Sloan, *Runaway Daughters: Seduction, Elopement, and Honor in Nineteenth-Century Mexico* (Albuquerque: University of New Mexico Press, 2008), 47.

29. Many legislators were in favor of modernization but were not willing to dispense with positivist ideology that emphasized order and progress. See Robert Buffington, *Criminal and Citizen in Modern Mexico* (Lincoln: University of Nebraska Press, 2000). See also José Ángel Ceniceros, *Tres estudios de criminología* (Mexico City: Cuadernos Criminalia, 1941). Ceniceros explores the continued influence of positivism on penal reform in Mexico. For more on sexual violence during the Porfirian period, see Trujillo Bretón, "Los excesos del deseo."

30. Mary Kay Vaughan, *The State, Education, and Social Class in Mexico, 1880–1928* (DeKalb: Northern Illinois University Press, 1982), 204.

31. Ibid.

32. Buffington, *Criminal and Citizen in Modern Mexico*, 124–25.

33. Ibid.

34. Ibid, 110. For more on the debate surrounding the Penal Code of 1929, see Elisa Speckman Guerra, "Justice Reform and Legal Opinion: The Mexican Criminal Codes of 1871, 1929, and 1931," in *Reforming the Administration of Justice in Mexico*, ed. Wayne Cornelius and David Shirk, 225–50 (Notre Dame: University of Notre Dame Press / San Diego: Center for U.S/Mexican Studies, UC San Diego, 2007). See also Sergio López Ayllón, *Las transformaciones del sistema jurídico y los significados sociales del derecho en México: La encrucijada entre tradición y modernidad* (México: Universidad Nacional Autónoma de México, 1997), 237–72.

35. Buffington, *Criminal and Citizen in Modern Mexico*, 126. Also see Miguel S. Macedo and José Ángel Ceniceros, *Derechos, penal y procedimientos penales: Programa y conferencias de 1926* (Mexico City: Escuela Libere de Derecho, 1928). For an early analysis of the Mexican Penal Code of 1929, see Salvador Mendoza, "El Nuevo Código Penal de México," *Hispanic American Historical Review* 10, no. 3 (1930): 299–312; Robert Buffington, "Looking Forward, Looking Back: Judicial Discretion and State Legitimation in Modern Mexico," in *Crime, Histoires, & Sociétés / Crime, History, & Societies* 2, no. 2 (1998): 15–34.

36. Adalberto Tejeda, *Memoria de las labores del Gobierno Constitucional de Estado de Veracruz-Llave durante el cuatrienio 1928–1932* (Xalapa-Enriquez: Talleres Tipográficos del Gobierno del Estado, 1932), 29. Tejeda's position was not necessarily radical, as many legal officials sought to overturn Porifirian methods of detainment and punishment while accentuating rehabilitation.

37. The Penal Code of 1932 based fines and imprisonment on whether or not the victim had reached puberty. If the victim was "prepubescent," a conviction could yield one to three years in prison as opposed to four to six years in the 1896 code. See *Código penal del estado de Veracruz* Llave. See also Tejeda, *El Nuevo Código Civil: Códigos penal y de procedimientos penales: Leyes sobre la asistencia social y la atención jurídica de los menores, y de ejecución de sanciones* (Xalapa, 1948).

38. Karen Mead, "Gendering the Obstacles to Progress in Positivist Argentina, 1880–1920," *Hispanic American Historical Review* 77, no. 4 (November 1997): 645–75, and Judith Halberstam, *Female Masculinity* (Durham, NC: Duke University Press, 1998), 76.

39. Ibid.

40. See Sueann Caulfield, "Getting into Trouble: Dishonest Women, Modern Girls, and Women-Men in the Conceptual Language of Vida Policial, 1925–1927," *Signs* 19, no. 1 (Autumn 1993): 148.

41. Ibid., 148.

42. Francesca Miller, *Latin American Women and the Search for Social Justice* (Hanover, NH: University Press of New England, 1991), 58.

43. Patience Schell, "Gender, Class, and Anxiety at the Gabriela Mistral Vocational School, Revolutionary Mexico City," in *Gender, Politics, and Power in Modern Mexico*, ed. Jocelyn Olcott, Mary Kay Vaughan, and Gabriel Cano, 112–26 (Durham, NC: Duke University Press, 2006), 120.

44. Carlos Monsiváis, "When Gender Can't Be Seen amid the Symbols: Women and the Mexican Revolution," in *Sex in Revolution: Gender, Power, and Politics in Modern Mexico*, ed. Jocelyn Olcott, Mary Kay Vaughan, and Gabriela Cano, 1–20 (Durham, NC: Duke University Press, 2006), 8.

45. The cultural construction of La Malinche also shaped how Mexicans understood women's sexuality and vulnerability. See Joann Martin, "Motherhood and Power: The Production of a Women's Culture of Politics in a Mexican Community," *American Ethnologist* 17, no. 3 (August 1990): 470–90.

46. Extraordinary Session, *Diario de los debates de la XXVII Legislatura* 1, no. 12 (May 12, 1919), quoted in Katherine Elaine Bliss, "Theater of Operations: Reform Politics and the Battle for Prostitutes' Redemption at Revolutionary Mexico City's Syphilis Hospital," in *The Women's Revolution in Mexico, 1910–1953*, ed. Stephanie Mitchell and Patience A. Schell, 125–50 (Lanham, MD: Rowman and Littlefield, 2007), 131.

47. For a comparative analysis, see Arlene J. Díaz, "Women, Order, and Progress in Guzmán Blanco's Venezuela, 1870–1888," in *Crime and Punishment in Latin America: Law and Society Since Late Colonial Times*, ed. Ricardo D. Salvatore, Carlos Aguirre, and Gilbert M. Joseph, 56–82 (Durham, NC: Duke University Press, 2001).

48. Piccato, *City of Suspects*, 130.

49. AGEV, Tribunal Superior de Justicia, Orizaba, Juzgado Primero, Penales, años 1939–40, exp. 194, March 27, 1939.

50. AGEV, Tribunal Superior de Justicia, Orizaba, Juzgado Primero, Penales, años 1903–39, exp. 584, October 27, 1930.

51. Ibid.

52. Mexico's Criminal Code of 1929 no longer permitted police to conduct physical inspections of rape victims unless it was clear that they had been beaten. See Pablo Piccato, "'El Chalequero,' or the Mexican Jack the Ripper: The Meanings of Sexual Violence in Turn-of-the-Century Mexico City," *Hispanic American Historical Review* 81, no. 3–4 (2001): 621.

53. *Código Penal Federal*, Al margen un sello que dice: Poder Ejecutivo Federal, Estados Unidos Mexicanos (México: Secretaría de Gobernación, September 17, 1931), articles 259–66.

54. Penal law defined rape as sexual intercourse with the use of violence, regardless of the age and sex of the victim. As a result, many cases were downgraded to lesser charges where violence was not involved. *Código Penal Federal*, Al margen un sello que dice: Poder Ejecutivo Federal, Estados Unidos Mexicanos (México: Secretaría de Gobernación, September 17, 1931), articles 259–66. For an early analysis of penal law in Mexico, see Norman S. Hayner, "Criminogenic Zones in Mexico City," *American Sociological Review* 11, no. 4 (1946): 428–38, and Salvador Diego-Fernández, *La ciudad de Méjico a fines del siglo XIX* (Mexico City, 1937). For an examination of sexual crimes around the turn of the century, see Carlos Roumagnac, *Crímenes sexuales*, vol. 1 of *Crímenes sexuales y pasionales: Estudios de psicología morbosa* (México: Librería de Ch. Bouret, 1906–10).

55. AGEV, Tribunal Superior de Justicia, Orizaba, Juzgado Primero, Penales, años 1903–39, exp. 584, October 28, 1930.

56. Ibid., October 29, 1930.

57. AGEV, Tribunal Superior de Justicia, Orizaba, Juzgado Primero Penales, años 1903–39, exp. 584, October 28, 1930.

58. Ana Maria Alonso, "Love Sex, and Gossip," 55.

59. This case was litigated before the passage of the Penal Code of 1932. Therefore "chaste and honest" was still applied. Veracruz's Penal Code of 1932 removed the word "chaste" while retaining "honest." For more on how sexual difference shapes gendered categories, see Joan W. Scott, "Gender: A Useful Category of Historical Analysis," *American Historical Review* 91, no. 5 (December 1986): 1053–75.

60. In 1921, the number of women who were widowed in the state of Veracruz was nearly three times that of men. Archivo Municipal de Orizaba (AMO), Biblioteca, *Estado de Veracruz, Datos Geográficos*, 1921, 44–46.

61. Norman S. Hayner, "Notes on the Changing Mexican Family," *American Sociological Review* 7, no. 4 (August 1942): 489–97.

62. Pablo Piccato notes that in Mexico City judges often dismissed rape cases because of a women's public reputation or morality. See Piccato, *City of Suspects*. Also see Robert Buffington, "La violencia contra la mujer y la subjetividad masculina en la prensa popular de la ciudad de México en el cambio de siglo," in *De normas y transgresiones: Enfermedad y crimen en América Latina (1850–1950)*, ed. Elisa Speckman and Claudia Agostoni, 287–325 (México: UNAM, 2005).

63. Criminal charges against Marcelino Gomez for sexual abuse of a minor, AGEV, Tribunal Superior de Justicia, Orizaba, Juzgado Primero Penales, años 1903–39, exp. 584, October 27, 1930.

64. See Gustavo Rodriguez, "Perversiones sexuales," *Revista Jurídica Veracruzana* 1, no. 2 (April 30, 1940).

65. John B. Williman, "Adalberto Tejeda and the Third Phase of the Anticlerical Conflict in Twentieth Century Mexico," *Church and State* 15, no. 3 (Autumn 1973): 437–54; Matthew Butler, "Sotanas Rojinegras: Catholic Anticlericalism and Mexico's Revolutionary Schism," *The Americas* 65, no. 4 (April 2009): 535–58; Romana Falcón and Soledad García, *La semilla en el surco: Adalberto Tejeda y el radicalismo en Veracruz (1883–1960)* (Veracruz: Gobierno del Estado de Veracruz), 1986.

66. C. D. Ebaugh, "Mexico Studies Sex Education," *Social Forces* 15, no. 1 (October 1936): 81–83.

67. Monsiváis, "When Gender Can't Be Seen."

68. Rodríguez, "Perversiones sexuales."

69. AGEV, Tribunal Superior de Justicia, Orizaba, Juzgado Segundo, año 1929, exp. 189.

70. The confusion over Josefina's name is obvious in the lower court's ruling. When María explained that she sent for the civil registration of her daughter's birth in Tlaxcala, the document lacked a legal signature. This case is also complicated because Josefina was either seventeen or eighteen years old when the alleged rape took place. Sanchez made this point in his defense when he claimed that there was no crime because Josefina was of legal consensual age.

71. Ibid.

72. Ibid.

73. Ibid.

74. AGEV, Tribunal Superior de Justicia, Orizaba, Juzgado Segundo, año 1929, exp. 189.

75. Sonya Lipsett-Rivera found in her research on early republican Mexico that marriage between a perpetrator and a rape victim could redeem a family's honor. The evidence presented in this chapter indicates that this persisted into the postrevolutionary period. See Lipsett-Rivera, "The Intersection of Rape and Marriage in Late Colonial and Early National Mexico," *Colonial Latin American Historical Review* 6, no. 4 (Fall 1997): 559–90.

76. "Fue confirmada la sentencia contra un jovencito que fue raptado [*sic*] por una chica," *Los Sucesos* (August 10, 1934), tomo 14, pp. 1–2.

77. AGEV, Tribunal Superior de Justicia, Orizaba, Juzgado Primero, Penales, April 8, 1941, exp 99.

78. Ibid.

79. *Códigos penal y de procedimientos penales: Leyes sobre la asistencia social y la atención jurídica de los menores.* For an analysis of legal changes pertaining to estupro, see Gerardo Gil Ortiz, "Estudio dogmatico jurídico del delito de estupro" (thesis, Universidad de Veracruzana, Xalapa, 1973).

80. AGEV, Tribunal Superior de Justicia, Veracruz, Juzgado Primero Penales, año 1947, exp 150.

81. AGEV, Tribunal Superior de Justicia, Juzgado Primero, Penales, Tuxpan, año 1949, exp. 73.

82. Ibid., appealed ruling June 27, 1951.

83. Beda Ponce de Mendez, "La mujer en nuestro derecho positivo," tesis que para su Examen Recepcional de Abogado (Xalapa-Enriquez, 1947).

8

BETWEEN BARBARITY
AND TRADITION

乇

Past and Present Representations of Lynching in Mexico

GEMA SANTAMARÍA

T HE AIM OF THIS CHAPTER is to analyze media and official representations of lynching in twentieth- and twentieth-first-century Mexico. Lynching can be defined as a public, gruesome, and often ritualized form of collective violence. Its aim is to punish a person who is considered to threaten or offend a community's norms and well-being.[1] In spite of its illegality, those who lynch suspected perpetrators do not consider their actions to be a crime but in fact a legitimate way to attain justice. Thus, similarly to the historical trajectory of lynching in the United States and in contemporary Latin America, lynchings in Mexico are often carried out in prominent public spaces and, not rarely, even in the presence of state authorities. Although they may not lead to the victim's death, lynchings are by and large characterized by what seems to be a disproportionate and particularly cruel use of violence, involving the torture, mutilation, burning, or hanging of the victim. In all, lynching serves to illuminate a central theme of the present volume: namely, the dissonance between popular and official understandings of crime and justice in modern Latin America.

This chapter will focus on two different episodes of lynching that, given their historical and political significance, constitute pertinent case studies by which to analyze public debates and understandings of lynching violence in contemporary Mexico. The first, focused on the period from 1932 to 1936, comprises a series of attacks against so-called socialist teachers in different rural communities of Mexico. The second consists of a single case of lynching perpetrated in 2004 against three police officers in Mexico City. Both instances involved the victimization of public officials whose presence or actions within their respective communities foregrounded the state's authority and legitimacy (there were multiple incidents of lynching during the 1930s, most of which were associated with former Cristeros). Socialist teachers were central to the process of modernization and secularization promoted by the Lázaro Cárdenas government (1934–40), which sought to incorporate rural and Indian communities into the centralized structure created by the postrevolutionary elites.[2] Police officers, for their part, were instrumental in the implementation of security policies that sought to assert the government's legitimacy in light of increasing levels of insecurity and citizens' distrust in the justice and security apparatus.[3]

Despite their temporal and contextual differences, both episodes of lynching were represented by media and official accounts as acts driven by the traditions, religious backwardness, or the "*usos y costumbres*" (literally "uses and customs") of given communities. I argue that these accounts and their references to the "traditions" of certain groups have contributed to a racialized understanding of lynching and its perpetrators. In Mexico's historical present, where race has become a somehow "unsayable" marker of social difference, references to the alleged "traditions" of certain communities in cases of collective acts of violence hinge on a discourse that sees and produces racialized subjects through naturalized or reified cultural traces such as language, dress, religion, and culture.[4] This chapter points out the continuities between past and present representations of lynching and the impact these representations have had in obscuring the state's responsibility in provoking this form of violence.

Scholarship on lynching in Latin America first appeared in the 1980s and interpreted these acts as a reaction by citizens and communities to high levels of delinquency, police corruption, and limited access to justice.[5] As such, this literature has called into question media and official representations of these acts as manifestations of "pre-modern" or "backward" indigenous cultures and has instead demonstrated their connection to the current security crisis impacting various countries in Latin America.[6] In the context of Bolivia, Guatemala, Ecuador, and Mexico, for instance, newspaper reports and government officials have tended to associate lynching with residual traditions of indigenous communities. The existing scholarly literature has demonstrated that lynchings are not part of indigenous customary laws and that this collective and extrajudicial form of violence is practiced in both indigenous and nonindigenous communities facing high levels of insecurity and crime.[7] As scholar Christopher Krupa has suggested for the case of Ecuador, depictions of lynching as "Indian-like acts" not only misrepresent this phenomenon but also serve to reify a public image of indigenous communities as "barbaric" and as incapable of participating in a white-mestizo society that claims for itself the values of modernity and order.[8]

This chapter seeks to contribute to this scholarship by introducing a historical perspective capable of highlighting the tenacity of certain racialized representations of lynching. With a few exceptions, most works on lynching in Mexico and Latin America have focused on cases within the last three decades. In the case of Mexico these exceptions include works dealing with the above-mentioned attacks against socialist teachers (during La Segunda),[9] studies based on a lynching that took place in 1968 in the context of the political violence and unrest surrounding Mexico's student movement,[10] and, more recently, a study of what the national press considered to be, at the time, the country's "first lynching" in 1897.[11] In the case of Peru, the work of Hinnerk Onken has traced the history of this practice to the nineteenth and early twentieth centuries, when lynching operated as a form of social protest enacted by socially marginalized groups against members of the economic and political elites.[12] None of these works, however, has attempted a comparative reading of past and present cases of lynching. This chapter seeks to offer such a reading by highlighting similarities or continuities in the ways in which lynching has been discussed or represented.

The argument will be presented as follows: The first section will introduce the two instances of collective violence and provide a critical reading of their media and official representations through the use of primary and secondary sources. For the period from 1932 to 1936, I consulted two of the most important national newspapers printed at the time: *Excélsior* and *El Universal*. My research was focused mainly on the years 1935 and 1936, when some of the most important attacks against socialist teachers took place in five states. Because they had national coverage and were printed in Mexico City, both newspapers operated under the influence of the dominant political elites and hence were characterized, overall, by an official tone. For this period, I also reviewed letters and security reports addressed to President Cárdenas, which are located in the National Archive of Mexico. My analysis of the 2004 case is, on the other hand, based on news and articles published in the Mexican newspapers *La Jornada* and *El Universal* from November 2004 to December of 2005.[13] The second section will establish the alternative interpretations that these representations obscured or undermined and point to those elements that can contribute to a more political understanding of these acts. That is, to an understanding that highlights how these episodes of collective violence constituted, in spite of their illegality, a means of resisting or counteracting state policies that were considered illegitimate or even threatening by given communities.

TWO INSTANCES OF COLLECTIVE VIOLENCE

From 1932 to 1936 a series of attacks against so-called socialist teachers took place within various rural communities in states such as Puebla, Sonora, Michoacán, Veracruz, and Chiapas. The attacks included beatings, hangings, and shootings, as well as the cutting off of ears by mobs or groups of bandits in visible public spaces.[14] The exact number of teachers who were either killed or injured by these attacks is difficult to establish, but some accounts refer to one hundred assassinations and two hundred cases of lacerated or mutilated teachers.[15] These violent incidents constituted a direct response to the implementation of the "socialist education" project (1934–36) promoted by the Lázaro Cárdenas government.

The socialist education project was an ambitious and multilayered program that included the creation of a national, homogeneous, and centralized model of education. Its aim was to "modernize" the countryside and to integrate indigenous populations through the implementation of agrarian reform and the secularization of social life.[16] Socialist teachers, most of them young, urban, and educated, played pivotal roles in these tasks and, as such, were celebrated by the Cárdenas government both as "bearers of progress" and eventually as "martyrs" at the hands of the so-called ignorance of the people. The project affected not only the clergy and lay members of the Catholic Church, who considered a secular and socialist model of education offensive to the religious and moral values held by given communities; it also had an impact on the material well-being of large landowners whose properties were being threatened by the agrarian reform and by the social changes brought about by so-called socialist ideology.[17]

As historian Ben Fallaw points out, attacks against socialist teachers included offensive tactics organized by well-armed groups of bandits as well as more spontaneous actions that involved the participation of peasants, impoverished indigenous people, and lay members of the Catholic Church.[18] Despite this, most official and media reports referred to these attacks as episodes driven by the religious fanaticism and backwardness of these rural communities. For instance, on November 15, 1935, in the town of Teziutlán, in Sierra Norte, teachers Carlos Pastrana, Carlos Sayago, and Librado Labastida were killed with pistols and machetes. According to the report filed by the federal inspector in charge of the investigation, there had been disturbances in the town since April of the same year. Parents stopped sending their children to school, and some local religious associations, with the support of the priests, circulated leaflets that denounced socialist education. The report stated, "The dominion that the clergy exercises over the indigenous people of the area is absolute . . . leading them to perpetrate crimes, like those that took place against the teachers."[19] The virtually simultaneous killing of the three teachers at three different places led the inspector to conclude that the attacks were carefully premeditated. Twenty-three-year-old Carlos Sayago was killed by a group of armed men just two hundred meters away from the school where he was teaching; Carlos Pastrana was nearly decapitated with a machete, ending his life close to his residence; and Librado Labastida, approximately twenty-eight years old, was shot only thirty meters from his assigned school.

In reference to the same case, one newspaper reported that three *maestros socialistas* (socialist teachers) had been attacked in Puebla by a "tumulto de indígenas fanáticos" (a tumult of fanatic Indians).[20] No reason besides the alleged fanaticism of the perpetrators was given to explain this violent episode. The note omits any reference to how socialist education had been implemented or received by this or other rural communities. Moreover, the use of the words "tumulto" and "indígenas" is worthy of mention. In Spanish, *tumulto* denotes disorganization and messiness and resembles other words such as *turba* (mob) or *chusma* (the lower class), also frequently used to refer to this type of act. As explored by sociologist Francesca Polletta, acts that are described as "unplanned, impulsive, and . . . spontaneous" are usually set in opposition to planned, calculated, and so-called rational political acts.[21] As such, the categorization of these acts as impulsive or irrational served to obscure the political drivers behind these events. As for the word "indígenas," it is interesting to note that both newspaper reporters and government officials felt the need to specify the race of the perpetrators. The historiography of these periods indicates that not only Indians but mestizos were involved in these acts.[22] And, yet, the word "mestizos" is never used in the newspaper articles analyzed, an omission that may confirm Alan Knight's suggestion that only indigenous populations were racialized in 1930s Mexico, based on sociological and cultural attributes that were considered deterministic for the behavior of these groups.[23]

In March 1936, another newspaper reported that a group of Catholics armed with stones, knives, and pistols had attacked the maestros of a "cultural mission" in Guanajuato, killing thirteen people and injuring at least twenty-nine. According to this news story, the priest of the place "*influenced the temper* of the believers so they would fight the official elements, since *otherwise it is inexplicable* that they came out of the mass armed . . . and immediately attacked the professors and neighbors."[24] It is important to mention that the same article quotes President Lázaro Cárdenas, who, in tune with this explanation, expressed that "the only group responsible for this *zafarrancho* [or "mess"] were the priests who had provoked the parishioners against the maestros of the rural mission."[25]

These statements coincided with an official discourse that tended to attribute any type of resistance, violent or otherwise, against the socialist education to the influence or "manipulation" exercised by the Catholic Church. In particular, letters, or *oficios*, written by both federally commissioned rural maestros and local officials pointed to local priests as the main actors responsible for "fanaticizing," provoking, or inciting the children and the people of the community against the *escuela socialista*. In some cases, they were even accused of being the "intellectual authors" of some of the maestros' homicides.[26] In May 1935, the federal inspector José Ventura, in charge of the federal rural school "Carlos Marx" in Queréndaro, Michoacán, asked the minister of government to either punish or exile the local priest, who, he claimed, was responsible for "agitating the residents" and inciting them to withdraw their children from school. According to him, it was the propaganda promoted by the priest that made the inhabitants of this town behave like *"fanáticos"* and react with hatred against the rural school and its professors.[27] In Zacán, Michoacán, the federally commissioned rural maestro Jesús Torres Cárdenas also accused the local priest of "fanaticizing" the "children of this town" and requested that the government exile him, since he was nothing less than an "enemy of the progress and betterment of the proletariat."[28]

References to the alleged manipulation by the local priests within given communities served to characterize so-called religious fanatics and Indians as both guilty and innocent of their actions. They were guilty of their violent and irrational behavior, but they were innocent because their behavior derived from their ignorance and from their entrapment in what reformers considered a false ideology (i.e., Catholicism). As indicated by Mara Loveman, the use by political elites of expressions such as "ignorant" and "irrational" to refer to the rural communities whom they were supposed to be modernizing operated as a discourse that denied these groups any "capacity of autonomous [political] actions."[29] Since the pueblo was considered ignorant, it was "unpoliticized and unaware," and hence its actions could only be the result of some exterior influence. In other words, the attacks against the teachers could not be expressions of the community's own agency.

Along the same lines, another newspaper article referred to statements made by a government official speaking at the 1935 Scientific Congress, who expressed that it was difficult to know how effective the process of "de-fanatization" of the Indian had been since "the Catholic Church has occupied a great part of the time of the pueblo." He also stated that the Indians did not "understand the spirit of the constitutional reform" (which introduced secular and socialist education), confusing the "war against *fanatismo*" and all religion with a war fought exclusively against the Catholic Church.[30] The use of warfare rhetoric to refer to the implementation of the socialist education at a national level also informed other statements made by President Cárdenas when he called teachers the ultimate bearers of the modern principles of the 1910 Mexican Revolution[31] and authorized them to use arms to defend themselves against the so-called fanatics.[32]

Despite temporal and contextual differences, this representation, wherein acts of collective violence were associated with the backward or traditional beliefs of certain communities, was also present in the lynching of three police officers on November 23, 2004, in San Juan Ixtapoyan, a small town located in the borough of Tláhuac in Mexico City. According to the version provided by some of the town's inhabitants, the three men had been seen outside the local school taking pictures of children. Allegedly, there were reasons to believe they formed part of a criminal network associated with the kidnapping of minors and trafficking of human organs.[33] The three men turned out to be police officers of the Federal Preventive Police (Policia Federal Preventiva, PFP), one of the most specialized and highly ranked security units combating organized crime and terrorism in Mexico. The event was videotaped by one of the witnesses of the lynching as well as by reporters of one of the largest TV networks in the country, Televisa, whose personnel managed to arrive in San Juan Ixtapoyan two hours before the local and federal police forces. Two of the victims were interviewed before being assassinated and stated before the cameras that they were federal cops working undercover in a security operation to detect drug-trafficking activities in the area. Their statement, however, did not dissuade the group of attackers, who, according to media accounts, included more than three hundred people.[34]

The lynching in San Juan Ixtapoyan, commonly referred to by the media as the "Tláhuac case," can be interpreted in light of the recent increase in vigilantism and private mechanisms of security in Mexico over the last thirty years. This includes self-defense groups, neighborhood-based forms of policing, and private security guards.[35] The cases of lethal and nonlethal lynchings increased from 107 between 1988 and 1999 to 129 between 2000 and 2010.[36] Considering that crimes and violent deaths are significantly underreported in Mexico, it is fair to speculate that the number of lynchings is significantly higher than what is officially portrayed. In fact, Mexico has been identified, together with Guatemala, Bolivia, and Ecuador, as one of the Latin American countries where these acts have become more frequent over the last decades.[37]

In Mexico, the intensification of lynchings against so-called criminals can be explained by the sudden rise in crime rates, particularly robberies, in the mid-1980s at both the national and local levels,[38] as well as by the growing distrust in the state's capacity to control crime and violence.[39] Although the state's incapacity to uphold the rule of law effectively is certainly not new to the country,[40] the relation between this lack of capacity and Mexico's process of democratization does prove unique in its recent configuration. Specifically, the process of democratization brought about bureaucratic impasse, decentralization, and an unreformed security sector that has contributed to the privatization of security and citizens' adoption of self-help mechanisms of justice.[41]

The Tláhuac case is one among many that have taken place in Mexico over the last decades. However, a number of particularities make it a salient case for studying the relationship between lynching and insecurity in contemporary Mexico. For instance, the lynching in San Juan Ixtapoyan was one of only two that had been filmed and broadcast in Mexico at the time,[42] and it was the first to involve the assassination of two highly ranked police officers (the third officer survived). Moreover, it happened at the heart of what is considered to be a "modern Mexico," and the case exemplified the rivalry between the federal government and the local government and between two highly politicized police institutions, the PFP and Mexico City's police.[43]

As explained above, and similarly to the 1930s attacks against socialist teachers, the lynching in San Juan Ixtapoyan was represented as an expression of the backwardness of those who perpetrated it. Andrés Manuel López Obrador, then mayor of Mexico

City (2000–2005), played a pivotal role in the articulation of this discourse. Three years before the Tláhuac case, in reference to the lynching of a man caught trying to steal a religious image from a church in Mexico City, López Obrador stated that this type of act needed to be understood "as part of the history of the pueblos of Mexico" and that the government should not interfere with the "traditions of the people."[44] In 2004, this statement reappeared and quickly gained a hegemonic position, being quoted and used by representatives from both the right and left of the political spectrum in reference to the lynching in San Juan Ixtapoyan.

For instance, when interviewed about the lynching acts in San Juan Ixtapoyan, the main leader at the local assembly of the left-wing party, Partido Revolucionario Democrático (PRD), claimed that "it was unjustifiable that under the logic of traditions (usos y costumbres)" crimes like this would be carried out.[45] The same speaker added that "it had already become a constant that in these pueblos the logic of the community imposes itself on the logic of the law." Two days after the event, another newspaper article quoted one of the main representatives of the right-wing party, Partido Acción Nacional (PAN), who declared that it was outrageous to hear politicians, in the context of such "abhorrent" crimes, claiming that "the pueblo was always right" and that these acts could be justified as part of their traditions. He added that, after this act, "it was clear that a distinction must be made between what the *pueblo* of Mexico is and what the *mob* is."[46] By the same token, President Vicente Fox from the PAN party claimed he would "end the painful practice of the usos y costumbres" and that his government would eliminate the "shameful practice of taking justice into one's own hands."[47] As should be clear by now, these politicians only seemed to disagree on making usos y costumbres a justification for lynching or self-help justice but did not really challenge the idea that traditions were the main drivers behind these acts. In other words, they did not deny that the pueblo, the mob, or the multitude behaved violently owing to its particular traditions, only that this should not be used as an excuse to pardon or leave these acts unpunished. This is particularly salient in the case of the president who, by claiming he would "end" those "usos y costumbres" only echoed the statement made by his rival, the mayor of Mexico City.

Newspaper columnists and other public figures echoed this representation of lynching as an expression of people's traditions. For instance, a columnist writing on the Tláhuac case under the headline "Mexico bronco" ("Rough Mexico"), rejected these types of "atrocities" by crowds that want to take justice in their own hands and critiqued Mexico City's mayor for justifying these acts under the logic of "usos y costumbres."[48] The same day, another columnist also referred to the "*multitud y barbarie*" ("multitude and barbarity") mentioned in the mayor's statement and lamented the fact that "the multitude uses violence every time it feels threatened."[49] By the same token, the director of the National Human Rights Commission (Comisión Nacional de los Derechos Humanos, CNDH) suggested critically analyzing the "cultural forms" behind violent practices and asserted that "as a civilized nation, we do not accept the logic of usos y costumbres when human rights are violated."[50] The impact of this discourse was such that, even two years after the lynching, Carlos Monsiváis, one of the most influential public intellectuals in Mexico, stated in an article that "nothing justifies a lynching" and that to "argue that the usos y costumbres of the community . . . redeems the intolerance of centuries in the name of idolatry: the voice of the Pueblo is the voice of God."[51] Similar to the ways the criminalization of black Cuban veterans delegitimized racial protest and facilitated racist state violence (chapter 5, this volume), the discourse on traditions here depoliticized the actions of the perpetrators of lynching as backward.

DESTABILIZING DISCOURSE: TOWARD A CRITICAL INTERPRETATION

Thus far, I have presented two different episodes of lynching and their representations in the media and official discourses as acts that reflected either the religious fanaticism or the backwardness and traditions of given communities. In contrast to the attacks against socialist teachers, the lynching of the police officers in San Juan Ixtapoyan was not overtly represented in terms of the race or ethnicity of perpetrators. Nevertheless, given that the "race question" was "de-biologized" in Mexico at the outset of the twentieth century and was instead 'naturalized' or reified based on cultural markers such as language, dress, religion, and culture,[52] it is possible to assert that references to the *usos* and *costumbres* of given communities were indeed informed by racialized constructs. In other words, in contemporary Mexico, where race has become an "unsayable" and yet well-known category, references to the "traditions" of some groups or communities allows for the reinscription of these "naturalized" cultural markers. In Mexico, as in other Latin American countries such as Guatemala, Bolivia, and Ecuador, lynchings are not grounded in racial or ethnic differences; nor are they informed by customary laws. Rather, lynchings and their perpetrators have been "racialized" in particular ways as an *effect* of certain media and official representations.[53]

Representations of violence and crime have particular consequences for how we come to understand their origins and potential causes. In the case of the series of attacks against socialist teachers, the fact that media and official representations centered on the so-called religious fanaticism of the perpetrators resulted in the invisibility of the nonreligious factors that informed these acts. As mentioned above, the resistance to the socialist education project was not based solely on religious beliefs but was also driven by a strong opposition to agrarian reform and the negative impact this had on the material interests of landowners.[54] What is more, even if religious beliefs motivated these acts, a discourse that reduced religion to "false ideology," irrationality, or ignorance denied the fact that entire worldviews and forms of communal ties were fundamentally threatened by the implementation of these secularist and at times anticlerical policies.[55] By the same token, the fact that perpetrators were represented simply as "fanatics" created a depoliticized image of their actions that enabled the government to disavow them, undermining these communities' attempts to question the legitimacy of the postrevolutionary modernizing project. In other words, the categorization of these events as expressions of "religious fanaticism" reduced them to backward, irrational, and unpredictable incidents that, as such, had no bearing on the policies of state officials who claimed to represent reason, modernity, and legitimacy. As Paul Gillingham has suggested, representations of violence as expressions of cultural determinism or so-called regional traditions enabled the elites to "remove (their) agency from the commission of violence."[56] Although President Cárdenas would eventually revisit the socialist education project and eliminate some of its anticlerical elements, his first reaction to the attacks against the maestros was to authorize and even promote the use of arms among them.[57] This demonstrates that representations can exert a powerful impact on specific practices and actions.

In the case of the 2004 lynching in San Juan Ixtapoyan, in Mexico City, the emphasis on the alleged traditions and customs of this town served to obscure the statements the town's inhabitants made. Far from referring to "usos y costumbres," the inhabitants of San Juan Ixtapoyan repeatedly stated that their actions were based on the conviction that the three men were, in effect, attempting to kidnap their children from the school. When a journalist interrogated two women, for instance, and asked them if they were afraid of living next to neighbors who were capable of lynching so-called criminals, they responded, "No," they were not afraid of them. Instead, they stated: "We are afraid of the police, who are going to come after us now. . . . No, we are not afraid of them. They were just defending our children. They did it in self-defense and did not act malevolently."[58] What is more, the town's inhabitants declared the reason they would not turn in the alleged criminals to the police was that they did not trust law officials. They declared that, on previous occasions, the police had released alleged criminals in exchange for money.[59] That these statements were not taken up by any of the politicians mentioned above confirms the hegemonic position of the discourse on traditions. It also reflects the political elites' unwillingness to address the need to reform the police forces at both local and federal levels or to acknowledge the lack of legitimacy of the justice and security apparatus.

Furthermore, since this event was depicted as being driven by cultural traditions, as opposed to rational or calculated reasons, political elites were capable of applying a "guilty and innocent" logic similar to the one used in the case of the attacks against socialist teachers. That is, the inhabitants of San Juan Ixtapoyan, just like the so-called religious fanatics of the 1930s, were "guilty" of their violent and irrational acts but were also "innocent" since their acts were unplanned and impulsive. In a word, they were nonpolitical. Moreover, as in the 1930s case, the political elites not only missed an opportunity to critically assess their performance but also decided to respond to these actions with violence. While in the 1930s the government decided to arm the socialist teachers, in 2004 the reaction was to send a large security force, which included members of the Federal Preventive Police, the day after the lynching. During this operation, which was carried out at night and included unauthorized intrusions and several private property damages, thirty-five people were arrested based on the "matching" of these guilty parties with images from the television videos transmitted the night before.[60] Moreover, both federal and local governments stated that this event demonstrated that the presence of police and security forces had to be strengthened in the area, a decision that illustrates that the statements made by the town's inhabitants regarding the lack of trust in the police went unheeded.

Despite the prevalence of these representations of lynching in newspaper reports and official discourses, a critical reading of both primary and secondary material makes an alternative interpretation of the events possible. In the final section of this chapter, I would like to follow the articulation of an alternative discourse that may help evince the limits and incompleteness of the discourse on traditions and religious fanaticism and illuminate a political dimension that is central to understand both incidents of collective violence.

In the case of the 1930s, the same newspapers contained references to episodes of lynching that were directly organized by "*bandas de pistoleros*" (armed gangs), "*insurrectos*" (insurgents), or "*grupos de alzados*" (groups of rebels). In this case, lynchings were no longer depicted as irrational reactions of the "mob" but rather as purposeful and well-planned actions organized by armed bandits who, among other things, aimed at resisting the agrarian reform promoted by President Cárdenas. Interestingly enough, in all the references I found to these groups of so-called bandits, no mention is made of their ethnicity and no emphasis is put on their religious beliefs. For instance, a newspaper reported that in April 1936, seventy armed individuals in Tlapacoyan, Veracruz, burned a professor alive and cut off the ears of another.[61] The year before and in reference to the town of San Martín Hidalgo in Jalisco, the same newspaper reported that a "group of rebels" (*alzados*) attacked two maestras and their father for promoting socialist education. According to the report, the teachers' ears were also cut off and the father's body was mutilated and hanged by a noose.[62] A group of "*bandoleros*" was also identified as responsible for the killing of a rural maestro on November 26, 1935, in Puebla. According to the report, the leader of the group killed the rural maestro by cutting off his head with a machete in front of his class. The group of "bandoleros," apprehended and executed by the federal forces the following day, allegedly had in their possession a list of people whom they were planning to assassinate.[63] Letters addressing President Cárdenas also reveal the participation of organized groups of pistoleros. For instance, on November 25, 1937, a peasant organization of Atlixco, Puebla, addressed the president to ask for justice for the assassination of teacher Jerónimo Meléndez at the hands of a group of pistoleros. The president of the organization requested arms be provided to defend teachers.[64] By the same token, the revolutionary party, Partido Nacional Revolucionario (PNR), denounced the killing of a socialist teacher by bandits under the command of Enrique Rodriguez, alias "El Tallarín." Rodriguez was known for subjecting teachers to different forms of torture, including hanging them in public plazas and cutting off their ears.[65]

In the case of the lynching in San Juan Ixtapoyan, this alternative discourse on politics was articulated by politicians themselves and put into circulation by newspapers. For instance, on December of 2004, a polemic among leaders of different political parties and between the federal and local police forces revealed that the federal government had been carrying out undercover operations in San Juan Ixtapoyan, not only to prevent drug-trafficking activities but also to counter the alleged presence of insurrectionary groups such as the Ejército Revolucionario del Pueblo, known as EPR (People's Revolutionary Army) in the area. Francisco Labastida, one of the most notorious leaders of the PRI, declared that Tláhuac had been under constant surveillance, because the EPR kept one of its main cells in this area.[66] Following his statement, a member of Mexico City's security agency declared that, in effect, the federal government had maintained security operations in the area to watch and control the activities of this group without informing the local government as it should have.[67] Finally, the director of security forces in Mexico City even declared that the lynching had probably been carried out or planned by EPR members themselves.[68] No reasons were offered for why a revolutionary group, known in the country for carrying out large terrorist operations against the state's gas and oil infrastructure, would be behind a lynching in the small municipality of San Juan Ixtapoyan. No reasons were given either as to how to reconcile this version with the fact that locals themselves seemed to have supported the lynching, as attested by the video and by their declarations to the newspapers.

How should we interpret this rather alien reference to more "organized" political actors at the margins of a discourse that represents perpetrators and their actions as unpredictable, irrational, and unorganized? My interpretation is twofold. On the one hand, this alternative discourse reveals the limits and partial character of the discourse on traditions. In the first case, it serves to confirm that violent acts against socialist teachers did not follow exclusively religious motives but were also connected to political disputes over the agrarian reform promoted by President Cárdenas through the socialist education project.[69] In the second case, even if we remain skeptical about the real presence of the EPR in this area and more so about its alleged participation in the lynching, the careful and high-level covert operations carried out by the federal government in San Juan Ixtapoyan problematize the image of this municipality as a place caught in traditional usos y costumbres. Instead, this representation seems to reveal a town caught in a complex dispute between different police forces and shaped by the alleged presence of drug-trafficking activities or so-called guerrillas.

On the other hand, if the discourse of traditions renders lynchings as irrational, unpredictable, and nonpolitical by associating them with perpetrators who are mobilized by their religious beliefs, this "discourse on politics" excludes cultural reasons and any racialized underpinnings in order to account for perpetrators who are depicted, in this case, as more rational and political (the bandits in the 1930s, the guerrilla members in 2004). In this sense, instead of claiming that all lynchings are nonpolitical, this discourse seems to suggest that they can be political if they are planned, rational, and predictable. Moreover, it excludes culturalist and racialized claims only when the latter characteristics hold. In so doing, I believe, the latter discourse leaves untouched an understanding that reiterates unplanned and impulsive acts as nonpolitical. More importantly perhaps, it confirms that, when it comes to analyzing violent acts, the category of "race" exists and is inscribed through the use of a certain discourse on traditions, since ethnic or racial constructs are not mentioned overtly or covertly in reference to the violence perpetrated by these other more "political" actors. Finally, it should be said that in both cases the references to these more organized groups did not do away with the hegemonic position of the discourse on religious fanaticism or traditions; these "other" actors were only mentioned in the marginalia of the main statements made by high-level state officials (i.e., the president and the mayor), which kept referring to either "religious fanaticism" or to "usos y costumbres." It is up to the researcher, then, to "intervene" or revise the discourse on traditions through the discourse on politics and question the underlying assumptions of both.

CONCLUSIONS

In this chapter, I have taken two historically distant and apparently different acts of collective violence and analyzed them through the lens of a hegemonic discourse on tradition that, based on culturalist and racialized claims, excluded the possibility of understanding these acts as related to the policies and lines of action of the state. I discussed how this discourse attained its hegemonic position and some of its possible effects and finally introduced an alternative discourse that contaminated, albeit did not destabilize entirely, the discourse on traditions.

Violent acts live and circulate through their representations. They are reiterated, spoken, and represented through discourses that pretend to be able to grasp or contain their complexity. Based on the two different examples discussed here, it may be that we are witnessing the historical tenacity and persuasiveness of a discourse that offers only a limited and partial degree of legibility through the overt and covert uses of race and the so-called traditions associated with it. As suggested by Pablo Piccato, abhorrent or irrational criminal or violent acts have been traditionally excluded from central debates about politics and civil society in Mexico.[70] Nonetheless, the recent upsurge in lethal and nonlethal forms of violence in Mexico, related particularly to drug trafficking, but also to kidnappings, extortions, self-defense forces, and lynchings, has highlighted the need to rethink the place of violence within Mexico's past and present sociopolitical landscape.[71]

Vigilantism and self-help forms of justice such as lynching constitute unique sites to analyze why and how the state's legality and legitimacy is questioned, resisted, and contested. To subsume these acts within a narrative of backwardness and irrationality is to deny their political dimension and to further contribute to a racialized understanding of collective acts of violence. In contemporary Mexico, where groups of armed vigilantes have emerged in different states of the Mexican territory such as Guerrero, Michoacán, Morelos, and Chiapas as a reaction to the country's security crisis, it becomes pressing to develop a critical understanding of violence and crime capable of highlighting the political drivers of perpetrators as well as the state's responsibility in the perpetuation of violence. It is my hope that through the analysis presented in this chapter a further step has been taken to think critically about how discourses may affect and limit our understanding of crime and violence.

NOTES

1. David Garland, "Penal Excess and Surplus Meaning: Public Torture Lynchings in Twentieth-Century America," *Law and Society Review* 39, no. 4 (2005): 793–833; Roberta Senechal de la Roche, "Collective Violence as Social Control," *Sociological Forum* 11, no. 1 (1996): 97–128.

2. Mary K. Vaughan, "El papel político del magisterio socialista de México, 1934–1940: Un estudio comparativo de los casos de Puebla y Sonora," in *Memoria del XII Simposio de Historia y Antropología* (Sonora: Universidad de Sonora, Departamento de Historia y Antropología, 1988), 2:175–97.

3. Diane E. Davis, "Undermining the Rule of Law: Democratization and the Dark Side of Police Reform in Mexico," *Latin American Politics and Society* 48, no. 1 (2006): 55–86.

4. Alan Knight has argued that the racist underpinnings of what was known as "Indigenismo" shifted during the 1930s from biological to so-called sociological attributes (i.e., culture, religion, social organization) but retained its deterministic undertones. See Knight, "Racism, Revolution, and Indigenismo: Mexico, 1910–1940," in *The Idea of Race in Latin America, 1870–1940*, ed. Richard Graham, 71–113 (Austin: University of Texas Press, 1990), 72–73, 92–94.

5. See Leigh Binford and Nancy Churchill, "Lynching and States of Fear in Urban Mexico," *Anthropologica* 51, no. 2 (2009): 1–12; Knight, "Racism, Revolution, and Indigenismo," 72–73, 92–94, 1–12; Antonio Fuentes Díaz, *Linchamientos: Fragmentación y respuesta en el México neoliberal* (Puebla: Benemérita Universidad Autónoma de Puebla, 2005); Daniel M. Goldstein, *The Spectacular City: Violence and Performance in Urban Bolivia* (Durham, NC: Duke University Press, 2004); Jose de Souza Martins, "Lynchings—Life by a Thread: Street Justice in Brazil, 1979–1988," in *Vigilantism and the State in Modern Latin America*, ed. Martha Huggins, 21–32 (New York: Praeger 1999).

6. Maria Teresa Sierra, "The Revival of Indigenous Justice in Mexico: Challenges for Human Rights and the State," *Political and Legal Anthropology Review* 28, no. 1 (2005): 52–72; Christopher Krupa, "Histories in Red: Ways of Seeing Lynching in Ecuador," *American Ethnologist* 36, no. 1 (2009): 20–39.

7. Ibid.

8. Krupa, "Histories in Red," 21–22.

9. Ben Fallaw, *Religion and State Formation in Postrevolutionary Mexico* (Durham, NC: Duke University Press, 2013); Marjorie Becker, *Setting the Virgin on Fire: Lázaro Cárdenas, Michoacán Peasants, and the Redemption of the Mexican Revolution* (Berkeley: University of California Press, 1996); Stephen Lewis, "A Window into the Recent Past in Chiapas: Federal Education and Indigenismo in the Highlands, 1921–1940," *Journal of Latin American Anthropology* 6, no. 1 (2001): 67; Vaughan, "El papel politico del magisterio."

10. On September 14, 1968, in the town of San Miguel Canoa in Puebla, Mexico, hundreds of members of the community lynched five university workers from the Universidad Autónoma de Puebla. The lynching was triggered by the belief that these university workers were actually communist students from the university. Guillermina Meaney, *Canoa: El crimen impune* (México: Editorial Posada, 1977); Osvaldo Romero, *La violencia como fenómeno social: El linchamiento en San Miguel Canoa, Puebla* (México: Jorale, 2006).

11. Claudio Lomnitz, "Mexico's First Lynching: Sovereignty, Criminality, Moral Panic," *Critical Historical Studies* 1, no. 1 (2014): 85–123. As explained by Lomnitz, the case was not really a lynching but an execution carried out by a group of policemen against the victim while in their custody. However, the case did trigger a national debate about the nature of collective violence in Mexico and its relation to "el pueblo" or to the state.

12. Hinnerk Onken, "Lynching in Peru in the Nineteenth and Early Twentieth Centuries," in *Globalizing Lynching History: Vigilantism and Extralegal Punishment from an International Perspective*, ed. Manfred Berg and Simon Wendt, 173–86 (New York: Palgrave Macmillan, 2011).

13. *La Jornada* is associated with a more leftist or critical political ideology, whereas *El Universal* is informed by a more center-right discourse or ideology. The searching criteria were the words "Tláhuac," "lynching" (*linchamiento*), and "San Juan Ixtapoyan." Coverage from 2004–5 was taken from the newspapers' official Web sites: http://www.jornada.unam.mx and http://www.eluniversal.com.mx.

14. References to the cutting off of ears of teachers were particularly salient in the press. This distinct form of mutilation might be interpreted as a means to denounce the government's "deafness" to those who opposed the socialist education or simply a way to mark the teachers' bodies in order to send a message to a broader audience.

15. Jean Meyer, "An Idea of Mexico: Catholics in the Revolution," in *The Eagle and the Virgin: Nation and Cultural Revolution in Mexico, 1910–1940*, ed. Mary Kay Vaughan and Stephen E. Lewis, 281–96 (Durham, NC: Duke University Press, 2006), 291.

16. Lewis, "A Window into the Recent Past in Chiapas"; Ana María Alonso, "Territorializing the Nation and 'Integrating the Indian': 'Mestizaje' in Mexican Official Discourses and Public Culture," in *Sovereign Bodies: Citizens, Migrants, and States in the Postcolonial World*, ed. Thomas Blom Hansen and Finn Stepputat, 39–60 (Princeton, NJ: Princeton University Press, 2005); Knight "Racism, Revolution, and Indigenismo."

17. Enrique Guerra Manzo, "The Resistance of the Marginalised: Catholics in Eastern Michoacán and the Mexican State, 1920–1940," *Journal of Latin American Studies* 40, no. 1 (2008): 109–33; Vaughan, "El papel político del magisterio."

18. Fallaw, *Religion and State Formation*.

19. "Rinde informe de la investigación practicada en la zona de Teziutlán, Puebla," November 26, 1935, Archivo Nacional de México, Fondo Investigaciones Políticas y Sociales, caja 71, exp. 2 (hereafter AGN/FIPS).

20. "Tres maestros fueron asesinados en Puebla," *El Universal*, November 17, 1935.

21. Francesca Polletta, "'It Was Like a Fever': Why People Protest," in *It Was Like a Fever: Storytelling in Protest and Politics* (Chicago: University of Chicago Press, 2006), 32.

22. Fallaw, *Religion and State Formation*; Lewis, "A Window into the Recent Past in Chiapas"; Vaughan, "El papel político del magisterio."

23. Knight, "Racism, Revolution, and Indigenismo." See also Keith Brewster, "Redeeming the 'Indian': Sport and Ethnicity in Post-Revolutionary Mexico," *Patterns of Prejudice* 38, no. 3 (2004): 213–31.

24. "Numerosos muertos y heridos en Ciudad Gonzales: Zafarrancho sangriento por causa religiosa," *Excélsior*, March 31, 1936. Emphasis mine.

25. Ibid.

26. Antonio Morales, "Pídase separación inmediata cura Pamatacuaro," July 8, 1939, AGN, Dirección General de Gobierno (hereafter DGN), Asesinatos, caja 56, exp. 42.

27. "Se consigna al Cura José María Núñez de Queréndaro, Michoacán," May 4, 1935, AGN, DGN, Quejas, caja 54, exp. 45.

28. Jesús Torres Cárdenas y Quirino Méndez, "Queja en contra del cura Ignacio Crezco por fanatizar a la población, oponerse al progreso y la renovación de las masas campesinas," October 19, 1934, AGN, DGN, Quejas, caja 54, exp. 45.

29. Loveman argues that Brazil's modernizing elites were unable to recognize certain acts of resistance among rural populations *qua acts of resistance* that attempted to question the elites' modernizing techniques. Instead, these elites imposed categories such as "*povo ignorante*," "stupid," and "fanatic" to explain mobilizations that were neither irrational nor determined exclusively by religious beliefs but purposefully political and built on legitimate grounds. Mara Loveman, "Blinded Like a State: The Revolt Against Civil Registration in Nineteenth-Century Brazil," *Comparative Studies in Society and History* 49, no. 1 (2007): 5–39.

30. "No es posible declarar si se ha logrado algo con la desfanatización de indios," *Excelsior*, September 11, 1935. See also Matthew Butler, "God's Campesinos? Mexico's Revolutionary Church in the Countryside," *Bulletin of Latin American Research* 28, no. 2 (2009): 165–84; Roberto Blancarte, "Intransigence, Anticommunism, and Reconciliation: Church/State Relations in Transition," in *Dictablanda: Politics, Work, and Culture in Mexico, 1938–1968*, ed. Paul Gillingham and Benjamin T. Smith, 70–88 (Durham, NC: Duke University Press, 2014).

31. "Los maestros rurales ante el presidente Cárdenas," *El Universal*, December 5, 1935.

32. "Se autoriza a los maestros rurales para usar armas," *Excelsior*, November 8, 1935.

33. "Turba quema vivos a dos agentes de la PFP; otro en estado grave," *La Jornada*, November 24, 2004; "Detienen a 33 presuntos implicados en el linchamiento de dos policías," *La Jornada*, November 25, 2004.

34. "Turba quema vivos a dos agentes de la PFP," *La Jornada*, November 24, 2004.

35. For an analysis of this trend in Latin America, see Mark Ungar, "The Privatization of Citizen Security in Latin America: From Elite Guards to Neighborhood Vigilantes," *Social Justice* 34, no. 3–4 (2007): 20–37.

36. Raúl Rodríguez Guillén, "Crisis de autoridad y violencia social: Los linchamientos en México," *Polis: Investigación y Análisis Sociopolítico y Psicosocial* 8, no. 2 (2012): 48–49.

37. Angelina Snodgrass Godoy, "When 'Justice' Is Criminal: Lynchings in Contemporary Latin America," *Theory and Society* 33, no. 6 (2004): 621–51.

38. Pablo Piccato, "Estadísticas del crimen en México: Series históricas, 1901–2001," http://www.columbia.edu/~pp143/estadisticascrimen/EstadisticasSigloXX.htm.

39. Data from the World Value Survey indicates that the percentage of Mexican citizens expressing distrust in the legal system increased from 12 percent to 25.3 percent from 1981 to

1997. In other words, distrust in the legal system more than doubled during this period. See Robert Kossick, "The Rule of Law and Development in Mexico," *Arizona Journal of International and Comparative Law* 21, no. 3 (2004): 718.

40. Pilar Domingo, "Rule of Law, Citizenship, and Access to Justice in Mexico," *Mexican Studies* 15, no. 1 (1999): 151–91; Diane Davis, "Policing and Regime Transition: From Postauthoritarianism to Populism to Neoliberalism," in *Violence, Coercion, and State-Making in Twentieth-Century Mexico: The Other Half of the Centaur*, ed. Will G. Pansters, 68–90 (Stanford, CA: Stanford University Press, 2012).

41. Davis, "Undermining the Rule of Law."

42. The first refers to the lynching of a man who was accused of having raped a woman in a small town in Veracruz, Mexico, in 1996. A "passive participant" in the lynching filmed the event, and the video was distributed between the two main TV networks in Mexico, Televisa and Television Azteca. See Comisión Nacional de Derechos Humanos, *Linchamiento: Justicia por propia mano (casos específicos)* (México: Comisión Nacional de los Derechos Humanos, 2003), 36.

43. The 2000–2005 period was characterized by a strong rivalry between the president and the mayor of Mexico City. At the federal level, Vicente Fox became the first elected president (2000–2006) from a political party opposing the Partido Revolucionario Institucional (PRI), the party that had ruled the country for seventy-one years without interruption. At the local level, Andrés Manuel López Obrador (2000–2005) was the third head of government in Mexico City who belonged to a non-PRI party. Davis, "Undermining the Rule of Law."

44. Quoted in Snodgrass Godoy, "When 'Justice' Is Criminal," 626.

45. "Turba quema vivos a dos agentes de la PFP," *La Jornada*, November 24, 2004.

46. "Mandos superiores nos ordenaron esperar, acusan agentes de la PFP," *La Jornada*, November 26, 2004. Emphasis mine. This impulse on behalf of political elites to differentiate the mob from the "pueblo" can be traced back to the turn of the twentieth century in Mexico. In reference to the alleged lynching against Arnulfo Arrullo, a man who assailed President Porfirio Díaz, Lomnitz (2014) describes the political class's condemnation of the lynching as an act that stained the dignity of Mexico's "pueblo" and brought it dangerously close to the "mob rule" that characterized the American South at the time. See Lomnitz, "Mexico's First Lynching," 105–6.

47. "Ofrece Fox acabar con la *dolosa práctica* de los usos y costumbres," *La Jornada*, December 3, 2004.

48. Francisco Ugalde, "México Bronco," *El Universal*, December 26, 2004.

49. Laura Elena Herrejón, "Multitud y barbarie," *El Universal*, December 26, 2004.

50. "La estabilidad social y política, en riesgo por la violencia: CNDH," *La Jornada*, January 26, 2005.

51. Carlos Monsiváis, "La tolerancia y las sociedades de convivencia," *La Jornada*, November 19, 2006.

52. Knight, "Racism, Revolution, and Indigenismo."

53. Krupa "Histories in Red"; Goldstein, *The Spectacular City*; Snodgrass Godoy, "When 'Justice' Is Criminal."

54. The agrarian reform produced tremendous violence, which intersected with clericalism. See Romana Falcón and Soledad García, *La semilla en el surco: Adalberto Tejeda y el radicalism en Veracruz, 1883–1960* (Mexico City: El Colegio de México, 1986); John B. Williman, "Adalberto Tejeda and the Third Phase of the Anticlerical Conflict in Twentieth Century Mexico," *Journal of Church and State* 15, no. 3 (1973): 437–54.

55. Meyer, "An Idea of Mexico."

56. Paul Gillingham, "Who Killed Crispín Aguilar? Violence and Order in the Postrevolutionary Countryside," in Pansters, *Violence, Coercion, and State-Making in Twentieth-Century Mexico*, 110.

57. "Los maestros rurales ante el presidente Cárdenas," *El Universal*, December 5, 1935; "Garantías de mejoramiento de los maestros," *El Universal*, December 11, 1935; "Se autoriza a los maestros rurales para usar armas," *Excélsior*, November 8, 1935.

58. "Linchamiento en Tláhuac: Del rumor a la barbarie," *La Jornada*, November 28, 2004.

59. "Pedirán datos de Tláhuac a próximo titula de SSP," *El Universal*, December 6, 2004.

60. "Identifican a seis implicados en linchamiento," *El Universal*, November 25, 2004; "Puedo identificar a algunos culpables," *El Universal*, December 6, 2004.

61. "Fue quemado vivo un maestro rural y otro más fue vilmente mutilado," *Excélsior*, April 22, 1936; and "Fue duramente batida la gavilla que quemó a un maestro y amputó las orejas de otro en Tlapacoyan," *Excélsior*, April 23, 1936. See also Heather Fowler-Salamini, *Agrarian Radicalism in Veracruz* (Lincoln: University of Nebraska Press, 1978).

62. "Maestros socialistas sin orejas: Se las cortó un núcleo de gente alzada," *Excélsior*, November 19, 1935.

63. "Los asesinos de maestros muertos por las tropas," *El Universal*, November 19, 1935.

64. Antonio Echegaray, "Coreograma dirigido al Presidente Cárdenas," November 25, 1937, AGN, Documentación de la Administración Pública, caja 53, fol. 2/012.2(18), exp. 62.

65. Flaviano García, "Carta de protesta," March 5, 1938, AGN, Documentación de la Administración Pública, caja 53, fol. 2/012.2(18), exp. 57.

66. "Labastida: Desde 98 indicios de grupos extremistas en Tláhuac," *La Jornada*, December 17, 2004.

67. "El linchamiento en Tláhuac, acto dirigido e intencionado: Regino," *La Jornada*, December 23, 2004.

68. "En marcha, investigación sobre la presunta presencia del EPR en Tláhuac," *La Jornada*, March 5, 2005.

69. Vaughan, "El papel político del magisterio," 179.

70. Pablo Piccato, "Homicide as Politics in Modern Mexico," in *Murder and Violence in Modern Latin America*, ed. Eric A. Johnson et al., 104–25 (West Sussex: Wiley-Blackwell, 2013).

71. Will G. Pansters, "Zones of State-Making: Violence, Coercion, and Hegemony in Twentieth Century Mexico," in Pansters, *Violence, Coercion, and State-Making in Twentieth-Century Mexico*, 3–39.

CONCLUSION

৯৯

Toward an Intersectional Vision of Crime

BONNIE A. LUCERO

ONE OF the most powerful themes in modern Latin American history is the stark and persisting tension between inclusive discourse and exclusionary practice. The Enlightenment ideas that inspired the wars for independence in mainland Spanish America in the early nineteenth century provided the intellectual groundwork for the construction of socially inclusive nationalist discourses in many Latin American countries—ones that rarely translated into substantial political inclusion, economic mobility, and social status for nonwhite, poor, working-class, and rural peoples.[1]

A compelling explanation for the ways national elites reconciled liberal nationalist ideologies with exclusionary practices can be found in the concept of hegemony articulated by Italian intellectual Antonio Gramsci.[2] Hegemony has come to connote the popular acceptance and internalization of the interests of the ruling group as universal, rational, and natural as a result of such nonviolent means as co-opting and incorporating special interest groups into the dominant order.[3] Those nonviolent, often implicit forms of control that produce popular consent are usually buttressed by actual or threatened state violence, such as policing, military force, arrest, and imprisonment. But effective ideology preempts the need for such violence, thereby reproducing the dominant order as popular sectors police themselves.[4]

Historians have zeroed in on nationalist discourses as a key terrain on which Latin American elites constructed state hegemony. In particular, elites in countries like Argentina, Brazil, Cuba, and Mexico developed national myths of racial harmony, inclusion, and equality, often nationalizing sanitized versions of nonwhite cultures to prove how insignificant race had become. In countries with dense indigenous populations such as Mexico and Peru, the mestizo emerged as a celebrated national type.[5] In countries like Brazil and Cuba, where people of African descent constituted a significant portion of the national populations, ideals of racial brotherhood and racial democracy offered black peoples theoretical inclusion.[6] Still others like Argentina and Chile constructed their national identities around their histories of European immigration, downplaying the presence of significant black and indigenous minorities.[7]

At the same time as elites across Latin America constructed inclusive nationalist discourses, they confronted prevailing Euro-American views that black and indigenous populations were incompatible with civilization and self-government.[8] They attempted to reconcile this paradox by limiting the practical applications of discourses of raceless nationalism. They used discourses of *mestizaje* and racial brotherhood to erase nonwhites from conversations about ideal national identities and to appropriate indigeneity and blackness for their own purposes.[9] They excluded enslaved, indigenous, and propertyless men (not to mention all women until the twentieth century) from many of the rights of citizenship, while continuing to define civic virtue as the domain of "cultured and educated men." Indeed, these very myths of inclusion enabled elites to veil periodic state violence against nonwhite groups alternately in a cloak of nationalist myths of racial democracy and positivist propaganda in favor of European immigration to "improve" the national population and foster economic growth.[10] Despite rhetoric of inclusivity, these nationalist discourses helped reproduce the social exclusion they seemingly preempted.[11]

A striking corollary to this gap between inclusive theory and exclusionary practice was the increasing criminalization of the poor and nonwhites. The rising tide of state force suggests that these marginalized populations did not tacitly accept their exclusion. Some scholars have argued that state violence in the form of surveillance, policing, disciplining, and incarceration (to repress crime) highlights the failures of hegemony, or at very least its incomplete reign over the masses.[12] The now-famous refrain that "a functioning police state needs no police" encapsulates this common-sense perspective.[13] By the same logic, pervasive violent encounters between agents of the state and criminalized subjects reveal the incomplete, contested, and uneven development of consensus about what and who is criminal, rather than symbolizing the total hegemony of dominant notions of criminality.

To a certain extent, the notion that state violence against criminals reflects the incompleteness of state hegemony makes sense given the growing rift between raceless nationalism and criminalizing discourses disproportionately targeting racial others and the poor. However, the research in the present volume points to the limitations of this approach. This book has explored the tension between inclusive discourse and exclusionary practice by examining the ongoing, intersecting, and often conflicting processes of constructing and contesting criminality in modern Latin America. The chapters in the first part of the book explore the construction of criminalizing discourses by state authorities, scientists and intellectuals, and the media. These chapters expose the internal contradictions within these criminological discourses and challenge the assumed coherence and homogeneity of the elite groups who produced them. The chapters in the second part assess the myriad ways that popular sectors—whether workers, mothers, racial "others," or some combination of these—negotiated and confronted these dominant visions of crime. The authors reveal significant degrees of individual agency in confronting scientific, legal, and policing practices that targeted them as actual or potential criminals and subverting the neat assumptions articulated in criminological theories. These chapters also show that popular actors occasionally faced overt state violence to silence their attempts to negotiate the social hierarchy.

Following historians of crime like Robert Buffington and Carlos Aguirre, the scholarship presented in this volume suggests that criminalization afforded elites across Latin America a powerful way of *legitimizing*, rather than ameliorating, social hierarchies that privileged them while seeming to adhere to inclusive nationalist ideologies.[14] I would like to extend this idea by arguing that criminalizing discourses themselves served as powerful ideological tools of hegemony, rather than reflections of its incompleteness. While the state's need to resort to violence might betray popular disagreements with dominant notions of criminality, the discord is not inconsistent with Gramsci's notion of hegemony, which he insisted was defined by negotiation rather than consensus.[15]

The significance of criminalization for consolidating an existing social and political order is twofold. First, criminalizing certain acts through scientific discourse, media representations, and legislation effectively contributes to the construction of hegemony by communicating what kinds of conduct are unacceptable, and by extension how good citizens *should* behave.[16] In this way, law dichotomizes the possibilities of human behavior into legal and illegal, scientists and intellectuals create theories to explain who commits crimes and why, and sensationalized media representations of crime help circulate these "truths," in service of conflating illegality with immorality.[17] Even when subordinate groups challenged the visions of criminality concocted by the ruling elites, intellectuals, and the media, most of the time these protests at least nominally acknowledged crime as an act that could and should be punished.

Second, part of the power of criminalization is that it not only establishes the guidelines of acceptable behavior but also validates the use of violence against certain groups who challenge the dominant order by criminalizing their forms of resistance and subsistence strategies. Defining criminality allowed national elites to fold violence against internal enemies into the justifiable and accepted everyday practices of the state, ironically all in the name of progress and the minimization of future disorder and violence. Because prevailing ideas about crime justified and validated the punishment of suspected or potential criminals, the violence of these forms of control was rendered less visible, so long as the majority of the population had internalized the dominant understanding of crime. Policing, legally prescribed punishments, and even assault or assassination of individuals refusing to conform were no longer officially considered violent acts but rather widely accepted instances of the state's legitimate use of force in service of order, progress, modernity, national security, and the prevention of disorder.

If criminalization functions as an ideological tool of hegemony, then understanding how criminality is defined, rationalized, and reproduced is essential for deciphering how it helps sustain the dominant order. Scholars have rightly noted that categories of difference such as class and race have been central to notions of criminality and thereby reinforce the prevailing social order. However, one of the reasons it has been so difficult to discern the role of criminalizing discourses in the construction of state hegemony is that most studies of crime focus on the classist and racist dimensions of criminalization alone. Studies of race and class as isolated systems of difference in criminalizing discourses necessarily face challenges in explaining how these categories could form such compelling and explicit features of ideas about crime, precisely because they existed in societies whose prevailing ideology eschewed race and embraced liberal inclusiveness, at least for men.

Despite the seeming conflation of crime with men's experiences in the existing scholarship, ideas about gender also served as a crucial, if understudied, dimension of criminalizing discourses, and they simultaneously intersected with and helped produce racial and class hierarchies. Nevertheless, scholars have paid less attention to these significant gendered undertones, which sometimes served to obscure and naturalize the supposed link between nonwhiteness and criminality. Even fewer studies explore the ways the intersections of these axes of difference render certain populations uniquely vulnerable to criminalization and the violence it mobilizes. I contend that studying the gendered underpinnings of the construction and contestation of criminality holds the key to understanding how criminalization served as a tool of hegemony precisely because of gender's implicit entwinement with race and class. Thus, the authors in this volume have emulated the pioneers of crime history by paying careful attention to race and class as systems of oppression through which criminalization operated. Building on that foundation, I seek to incorporate some of the insights from recent feminist scholarship on Latin America and U.S. black feminist critiques by paying attention to the gendered dimensions of what has been a decidedly male-centered narrative.[18]

In this conclusion, I argue for a more intersectional approach to the history of crime. I survey some of the existing historiography on social inequality and crime in

Latin America in order to trace the gradual incorporation of attention to gender as well as the implications of this shift for understandings of the role of crime in state consolidation. In the first section I show that most histories of the raced and classed dimensions of crime focus exclusively on men, usually without acknowledgement of this perspective and typically without engaging in gendered analysis. The second section examines some of the most important works on women's and gender histories of crime. A survey of the existing scholarship suggests that the conflation of women and gender still serves as a prevailing paradigm guiding the majority of studies of crime. Moving toward a truly *gendered* analysis of crime—which considers both men and women as gendered subjects—can help foreground the ways in which the exclusion of poor and nonwhite men from the rights of citizenship could be reproduced, naturalized, and ultimately justified in terms of their inadequate, excessive, or deficient gendered practices rather than on the basis of their race.

The third section examines some of the foundational studies analyzing race, class, and gender. I use this discussion to suggest ways to elaborate a more deliberate and methodical analysis of the ways the intersection of these systems of inequality shapes nonelite experiences and informs their strategies to subvert criminalization.[19] I offer some reflections on the ways in which this book has carved out space for, and, in modest ways, has helped construct an emerging intersectional perspective on criminality in Latin America. This perspective, at its best, foregrounds the intersections of race, class, and gender in ideas of criminality and in the tangible consequences of criminalization and persecution. The intersectional approach to studying the history of crime proposed here has the potential to reveal the ways state violence against criminals could be discursively transformed into the legitimate defense of the state.

CLASS AND RACE IN IDEAS ABOUT CRIMINALITY

One of the most salient themes in this volume has been the centrality of social difference to ruminations on, practices regarding, and prosecutions of crime. Existing historical studies of crime in modern Latin America foreground class as one of the most significant mechanisms of difference in processes of criminalization. Between the 1960s and the 1980s, many legal historians envisioned state institutions, particularly law and law enforcement, as "tools of domination, time-worn expressions of class rule"—a view that Gil Joseph noted still proves compelling given the differential access to legal justice the wealthy enjoy. Indeed, recent research shows that in cases such as Mexico, ruling elites deployed an initially contentious but ultimately effective classed vision of crime to impose their own visions of order and civilization on the supposed internal enemies within their societies.[20] As the scholarship contained in the pathbreaking edited collection *Crime and Punishment in Latin America* suggests, class hierarchy provided a fruitful analytical perspective. It allowed scholars to elucidate the ways individuals and groups labeled as dangerous used the legal system to lay claim to the rights of citizenship while challenging the unilaterality of elite power.[21]

Almost all the chapters in the present volume draw on this dense and insightful historiography on socioeconomic inequality in modern Latin America to highlight issues of class in both elite conceptualizations of crime and police prosecutions of supposed criminals as well as in poor and working-class people's negotiation of these ideas. Class distinctions proved essential to the creation of what James Garza calls the "underworld," a realm completely distinct from that of peaceful citizens and devoid of modernity. It was also crucial in Teresa P. R. Caldeira's ethnographical research in São Paulo, where elites responded to the presumed threat of poor migrants and urban dwellers by walling off and segregating the urban landscape.[22] This moral distinction between criminals and law-abiding people undergirded the fantastical press coverage of criminals that Sönke Hansen charts in midcentury Peruvian *policiales*, while also offering a source of tensions between beat policemen and police administrators, as Juandrea Bates shows for early twentieth-century Argentina.

Although national states in Latin American countries certainly faced limitations to their legitimacy and the totality of their power beyond the reach of the capital cities, several authors highlight the expansion of state surveillance and violence against marginalized populations in urban centers and regions considered central to strategic interests at the turn of the twentieth century. Certainly, scholars have recognized the centrality of violence to state formation.[23] However, much of the existing scholarship on crime, with the exception of studies of banditry, has focused on crime in urban zones—particularly the capital cities. This implicit association between crime and urban space obscures the diverse ways in which the construction and contestation of ideas about crime shaped the relationship between state formation and violence. Following the lead of the recent wave of microhistorical studies of provincial cities and rural zones, which have made a compelling case for the inclusion and consideration of Latin American historical experiences beyond capital cities, the present volume offers a multidimensional view of crime from major urban centers as well as provincial cities and rural areas.[24] This book has challenged the conflation of crime with urban space, offering a more multivalent view of the ways constructions of crime relied on class stratification.

By expanding the geographical framework beyond Latin America's major capital cities, this volume explores the ways ruling elites employed nonviolent as well as coercive means to legitimize, rationalize, justify, and naturalize such violence in service of the consolidation of state interests, which oftentimes conflicted with popular needs and desires. Several chapters of this book challenge the dominant paradigm linking urban space to criminality. My own chapter as well as that of Gregory Swedberg decenter capital cities by offering nuanced narratives of regional hubs, while Gema Santamaría interrogates the extent to which the vision of law and order developed in Mexico's capital applied to remote rural areas. Moreover, while Marcos Fernández Labbé explores the liminal spaces of international boundaries, Diego Galeano examines the tensions and international cooperation among South American capital cities and provincial hubs. By placing in dialogue provincial, rural, and internationally oriented studies with ones focusing on capitals and megacities, this volume has underscored the significance of the tensions between local, national, and international elites in defining crime and imposing order on populations deemed to be transgressive. Together, our interrogation of competing notions of criminality, emphasis on the relations between theory and experiences, as well as the broader geographical approach to the problem of crime in Latin America has helped highlight the limits of the state in imposing and enforcing elite notions of criminality on rural and provincial populations. These examples suggest that criminality emerged as a powerful, but ultimately incomplete, tool of the construction and perpetuation of the prevailing order at a given historical moment and place.

While class remains central to any analysis of modern Latin American criminality, this volume has articulated a certain challenge to the exclusivity of class as the driving force behind criminality and the main motor of subaltern contestation of criminalization. Conventional historiographical views of the transition from colony to republic emphasize the emergence of class as the primary unit of social hierarchy, and suggest that race and ethnicity became less salient after national independence. The shift away from colonial notions of race supposedly enabled the birth of liberal nations founded on myths of racial democracy.[25] This ideology remained discursively powerful despite its practical limitations. Even as elites upheld mestizos as quintessential national types, they promoted policies of white immigration to offset black and brown populations and implicitly envisioned miscegenation as a way to "improve" the national racial stock through gradual whitening. These changes would help bring Latin American societies' into conformity with "European" civilizing projects.[26]

One of the points of consensus that this book challenges is the neat division between racial caste systems of the colonial period and the liberal, color-blind class systems of the republican era. The research presented here has suggested that racial and ethnic categorizations and subjectivities intersected with class and remained critical in defining dominant notions of accused and accuser and in distinguishing between criminal acts and legitimate ones. This observation suggests greater continuity between the republican era and the colonial period than previously thought. Even though earlier generations of scholars have argued that the transition from colony to republic brought greater emphasis on class over caste, this volume contributes to a growing body of scholarship underscoring the persisting salience of race in the midst of emerging republican ideas about class following independence. Luz Huertas demonstrates this in her examination of intellectual debates on criminality in early twentieth-century Lima, and both Fernández Labbé and Hansen show the persistence of this type of racial thinking well into the mid-twentieth century in Chile and Peru, respectively. While Chilean authorities justified tighter surveillance of drug trafficking by claiming a role in protecting the "Chilean race" from a constructed foreign menace, yellow journalism in 1950s Peru drew on expanding literacy among the popular classes to reinforce racialized images of crime through nearly fictionalized news reports. The centrality of race—in its myriad intersections with class—in constructions of crime reinforced already established patterns of discrimination even within emerging inclusive liberal states, as criminality became a proxy for racialized and classed notions of danger. As illustrated in the work of Bonnie A. Lucero and Juandrea Bates, in spite of inclusive nationalist ideologies, there were profound continuities in the everyday experiences of poor and working-class Cubans and Argentineans, who were often black or racially mixed. In Cuba, African-descended veterans of the War of Independence encountered stark contrasts to the wartime discourse of racial brotherhood as they attempted to reintegrate themselves into civilian life. State violence against poor and working-class populations—often black—provided a means for the Cuban state to fortify inequalities without mentioning race. In the same vein, the divergence between popular and elite conceptions of crime in Argentina contributed to the increasing alienation of poor and working-class people from the rights of citizenship and the benefits of the state and also decreased the effectiveness of police reforms. Today most scholars can agree that neither race nor class acted in isolation; rather, they were intimately intertwined in the production and preservation of inequality.[27]

Despite the attention to the parallel workings of race and class in projects of criminalization and policing, one of the main problems with the historiography on race and crime is its implicit male perspective. The vast majority of the scholarship on the criminalization of African-descended, indigenous, mestizo, or immigrant groups, though purporting to be universal, focuses exclusively on men. Race and class certainly occupied a privileged place in conceptions of criminality, but criminalization was not merely a question of poverty and racial otherness, even if poor and working-class men and women of indigenous, African, and Asian ancestry did face greater scrutiny over their everyday lives than did members of whiter higher classes. In the next section, I explore the ways scholars in this volume and its predecessors have attempted to address the role of gender in the history of crime.

WOMEN AND GENDER IN THE HISTORY OF CRIME

One of the major challenges Latin American historians have confronted in the last decades has involved paying attention to the ways historical narratives so often considered universal are actually particularly gendered, masculinist ones. In the existing historiography on criminality in Latin America, this could not be truer. Historical writing in general, and studies of traditionally "masculine" areas such as war, politics, and crime in particular, has until recently been about men.[28] Nowhere are these implicit assumptions of maleness more profound than in studies of crime, which tend to reproduce what Huertas and others have identified a reluctance among elites to label women straightforwardly as criminals.[29] Despite this decidedly masculine slant in histories of crime in Latin America, scholars have gradually begun to incorporate women, and more recently gendered perspectives, into the field.

One of the most common ways historians have examined the intersection of women's experiences with crime is through the history of patriarchal control exercised through laws and practices related to sexual honor.[30] Verena Stolcke's pioneering study of sexual values in pre-emancipation Cuba underscored how the societal value placed on white women's sexual honor afforded certain white colonial women access to legal protections of their sexual honor while facilitating the sexual exploitation of women of color.[31] This work prompted a wave of research on the intersections of law and sexual honor. Studies of rape, sexual assault (*estupro*), abduction (*rapto*), deflowering, and other violations of women's sexual honor have painted a compelling portrait of the unique dangers and protections experienced by women of diverse social backgrounds within the patriarchal system of honor/shame in its intersections with class and racial hierarchies.[32]

Yet, women were more than victims of crime; some perpetrated criminal acts, or engaged in everyday subsistence strategies that agents of the state criminalized. Marcos Luiz Bretas points out that police in nineteenth-century Rio de Janeiro commonly mentioned their encounters with women, not only as victims of sexual assault and domestic violence but as suspected agents of immorality or disorder in their engagement with prostitution.[33] Although women undoubtedly participated in nearly all aspects of criminality, the existing historical research on the experiences of female criminals has been remarkably narrow. Indeed, most studies that depart from the conventional male-centered narrative of crime in Latin American history focus on women in distinctly "female" realms—fertility control, prostitution, motherhood, and sexual transgression. Women appear in much of the historiography as corrupting factors in criminal behavior, as individuals who fail in their gendered duties as wives, mothers, and educators, becoming negative forces in society. Perhaps the most significant branch of this scholarship has examined women's experiences and negotiation of prostitution in the nineteenth and twentieth centuries. Donna Guy demonstrated that policies aimed at rehabilitating prostitutes, preventing the spread of venereal disease, and reforming prostitution law ultimately stigmatized and repressed marginal women in Buenos Aires at the turn of the twentieth century.[34] These and similar "reforms" carried out across Latin America and the Caribbean responded to prostitution by surveilling and restricting women, rather than ameliorating their poverty or addressing the demands side of prostitution.[35] Subsequently, the historical study of prostitution has flourished to include countries as diverse as Brazil, Chile, Colombia, Cuba, Mexico, and Puerto Rico, though it is worth mentioning that not all studies consider prostitution within a framework of criminality because in many places it was not totally prohibited until the early twentieth century.[36]

Beyond the proliferation of scholarship on prostitution, historians have also begun to explore the points of contact between women and the state in the realms of reproduction, fertility control, and mental health. Kristin Ruggiero, Mala Htun, David Carey, and Cassia Roth, among others, have productively interrogated state policing of women's—particularly poor and nonwhite women's—reproductive and child-rearing practices, including the criminalization of abortion and infanticide in nineteenth-century Argentina, twentieth-century Guatemala and Brazil, and beyond.[37] Although the indices of crimes that women committed were typically significantly lower than for crimes that men committed, Elisa Speckman notes that women tended to commit different kinds of crimes than men. These "women's crimes" were usually, though not always, less violent, or at least usually resulted in less severe injuries. Women were also prosecuted for fertility control, particularly infanticide and abortion, or for crimes involving their roles as mothers, such as neglect or abandonment and corruption of minors. In Mexico, for example, women who committed these crimes were typically poor or working-class women, mainly mestizas, who worked outside their homes and were generally illiterate.[38] Other studies have similarly examined the criminalization of abortion and infanticide in nineteenth-century Argentina, twentieth-century Brazil, and beyond. The study of women has gained ground in the fields of mental health and institutionalization.[39]

While studies of women have slowly trickled into the historiography on crime and criminality in Latin America, no systematic attempt to analyze the unique ways in which women experienced and contested criminalization exists. In the two major edited volumes on crime in Latin America, for example, chapters on women seem almost randomly interspersed throughout collections focused more on developing a social history perspective concerned with how subaltern actors of all kinds experienced and navigated the structures of oppression. This approach lent itself to the study of subaltern classes and racial groups, usually men, treated in an implicitly universalist, unmarked way, while women's experiences appeared as particular cases, anomalies.[40] Because so much of the existing scholarship on crime focuses on male experiences, often without treating men as gendered subjects, this field has suffered from an intense neglect of the possibilities of using gender as a category of historical analysis.[41]

Adding women's experiences into the historiography on crime, while possibly offering challenges to the conflation of crime with men, does not necessarily equate to gendering the history of crime. It is not enough to apply a gender analysis only to women and activities supposedly associated with women, in part because this reinforces the conventional vision of the universality of the male experience and the particularity of the female experience.[42] Moreover, narrowly focusing on "women's crimes," such as prostitution, fertility control, and poor child-rearing, without equal attention to women's experiences beyond being sexual objects and reproducers renders women one-dimensional historical figures who were either victimized by agents of patriarchy or whose only meaningful actions lay in their sexual transgressions. Continually emphasizing women's criminalization as sexual deviants and poor mothers reinforces dangerous stereotypes that women's only value lies between their legs.

Histories of crime need to account for the significance of gender beyond oppression and victimization, beyond activities and spaces typically labeled as feminine, and beyond women and girls. After all, gender historians have repeatedly emphasized the relational character of gender in order to challenge the universality of male narratives and to unravel the assumption that women's experience was somehow more particular than that of men. As Joan Scott's call for the use of gender as an analytical tool suggests, an intersectional history of criminality must envision both men and women as gendered subjects. A few scholars have begun to heed this call by examining women's experiences beyond the confines of the domestic sphere, by paying attention to their relationships with men, and by considering men as gendered subjects in their own right. For example, Arlene J. Díaz's recent research on early republican Venezuela underscores the relationality of gender to highlight the ways in which women's engagement with the courts was influenced by and itself shaped men's negotiations over patriarchal and political control.[43]

Some of the most promising historical research on men as gendered subjects focuses on sexuality. One branch of this scholarship examines men's negotiations or transgressions of their expected roles as breadwinners in heterosexual patriarchal family units. In this vein, Steve Stern's pioneering 1995 study of men, women, and violence in late colonial Mexico is instructive because it situates men's violence within a gendered framework alongside the experiences of women. Through his study of the workers at El Teniente mine in Chile, Thomas Miller Klubbock shows how the imposition of bourgeois gender roles embodied in the patriarchal family through an American company's corporate welfare policies aimed to reduce male criminality and labor resistance.[44] Natalia Milenesio defied the conventional conflation of studies of prostitution with a focus on women by examining men's sexuality in relation to prostitution and venereal disease campaigns in twentieth-century Argentina. She demonstrated the ways that prevailing ideas about the regulation of female sexuality—embodied in ineffective prostitution reglamentation and indecent premarital examination of (virgin) women—resulted in the promulgation of a law in 1936 mandating premarital inspection of men for venereal disease in order to protect the future population of Argentina.[45]

The recent proliferation of studies of homosexual masculinities in Latin America, especially Mexico and Brazil, also holds promise for the field of crime history.[46] James N. Green, for example, explores ideas linking homosexuality to criminality in twentieth-century Brazil. He shows that Brazilian criminologists not only sought to criminalize supposedly deviant sexualities but also linked homosexual acts to other criminal behavior like murder, leading to the conflation of confinement with medical "rehabilitation" efforts.[47] These studies show how gendering men's experiences can bring new insights into the construction and contestation of criminality.

So much more can and must be done in order to gender the history of criminality in Latin America. One way we can begin to create space for more comprehensively gendered approaches to crime is by paying careful attention to how we define crime and criminality as well as the assumptions we make about who perpetrates crime and why. Literary critics, and to a lesser extent some historians of Latin America, have begun to examine the relationship between masculinity and crimes committed by men.[48] Historians of crime have ample material for further developing this line of inquiry. Consider the example of vagrancy—a common category of crime that few historians have considered in terms of gender. Understandings of vagrancy usually rested on profoundly masculinist assumptions related to the patriarchal duties of men, not to mention the racial presumption that poor and nonwhite men were inherently lazy and less inclined to take up formal work. Because vagrancy was quintessentially about policing the everyday productive labor of subordinate populations, the gendered, classed, and racial assumption that a man's duty included reporting to work every day to fulfill his function as a breadwinner for a supposedly domestic housewife demonstrates the ways a focus on this form of criminality might offer an exclusionary or incomplete vision of crime if it were presented in a universalist way. Most research on vagrancy unsurprisingly has focused on men, but few of these studies explicitly acknowledge the gender-specific nature of their work and fewer actively engage gender scholarship to explore the ways men as gendered subjects navigated this criminalized category.

Certainly, some exceptions existed in which vagrancy laws explicitly applied to both men and women, such as in early republican Venezuela, but the existing historiography does not address the extent to which authorities actually applied these laws to prosecute women for vagrancy.[49] Olivia María Gomes da Cunha examines cases in which Rio de Janeiro police detained women for vagrancy, but the assumptions these male police made—such as that the female suspects could not possibly already have criminal records—speak to the prevailing view of vagrancy as a crime committed by men.[50] Indeed, my own research on jail and prison records in American-occupied and early republican Cuba has not uncovered a single instance of a woman convicted of vagrancy—a crime of which men of the working class, of African descent, and of foreign birth were more commonly accused.[51] Studies of banditry show a similar pattern.[52]

Analyzing some of the research presented in this volume through a gendered lens might offer new insights on these fascinating case studies. What would the story of international crime in South America, for example, look like if gender became a consideration not only in noting the embarrassment of José Ferrari's nameless wife but also in helping decode the activities of Minga-Minga? Did international thieves like Minga-Minga and Narigueta (chap. 1) steal to support a family, or were their activities, mobility, and willingness to transgress law facilitated by their relative freedom from patriarchal responsibilities? How might we understand the significance of the presumably homosocial networks of international criminals? Likewise, how might examining the power relations among beat policemen and administrators transform the way we understand the seeming disparity between policy and practice in turn-of-the-century Buenos Aires? Might it partially be understood as a form of thwarting superior authority and challenging emasculating subordination by these working-class policemen?

These questions suggest the rich possibilities of gendered approaches to the history of crime. Yet, gender, like class and like race, cannot stand alone as a tool for analyzing crime. Indeed, conventional approaches to women's and even some gender histories suffer from the conflation of gender with the normative, white, middle-class experience. Moreover, a critical gendered approach must also analyze the ways in which gender not only constitutes power inequalities based on perceived differences but also the ways in which it transcends differences between men and women to shape other systems of inequality—race, class, sexuality, to name a few.[53] The next section offers some reflections on the possibilities for developing a perspective on the history of crime that gives more equal weight to race *and* gender.

SOME TRAJECTORIES FOR FUTURE
INTERSECTIONAL SCHOLARSHIP

One of the main challenges in this incipient historiography of gender and crime in Latin America is the relatively scant attention to the ways other systems of inequality—namely racial hierarchy—shape the experiences of diverse groups of women and men. Indeed, the assumption in much of this work is one that has plagued feminist scholars for decades—the implicit assumption that white women's experiences can adequately represent women more broadly. As yet, the historiography on crime in Latin America has neglected one of the key insights of intersectional feminism, namely that race (and other systems of inequality like sexuality) fundamentally transforms the ways women and men experience power relations in their relationships with one another. In other words, experiences of race and gender are mutually constitutive and multiplicative, rather than summative.[54]

Part of the problem is that racial inequality in Latin America is often expressed covertly or coded within other language to comply with the prevailing liberal nationalist discourses of racial harmony, mestizaje, mestiçagem, and multiculturalism. The recent work of Marisol de la Cadena exposes the ways in which the prevailing vision of education as a tool for improving one's racial and cultural subordination both challenged and reinforced racial hierarchy in Cuzco, Peru, by enabling educated mestizos to claim a higher social status while legitimizing the continued subordination of the majority of indigenous people and disparagement of indianness.[55] Charles Hale similarly argues that state-sponsored multiculturalism in Guatemala constituted a core tool of neoliberal economic and political policies by fostering the recognition of the most basic human rights under the guise of inclusion while rejecting other more substantive claims to inclusion by nonelite actors. Rather than gaining inclusion on their own terms, these marginal actors were simply expected to assimilate.[56] Marilyn Grace Miller and Frances Twine likewise interrogate the discourses of mestizaje in Mexico and racial democracy in Brazil, respectively, revealing their power to obfuscate race while reinforcing racial hierarchy.[57] These inclusive discourses tend to obscure the way racism functions in these societies, while also fostering the social production of alternate idioms of racism. Sometimes, these idioms themselves are gendered, as my work suggests, but often they obscure the tangible intersections of race and gender in terrains such as honor, sex, and science—the very sites at which inequality is produced.[58]

The slipperiness of race in Latin America has complicated but not prevented scholars from examining the intersections of race and gender, though less attention has been paid to the ways these insights illuminate criminality. Peter Wade has noted that the emergence of scientific discourses and practices such as eugenics, hygiene, and medicine offers fertile terrain for exploring the intersections of race and gender, even as assumptions linking whiteness to honor persisted.[59] Studies of Latin American eugenics movements, for example, suggest that eugenics emerged as a terrain in which race and gender interacted, in a similar way to, as historians have noted, how honor functioned during the colonial and early republican periods.[60] Historians have often focused on the construction of national myths while paying less attention to their gendered applications. A growing number of literary scholars have emphasized the centrality of the sexualization and vilification of black women in the construction of the sanctified, desexualized image of white women. Joan Dayan, for example, notes that the prostitution and sexual exploitation of black women proved central to the reproduction of spiritualized images of white women in Haiti. Similarly, Vera Kutzinski illustrates the ways in which the sexualization of mulata women helped entrench a racial hierarchy while also reinforcing racially unequal access to patriarchy.[61]

A small number of recent studies of elite projects for hygiene and morality evince an important foundation for future research on the intersections of race and gender in histories of criminality, though few of them sit squarely within the field of criminality. Scholars examining female deviance have interrogated the ways in which control over women's sexuality underpinned neocolonial projects. Laura Briggs shows that gendered policies on family planning, sexuality, and reproduction directed mainly toward mixed-race, working-class women proved central to the preservation of U.S. empire in early twentieth-century Puerto Rico. Laura Putnam analyzes the efforts of working-class women to claim honor in the courts of Limón, Costa Rica, implicitly elucidating the ways race and gender operated at two distinct social levels—the intimate and the public. In her study of race and sexual politics in Puerto Rico, Eileen Suárez Findlay shows that ideas linking whiteness to sexual morality persisted through the transition from Spanish colony to American neocolony, forming the centerpiece of bourgeois policy to "de-Africanize" the Puerto Rican masses. Her research suggests that applying gender ideals unevenly to women of different racial backgrounds served to reinforce racial hierarchy, which continued to rest on the conceptual conflation of honor and whiteness.[62] While these and other similar studies have faced criticism for treating race as secondary to gender in some cases, or treating these systems unevenly or separately, this theoretical point illustrates an important insight about the difficulty of studying the intersections of race and gender in a context in which, for the most part, race operates silently.[63]

Several chapters in the present volume demonstrate an incipient attention to gender and its intersections with race and class as an important theme in studying criminality, expanding the conventional limits of studying women's deviance to a more comprehensive gendered approach. These chapters challenge the default view of practices, debates, and constructions of criminality as a predominantly male domain. In particular, Gregory Swedberg's analysis of sexual assault criminal proceedings involving working-class women in Veracruz, Mexico, demonstrates the continuities of virginity and familial honor in defining and punishing cases of sexual violence, despite the increasing legal rights for women in postrevolutionary Mexico. He also casts light on the efforts of individual women, many times mothers, in the face of the legal system run by, and frequently favoring, men. By appropriating discourses on virginity and honesty, these women co-opted one of the very roles that elites occasionally used against them—their role as mothers—and sometimes succeeded in securing legal action against offenders.

While the documents in Swedberg's study rarely indicate race and ethnicity,[64] other studies of women's efforts to obtain legal redress for sexual assault present a picture in which race and gender clearly intersect with each other. The pioneering work of Verena Stolcke on race and sexual values in nineteenth-century Cuba, for one, elucidates the uniquely raced and gendered ways in which marriage and concubinage operated in that nineteenth-century slave society. Whereas white men routinely exploited their preferential access to the bodies of nonwhite and poor women through relations of concubinage, they usually married women of similar racial and class status.[65] While most would read this dynamic of intraracial marriage and interracial concubinage as an indicator of racial hierarchy, Patricia Hill Collins points out that viewing it in this way implicitly privileges a masculinist view of race. In her contemporary analysis of race and women's ability to obtain convictions for rape accusations, Kimberlé Crenshaw shows that the lower rates of convictions in cases involving black female rape survivors illustrates the systematic devaluation of black women through not only racial and gendered oppression but through their unique intersection that renders black women as both less believable and less worthy of protection.[66] These insights provide a useful framework for examining the ways gender operated in the construction of female criminality and deviance, whether in the persisting official emphasis on (white) middle-class notions of female chastity or in the masculinizing language used to describe female criminals in early twentieth-century Cuba.[67]

In modest ways, the inclusion and acknowledgement of particularly gendered spaces and ideas evident in several chapters in this volume evince a growing awareness of the gendered dimensions of implicitly racialized notions of crime. Fernández Labbé, for example, unveils the fluidity of racialized sexual spaces like brothels in the official images of illicit drug trafficking in mid-twentieth-century Chile. Similarly, Huertas finds that the Peruvian criminologists' gendered perspectives on largely nonwhite criminal subjects helped produce a masculinist discourse that implicitly assumed the maleness of criminals while, most of the time, limiting the application of criminal labeling to women. In the rare cases in which women appeared in criminologists' musings, the differential gendered construction of criminal types centered on female irrationality, which compounded the atavism and racial degeneracy afflicting male criminals, or alternatively on the failures of the education system. Research on the same period in Brazil confirms these insights.[68]

Yet greater attention must be paid to the ways gender, class, and race operated as mutually constitutive systems of oppression. In this vein, Huertas's research suggests one possible trajectory for future research: analyzing how the elite focus on predominantly nonwhite, poor, and working-class male criminal subjects was in itself gendered. Future studies might interrogate the extent to which elite criminologists interpreted the social subordination and deviance of these men as indications of their failed and pathological masculinity or effeminacy. Recent research by Marisol de la Cadena also suggests the need to interrogate how the theoretical reluctance to label women as criminals actually translated into practice. In her analysis of the politics of insolence among Cuzco market women in the mid-twentieth century, de la Cadena demonstrates that criminalization of gendered misbehavior by these women depoliticized the actions of these women by playing on racial stereotypes of mestiza women.[69] Moreover, if the dismissal of women—particularly nonwhite women—as inherently irrational contributed to the difficulty of applying a masculinist criminal concept to them (one that was inherently rational), future research might examine how ideas about civilization that prevailed at the turn of the twentieth century similarly feminized nonwhite men.

In addition to examining women's experiences through a gendered lens, this volume also evinces an incipient attempt to gender spheres conventionally associated with men. In the case of Cuba, I examine the ways in which gendered discourses blurred the role of racial discrimination in the efforts of white veterans of the War of Independence to consolidate their own local authority during the American military occupation. Whereas references to a shared history of patriotic military service theoretically offered a level foundation for black and white Cubans to claim political power, the conflation of whiteness and honor remained a core assumption underlying assessments of fitness for citizenship. The slaying of the black general Dionisio Gil in the middle of a provincial Cuban city, though publicly recognized as a racial killing, emerged in official discourse as an example of gender transgression, which not only demonstrated a lack of patriotism but also threatened the fragile national unity.

While the slaying of Gil is perhaps an extreme example of denying subordinate claims to masculine authority, it illustrates a broader point implicit in the historiography: criminalizing nonwhite men facilitated their prosecution and exclusion on the grounds of their gendered transgression, while also denying them the privileges of masculinity through incarceration, political exclusion, or outright annihilation.[70] In this respect, studies of particularly masculine experiences, including vagrancy, prison labor, and deportation, should give more explicit attention to the gendered roots and consequences of these practices of criminalization. Robert Buffington's study of vagrancy in Mexico offers an excellent example of how gender analysis could transform and extend the significance of historical perspectives on crime. While Buffington clearly notes that police prosecution of vagrancy helped justify the political exclusion of presumably poor and nonwhite deviants, a gendered approach would help underscore the dual marginalization implied in a man's incarceration. Not only were imprisoned men excluded from exercising the masculine right of political enfranchisement, they were also excluded from performing their patriarchal duties of breadwinning, and therefore were forcibly separated from the male privilege of controlling women's bodies and labor.[71] Peter Beattie's recent work on the Brazilian penal colony Fernando de Noronha suggests similar gendered visions and consequences for crime.[72]

Gema Santamaría's examination of implicitly racialized discourses of tradition presents another opportunity to deploy gender as a lens of analysis. Scholars such as Robyn Weigman have emphasized the discursive parallels of gender and racial othering in the conflation of blacks and women in the United States.[73] How might the display of violence in lynching constitute a symbolic rejection of the feminized and racialized status imposed on rural dwellers, whom the state labeled "traditional"? Is it possible to view lynching in postrevolutionary Mexico independently of its presumed sexual politics? To what extent does reading violence as inherently masculine limit our view of women's participation and even leadership in violent events such as lynching?[74]

Several recent studies of the criminalization of homosexual practices suggest the need to challenge and transcend the confines of the heteronormative nuclear family as a framework for analyzing criminalized groups of men. In this regard, the research on Brazil and Mexico has offered the most cogent insights. Peter Beattie's study of military impressment in late nineteenth and early twentieth-century Brazil elucidates the reciprocal relations connecting criminality and homosexuality among poor and nonwhite Brazilians. James Green notes the overwhelming discursive association between blackness, criminality, and homosexuality in the mid-twentieth century, which led black men to be disproportionately prosecuted for homosexuality despite their relatively low representation in homosexual communities.[75]

The two approaches mentioned above—the first of which calls for examining how race functions to constitute women's subordination and the second of which entails exposing the implicitly masculine domains of racial exclusion as gendered rather than universal—represent two potential trajectories through which future studies of crime can interrogate the intersections of race and gender. A gendered analysis of crime helps foreground the ways in which the exclusion of poor and nonwhite men from the rights of citizenship could be reproduced, naturalized, and ultimately justified in terms of their inadequate, excessive, or deficient gendered practices rather than on the basis of their race. Hence, employing an intersectional approach to the study of crime in Latin America helps reveal how the often unstated gendered undertones of criminalizing discourses helped validate the criminalization of racial others in societies that supposedly celebrated racial harmony. In this way, crime and criminality emerged not merely as a product of Latin American state formation but as a cornerstone of state hegemony in these evolving "imagined communities."[76] During the transformative age of "order and progress" at the turn of the twentieth century, criminalization emerged as a powerful tool of state (re)consolidation.

Ultimately, analyzing the history of Latin American criminality from an intersectional perspective has the potential to help scholars find new answers to old questions, such as how racism and racial democracy could coexist, or why a question about race, as Wade puts it, so often evokes an answer of sex. Yet, an intersectional approach also has the power to evoke new questions about crime, challenge how we define it, and shape the practical implications historical research might offer for creating more peaceful if not more equitable societies.

NOTES

1. See, for example, Aline Helg, *Liberty and Equality in Caribbean Colombia, 1770–1835* (Chapel Hill: University of North Carolina Press, 2004); Mark Thurner, *From Two Republics to One Divided: Contradictions of Postcolonial Nationmaking in Andean Peru* (Durham, NC: Duke University Press, 1997).

2. Derek Sayer, "Everyday Forms of State Formation: Some Dissident Remarks on 'Hegemony,'" in *Everyday Forms of State Formation: Revolution and the Negotiation of Rule in Modern Mexico*, ed. Gilbert Joseph and Daniel Nugent, 367–78 (Durham, NC: Duke University Press, 2004).

3. Douglas Litowitz, "Gramsci, Hegemony, and the Law," *BYU Law Review* 2 (2000): 525–26.

4. Hannah Arendt, *On Violence* (New York: Houghton Mifflin Harcourt, 1970).

5. Marisol de la Cadena, *Indigenous Mestizos: The Politics of Race and Culture in Cuzco, Peru, 1919–1991* (Durham, NC: Duke University Press, 2000).

6. Edward E. Telles, *Race in Another America: The Significance of Skin Color in Brazil* (Princeton, NJ: Princeton University Press, 2004); Thomas E. Skidmore, *Black into White: Race and Nationality in Brazilian Thought* (Durham, NC: Duke University Press, 1992); Alejandro de la Fuente, *A Nation for All: Race, Inequality, and Politics in Twentieth-Century Cuba* (Chapel Hill: University of North Carolina Press, 2001).

7. John C. Chasteen, *National Rhythms, African Roots: The Deep History of Latin American Popular Dance* (Albuquerque: University of New Mexico Press, 2004); George Reid

Andrews, *The Afro-Argentines of Buenos Aires, 1800–1900* (Madison: University of Wisconsin Press, 1980).

8. Fredrick B. Pike, *The United States and Latin America: Myths and Stereotypes of Civilization and Nature* (Austin: University of Texas Press, 1992), 168–71.

9. Marilyn Grace Miller, *The Rise and Fall of the Cosmic Race: The Cult of Mestizaje in Latin America* (Austin: University of Texas Press, 2004); De la Cadena, *Indigenous Mestizos*.

10. Aline Helg, *Our Rightful Share: The Afro-Cuban Struggle for Equality, 1886–1912* (Chapel Hill: University of North Carolina Press, 1995); Robert M. Levine, *Vale of Tears: Revisiting the Canudos Massacre in Northeastern Brazil, 1893–1897* (Berkeley: University of California Press, 1992); Todd Diacon, *Millenarian Vision, Capitalist Reality: Brazil's Contestado Rebellion, 1912–1916* (Durham, NC: Duke University Press, 1991).

11. Nancy Appelbaum, Anne Macpherson, and Karin Alejandra Rosemblatt, "Introduction: Racial Nations," in Appelbaum, Macpherson, and Rosemblatt, eds., *Race and Nation in Modern Latin America*, 3–9 (Chapel Hill: University of North Carolina Press, 2003). See also Sarah C. Chambers, *From Subjects to Citizens: Honor, Gender, and Politics in Arequipa, Peru, 1780–1854* (University Park: Pennsylvania State University Press, 1999).

12. Litowitz, "Gramsci," 524. See also R. W. Connell, *Masculinities* (Berkeley: University of California Press, 1995), 77–78.

13. Willian S. Burroughs, *Naked Lunch* (1959; New York: Grove, 2004), 31. Also quoted in Litowitz, "Gramsci."

14. Robert Buffington, *Criminal and Citizen in Modern Mexico* (Lincoln: University of Nebraska Press, 2000); Carlos Aguirre, *The Criminals of Lima and Their Worlds: The Prison Experience, 1850–1935* (Durham, NC: Duke University Press, 2005).

15. William Rosenberry, "Hegemony and the Language of Contention," in Joseph and Nugent, *Everyday Forms of State Formation*, 361.

16. Litowitz, "Gramsci," 546.

17. Alejandra Bronfman, *Measures of Equality: Social Science, Citizenship, and Race in Cuba, 1902–1940* (Chapel Hill: University of North Carolina Press, 2004); Nancy Leys Stepan, *"The Hour of Eugenics": Race, Gender, and Nation in Latin America* (Ithaca, NY: Cornell University Press, 1991); Pablo Piccato, *City of Suspects: Crime in Mexico City, 1900–1931* (Durham, NC: Duke University Press 2001); Olivia Maria Gomes da Cunha, *Intenção e gesto: Pessoa, cor e a produção cotidiana da (in)diferença no Rio de Janeiro, 1927–1942* (Rio de Janeiro: Arquivo Nacional, 2002); Lilia M. Schwarcz, *O espetáculo das raças: Cientistas, instituições e questão racial no Brasil, 1870–1930* (São Paulo: Companhia das Letras, 1993).

18. Sueann Caulfield, *In Defense of Honor: Sexual Morality, Modernity, and Nation in Early-Twentieth-Century Brazil* (Durham, NC: Duke University Press, 2000); Kristin Ruggiero, *Modernity in the Flesh: Medicine, Law, and Society in Turn-of-the-Century Argentina* (Stanford, CA: Stanford University Press, 2003); Julia Rodríguez, *Civilizing Argentina: Science, Medicine, and the Modern State* (Chapel Hill: University of North Carolina Press, 2005);

Eileen Suárez Findlay, *Imposing Decency: The Politics of Sexuality and Race in Puerto Rico, 1870–1920* (Durham, NC: Duke University Press, 1999); David Carey Jr., *I Ask for Justice: Maya Women, Dictators, and Crime in Guatemala, 1898–1944* (Austin: University of Texas Press, 2014). See also William E. French and Katherine Elaine Bliss, eds. *Gender, Sexuality, and Power in Latin America Since Independence* (Lanham, MD: Rowman and Littlefield, 2006).

19. Peter Wade, *Race and Sex in Latin America* (New York: Pluto Press, 2009).

20. Piccato, *City of Suspects*; Buffington, *Criminal and Citizen in Modern Mexico*.

21. Gil Joseph, preface to *Crime and Punishment in Latin America: Law and Society Since Late Colonial Times*, ed. Ricardo D. Salvatore, Carlos Aguirre, and Gilbert M. Joseph (Durham, NC: Duke University Press, 2001), ix–x.

22. James A. Garza, *The Imagined Underworld: Sex, Crime, and Vice in Porfirian Mexico City* (Lincoln: University of Nebraska Press, 2007), 4; Teresa P. R. Caldeira, *City of Walls: Crime, Segregation, and Citizenship in São Paulo* (Berkeley: University of California Press, 2000).

23. See, for example, Wil G. Pansters, ed., *Violence, Coercion, and State-Making in Twentieth-Century Mexico: The Other Half of the Centaur* (Stanford, CA: Stanford University Press, 2012).

24. For provincial studies of fields adjacent to crime, see Florencia Mallon, *Peasant and Nation: The Making of Postcolonial Mexico and Peru* (Berkeley: University of California Press, 1995); Lara Putnam, *The Company They Kept: Migrants and the Politics of Gender in Caribbean Costa Rica, 1870–1960* (Chapel Hill: University of North Carolina Press, 2002); Findlay, *Imposing Decency*.

25. See, for example, George Reid Andrews, "Race Versus Class Association: The Afro-Argentines of Buenos Aires, 1850–1900," *Journal of Latin American Studies* 11, no. 1 (1979): 19–39. For an overview of some of the most important studies interrogating Latin American racial democracy, see Alejandro de la Fuente, "From Slaves to Citizens? Tannenbaum and the Debates on Slavery, Emancipation, and Race Relations in Latin America," *International Labor and Working-Class History* 77 (2010): 154–73.

26. Teresa A. Meade, *"Civilizing" Rio: Reform and Resistance in a Brazilian City, 1889–1930* (University Park: Pennsylvania State University Press, 1997).

27. Edward E. Telles, *Race in Another America: The Significance of Skin Color in Brazil* (Princeton, NJ: Princeton University Press, 2004), 5–10; Wade, *Race and Sex in Latin America*, 1.

28. R. W. Connell, *Masculinities* (Berkeley: University of California Press, 1995).

29. Rebecca Biron, *Murder and Masculinity: Violent Fictions in Twentieth-Century Latin America* (Nashville, TN: Vanderbilt University Press, 2000).

30. See Ricardo Salvatore, "Criminal Justice History in Latin America: Promising Notes," *Crime, Histoire, & Sociétés / Crime, History, & Societies* 2, no. 2 (1998): 5–11.

31. Verena Martínez-Alier (Stolcke), *Marriage, Class, and Colour in Nineteenth-Century Cuba: A Study of Racial Attitudes and Sexual Value in a Slave Society* (Cambridge: Cambridge University Press, 1974).

32. Sueann Caulfield, Sarah C. Chambers, and Lara Putnam, eds., *Honor, Status, and Law in Modern Latin America* (Durham, NC: Duke University Press, 2005); Caulfield, *In Defense of Honor*; Martha de Abreu Esteves, *Meninas perdidas: Os populares e o cotidiano do amor no Rio de Janeiro da Belle Epoque* (Rio de Janeiro: Editora Paz e Terra, 1989); Findlay, *Imposing Decency*. See also Kathryn A. Sloan, *Runaway Daughters: Seduction, Elopement, and Honor in Nineteenth-Century Mexico* (Albuquerque: University of New Mexico Press, 2008); Ana María Alonso, *Thread of Blood: Colonialism, Revolution, and Gender on Mexico's Northern Frontier* (Tucson: University of Arizona Press, 1995).

33. Marcos Luiz Bretas, "The Sovereign's Vigilant Eye? Daily Policing and Women in Rio de Janeiro, 1907–1930," *Crime, Histoire, & Sociétés / Crime, History, & Societies* 2, no. 2 (1998): 55–71.

34. Donna J. Guy, *Sex and Danger in Buenos Aires: Prostitution, Family, and Nation in Argentina* (Lincoln: University of Nebraska Press, 1991).

35. An important exception to this pattern was the medical recommendation in the early twentieth century for prenuptial certificates to confirm that men were fit for marriage (free of venereal disease). See Asunción Lavrín, *Women, Feminism, and Social Change in Argentina, Chile, and Uruguay, 1890–1940* (Lincoln: University of Nebraska Press, 1995), 168–73; Stepan, "The Hour of Eugenics," 122–28.

36. Cristiani Schettini, *"Que tenhas teu corpo": Uma história social da prostituição no Rio de Janeiro das primeiras décadas republicanas* (Rio de Janeiro: Arquivo Nacional, 2006); Sueann Caulfield, "O nascimento do Mangue: Raça, nação e o controle da prostituição no Rio de Janeiro, 1850–1942," *Tempo* 9 (2002): 43–63; Sandra Lauderdale Graham, "Dangerous Fantasies: The Altered Vocabulary of Commercial Sex," *Luso-Brazilian Review* 30, no. 1 (1993): 133–39; Lená Medeiros de Menezes, *Os estrangeiros e o comercio do prazer nas ruas do Rio de Janeiro, 1890–1930* (Rio de Janeiro: Arquivo Nacional, 1992); Katherine Elaine Bliss, *Compromised Positions: Prostitution, Public Health, and Gender Politics in Revolutionary Mexico City* (University Park: Pennsylvania State University, 2001); Katherine Elaine Bliss, "'Guided by an Imperious, Moral Need': Prostitutes, Motherhood, and Nationalism in Revolutionary Mexico," in *Reconstructing Criminality in Latin America*, ed. Carlos Aguirre and Robert Buffington, 167–94 (Wilmington, DE: Scholarly Resources, 2000); Cristina Rivera-Garza, "The Criminalization of the Syphilitic Body: Prostitutes, Health Crimes, and Society in Mexico City, 1867–1930," in Salvatore, Aguirre, and Joseph, *Crime and Punishment in Latin America*; Tiffany Sippial, *Prostitution, Modernity, and the Making of the Cuban Republic, 1840–1920* (Chapel Hill: University of North Carolina, 2013); María del Cármen Barcia, "Entre el poder y la

crisis: Las prostitutas se defienden," *Contrastes, Revista de Historia* 7–8 (1991–93): 7–20; Findlay, *Imposing Decency*.

37. Kristin Ruggiero, "Not Guilty: Abortion and Infanticide in Nineteenth-Century Argentina," in Aguirre and Buffington, *Reconstructing Criminality in Latin America*, 149–66; Fabíola Rohden, *A arte de enganar a natureza: Contracepção, aborto e infanticídio no início do século XX* (Rio de Janeiro: Editora Fiocruz, 2003); Mala Htun, *Sex and the State: Abortion, Divorce, and the Family Under Latin American Dictatorships and Democracies* (Cambridge: Cambridge University Press, 2003); Carey, *I Ask for Justice*, 118–52; Natalie Kimball, "An Open Secret: The Hidden History of Unwanted Pregnancy and Abortion in Highland Bolivia, 1952–2010" (PhD diss., University of Pittsburgh, 2013); Cassia Roth, "Policing Pregnancy: Poverty, Reproduction, and the Law in Early-Twentieth-Century Rio de Janeiro," *Journal of Women's History* (forthcoming).

38. Elisa Speckman Guerra, "Las flores del mal: Mujeres criminales en el porfiriato," *Historia Mexicana* 47, no. 1 (1997): 187–90.

39. Cristina Rivera-Garza, "'She Neither Respected Nor Obeyed Anyone': Inmates and Psychiatrists Debate Gender and Class at the General Insane Asylum La Castañeda, Mexico, 1910–1930," *Hispanic American Historical Review* 81, no. 3–4 (2001): 653–88; Donna J. Guy, "Girls in Prison: The Role of the Buenos Aires Casa Correccional de Mujeres as an Institution for Child Rescue, 1890–1940," in Salvatore, Aguirre, and Joseph, *Crime and Punishment in Latin America*, 369–90; Jennifer Lambe, "A Century of Work: Reconstructing Mazorra, 1857–1959," *Cuban Studies* 43 (2015): 90–117.

40. Ruggiero, "Not Guilty"; Bliss, "'Guided by an Imperious, Moral Need'"; Arlene J. Díaz, "Women, Order, and Progress in Guzmán Blanco's Venezuela, 1870–1888," in Salvatore, Aguirre, and Joseph, *Crime and Punishment in Latin America*, 56–82; Rivera-Garza, "The Criminalization of the Syphilitic Body"; Dain Borges, "Healing and Mischief: Witchcraft in Brazilian Law and Literature, 1890–1922," in Salvatore, Aguirre, and Joseph, *Crime and Punishment in Latin America*, 181–210; Guy, "Girls in Prison."

41. Joan W. Scott, *Gender and the Politics of History* (New York: Columbia University Press, 1989).

42. Scott, *Gender*, 25

43. Steve Stern, *The Secret History of Gender: Women, Men, and Power in Late Colonial Mexico* (Chapel Hill: University of North Carolina Press, 1995); Arlene J. Díaz, *Female Citizens, Patriarchs, and the Law in Venezuela, 1786–1904* (Lincoln: University of Nebraska Press, 2009).

44. Thomas Miller Klubbock, *Contested Communities: Class, Gender, and Politics in Chile's El Teniente Copper Mine, 1904–1951* (Durham, NC: Duke University Press, 1998), 73.

45. Natalia Milenesio, "Redefining Men's Sexuality, Resignifying Male Bodies: The Argentine Law of Anti-Venereal Profylaxis, 1936," *Gender and History* 17, no. 2 (2005): 463–91.

46. Matthew C. Gutmann, *The Meanings of Macho: Being a Man in Mexico City* (Berkeley: University of California Press, 1996); Matthew C. Guttman, ed., *Changing Men and Masculinities in Latin America* (Durham, NC: Duke University Press, 2003); Victor M. Macías-González and Anne Rubenstein, eds., *Masculinity and Sexuality in Modern Mexico* (Albuquerque: University of New Mexico, 2012).

47. James N. Green, *Beyond Carnival: Male Homosexuality in Twentieth-Century Brazil* (Chicago: University of Chicago Press, 1999), 121–35.

48. Biron, *Murder and Masculinity*; Piccato, *City of Suspects*; Martine Jean, "Guardians of Order: Police and Society in Rio de Janeiro, Brazil, 1907–1930" (PhD diss., Yale University, 2010).

49. Díaz, *Female Citizens*, 149.

50. Olivia Maria Gomes da Cunha, "The Stigmas of Dishonor: Criminal Records, Civil Rights, and Forensic Identification in Rio de Janeiro, 1903–1940," in Caulfield, Chambers, and Putnam, *Honor, Status, and Law in Modern Latin America*, 295–315. Also see Martine Jean, "Guardians of Order."

51. See Bonnie A. Lucero, "Engendering Inequality: Masculinity and Racial Exclusion in Cuba, 1895–1902" (PhD diss., University of North Carolina–Chapel Hill, 2013).

52. Richard W. Slatta, ed., *Bandidos: The Varieties of Latin American Banditry* (New York: Greenwood Press, 1987); Chris Frazer, *Bandit Nation: A History of Outlaws and Cultural Struggle in Mexico, 1810–1920* (Lincoln: University of Nebraska Press, 2006).

53. Scott, *Gender*, 42.

54. Patricia Hill Collins, *Black Feminist Thought: Knowledge, Consciousness, and the Politics of Empowerment* (New York: Routledge, 2010); Kimberlé Crenshaw, "Mapping the Margins: Intersectionality, Identity Politics, and Violence Against Women of Color," *Stanford Law Review* 43, no. 6 (1991): 1241–99.

55. De la Cadena, *Indigenous Mestizos*.

56. Charles Hale, "Does Multiculturalism Menace? Governance, Cultural Rights, and the Politics of Identity in Guatemala," *Journal of Latin American Studies* 34, no. 3 (2002): 485–524.

57. Miller, *The Rise and Fall of the Cosmic Race*; Frances W. Twine, *Racism in a Racial Democracy: The Maintenance of White Supremacy in Brazil* (New Brunswick, NJ: Rutgers University Press, 1998).

58. Lucero, "Engendering Inequality"; see also Wade, *Race and Sex*.

59. Wade, *Race and Sex*, 110–13, 128.

60. Stepan, *"The Hour of Eugenics"*; Stern, *Eugenic Nation*.

61. Joan Dayan, "Erzulie: A Women's History of Haiti," *Research in African Literatures* 25, no. 2 (1994): 5–31; Vera Kutzinski, *Sugar's Secrets: Race and the Erotics of Cuban Nationalism* (Charlottesville: University of Virginia Press, 1993).

62. Findlay, *Imposing Decency*.

63. Wade, *Race and Sex*, 136–37.

64. Gomes da Cunha, *Intenção e gesto*.

65. Martínez-Alier [Stolcke], *Marriage, Class, and Colour*.

66. Collins, *Black Feminist Thought*; Crenshaw, "Mapping the Margins," 1277–78.

67. Israel Castellanos, *La delincuencia feminina en Cuba* (Havana: Imprenta Ojeda, 1929).

68. Cassia Roth, "A Miscarriage of Justice: Reproduction, Medicine, and the Law in Rio de Janeiro, Brazil (1890–1940)" (PhD diss., University of California–Los Angeles, 2016).

69. De la Cadena, *Indigenous Mestizos*, 208–14.

70. Piccato, *City of Suspects*.

71. Buffington, *Criminal and Citizen in Modern Mexico*.

72. Peter M. Beattie, *Punishment in Paradise: Race, Slavery, Human Rights, and a Nineteenth-Century Brazilian Penal Colony* (Durham, NC: Duke University Press, 2015).

73. Robyn Weigman, *American Anatomies: Theorizing Race and Gender* (Durham, NC: Duke University Press, 1995).

74. For a compelling critique, see Aisha K. Finch, "'What Looks Like a Revolution': Enslaved Women and the Gendered Terrain of Slave Insurgencies in Cuba, 1843–1844," *Journal of Women's History* 26, no. 1 (2014): 112–34.

75. Peter Beattie, *The Tribute of Blood: Army, Honor, Race, and Nation in Brazil, 1864–1945* (Durham, NC: Duke University Press, 2001); Green, *Beyond Carnival*.

76. Benedict Anderson, *Imagined Communities* (London: Verso, 1983).

SELECTED BIBLIOGRAPHY

Abreu Esteves, Martha de. *Meninas perdidas: Os populares e o cotidiano do amor no Rio de Janeiro da Belle Epoque.* Rio de Janeiro: Editora Paz e Terra, 1989.

Adelman, Jeremy. *Essays in Argentine Labor History, 1870–1930.* Oxford: Macmillan Press, 1992.

Agostoni, Claudia. *Monuments of Progress: Modernization and Public Health in Mexico City, 1876–1910.* Boulder: University Press of Colorado, 2003.

Aguirre, Carlos. "Crime, Race, and Morals: The Development of Criminology in Peru (1890–1930)." *Crime, Histoires, & Sociétés / Crime, History, & Societies* 2, no. 2 (1998): 73–90.

———. *The Criminals of Lima and Their Worlds: The Prison Experience, 1850–1935.* Durham, NC: Duke University Press, 2005.

———. "Delito, raza y cultura: El desarrollo de la criminología en el Perú." *Diálogos en Historia* 2 (2000): 179–206.

Aguirre, Carlos, and Robert Buffington, eds. *Reconstructing Criminality in Latin America.* Wilmington, DE: Scholarly Resources, 2000.

Aguirre, Carlos, and Charles Walker, eds. *Bandoleros, abigeos y montoneros: Criminalidad y violencia en el Perú, siglos XVIII–XX.* Lima: Instituto de Apoyo Agrario / Instituto Pasado y Presente, 1990.

Aibar Valdez, César. *Diez años de criminalidad en Arequipa (interpretación).* Arequipa: Tipografía Librería Quiroz Perea, 1935.

Alonso, Ana María. "Love, Sex, and Gossip in Legal Cases from Namiquipa, Chihuahua." In *Decoding Gender, Law, and Practice in Contemporary Mexico,* edited by Helga Baitenmann, Victoria Chenaut, and Ann Varley, 43–58. New Brunswick, NJ: Rutgers University Press, 2007.

———. "Territorializing the Nation and 'Integrating the Indian': 'Mestizaje' in Mexican Official Discourses and Public Culture." In *Sovereign Bodies: Citizens, Migrants, and States in the Postcolonial World*, edited by Thomas Blom Hansen and Finn Stepputat, 39–60. Princeton, NJ: Princeton University Press, 2005.

———. *Thread of Blood: Colonialism, Revolution, and Gender on Mexico's Northern Frontier.* Tucson: University of Arizona Press, 1995.

———. "'What the Strong Owe to the Weak': Rationality, Domestic Violence, and Governmentality in Nineteenth-Century Mexico." In *Gender's Place: Feminist Anthropologies of Latin America*, edited by Rosario Montoya, Lessie Jo Frazier, and Janise Hurtig, 115–34. New York: Palgrave, 2002.

Anderson, Benedict. *Imagined Communities.* London: Verso, 1983.

Andreas, Peter, and Ethan Nadelman. *Policing the Globe: Criminalization and Crime Control in International Relations.* Oxford: Oxford University Press, 2008.

Andrews, George Reid. *The Afro-Argentines of Buenos Aires, 1800–1900.* Madison: University of Wisconsin Press, 1980.

———. "Race versus Class Association: The Afro-Argentines of Buenos Aires, 1850–1900." *Journal of Latin American Studies* 11, no. 1 (1979): 19–39.

Appelbaum, Nancy P., Anne S. Macpherson, and Karin Alejandra Rosemblatt, eds. *Race and Nation in Modern Latin America.* Chapel Hill: University of North Carolina Press, 2003.

Armitage, David. "Three Concepts of Atlantic History." In *The British Atlantic World, 1500–1800*, edited by David Armitage and Michael J. Braddick. Basingstoke: Palgrave Macmillan, 2002.

Baily, Samuel L., and Eduardo José Míguez, eds., *Mass Migration to Modern Latin America.* New York: Rowman and Littlefield, 2003.

Baines, Dudley. *Emigration from Europe, 1815–1930.* Cambridge: Cambridge University Press, 1995.

Barcia, María del Cármen. "Entre el poder y la crisis: Las prostitutas se defienden." *Contrastes: Revista de Historia* 7–8 (1991–93): 7–20.

Barra-Melej, Patrick. "Hippismo a la chilena: Juventud y heterodoxia cultural en un contexto trasnacional (1970–1973)." In *Ampliando Miradas: Chile y su historia en un tiempo global*, edited by Fernando Purcell and Alfredo Riquelme, 305–25. Santiago: PUC-RIL, 2009.

Barreneche, Osvaldo. "De brava a dura: La policía de la provincia de Buenos Aires durante la primera mitad del siglo XX." *Cuadernos de Antropología Social* 32 (2010): 31–56.

Beattie, Peter M. *Punishment in Paradise: Race, Slavery, Human Rights, and a Nineteenth-Century Brazilian Penal Colony.* Durham, NC: Duke University Press, 2015.

———. *The Tribute of Blood: Army, Honor, Race, and Nation in Brazil, 1864–1945.* Durham, NC: Duke University Press, 2001.

Becker, Marjorie. *Setting the Virgin on Fire: Lázaro Cárdenas, Michoacán Peasants, and the Redemption of the Mexican Revolution.* Berkeley: University of California Press, 1995.

Beirne, Piers. *Inventing Criminology: Essays on the Rise of "Homo Criminalis."* Albany: State University of New York Press, 1993.

Bell, David F. "Technologies of Speed, Technologies of Crime." *Yale French Studies* 108 (2005): 8–19.

Belmonte, Emilio. *Capacidad y responsabilidad del morfinómano, cocainómano y opiómano.* Santiago de Chile: Imprenta Lagunas & Cía, 1920.

Binford, Leigh, and Nancy Churchill. "Lynching and States of Fear in Urban Mexico." *Anthropologica* 51, no. 6 (2009): 1–12.

Biron, Rebecca. *Murder and Masculinity: Violent Fictions in Twentieth-Century Latin America.* Nashville, TN: Vanderbilt University Press, 2000.

Blackwelder, Julia Kirk. "Urbanization, Crime, and Policing: Buenos Aires, 1880–1914." In *The Problem of Order in Changing Societies: Essays on Crime and Policing in Argentina and Uruguay,* edited by Lyman L. Johnson, 65–88. Albuquerque: University of New Mexico Press, 1990.

Blackwelder, Julia Kirk, and Lyman L. Johnson. "Changing Criminal Patterns in Buenos Aires, 1890 to 1914." *Journal of Latin American Studies* 14, no. 2 (1982): 359–79.

Bletz, May E. *Immigration and Acculturation in Brazil and Argentina, 1890–1920.* New York: Palgrave, 2010.

Bliss, Katherine Elaine. *Compromised Positions: Prostitution, Public Health, and Gender Politics in Revolutionary Mexico City.* University Park: Pennsylvania State University, 2001.

———. "'Guided by an Imperious, Moral Need': Prostitutes, Motherhood, and Nationalism in Revolutionary Mexico." In *Reconstructing Criminality in Latin America,* edited by Carlos Aguirre and Robert Buffington, 167–94. Wilmington, DE: Scholarly Resources, 2000.

———. "Theater of Operations: Reform Politics and the Battle for Prostitutes' Redemption at Revolutionary Mexico City's Syphilis Hospital." In *The Women's Revolution in Mexico, 1910–1953,* edited by Stephanie Mitchell and Patience A. Schell, 125–50. Lanham, MD: Rowman and Littlefield, 2007.

Blixen, Samuel. "La Operación Cóndor y la internacionalización de la represión en el Cono Sur." In *Memorias de la violencia en Uruguay y Argentina: Golpes, dictaduras y exilios (1973–2006),* edited by Eduardo Rey Tristán, 125–32. Santiago de Compostela: Universidad de Santiago de Compostela, 2007.

Borja, César. "La inmigración china es un mal necesario de evitar." In *Anales Universitarios del Perú* 10 (1877): 47–92.

Bretas, Marcos Luiz. *Ordem na cidade: O exercício cotidiano da autoridade policial no Rio de Janeiro: 1907–1930.* Rio de Janeiro: Rocco, 1997.

———. "The Sovereign's Vigilant Eye? Daily Policing and Women in Rio de Janeiro, 1907–1930." *Crime, Histoire, & Sociétés / Crime, History, & Societies* 2, no. 2 (1998): 55–71.

Brinks, Daniel M. "Informal Institutions and the Rule of Law: The Judicial Response to State Killing in Buenos Aires and São Paulo in the 1990s." *Comparative Politics* 36, no. 1 (2003): 1–19.

Bronfman, Alejandra. *Measures of Equality: Social Science, Citizenship, and Race in Cuba, 1902–1940.* Chapel Hill: University of North Carolina Press, 2004.

Bruce, Jorge. *Nos habíamos choleado tanto: Psicoanálisis y racismo*. Lima: Universidad de San Martin de Porres, 2007.

Buffington, Robert. *Criminal and Citizen in Modern Mexico*. Lincoln: University of Nebraska Press, 2000.

———. "Revolutionary Reform: The Mexican Revolution and the Discourse on Prison Reform." *Mexican Studies / Estudios Mexicanos* 9, no. 1 (1993): 71–93.

———. "La violencia contra la mujer y la subjetividad masculina en la prensa popular de la ciudad de México en el cambio de siglo." In *De normas y transgresiones: Enfermedad y crimen en América Latina (1850–1950)*, edited by Claudia Agostoni and Elisa Speckman, 287–325. México: UNAM, 2005.

Bustamante, Luis J. *Diccionario biográfico cienfueguero*. Cienfuegos, 1931.

Cabrera, Miguel Ángel. *Historia, lenguaje y teoría de la sociedad*. Valencia: Frónesis, 2001.

Caimari, Lila, ed. *La ley de los profanos: Delito, justicia y cultura en Buenos Aires (1870–1940)*. Buenos Aires: Universidad de San Andrés; Fondo de Cultura Económica, 2007.

———. "Remembering Freedom: Life as Seen from the Prison Cell (Buenos Aires Province 1930–1950)." In *Crime and Punishment in Latin America: Law and Society Since Late Colonial Times*, edited by Ricardo D. Salvatore, Carlos Aguirre, and Gilbert Joseph, 391–414. Durham, NC: Duke University Press, 2001.

Caldeira, Teresa P. R. *City of Walls: Crime, Segregation, and Citizenship in São Paulo*. Berkeley: University of California Press, 2000.

Calderón Cockburn, Julio. *La ciudad ilegal: Lima en el siglo XX*. Lima: Facultad de Ciencias Sociales–UNMSM, 2005.

Cambiazo Díaz, Juan. *El sentido subjetivo del derecho penal y el estado peligroso*. Chillán: Talleres Gráficos La Discusión, 1930.

Candea, Matei. *The Social after Gabriel Tarde: Debates and Assessments*. New York: Routledge, 2010.

Capelo, Joaquín. *La sociología de Lima*. Lima: J. Garland, 1895.

Carey, David, Jr. *I Ask for Justice: Maya Women, Dictators, and Crime in Guatemala, 1898–1944*. Austin: University of Texas Press, 2014.

Castells, Manuel. *The City and the Grassroots: A Cross-Cultural Theory of Urban Social Movements*. Berkeley: University of California Press, 1983.

Caulfield, Sueann. "Getting into Trouble: Dishonest Women, Modern Girls, and Women-Men in the Conceptual Language of Vida Policial, 1925–1927." *Signs* 19, no. 1 (Autumn 1993): 146–76.

———. *In Defense of Honor: Sexual Morality, Modernity, and Nation in Early-Twentieth-Century Brazil*. Durham, NC: Duke University Press, 2000.

———. "O nascimento do Mangue: Raça, nação e o controle da prostituição no Rio de Janeiro, 1850–1942." *Tempo* 9 (2002): 43–63.

Caulfield, Sueann, Sarah C. Chambers, and Lara Putnam, eds. *Honor, Status, and Law in Modern Latin America*. Durham, NC: Duke University Press, 2005.

Ceniceros, José Angel. *Tres estudios de criminología*. Mexico City, 1941.

Chambers, Sarah C. "Crime and Criminality: Judicial Practice in Arequipa, Peru, During the Transition from Colony to Republic." In *Reconstructing Crime in Latin America*, edited by Carlos Aguirre and Robert Buffington, 19–40. Wilmington, DE: Scholarly Resources, 2000.

———. *From Subjects to Citizens: Honor, Gender, and Politics in Arequipa, Peru, 1780–1854*. University Park: Pennsylvania State University Press, 1999.

Chambi, Oscar, Amelia Morimoto, and José Watanabe. *La memoria del ojo: Cien años de presencia japonesa en el Perú*. Lima: Congreso de la República del Perú, 1999.

Chasteen, John C. *National Rhythms, African Roots: The Deep History of Latin American Popular Dance*. Albuquerque: University of New Mexico Press, 2004.

Cohen, Stanley. *Folk Devils and Moral Panics: The Creation of the Mods and Rockers*. New York: Routledge, 2002.

Cole, Simon. *Suspect Identities: A History of Fingerprinting and Criminal Identification*. Cambridge: Harvard University Press, 2001.

Collins, Patricia Hill. *Black Feminist Thought: Knowledge, Consciousness, and the Politics of Empowerment*. New York: Routledge, 2010.

Comisión Parlamentaria Compuesta por Placido Jiménez y Gustavo Cornejo. *Proyecto de código penal*. Lima: Imprenta Minerva, 1928.

Connell, R. W. *Masculinities*. Berkeley: University of California Press, 1995.

Contreras, Carlos. *Centralismo y descentralismo en la historia del Perú independiente*. Lima: JCAS-IEP, 2000.

Cotler, Julio. *Clases, estado y nación en el Perú*. 5th ed. Lima: Instituto de Estudios Peruanos, 1988.

Crenshaw, Kimberlé. "Mapping the Margins: Intersectionality, Identity Politics, and Violence Against Women of Color." *Stanford Law Review* 43, no. 6 (1991): 1241–99.

Cueto, Marcos. "La reforma universitaria de 1919: Universidad y estudiantes a comienzos de siglo." Tesis de Licenciatura en Historia, Lima, PUCP, 1982.

Da Cunha, Euclides. *Os sertões: Campanha de canudos*. Sao Paulo: Ateliê Editorial, 2001.

Das Neves, Marcia. "A concepção de raça humana em Raimundo Nina Rodrigues." *Filosofia e história da biologia* 3 (2008): 241–61.

Davenport-Hines, Richard. *La búsqueda del olvido: Historia global de las drogas, 1500–2000*. Madrid: Fondo de Cultura Económica, 2003.

Davis, Diane E. "Policing and Regime Transition: From Postauthoritarianism to Populism to Neoliberalism." In *Violence, Coercion, and State-Making in Twentieth-Century Mexico: The Other Half of the Centaur*, edited by Will G. Pansters, 68–90. Stanford, CA: Stanford University Press, 2012.

———. "Undermining the Rule of Law: Democratization and the Dark Side of Police Reform in Mexico." *Latin American Politics and Society* 48, no. 1 (2006): 55–86.

Dawe, John, and Lewis Taylor. "Enrique López Albújar and the Study of Peruvian Brigandage." *Bulletin of Latin American Research* 13, no. 3 (1994): 247–80.

Dayan, Joan. "Erzulie: A Women's History of Haiti." *Research in African Literatures* 25, no. 2 (1994): 5–31.

Deflem, Mathieu. *Policing World Society: Historical Foundations of International Police Cooperation*. New York: Oxford University Press, 2004.

———. "Technology and the Internationalization of Policing: A Comparative-Historical Perspective." *Justice Quarterly* 19, no. 3 (2002): 453–75.

De la Cadena, Marisol. *Indigenous Mestizos: The Politics of Race and Culture in Cuzco, Peru, 1919–1991*. Durham, NC: Duke University Press, 2000.

———. "Silent Racism and Intellectual Superiority in Peru." *Bulletin of Latin American Research* 17, no. 2 (1998): 143–64.

De la Fuente, Alejandro. "From Slaves to Citizens? Tannenbaum and the Debates on Slavery, Emancipation, and Race Relations in Latin America." *International Labor and Working-Class History* 77 (2010): 154–73.

———. *A Nation for All: Race, Inequality, and Politics in Twentieth-Century Cuba*. Chapel Hill: University of North Carolina Press, 2001.

Derpich, Wilma. *El otro lado azul: Empresarios chinos en el Perú (1890–1930)*. Lima: Fondo Editorial del Congreso del Perú, 1999.

Diacon, Todd. *Millenarian Vision, Capitalist Reality: Brazil's Contestado Rebellion, 1912–1916*. Durham, NC: Duke University Press, 1991.

Díaz, Arlene J. *Female Citizens, Patriarchs, and the Law in Venezuela, 1786–1904*. Lincoln: University of Nebraska Press, 2004.

———. "Women, Order, and Progress in Guzmán Blanco's Venezuela, 1870–1888." In *Crime and Punishment in Latin America: Law and Society Since Late Colonial Times*, edited by Ricardo D. Salvatore, Carlos Aguirre, and Gilbert Joseph, 56–82. Durham, NC: Duke University Press, 2001.

Diego-Fernández, Salvador. *La ciudad de Méjico a fines del siglo XIX*. Mexico City, 1937.

Domingo, Pilar. "Rule of Law, Citizenship, and Access to Justice in Mexico." *Mexican Studies* 15, no. 1 (1999): 151–91.

Earle, Rebecca. "Rape and the Anxious Republic: Revolutionary Colombia, 1810–1830." In *Hidden Histories of Gender and the State in Latin America*, edited by Elizabeth Dore and Maxine Molyneux, 127–46. Durham, NC: Duke University Press, 1999.

Ebaugh, C. D. "Mexico Studies Sex Education." *Social Forces* 15, no. 1 (October 1936): 81–83.

Eley, Geoff, and Keith Nield. *El futuro de la clase en la historia: ¿Qué queda de lo social?* Valencia: PUV, 2010.

Elias, Norbert. *The Civilizing Process*. New York: Urizen Books, 1978.

Encinas, José Antonio. *Causas de la criminalidad indígena en el Perú: Ensayo de psicología experimental*. Lima: E. R. Villarán, 1919.

Fallaw, Ben. *Religion and State Formation in Postrevolutionary Mexico*. Durham, NC: Duke University Press, 2013.

Fausto, Boris. *Crime e cotidiano: A criminalidade em São Paulo (1880–1924)*. São Paulo: Edusp, 2001.

Fausto, Boris, and Fernando Devoto. *Brasil e Argentina: Um ensaio de história comparada (1850–2002)*. São Paulo: Editora 34, 2004.

Fentanes, Enrique. *Cuatrocientos años de Policía de Buenos Aires*. Buenos Aires: Biblioteca Policial, 1981.

Fernández Labbé, Marcos. "Asociales: Raza, exclusión y anormalidad en la construcción estatal chilena, 1920–1960." *Revista de Historia Social y de las Mentalidades*, 16, no. 2 (2012): 167–94.

———. *Drogas en Chile, 1900–1970: Mercado, consumo y representación*. Santiago: Ediciones Universidad Alberto Hurtado, 2011.

Ferrer, Ada. *Insurgent Cuba: Race, Nation, and Revolution, 1868–1898*. Chapel Hill: University of North Carolina Press, 1999.

Ferri, Enrico. *Criminal Sociology*. London: T. Fisher Unwin, 1895.

Finch, Aisha K. "What Looks Like a Revolution": Enslaved Women and the Gendered Terrain of Slave Insurgencies in Cuba, 1843–1844." *Journal of Women's History* 26, no. 1 (2014): 112–34.

Findlay, Eileen Suárez. *Imposing Decency: The Politics of Sexuality and Race in Puerto Rico, 1870–1920*. Durham, NC: Duke University Press, 1999.

Foucault, Michel. *Discipline and Punish: The Birth of the Prison*. Translated by Alan Sheridan. Vintage: New York, 1995.

Frazer, Chris. *Bandit Nation: A History of Outlaws and Cultural Struggle in Mexico, 1810–1920*. Lincoln: University of Nebraska Press, 2006.

French William E., and Katherine Elaine Bliss, eds. *Gender, Sexuality, and Power in Latin America Since Independence*. Lanham, MD: Rowman and Littlefield, 2006.

Fuentes Díaz, Antonio. *Linchamientos, fragmentación y respuesta en el México neoliberal*. Puebla: Benemérita Universidad Autónoma de Puebla, 2005.

Galeano, Diego. "As polícias estrangeiras." In *Criminosos viajantes, vigilantes modernos: Circulações policiais entre Rio de Janeiro e Buenos Aires, 1890–1930*. PhD diss., Universidade Federal do Rio de Janeiro, 2012.

———. *Escritores, detectives y archivistas: La cultura policial en Buenos Aires, 1821–1910*. Buenos Aires: Teseo, 2009.

———. "Voyages de policiers: Une route entre Paris et les villes sud américaines, 1880–1905." In *Circulations policières en Europe, 1750–1914*, edited by Catherine Denys, 41–62. Lille: Presses Universitaires du Septentrion, 2012.

Galeano, Diego, and Mercedes García Ferrari. "Cartographie du bertillonnage: Le système anthropométrique en Amérique latine: Circuits de diffusion, usages et résistances." In *Aux origines de la police scientifique: Alphonse Bertillon, précurseur de la science du crime*, edited by Pierre Piazza, 308–31. Paris: Karthala, 2011.

García, Guadalupe. "Urban *Guajiros*: Colonial *Reconcentración*, Rural Displacement, and Criminalisation in Western Cuba, 1895–1902." *Journal of Latin American Studies* 43, no. 2 (2011): 209–35.

García Ferrari, Mercedes. "Dissemination of the Argentine Dactyloscopy System in the Early Twentieth Century: Local, Regional, and International Dimensions." In *Identification and Registration Practices in Transnational Perspective: People, Papers, and Practices*, edited by Ilsen About, James Brown, and Gayle Lonergan, 40–58. London: Palgrave, 2013.

———. *Ladrones conocidos/sospechosos reservados: Identificación policial en Buenos Aires, 1880–1905*. Buenos Aires: Prometeo, 2010.

García Martínez, Orlando. "Caciques, elites, clientelas, y los problemas raciales: Veteranos negros en Cienfuegos entre 1902 y 1912." *Revista del Centro de Investigaciones Históricas* 15 (2004): 101–22.

Gargurevich Regal, Juan. *Última Hora: La fundación de un diario popular*. Lima: La Voz, 2005.

Gargurevich Regal, Juan, and Mercedes García Ferrari. "Cartographie du bertillonnage: Le système anthropométrique en Amérique latine: Circuits de diffusion, usages et résistances." In *Aux origines de la police scientifique: Alphonse Bertillon, précurseur de la science du crime*, edited by Pierre Piazza, 308–31. Paris: Karthala, 2011.

Garland, David. "Penal Excess and Surplus Meaning: Public Torture Lynchings in Twentieth-Century America." *Law and Society Review* 39, no. 4 (2005): 793–833.

Garza, James Alex. *The Imagined Underworld: Sex, Crime, and Vice in Porfirian Mexico City*. Lincoln: University of Nebraska Press, 2007.

Gay, Peter. *The Cultivation of Hatred*. Vol. 3 of *The Bourgeois Experience: Victoria to Freud*. New York: Norton, 1993.

Gil Maestre, Manuel. *Los malhechores de Madrid*. Gerona: Imprenta y Librería de Paciano Torres, 1889.

Goldstein, Daniel M. *The Spectacular City: Violence and Performance in Urban Bolivia*. Durham, NC: Duke University Press, 2004.

Gomes da Cunha, Olivia Maria. *Intenção e gesto: Pessoa, cor e a produção cotidiana da (in)diferença no Rio de Janeiro 1927–1942*. Rio de Janeiro: Arquivo Nacional, 2002.

González Miranda, Sergio. *El dios cautivo: Las Ligas Patrióticas en la chilenización compulsiva de Tarapacá (1910–1922)*. Santiago: LOM Ediciones, 2004.

Gootenberg, Paul. *Andean Cocaine: The Making of a Global Drug*. Chapel Hill: University of North Carolina Press, 2008.

Green, James N. *Beyond Carnival: Male Homosexuality in Twentieth-Century Brazil*. Chicago: University of Chicago Press, 1999.

Guerra, Lillian. *The Myth of José Martí: Conflicting Nationalisms in Early Twentieth-Century Cuba*. Chapel Hill: University of North Carolina Press, 2005.

Guerra Manzo, Enrique. "The Resistance of the Marginalised: Catholics in Eastern Michoacán and the Mexican State, 1920–1940." *Journal of Latin American Studies* 40, no. 1 (2008): 109–33.

Gumbrecht, Hans Ulrich. *Producción de presencia*. Mexico City: Universidad Iberoamericana, 2005.

Gutierrez, Leandro H., and Juan Suriano. "Workers' Housing and Living Conditions in Buenos Aires, 1880–1930." In *Essays in Argentine Labor History*, edited by Jeremy Adelman, 35–52. Oxford: Macmillan Press, 1992.

Gutmann, Matthew C., ed. *Changing Men and Masculinities in Latin America*. Durham, NC: Duke University Press, 2003.

———. *The Meanings of Macho: Being a Man in Mexico City*. Berkeley: University of California Press, 1996.

Guy, Donna. "Girls in Prison: The Role of the Buenos Aires Casa Correccional de Mujeres as an Institution for Child Rescue, 1890–1940." In *Crime and Punishment in Latin America: Law and Society Since Late Colonial Times*, edited by Ricardo D. Salvatore, Carlos Aguirre, and Gilbert M. Joseph, 369–90. Durham, NC: Duke University Press, 2001.

———. *Sex and Danger in Buenos Aires: Prostitution, Family, and Nation in Argentina*. Lincoln: University of Nebraska Press, 1991.

Habermas, Jürgen. *The Structural Transformation of the Public Sphere: An Inquiry into a Category of Bourgeois Society*. Cambridge: Polity Press, 1989.

Hague, Juan Luis. *"Estudios Policiales": Técnicas científicas aplicadas a la policiología y consideraciones sobre el mejoramiento de la institución policial en el Perú*. Lima: Impr. de la Escuela de la Guardia Civil, 1934.

———. *Hacia un nuevo concepto de la responsabilidad criminal y de la pena*. Lima: Imprenta y Litografía T. Scheuch, 1934.

Hale, Charles. "Does Multiculturalism Menace? Governance, Cultural Rights, and the Politics of Identity in Guatemala." *Journal of Latin American Studies* 34, no. 3 (2002): 485–524.

Hall, Gwendolyn Midlo. *Social Control in Slave Plantation Societies: A Comparison of St. Domingue and Cuba*. Baltimore: Johns Hopkins University Press, 1971.

Hansen, Sönke. *Die Arbeiterschichten von Lima (1940–1960): Eine Kultur-und Freizeitgeschichte*. Vol. 3. Berlin: Lit Verlag, 2011.

Haslip-Viera, Gabriel. "Crime and the Administration of Justice in Colonial Mexico City, 1616–1810." PhD diss., Columbia University, 1980.

Hay, Douglas, Peter Linebaugh, John G. Rule, E. P. Thompson, and Cal Winslow. *Albion's Fatal Tree: Crime and Society in Eighteenth-Century England*. New York: Pantheon Books, 1975.

Hayner, Norman S. "Criminogenic Zones in Mexico City." *American Sociological Review* 11, no. 4 (1946): 428–38.

———. "Notes on the Changing Mexican Family." *American Sociological Review* 7, no. 4 (1942): 489–97.

Helg, Aline. *Liberty and Equality in Caribbean Colombia, 1770–1835.* Chapel Hill: University of North Carolina Press, 2004.

———. *Our Rightful Share: The Afro-Cuban Struggle for Equality, 1886–1912.* Chapel Hill: University of North Carolina Press, 1995.

Hobsbawm, Eric. *Bandits.* New York: Delacorte Press, 1969.

———. *Primitive Rebels: Studies in Archaic Forms of Social Movement in the 19th and 20th Centuries.* Manchester: Manchester University Press, 1959.

Holloway, Thomas H. *Policing Rio de Janeiro: Repression and Resistance in a Nineteenth-Century City.* Stanford, CA: Stanford University Press, 1993.

———. "Punishment in Nineteenth-Century Rio de Janeiro: Judicial Action as Police Practice." In *Reconstructing Crime in Latin America*, edited by Carlos Aguirre and Robert Buffington, 85–112. Wilmington, DE: Scholarly Resources, 2000.

Horne, Gerald. *Race to Revolution: The United States and Cuba During Slavery and Jim Crow.* New York: Monthly Review Press, 2014.

Htun, Mala. *Sex and the State: Abortion, Divorce, and the Family Under Latin American Dictatorships and Democracies.* Cambridge: Cambridge University Press, 2003.

Hu-DeHart, Evelyn. "Opio y control social: Culíes en las haciendas de Perú y Cuba." *Istor* 7, no. 27 (Winter 2006): 28–45.

Huertas, Luz E. "Whistles and Clubs: The Institutional and Social History of the Police of Lima, 1890s–1910s." PhD diss., Texas Christian University, 2015.

Iglesias, Marial. *Las metáforas del cambio en la vida cotidiana: Cuba 1898–1902.* Havana: UNEAC, 2003.

Jankowiak, William, and Daniel Bradburn, eds. *Drugs, Labor, and Colonial Expansion.* Tucson: University of Arizona Press, 2003.

Jensen, Richard Bach. *The Battle Against Anarchist Terrorism: An International History, 1878–1934.* Cambridge: Cambridge University Press, 2014.

———. "The International Anti-Anarchist Conference of 1898 and the Origins of Interpol." *Journal of Contemporary History* 16, no. 2 (1981): 323–47.

Jiménez, Plácido. "La sociedad y el delito." In *Anales de la Universidad Mayor de San Marcos de Lima* 25 (1898): 107–354.

Johnson, Allan G. *The Blackwell Dictionary of Sociology: A User's Guide to Sociological Language.* Oxford: Blackwell, 1995.

Joyce, Patrick. "¿El final de la historia social?" *Historia Social* 50, no. 3 (2004): 25–45.

Kalmanowiecki, Laura. "Origins and Applications of Political Policing in Argentina." *Latin American Perspectives* 27, no. 2 (2000): 36–56.

———. "Police, Politics, and Repression in Modern Argentina." In *Reconstructing Criminality in Latin America*, edited by Carlos Aguirre and Robert Buffington, 195–218. Wilmington, DE: Scholarly Resources, 2000.

Kimball, Natalie. "An Open Secret: The Hidden History of Unwanted Pregnancy and Abortion in Highland Bolivia, 1952–2010." PhD diss., University of Pittsburgh, 2013.

Klarén, Peter. "The Origins of Modern Peru, 1880–1930." In *The Cambridge History of Latin America*, vol. 5, edited by Leslie Bethell, 587–640. Cambridge: Cambridge University Press, 1986.

Klubbock, Thomas Miller. *Contested Communities: Class, Gender, and Politics in Chile's El Teniente Copper Mine, 1904–1951*. Durham, NC: Duke University Press, 1998.

Knepper, Paul. *The Invention of International Crime: A Global Issue in the Making, 1881–1914*. London: Palgrave, 2010.

Knight, Alan. "Racism, Revolution, and Indigenismo: Mexico, 1910–1940." In *The Idea of Race in Latin America, 1870–1940*, edited by Richard Graham, 71–113. Austin: University of Texas Press, 1990.

Komisaruk, Catherine. "Rape Narratives, Rape Silences: Sexual Violence and Judicial Testimonies in Colonial Guatemala." *Biography* 31, no. 3 (2008): 369–96.

Kossick, Robert. "The Rule of Law and Development in Mexico." *Arizona Journal of International and Comparative Law* 21, no. 3 (2004): 715–834.

Krupa, Christopher. "Histories in Red: Ways of Seeing Lynching in Ecuador." *American Ethnologist* 36, no. 1 (2009): 20–39.

Kutzinski, Vera. *Sugar's Secrets: Race and the Erotics of Cuban Nationalism*. Charlottesville: University of Virginia Press, 1993.

Laclau, Ernesto, and Chantal Mouffe. *Hegemonía y estrategia socialista: Hacia una radicalización de la democracia*. Buenos Aires: FCE, 2004.

Larson, Brooke. *Trials on Nation Making: Liberalism, Race, and Ethnicity in the Andes, 1810–1910*. New York: Cambridge University Press, 2004.

Lauderdale Graham, Sandra. "Dangerous Fantasies: The Altered Vocabulary of Commercial Sex." *Luso-Brazilian Review* 30, no. 1 (1993): 133–39.

Lausent-Herrera, Isabelle. *Pasado y presente de la comunidad japonesa en el Perú*. Lima: Instituto Frances de Estudios Andinos 1991.

Lauvergne, Hubert. *Les forçats: Considérés sous le rapport physiologique, moral et intellectuel*. Paris: Baillière, 1841.

Leigh Raffo, Denise. "El miedo a la multitud: Dos provincianos en el Estadio Nacional, 1950–1970." In *El miedo en el Perú: Siglos XVI al XX*, edited by Claudia Rosas Lauro, 265–74. Lima: Fondo Editorial PUCP, 2005.

Levine, Robert M. *Vale of Tears: Revisiting the Canudos Massacre in Northeastern Brazil, 1893–1897*. Berkeley: University of California Press, 1992.

Lewis, Stephen. "A Window into the Recent Past in Chiapas: Federal Education and Indigenismo in the Highlands, 1921–1940." *Journal of Latin American Anthropology* 6, no. 1 (2001): 58–83.

Lin Chou, Diego. *Chile y China: Inmigración y relaciones bilaterales, 1845–1970*. Santiago: DIBAM, 2003.

Litowitz, Douglas. "Gramsci, Hegemony, and the Law." *BYU Law Review* 2 (2000): 525–26.

Lombroso, Césare. *Criminal Man*. Translated and edited by Mary Gibson and Nicole Hahn Rafter. Durham, NC: Duke University Press, 2006.

Lomnitz, Claudio. "Mexico's First Lynching: Sovereignty, Criminality, Moral Panic." *Critical Historical Studies* 1, no. 1 (2014): 85–123.

López, Leopoldo. *Reseña histórica de la policía en Buenos Aires*. Buenos Aires: Imprenta y Encuadernación de la Policía, 1911.

López Albújar, Enrique. *Los caballeros del delito*. Lima: Editorial Juan Mejía Baca, 1973.

Loveman, Mara. "Blinded Like a State: The Revolt Against Civil Registration in Nineteenth-Century Brazil." *Comparative Studies in Society and History* 49, no. 1 (2007): 5–39.

Lucero, Bonnie A. "Engendering Inequality: Masculinity and Racial Exclusion in Cuba, 1895–1902." PhD diss., University of North Carolina–Chapel Hill, 2013.

Macedo, Miguel S., and José Angel Ceniceros. *Derechos, Penal y Procedimientos Penales: Programa y conferencias de 1926*. México: Escuela Libere de Derecho, 1928.

Macías-González, Victor M., and Anne Rubenstein, eds. *Masculinity and Sexuality in Modern Mexico*. Albuquerque: University of New Mexico Press, 2012.

Mallon, Florencia. *Peasant and Nation: The Making of Postcolonial Mexico and Peru*. Berkeley: University of California Press, 1995.

Mannarelli, Maria Emma. *Limpias y modernas: Género, higiene y cultura en la Lima del novecientos*. Lima: Flora Tristán, 1999.

Manrique, Nelson. *La piel y la pluma: Escritos sobre literatura, etnicidad y racismo*. Lima: SUR Casa de Estudios del Socialismo, 1999.

Mariátegui, José Carlos. *Siete ensayos de interpretación de la realidad peruana*. 3rd ed. Caracas: Biblioteca Ayacucho, 2007.

Martin, Joann. "Motherhood and Power: The Production of a Women's Culture of Politics in a Mexican Community." *American Ethnologist* 17, no. 3 (August 1990): 470–90.

Martínez-Alier (Stolcke), Verena. *Marriage, Class, and Colour in Nineteenth-Century Cuba: A Study of Racial Attitudes and Sexual Value in a Slave Society*. Cambridge: Cambridge University Press, 1974.

Martins, Jose de Souza. "Lynchings, Life by a Thread: Street Justice in Brazil, 1979–1988." In *Vigilantism and the State in Modern Latin America*, edited by Martha Huggins, 21–32. New York: Praeger, 1999.

Matos Mar, José. *Desborde popular y crisis del Estado: El nuevo rostro del Perú en la década de 1980*. Lima: Instituto de Estudios Peruanos, 1984.

McGee, Sandra. "The Visible and Invisible Liga Patriotica Argentina, 1919–1928: Gender Roles and the Right Wing." *Hispanic American Historical Review* 64, no. 2 (1984): 233–58.

McSherry, J. Patrice. *Predatory States: Operation Condor and Covert War in Latin America.* New York: Rowman and Littlefield, 2005.

Mead, Karen. "Gendering the Obstacles to Progress in Positivist Argentina, 1880–1920." *Hispanic American Historical Review* 77, no. 4 (1997): 645–75.

Meade, Teresa A. *"Civilizing" Rio: Reform and Resistance in a Brazilian City, 1889–1930.* University Park: Pennsylvania State University Press, 1997.

Meaney, Guillermina. *Canoa: El crimen impune.* México: Editorial Posada, 1977.

Medeiros de Menezes, Lená. *Os estrangeiros e o comercio do prazer nas ruas do Rio de Janeiro, 1890–1930.* Rio de Janeiro: Arquivo Nacional, 1992.

Medina, Pío Máximo. *Causas del estacionarismo de la raza indígena y el remedio eficaz para su regeneración.* Lima: Imprenta La Industria, 1906.

———. *El tipo criminal.* Lima: Imprenta y Librería de San Pedro, 1907.

Mendoza, Salvador. "El Nuevo Código Penal de México." *Hispanic American Historical Review* 10, no. 3 (1930): 299–312.

Merino Rojas, Cristián. "Evolución histórica de la legislación nacional sobre tráfico ilícito de estupefacientes." Talca, 2000.

Meyer, Jean. "An Idea of Mexico: Catholics in the Revolution." In *The Eagle and the Virgin: Nation and Cultural Revolution in Mexico, 1910–1940*, edited by Mary Kay Vaughan and Stephen E. Lewis, 281–96. Durham, NC: Duke University Press, 2006.

Milanich, Nara. *Children of Fate: Childhood, Class, and the State in Chile, 1850–1930.* Durham, NC: Duke University Press, 2009.

Milenesio, Natalia. "Redefining Men's Sexuality, Resignifying Male Bodies: The Argentine Law of Anti-Venereal Profylaxis, 1936." *Gender and History* 17, no. 2 (2005): 463–91.

Miller, Francesca. *Latin American Women and the Search for Social Justice.* Hanover, NH: University Press of New England, 1991.

Miller, Marilyn Grace. *The Rise and Fall of the Cosmic Race: The Cult of Mestizaje in Latin America.* Austin: University of Texas Press, 2004.

Monsiváis, Carlos. "When Gender Can't Be Seen amid the Symbols: Women and the Mexican Revolution." In *Sex in Revolution: Gender, Politics, and Power in Modern Mexico*, edited by Jocelyn Olcott, Mary Kay Vaughan, and Gabriela Cano, 1–20. Durham, NC: Duke University Press, 2006.

Morales Salinas, Patricio. *La Dirección General de Investigaciones.* Santiago de Chile: Editorial Universitaria, 1956.

Morimoto, Amelia. *Los japoneses y sus descendientes en el Perú.* Lima: Congreso de la República del Perú, 1999.

Moya, Jose. *Cousins and Strangers: Spanish Immigration in Buenos Aires, 1850–1930.* Berkeley: University of California Press, 1998.

Mücke, Ulrich. *Asiaten in den Amerikas, 1850–1950.* FernUniversität Hagen, 2006.

Munck, Ronald. "Cycles of Class Struggle and the Making of the Working Class in Argentina, 1890–1920." *Journal of Latin American Studies* 19, no. 1 (1987): 19–39.

Muñiz, Pedro E. *Memoria del prefecto del departamento de Lima, 1893.* Lima: Imprenta del Universo, 1893.

Muñoz, Fanny. *Diversiones públicas en Lima, 1890–1920: La experiencia de la modernidad.* Lima: Red para el Desarrollo de las Ciencias Sociales en el Perú, 2001.

Munslow, Alun. *Desconstruindo a história.* Rio de Janeiro: Editora Vozes, 2006.

Musgrave, George Clarke. *Under Three Flags in Cuba: A Personal Account of the Cuban Insurrection and Spanish-American War.* Boston: Little, Brown, 1899.

Nina Rodrigues, Raimundo. *As Raças humanas e a responsabilidade penal no Brasil.* Sao Paulo: Companhia Editora Nacional, 1938.

Nye, Robert A. *Crime, Madness, and Politics in Modern France: The Medical Concept of National Decline.* Princeton, NJ: Princeton University Press, 1984.

O'Donnell, Guillermo. "On the State, Democratization, and Some Conceptual Problems: A Latin American View with Glances at Some Post-Communist Countries." *World Development* 21, no. 8 (1993): 13–57.

Ortiz, Fernando. "Consideraciones criminológicas positivistas acerca de la inmigración en Cuba." In *Memoria oficial: Quinta conferencia de beneficencia y corrección de la isla de Cuba,* 343–55. Havana: Librería y Papelería La Moderna Poesía, 1906.

———. *Hampa afro-cubana: Los negros brujos.* Madrid: Editorial América, 1917.

Ortiz, Gerardo Gil. "Estudio dogmatico jurídico del delito de estupro." Thesis, Universidad de Veracruzana, Xalapa, 1973.

Orum, Thomas T. "The Politics of Color: The Racial Dimension of Cuban Politics During the Early Republican Years, 1900–1912." PhD diss., New York University, 1975.

Padrón Valdés, Abelardo. *General de tres guerras.* Havana: Editorial de Ciencias Sociales, 1991.

Palacios, Cristian. "Entre Bertillon y Vucetich: Las tecnologías de identificación policial. Santiago de Chile, 1893–1924." *Revista Historia y Justicia* 1 (2013): 1–28.

Pansters, Will G. "Zones of State-Making: Violence, Coercion, and Hegemony in Twentieth-Century Mexico." In *Violence, Coercion, and State-Making in Twentieth-Century Mexico: The Other Half of the Centaur,* edited by Will G. Pansters, 3–39. Stanford, CA: Stanford University Press, 2012.

Pappademos, Melina. *Black Political Activism and the Cuban Republic.* Chapel Hill: University of North Carolina Press, 2010.

Paredes, Alejandro. "La Operación Cóndor y la guerra fría." *Universum* 1, no. 19 (2004): 122–37.

Pérez, Louis A., Jr. *Army and Politics in Cuba, 1898–1958.* Pittsburgh: University of Pittsburgh Press, 1976.

———. *Cuba Between Empires, 1978–1902.* Pittsburgh: University of Pittsburgh Press, 1985.

———. *Lords of the Mountain: Social Banditry and Peasant Protest in Cuba, 1878–1918.* Pittsburgh: University of Pittsburgh Press, 1989.

Peñaloza, Augusto. *Prevención eugénica de la criminalidad en el Perú.* Lima: La Voce D' Italia, 1916.

Piccato, Pablo. "'El Chalequero,' or the Mexican Jack the Ripper: The Meaning of Sexual Violence in Turn-of-the-Century Mexico City." *Hispanic American Historical Review* 81, no. 3–4 (2001): 623–51.

———. *City of Suspects: Crime in Mexico City, 1900–1931.* Durham, NC: Duke University Press, 2001.

———. "Homicide as Politics in Modern Mexico." In *Murder and Violence in Modern Latin America,* edited by Eric A. Johnson et al., 104–25. West Sussex: Wiley-Blackwell, 2013.

———. *The Tyranny of Opinion: Honor in the Construction of the Mexican Public Sphere.* Durham, NC: Duke University Press, 2010.

———. "Urbanistas, Ambulantes, and Mendigos: The Dispute for Urban Space in Mexico City, 1890–1930." In *Reconstructing Criminality in Latin America,* edited by Carlos Aguirre and Robert Buffington, 113–48. Wilmington, DE: Scholarly Resources, 2000.

Polletta, Francesca. "'It Was like a Fever . . . ': Why People Protest." In *It Was Like a Fever: Storytelling in Protest and Politics,* 32–52. Chicago: University of Chicago Press, 2006.

Ponce de Mendez, Beda. "La mujer en nuestro derecho positivo." Thesis, Xalapa-Enríquez, 1947.

Poole, Deborah. "Ciencia, peligrosidad y represión en la criminología indigenista peruana." In *Bandoleros, abigeos y montoneros: Criminalidad y violencia en el Perú, siglos XVIII-XX,* edited by Carlos Aguirre and Charles Walker, 335–67. Lima: Instituto de Apoyo Agrario, 1990.

———. "Paisajes de poder en la cultura Abigea del sur andino." *Debate Agrario* 3 (1988): 11–37.

Prado y Ugarteche, Javier. *El método positivo en el derecho penal.* 1890. Lima: Universidad Ricardo Palma, 2003.

———. "Estado social del Perú." In *Pensamiento positivista Latinoamericano,* vol. 1, edited by Leopoldo Zea, 324–35. Caracas: Biblioteca Ayacucho, 1980.

Prado y Ugarteche, Mariano Ignacio. *El tipo criminal.* Lima: Imprenta de E. Moreno, 1900.

Preuss, Ori. *Bridging the Island: Brazilian's Views of Spanish America and Themselves, 1865–1912.* Frankfurt/Madrid: Iberoamericana-Vervuert, 2011.

Putnam, Lara. *The Company They Kept: Migrants and the Politics of Gender in Caribbean Costa Rica, 1870–1960.* Chapel Hill: University of North Carolina Press, 2002.

Quijano, Aníbal. *La emergencia del grupo cholo y sus implicancias en la sociedad peruana.* Lima: Universidad San Marcos, 1967.

Quirós, Constancio Bernaldo de, and José María de Llanas Aguilaniedo. *La mala vida en Madrid: Estudio psico-sociológico con dibujos y fotograbados del natural.* Madrid: B. Rodríguez Serra, 1901.

Ramos, Carlos. *Historia del derecho civil peruano.* 2 vols. Lima: Pontificia Universidad Católica del Perú, 2005.

Ribot, Thédodule. *Heredity: A Psychological Study of Its Phenomena, Laws, Causes, and Consequences.* New York: Appleton, 1875.

Richard, Patricia, Ana María Viveros, and Liana Ortiz. *¿Fuma marihuana el estudiante chileno?* Santiago de Chile: Ediciones Nueva Universidad, PUC, 1972.

Rivera-Garza, Cristina. "The Criminalization of the Syphilitic Body: Prostitutes, Health Crimes, and Society in Mexico City, 1867–1930." In *Crime and Punishment in Latin America: Law and Society Since Late Colonial Times*, edited by Ricardo D. Salvatore, Carlos Aguirre, and Gilbert M. Joseph, 147–80. Durham, NC: Duke University Press, 2001.

———. "'She Neither Respected nor Obeyed Anyone': Inmates and Psychiatrists Debate Gender and Class at the General Insane Asylum La Castañeda, Mexico, 1910–1930." *Hispanic American Historical Review* 81, no. 3–4 (2001): 653–88.

Rock, David. *Argentina, 1516–1987: From Spanish Colonization to Alfonsín.* Berkeley: University of California Press, 1987.

———. "Lucha civil en la Argentina: La Semana Trágica de enero de 1919." *Desarrollo Económico* 11, no. 42–44 (1971–72): 165–215.

———. "Machine Politics in Buenos Aires and the Argentine Radical Party, 1912–1930." *Journal of Latin American Studies* 4, no. 2 (1972): 233–56.

———. *State Building and Political Movements in Argentina, 1860–1916.* Stanford, CA: Stanford University Press, 2002.

Rodriguez, Gustavo. "Perversiones sexuales." *Revista Jurídica Veracruzana* 1, no. 2 (1940).

Rodriguez, Julia. *Civilizing Argentina: Science, Medicine, and the Modern State.* Chapel Hill: University of North Carolina Press, 2006.

———. "South Atlantic Crossings: Fingerprints, Science, and the State in Turn-of the-Century Argentina." *American Historical Review* 109, no. 2 (2004): 387–416.

Rodríguez Guillén, Raúl. "Crisis de autoridad y violencia social: Los linchamientos en México." *Polis: Investigación y Análisis Sociopolítico y Psicosocial* 8 no. 2 (2012): 43–74.

Rodríguez Pastor, Humberto. *Herederos del dragón: Historia de la comunidad China en al Perú.* Lima: Fondo Editorial del Congreso del Perú, 2000.

Roger Zelada, Armando. *El problema de los estupefacientes.* Santiago de Chile: Imprenta El Imparcial, 1939.

Rohden, Fabíola. *A arte de enganar a natureza: Contracepção, aborto e infanticídio no início do século XX.* Rio de Janeiro: Editora Fiocruz, 2003.

Roloff y Mialofsky, Carlos. *Indice alfabético y defunciones del Ejército Libertador de Cuba, guerra de independencia, iniciada el 24 de febrero de 1895 y terminada oficialmente el 24 de Agosto de 1898.* Havana: Imprenta de Rambla y Bouza, 1901.

Romero, Osvaldo. *La violencia como fenómeno social: El linchamiento en San Miguel Canoa, Puebla.* México: Jorale, 2006.

Roumagnac, Carlos. *Crímenes sexuales.* Vol. 1 of *Crímenes sexuales y pasionales: Estudios de psicología morbosa.* Mexico City: Librería de Bouret, 1906–10.

Rudé, George. *The Crowd in History: A Study of Popular Disturbances in France and England.* New York: Wiley, 1964.

Ruggiero, Kristen. "Fingerprinting and the Argentine Plan for Universal Identification in the Late Nineteenth and Early Twentieth Centuries." In *Documenting Individual Identity: The Development of Practices in the Modern World*, edited by Jane Caplan and John Torpey, 184–96. Princeton, NJ: Princeton University Press, 2001.

———. *Modernity in the Flesh: Medicine, Law, and Society in Turn-of-the-Century Argentina*. Stanford, CA: Stanford University Press, 2003.

———. "Not Guilty: Abortion and Infanticide in Nineteenth-Century Argentina." In *Reconstructing Criminality in Latin America*, edited by Carlos Aguirre and Robert Buffington, 149–66. Wilmington, DE: Scholarly Resources, 2000.

———. "Passion, Perversity, and the Pace of Justice in Argentina in the Turn of the Last Century." In *Crime and Punishment in Latin America: Law and Society Since Late Colonial Times*, edited by Ricardo D. Salvatore, Carlos Aguirre, and Gilbert Joseph, 211–33. Durham, NC: Duke University Press, 2001.

Sáenz Rovner, Eduardo. *La conexión cubana: Narcotráfico, contrabando y juego en Cuba entre los años 20 y comienzos de la Revolución*. Bogotá: Centro de Estudios Sociales, Universidad Nacional de Colombia, 2005.

Salazar, Jorge. *De matar y morir*. Vol. 3 of *Historia de la noticia: Un siglo de homicidios en el Perú*. Lima: Universidad de San Martín de Porres, 2004.

———. *La medianoche del japonés*. Lima: Universidad de San Martín de Porres, 1991.

Salessi, Jorge. *Médicos, maleantes y maricas: Higiene, criminología y homosexualidad en la construcción de la nación Argentina (Buenos Aires, 1871–1914)*. Rosario: Beatríz Viterbo, 1995.

Salvatore, Ricardo D. "The Crimes of Poor *Paysanos* in Midnineteenth-Century Buenos Aires." In *Reconstructing Crime in Latin America: Essays on Criminology, Prison Reform, and Social Control, 1830–1940*, edited by Carlos Aguirre and Robert Buffington, 59–84. Wilmington, DE: Scholarly Resources, 2000.

———. "Criminal Justice History in Latin America: Promising Notes." *Crime, Histoire, & Sociétés / Crime, History, & Societies* 2, no. 2 (1998): 5–11.

———. "Criminology, Prison Reform, and the Buenos Aires Working Class." *Journal of Interdisciplinary History* 23, no. 2 (1992): 279–99.

———. "Sobre el surgimiento del estado médico legal en la argentina [1890–1940]." *Estudios sociales* 20, no. 1 (2005): 81–114.

Salvatore, Ricardo D., and Carlos Aguirre, eds. *The Birth of the Penitentiary in Latin America*. Austin: University of Texas Press, 1996.

Salvatore, Ricardo D., Carlos Aguirre, and Gilbert Joseph, eds. *Crime and Punishment in Latin America: Law and Society Since Late Colonial Times*. Durham, NC: Duke University Press, 2001.

Sargent, Charles S. *The Spatial Evolution of Greater Buenos Aires, Argentina, 1870–1930*. Tempe: Center for Latin American Studies, Arizona State University, 1972.

Sayer, Derek. "Everyday Forms of State Formation: Some Dissident Remarks on 'Hegemony.'" In *Everyday Forms of State Formation: Revolution and the Negotiation of Rule in Modern Mexico*, edited by Gilbert Joseph and Daniel Nugent, 367–78. Durham, NC: Duke University Press, 2004.

Scardaville, Michael. "Crime and the Urban Poor: Mexico City in the Late Colonial Period." PhD diss., University of Florida, 1977.

Scarzanella, Eugenia. *Ni gringos ni indios: Inmigración, criminalidad y racismo en la Argentina, 1890–1940*. Buenos Aires: Universidad Nacional de Quilmes Ediciones, 2004.

Schell, Patience. "Gender, Class, and Anxiety at the Gabriela Mistral Vocational School, Revolutionary Mexico City." In *Gender, Politics, and Power in Modern Mexico*, edited by Jocelyn Olcott, Mary Kay Vaughan, and Gabriel Cano, 112–26. Durham, NC: Duke University Press, 2006.

Schettini, Cristiana. *Que tenhas teu corpo: Uma historia social da prostituição no Rio de Janeiro das primeiras décadas republicanas*. Rio de Janeiro: Arquivo Nacional, 2006.

———. "South American Tours: Work Relations in the Entertainment Market in South America." *International Review of Social History* 57 (2012): 129–60.

Schwarcz, Lilia M. *O espetáculo das raças: Cientistas, instituições e questão racial no Brasil 1870–1930*. São Paulo: Companhia das Letras, 1993.

Scobie, James. *Buenos Aires: Plaza to Suburb, 1870–1910*. New York: Oxford University Press, 1974.

Scott, Joan W. *Gender and the Politics of History*. New York: Columbia University Press, 1989.

———. "Gender: A Useful Category of Historical Analysis." *American Historical Review* 91, no. 5 (1986): 1053–75.

Scott, Rebecca J. *Degrees of Freedom: Louisiana and Cuba After Slavery*. Cambridge: Harvard University Press 2005.

Seed, Patricia. *To Love, Honor, and Obey in Colonial Mexico*. Stanford, CA: Stanford University Press, 1988.

Senechal de la Roche, Roberta. "Collective Violence as Social Control." *Sociological Forum* 11, no. 1 (1996): 97–128.

Sierra, Maria Teresa. "The Revival of Indigenous Justice in Mexico: Challenges for Human Rights and the State." *Political and Legal Anthropology Review* 28, no. 1 (2005): 52–72.

Sippial, Tiffany A. *Prostitution, Modernity, and the Making of the Cuban Republic, 1840–1920*. Chapel Hill: University of North Carolina Press, 2013.

Slatta, Richard W., ed. *Bandidos: The Varieties of Latin American Banditry*. Westport, CT: Greenwood Press, 1987.

Sloan, Kathryn A. *Runaway Daughters: Seduction, Elopement, and Honor in Nineteenth-Century Mexico*. Albuquerque: University of New Mexico Press, 2008.

Smith, Stephanie. *Gender and the Mexican Revolution: Yucatán and the Realities of Patriarchy*. Chapel Hill: University of North Carolina Press, 2009.

Snodgrass Godoy, Angelina. "When 'Justice' Is Criminal: Lynchings in Contemporary Latin America." *Theory and Society* 33, no. 6 (2004): 621–51.

Solano, Susan. *El estado peligroso: Algunas de sus formas clínicas no delictivas.* Lima: Universidad de San Marcos de Lima, 1937.

Solf y Muro, Alfredo F. "Penalidad de la reincidencia." In *Anales de la Universidad Mayor de San Marcos de Lima* 25 (1898): 51–74.

Speckman Guerra, Elisa. *Crimen y castigo: Legislación penal, interpretaciones de la criminalidad y administración de justicia (Ciudad de México, 1872–1910).* Mexico City: El Colegio de México, 2002.

——. "Las flores del mal: Mujeres criminales en el porfiriato." *Historia Mexicana* 47, no. 1 (1997): 183–229.

——. "Justice Reform and Legal Opinion: The Mexican Criminal Codes of 1871, 1929, and 1931." In *Reforming the Administration of Justice in Mexico,* edited by Wayne Cornelius and David Shirk, 225–50. Notre Dame: University of Notre Dame Press / San Diego: Center for U.S./Mexican Studies, UC San Diego, 2007.

Staum, Martin S. *Labeling People: French Scholars on Society, Race, and Empire, 1815–1848.* Montreal: McGill-Queen's University Press, 2003.

Stepan, Nancy Leys. *"The Hour of Eugenics": Race, Gender, and Nation in Latin America.* Ithaca, NY: Cornell University Press, 1996.

Stern, Alexandra Minna. *Eugenic Nation: Faults and Frontiers of Better Breeding in Modern Latin America.* Berkeley: University of California Press, 2005.

——. "'The Hour of Eugenics' in Veracruz, Mexico: Radical Politics, Public Health, and Latin America's Only Sterilization Law." *Hispanic American Historical Review* 91, no. 3 (2011): 431–43.

Stern, Steve. *The Secret History of Gender: Women, Men, and Power in Late Colonial Mexico.* Chapel Hill: University of North Carolina Press, 1995.

Suriano, Juan. *Anarquistas: Cultura política y libertaria en Buenos Aires, 1890–1910.* Buenos Aires: Manantial, 2001.

——. *Trabajadores, anarquismo y Estado represor: De la Ley de residencia a la Ley de defensa social (1902–1910).* Buenos Aires: Centro Editor de América Latina, 1988.

Tamariz Lúcar, Domingo. *Memorias de una passion: La prensa peruana y sus protagonistas.* Vol. 1 (1948–1963). Lima: Campodónico, 1997.

Tarde, Gabriel. *Penal Philosophy.* New Brunswick, NJ: Transaction, 2001.

Taussig, Michael. *Law in a Lawless Land: Diary of a Limpieza in Colombia.* Chicago: University of Chicago Press, 2005.

Tejeda, Adalberto. *Memoria de las labores del Gobierno Constitucional de Estado de Veracruz Llave durante el cuatrienio 1928–1932.* Jalapa-Enríquez: Talleres Tipográficos del Gobierno del Estado, 1932.

———. *El Nuevo Código Civil del Estado de Veracruz-Llave*. Jalapa-Enríquez: Talleres Gráficos del Gobierno del Estado, 1932.

Temkin, Jennifer. *Rape and the Legal Process*. 2nd ed. New York: Oxford University Press, 2003.

Thorndike, Guillermo. *Los imperios del Sol: Una historia de los japoneses en el Perú*. Lima: Brasa, 1996.

Thurner, Mark. *From Two Republics to One Divided: Contradictions of Postcolonial Nationmaking in Andean Peru*. Durham, NC: Duke University Press, 1997.

Trujillo Bretón, Jorge Alberto. "Los excesos del deseo: Incontinencia y violencia sexual contra niños y jóvenes en Jalisco, 1885–1911." *Relaciones* 32, no. 127 (2011): 153–94.

Turner, Bryan S., ed. *The Cambridge Dictionary of Sociology*. Cambridge: Cambridge University Press, 2006.

Twine, Frances W. *Racism in a Racial Democracy: The Maintenance of White Supremacy in Brazil*. New Brunswick, NJ: Rutgers University Press, 1998.

Uribe-Uran, Victor M. "The Great Transformation of Law and Legal Culture: 'The Public' and 'the Private' in Transition from Empire to Nation in Mexico, Colombia, and Brazil, 1750–1850." In *Empire to Nation: Historical Perspectives on the Making of the Modern World*, edited by Joseph W. Esherwick, Hasan Kayali, and Eric Van Young, 68–105. Lanham, MD: Rowman and Littlefield, 2006.

Valdelomar, Anfiloquio. *La criminalidad indígena en el departamento de Puno: Estadística Judicial Criminal*. Puno: Tipografía Fournier, 1923.

Vanderwood, Paul J. *Disorder and Progress: Bandits, Police, and Mexican Development*. Lincoln: University of Nebraska Press, 1981.

Vargas, Joseph J. *Hell's Kitchen and the Battle for Urban Space: Class Struggle and Urban Reform in New York City, 1894–1914*. New York: Monthly Review Press, 2013.

Vaughan, Mary Kay. "El papel político del magisterio socialista de México, 1934–1940: Un estudio comparativo de los casos de Puebla y Sonora." In *Memoria del XII Simposio de Historia y Antropología*, vol. 2, 175–97. Sonora: Universidad de Sonora, Departamento de Historia y Antropología, 1988.

———. *The State, Education, and Social Class in Mexico, 1880–1928*. DeKalb: Northern Illinois University Press, 1982.

Wade, Peter. *Race and Sex in Latin America*. New York: Pluto Press, 2009.

———. *Raza y etnicidad en Latinoamérica*. Quito: Abya-Yala, 2000.

Walter, Richard. "Municipal Politics and Government in Buenos Aires, 1918–1930." *Journal of Interamerican Studies and World Affairs* 16, no. 2 (1974): 173–97.

Warren, Richard. "Mass Mobilization versus Social Control: Vagrancy and Political Order in Early Republican Mexico." In *Reconstructing Criminality in Latin America*, edited by Carlos Aguirre and Robert Buffington, 41–58. Wilmington, DE: Scholarly Resources, 2000.

Weigman, Robyn. *American Anatomies: Theorizing Race and Gender*. Durham, NC: Duke University Press, 1995.

Westin, Rubin Francis. *Racism in U.S. Imperialism: The Influence of Racial Assumptions on American Foreign Policy, 1893–1945.* Columbia: University of South Carolina Press, 1972.

Zamora, Stephen, José Ramón Cossío, Leonel Pereznieto, José Roldán-Xopa, and David Lopez. *Mexican Law.* Oxford: Oxford University Press, 2004.

Zeuske, Michael. "'Los negros hicimos la independencia': Aspectos de la movilización afrocubana en un hinterland cubano. Cienfuegos entre colonia y República." In *Espacios, silencios y los sentidos de la libertad: Cuba entre 1878 y 1912,* edited by Fernando Martínez Heredia, Rebecca J. Scott, and Orlando F. García Martínez. Havana: Ediciones Unión, 2001.

CONTRIBUTORS

DR. JUANDREA BATES is an assistant professor at Winona State University. She earned her PhD in history at the University of Texas at Austin. Her research focuses on the relationships between the police department, the urban poor, and the criminal justice system in turn-of-the-century Buenos Aires. Her current project explores the poor's interactions with civil law, investigating the role of poor families, particularly children and adolescents, in shaping judicial practice and custody law between 1871 and 1919. She has received generous funding from the Andrew W. Mellon Foundation as well as the Council on Library and Information Resources.

DR. MARCOS FERNÁNDEZ LABBÉ has published multiple articles about popular classes and the construction of discourses on deviant behavior in the nineteenth and the twentieth centuries. He is the author of *Prisión común, imaginario social e identidad: Chile, 1870–1920* (2003). His most recent scholarly interest centers on the production, regulation, and consumption of illegal drugs in Chile. He is currently a professor at Alberto Hurtado University in Chile.

DR. DIEGO GALEANO is a professor of modern and contemporary history at the Pontifical Catholic University (PUC) of Rio de Janeiro. He received his doctorate in social history from the Federal University of Rio de Janeiro. He holds a master's degree in historical research from the University of San Andrés and a bachelor's degree in sociology from the National University of La Plata. He is the author of *Escritores, detectives y archivistas: La cultura policial en Buenos Aires, 1821–1910* (2009) and is coeditor with Gregorio Kaminsky of the volume *Mirada (de) uniforme: Historia y crítica de la razón policial* (2011). His latest book, *Criminosos viajantes: Circulações transnacionais entre Rio de Janeiro e Buenos Aires, 1890–1930*, won the National Archives Research Award (Prêmio Arquivo Nacional de Pesquisa, 2013). He currently researches counterfeiters and swindlers in South America.

DR. SÖNKE HANSEN is a specialist in Peruvian history of the twentieth century. He completed his doctorate at the Universität Hamburg in Germany. He has a multidisciplinary background, with an emphasis on journalism, political sciences, and history. A former member of the Friedrich Ebert Foundation (Brussels, Belgium), Dr. Hansen has published several articles in edited volumes and journals in Peru and Europe and presented his research about Peruvian political culture at scholarly meetings.

DR. LUZ E. HUERTAS is a lecturer and coordinator of the Latin American Studies minor at Fairleigh Dickinson University. She is the recipient of several awards and acknowledgements, such as the Ross and Winnie Day Cannon Scholarship for exceptional achievement in graduate study of history (2010) and the Benjamin Schmidt Dissertation Fellowship (2013–14). She has published articles about Andean ethnohistory, justice, and punishment. Her current lines of interest center on criminology, law enforcement, and the social role of the police in Peru.

DR. BONNIE A. LUCERO is an assistant professor at the University of Texas–Rio Grande Valley. She specializes in Cuban history during the transition from colony to republic. At the interstices of race and gender studies, her research centers on the experiences of men and women of African descent and engages the themes of masculinity, political activism, and anticolonial struggle. She is the author of several articles on Cuban history, which have appeared in the *Journal of Transnational American Studies* and *Atlantic Studies*.

DR. GEMA SANTAMARÍA is an assistant professor in the Department of International Studies at the Instituto Tecnológico Autónomo de México (ITAM). She holds a PhD in sociology and historical studies from the New School for Social Research as well as a masters in gender and social policy from the London School of Economics. She has been a consultant for the United Nations Development Program and has developed specialized reports for the Woodrow Wilson Center for International Scholars and the Norwegian Peacebuilding Resource Center (NOREF). She works on vigilantism, extrajudicial violence, and twentieth-century state-building in Mexico and Central America.

DR. GREGORY J. SWEDBERG has published numerous articles about violence, repression, and marital equality in twentieth-century Mexico. Associate professor at Manhattanville College and a former Fulbright-Hays Doctoral Dissertation Research Abroad fellow, he has also organized panels for and presented papers at several congresses and conferences. His teaching experience includes appointments at Princeton University, Rutgers University, and several other institutions.

INDEX